Riding High

Riding High

Horses, Humans and
History in South Africa

Sandra Swart

WITS UNIVERSITY PRESS

Published in South Africa by:

Wits University Press
1 Jan Smuts Avenue
Johannesburg
2001
http://witspress.wits.ac.za

Cover design by Hothouse South Africa.
Book design and layout by Sheaf Publishing.
Printed and bound by Ultra Litho (Pty) Ltd.

Contents

Acknowledgements

M Y RESEARCH IS only one voice in what I hope will become a conversation about animals in history in southern Africa. As they say in Lesotho, *Petsane e gola kago amusa*: 'a foal only grows by suckling'. I would like to thank the horse riders, breeders, owners and experts who received me so generously in my journeys to Lesotho, the Free State, Kwa-Zulu Natal, the Western Cape and the Eastern Cape. Although we debate and differ on many points, they are always willing to 'talk horse'. I single out especially Frans van der Merwe, and also Ezelle Marais, Cecily Norden and Koof Snyman.

I am grateful for an Oppenheimer Grant, an HB Thom Grant, a National Research Foundation Grant and the support of the office of the dean of the Faculty of Arts and Social Sciences at the University of Stellenbosch, Hennie Kotzé. Thanks to the National Research Foundation, the Research Office of the University of Stellenbosch and the wonderful academic staff of Stellenbosch University History Department.

My friends and colleagues, especially, need a damn good thanking. Particular thanks to Pete Edwards, Bill Storey and Dan Wylie for commenting closely on the manuscript. Thanks also to Andrew Bank, Greg Bankoff, William Beinart, Karen Brown, Sam Challis, William Clarence-Smith, Bob Edgar, Malcolm Draper, Erica Fudge, Rob Gordon, Fraser Griffin-Gulston, Albert and Annamari Grundlingh, Lindy Heinecken, Nancy Jacobs, Donna Landry, Helena Lategan, Jesmael Mataga, Clay McShane, Bill Nasson, Gordon Pirie, Harriet Ritvo, Joel Tarr, Motlatsi Thabane, Liz Tobey, the late Stanley Trapido, Treva Tucker, Karen Raber, Ian van der Waag, Lance van Sittert and Wendy Woodward. Thanks also to our wonderful students who shared parts of this experience: Sarah Duff, Danelle van Zyl, Chet Fransch, Christina Kgari-Masondo, Lindie Korf, Stef Vandenbergh and Lize-Marie Van der Watt. Thanks to the Swart family, easily my favourite critics. Thank you to Adrian Ryan, the best friend I ever had. And also appreciation to my partner, Graham Walker. Thank you for accompanying me to the field when you could and, when you could not, thank you for being there when I returned. May all my journeys end in your arms.

Preface

Toni Morrison once observed: 'If there's a book you really want to read but it hasn't been written yet, then you must write it.' This is what I have set out to do in filling the historiographical lacuna in the literature on horses, and indeed the role of animals and the environment more generally, in the history of southern Africa. Horses act as a way into understanding social and political processes, as part of what has been termed the 'animal turn' in the social sciences. Recent historiography is beginning to explore the importance of animals in human affairs and has found that they have their own histories both independently of and profoundly revealing of human history. My principal research interest lies simply in the effects of an inter-species relationship between a particularly well-evolved primate (*Homo sapiens*) and an evolving odd-toed ungulate of the family *Equidae* (*Equus caballus*). In this book, I explore the ramifications of this relationship for both species and its significance in effecting change within their social and natural environments.

Adventures in fieldwork

Any research project that requires intense archival and field research faces constraints imposed on one's time – not by teaching, which is a pleasure, but by the continual hunt for funding and endless administrative duties of today's university. The shell-shocked state of academia is reminiscent of Marshall Foch's defiant summation at the Battle of the Marne: 'Hard pressed on my right. My centre is yielding. Impossible to manoeuvre. Situation excellent. I shall attack.' In much the same spirit, I embarked on this project.

So, to the surprise of my colleagues and the anxiety of my friends, I set off to pursue the stories about horses in southern Africa. I went from the more sedate state archives of Maseru, Cape Town, Bloemfontein, Durban, Pretoria and London to the saddler and hackney communities of the Western Cape, to the race track, to the Boerperde of the Eastern Cape and Free State, to the Nooitgedacht enthusiasts of the north, to the mountain villages of the Highlands of Lesotho. One theme generated by far the greatest quantity of paper (the diet on which historians, like *Coleoptera*, feed) – the racing industry.

vii

However, this is discussed here only as it pertains to the broader societal role of horses, as even a cursory examination of the paperwork would cause it to loom disproportionately large compared to its actual impact.[1]

My methodology includes the use of oral history, with research trips to a variety of places in South Africa and Lesotho, often pursuing fieldwork on horseback in otherwise inaccessible areas. Unlike some other historians (like Robin Law, for example, who wrote the history of the horse in West Africa, but was at pains to point out that he 'did not undertake this project because [he was] an enthusiast for horses' and had 'in fact, no special affections for these animals'),[2] I have an unabashed fondness for these creatures. But I approach this project first and foremost as an historian, with my affection following, like a dog, at my heels.

The not so small matter of a horse

Perhaps for some, this project skirts perilously close to the 'strangely neglected topic' that Kingsley Amis's hapless young academic Lucky Jim tried to hammer into a publishable article entitled 'The economic influence of the developments in shipbuilding techniques, 1450–1485'. Jim starts his article with the words: 'In considering this strangely neglected topic …' Then he pauses and anguishes: 'This what neglected topic? This strangely what topic? This strangely neglected what?' Like Jim, I have sometimes worried that my attentiveness to the apparently marginal might seem like nothing more than the self-indulgence, quite literally, of riding my own hobbyhorse. But I believe this research does indeed reveal the significance of the horse to human history. Insights about the contingency of history, seen through the agency of animals themselves and the human ideas about them, resonate with much of the recent scholarship about human–animal relationships, which has revealed the profound connections between how we think about and interact with animals and how we think about ourselves, our cultures and those of other humans. The history of horses is the history of desire – and the desire for power in particular, so effectively analysed in social history.

I took to socio-environmental history the way some people take to whisky. The strong emphasis it offers on how power operates through differences embedded in class, race, gender and generation provides a framework for analysis. The title *Riding High* reflects the focus on power and class that runs through the chapters and the hunger to understand it. This is because history is not so much a discipline as a pathology. It engenders obsession. This work grew into my passion, filling several years of my life. And with passion comes pain. I have been bored, lonely or terrified as often as I have been happy while doing my fieldwork. This brings me to the everyday dangers of fieldwork. For years there has been a poster on my door:

FIELDWORKER WANTED
To accompany environmental historian working
on horses in eastern Free State and Lesotho.
The pay is low, the area fairly dangerous,
the hours long and the work physically challenging.
A week- to two-week-long periods at a time –
usually during university holidays.

Oddly, I have never had any enquiries.

To turn from academia and to borrow an anecdote from another arena of unnecessary conflict: in about 1973, former heavyweight boxing champion Joe Frazier and a non-boxing friend were watching a match, and the friend exclaimed how easy it looked to fight in the ring. 'It's harder than it looks', Frazier said dryly. The same is true of writing history. And, sometimes, it can be just as painful. The final product – the 'story' – is presented as seamless – but the process of achieving this seamless appearance is bruising. Conducting research in isolated and liminal places comes with its own perils. For example, I proved a constant disappointment to my informants by focusing on horses rather than cattle. After answering, brusquely, a few equine-themed questions, southern African men (of many different classes and ethnicities) would lean back and with an expansive gesture, say fondly: 'Ah, cattle, now …' Even when I could get them to talk about horses during fieldwork, I found that everything is a shake down. On rich stud farms I had to keep explaining that I could not afford to leave with one of their glossy products and in poor rural areas where tourists are ambulatory sources of income I had to justify my parsimony – there was a singular failure to differentiate between rich tourists and academics on a shoe-string budget.

Moreover, fieldwork done on jaded horses wearing ill-fitting tack in precipitous areas carries its own hazards. Along with historiographical methodology, one had to learn more practical things – like how to fashion a makeshift bridle out of a jersey and how to keep your field notebooks dry in a damp saddlebag. (Often, to add to my indignity, I became ill, with a spell of bronchitis once earning me, from my heartless students, the temporary sobriquet 'the hoarse whisperer'.)

Then there are the horses themselves. Galloping horses may look like rapture in motion, but that is not how they feel. Death feels a close companion as the horse grabs the ground and the earth rises up at you like an appointment in Samarra.

Although one quickly learns phrases like '*Kabatla pere e bonolo*' (I need a quiet horse), this is often insufficient protection. This is because for horses as a species, aggression is an important career move. Successful acts of animosity allow one to move up the horse hierarchy. So if you meet your horse's belligerence with submission, then he moves up the pecking order and you move down. Luckily, university academics are uniquely trained to handle such petty power struggles.

In any event, something I learned quickly about horse riding in Lesotho is that a fear of rogue horses is not the problem; it is a fear of heights. Lesotho has the highest lowest point of anywhere in the world.[3] Two-thirds of its land area is mountainous, and all this orographic liveliness precipitates unusual weather patterns. While the country has 300 days of sunshine a year, it is often in bitter conditions. (All the guidebooks counsel one to avoid being hit by lightening, which is sound – if perhaps superfluous – advice.) Moreover, in Lesotho, the traditional remedy for horses' diseases is *matekoane* or dagga/marijuana (which lends another nuance to the title of this volume). As one ascends, the trail becomes narrower and the path more slippery, with vertiginous drops in sometimes freezing conditions. Often I would simply close my eyes, as one does during a horror film, and, upon opening them, quietly ululate with fear. On many occasions, the view to my left consisted solely of a saddlebag, my left boot – and clear mountain air. Trusting my life to a (potentially stoned) horse required a serious level of commitment to my research.

Quite aside from these physical dangers of data gathering, there are intellectual hazards.

The Margaret Mead syndrome

As Dr Johnson once said in his confident way: 'Great abilities are not requisite for an historian; for in historical composition, all the greatest powers of the human mind are quiescent.'[4] Essentially, I think he meant we simply use advanced listening skills when being historians, letting the sources, both human and paper, talk for themselves. We historians are, after all, in the memory business. Along with telling people what happened, we also want to establish why some past events resonate more than others. My work relied most heavily on archival sources, but the oral history component served a slightly different role. Often, it simply added verisimilitude without veracity. As Alessandro Portelli noted: 'The importance of oral testimony may lie not in its adherence to fact, but rather in its departure from it, as imagination, symbolism, and desire emerge.' The problem is, of course, that fairly often the sources talk nonsense. For example, in an illuminating case study, the Australian anthropologist Derek Freeman critiqued Margaret Mead's 1928 bestseller and canonical classic, *Coming of Age in Samoa*. The book, which detailed the uninhibited – not to say frankly saucy – sexual behaviour of young Samoans, was wildly wrong. Freeman argues that Mead was quite simply deluded by some lighthearted Samoans who thoroughly enjoyed spinning these romances and shocking the poor woman.[5] More importantly, she made the paradigmatic mistake of imposing the cultural determinism of her mentor, Franz Boas, on her empirical research.

A similar and pressing risk lurks for the southern African researcher. In rural areas I engaged in an often futile search for 'indigenous knowledge', particularly local traditions of healing. In the Lesotho Highlands, for example, I had heard rumours of an old man greatly skilled in the arts of healing and travelled to a remote homestead to interview him. I was hoping to learn more about local remedies like pumpkin seed usage in the treatment of intestinal parasites. Through an interpreter, I asked the old man how the community contended with the 'terrible trouble of worms in the stomach of the beasts'. The old man looked at me incredulously and said, in English: 'I use Equimax. What do you use?'

On another occasion, I was following up research on the symbolism and cultural totems of the horse. Immersed in the cross-cultural anthropological literature, I asked whether any particular horse colours were avoided by local riders, to which the interviewee responded 'yes', and added that the colour white was eschewed. I became extremely excited. This fitted the categories of bovine avoidance found in several closely linked social groups! I burst out breathlessly: 'Is it because white horses symbolise death?' 'No,' he said gently 'it is because white hair is hard to get off your pants.'

Talking horse

Such disappointments abounded, but at least the sources were talking to me – largely because we shared a certain understanding. I have found that many people are able to get through life without knowing the definition of a horse. For those that are not, the redoubtable Dr Johnson has provided the following: *'horse: [Sx] a neighing quadruped used for draught, carriage, and warfare.'* This definition is helpful, but perhaps a trifle insufficient. Each horse society has its own idiosyncratic language that changes over time. For example, the Kazaks, who are particular about these things, have 62 words for the varying shades of dark brown horses alone.[6] In English, the equestrian vocabulary has yielded a wonderful miscellany of words. The diseases alone are magnificently named: 'poll evil', 'farcy', 'sweeney', 'wind puff' and, my personal favourite (and the pseudonym I adopt when writing outraged letters to the newspapers), 'fistulous withers'.

Such words create a jargon, a secret language that both includes and excludes. Historically, this was evident in horse cultures as various as those, for example, of the secret horseman societies of Ireland, the plains and pampas of the Americas, the Mongolian steppes and the Lesotho Highlands. Horsemanship was both a way of entrenching societal divides, as the discussion will show, and, much more occasionally, a way of crossing divides.[7] Similarly, knowledge about horses can unite, but it can also divide. But my knowledge, limited as it is, offered a way into understanding and opened up conversations that were otherwise impossible for an outsider to participate in. (As 'Banjo' Paterson, the Australian 'bush poet' and eyewitness to the South African War, remarked upon meeting strangers: 'So we talked about horses, that one unfailing topic ... [that] is a better passport than any letter of introduction.')[8]

This was vital because, after a long age of suspicion, historians have begun to use the technique of *asking people things*. We began to view oral interviewing more benignly after 1945, and introduced techniques like building rapport, asking open-ended questions, exercising scrupulous note taking and eliciting memories through introducing photographs. Oral historians have written about outsider–insider status in acquiring data through interviewing. While outsider status is believed to afford detachment and objectivity, insider status (like being a horse rider) allows a path to otherwise taboo knowledge. Ideally, a balance between the two is sought: Belinda Bozzoli, for example, showed in *Women of Phokeng*, a study of power relations among black women in apartheid South Africa, that the nuanced interviews of her colleague, Mmantho Nkotsoe, were due to her 'insider' status, because she shared ethnicity, class, dialect and gender, and, most significantly, an understanding of what it means to be oppressed with her interviewees.[9] Similarly, the horseman/-woman historian listens for the truths that reveal themselves only in the rare intimacy of being passionate about the same thing.

This research has led me to encounter a variety of interesting people, both living and dead: scientists, horse thieves, soldiers, settlers, sailors, bureaucrats, family men and women, nation builders, peasant farmers, wealthy stud farm owners, wild-eyed punters and even the leader of a paramilitary terrorist group, who wrote to me from his gaol cell.

Although thankfully unable to enrage the deceased, occasionally I did enrage the living. The horse world is a strange and perilous place. Entering the horse-breeding world is reminiscent of Van Leeuwenhoek looking through the microscope he had just invented at a drop of apparently clear and tranquil water and finding the predatory jungle of bacteria that was to be found there. Of course, just accepting the well-liked Whig narrative models of breed development gelds analysis. But when one analyses the recent past in particular, one faces the simple danger of making people angry. This is exacerbated by the passions aroused by the two most important themes in this book: horses and power. This is why, historiographically, one tries to be heretical without being blasphemous.[10]

Delightfully, Chekhov maintained that '[c]ritics are like horse-flies which prevent the horse from ploughing'. However, the critics need to buzz. That is why the word 'essays' deployed to describe the chapters in the book is key. I use the word in the style originally intended by Montaigne when he coined the term 'essay', which translates to 'endeavours' or 'little projects of trial and error'.[11] This sixteenth-century approach is useful in opening up fresh terrain in social history, where new territory is opened up (but never conquered) by the historiographical pioneers. This book is part of the long conversation historians need to have to understand the changing and pivotal relationship between animals and human society and the impact that their relationship has had on their environment.

Particular truths and legends have become entrenched in the various oral traditions – Basotho, Afrikaans and so on. About two-and-a-half thousand years ago, historians decided to try and tell the truth about the past.[12] This endeavour got off to a shaky start. The mythical tales people told to comfort, to affirm, to correct and to police themselves were replaced with stuttering efforts towards 'history' as we understand it. Just as today, they were frequently partial, biased and often just plain wrong. But they were part of a conversation that tried to tell the 'real stories'. This study attempts to extract the facts as far as possible and, moreover, explain the process of myth making by contextualising it within the material changes in society. Fact is no less beautiful than legend, but it is more untidy, more difficult to gather, needs more funding to get hold of and is a lot harder to explain. Moreover, it would be wrong to insist that this is the final word: this book is just the start of a conversation. After all, as 'Banjo' Paterson said about his own experiences in the South African War, 'nobody believes anything that a man says about a horse'.[13]

Chapter 1

'But where's the bloody horse?'

Humans, Horses and Historiography

You praise the firm restraint with which they write –
   I'm with you there, of course:
They use the snaffle and the curb all right,
   But where's the bloody horse?
          Roy Campbell (1901–57), 'On some South African novelists'

IN THE DUNES outside the Namibian town of Swakopmund on the south-west Atlantic coast there is a mass grave of horses dating back almost a century. Strong winds blow the desert sands, exposing and then concealing the weathered bones from time to time. Each skull has a bullet hole in the forehead. These are the remains of over 2,000 horses and mules destroyed in the summer of 1915 to halt the epidemic spread of virulent glanders among South African Defence Force animals.[1] Like the shifting desert sands, the historical record reveals and conceals the history of horses in southern Africa.

There is a strange concealment when historians write about the past.[2] It is the absence – perhaps forgivable – of the obvious. Horses have been too ubiquitous, in a way, to catch the historian's eye. Perhaps it is the very centrality of animals to human lives that has previously rendered them invisible – at least invisible to scholars intent on mainstream history or the (aptly labelled) humanities more generally. Horses are absent from the official historical record in southern Africa, except when one detects their hoofprints in some battle, finds an allusion to the gallant exploits of a particular horse or the tragic slaughter of horses in war, or reads of them amalgamated in a much desired commodity on the shifting colonial frontiers, the dyad of 'guns and horses'. Sometimes one hears a distant whinny in travellers' descriptions, in personal letters and in diaries.

Yet horses are everywhere in the primary sources. They were significant within the colonial economies of southern Africa. They occupied material and symbolic spaces, helping to buttress the shifting socio-political orders and looming large in rituals of social differentiation. It is widely accepted that horses played a significant role in human history (and, though less remarked, that humans played a pivotal role in horses' history). As Alfred Crosby has noted of the broad global processes of human settler invasions of new lands, human colonists came to the 'new worlds' not as individual immigrants, but 'as part of a grunting, lowing, neighing, crowing, chirping, snarling, buzzing, self-replicating and world-altering avalanche'.[3] Just as they had done in Europe, Asia, the Americas and North Africa, in southern Africa the equine colonisers who accompanied the human ones not only provided power and transportation, but also altered their new biophysical and social environments in a range of ways.[4] Although, as the chapters that follow will show, not as economically important as cattle, not as ecologically damaging as sheep, and not as familiar as dogs and cats in the domestic sphere, nevertheless the horse has played an inescapable role. In their three-and-a-half centuries in southern Africa horses have in fact managed to leave visible socio-political and economic tracks. Until the mid-twentieth century they were integral to civic functioning and public recreation. They were replaced by mechanised devices only after lively debate, staying significant in the high-end leisure sector; subsistence agriculture; the low-cost transport of goods in some urban locales and transport, e.g. in the Lesotho Highlands; and in the South African military and policing sectors. Until the present horses have remained elemental to certain public rituals of power, from military parades to intensely personal acts of healing in riding for the disabled. Since the late eighteenth century racehorses have remained a popular way for people to correlate inversely their hopes and their wages every week.

The 'animal turn'

A generation ago, in order to caricature the new social history, a historian wrote a satirical essay (under the pseudonym Charles Phineas) on 'Household pets and urban alienation' in which he declared that the history of pets remained too much the history of their owners, illuminating more about the owning than the owned.[5] His words now resonate without irony, because – drawing eclectically on the fields of environmental history,[6] literary criticism, psychology, cultural geography, bioethics and anthropology – recent historiography is beginning to give greater emphasis to the importance of animal-centred research. Animals are roaming the groves of academe; they bark and paw at the doors of the ivory tower.

Historians have begun to open these doors a trifle. No longer is the mention of an animal-related topic likely to provoke 'surprise and amusement', as was the case 20 years ago.[7] Instead of being dismissed as simply a fad, the increasing inclusion of animals is gaining momentum as part of our social and political narratives, from the early movement of hunters and gatherers; through the grand narrative of domestication and agricultural transformation; to figuring allegorically and materially in religions, social rituals and literature.[8] Animal Studies is now a growing academic field. It has its own journals and is wide ranging in disciplinary terms, extending from, for example, anthropologies of human–animal interactions, animal geographies and the position of animals in the construction of identity to animals in popular culture.[9] Analysis is becoming progressively more diverse, including rural and urban locales and literary, cinematic and cyberspace arenas, and touching on themes like the commercial food chain, ecotourism and the construction of national identities. Some of the new historical scholarship on animals has been the work of historians (like Ritvo and Thomas); some the work of literary and cultural studies practitioners (like Fudge and Baker). Nevertheless, whether the 'animal turn' is manifested in eco-criticism or environmental history, or featured in the interdisciplinary domain of Animal Studies, it remains the case, as Ritvo has observed, that historical research provides much of the bedrock for more exclusively interpretive scholarship. To understand developments in the field to date, with particular focus on the discipline of history, we need to ask not only 'Why *animals*?', but also 'Why *now*?'

Historians, like artists, often fall in love with their models. Lately, however, there has been a significant move away from old models towards embracing new forms, and concomitant new sources, in history writing in southern Africa. Certainly, the international green movement has effected change within academe, with scholars focusing on the history of science, technology and the environment. Human practices now threaten animal worlds – indeed, the global environment – to such an extent that humans have now both an 'intellectual responsibility' and 'ethical duty' to consider animals closely.[10] Additionally, the twentieth century's ethological observations of animals as closer to humans than we have previously acknowledged leads towards a gradual rejection of the nature/culture distinction that has been a central part of C.P. Snow's 'two cultures', the distinction between social and natural sciences.[11]

Other theorists have argued that animals were never part of the twentieth century's modernist project – except, arguably, as commodities – and now, particularly coupled to the rise of the animal rights movement, increasing attention is being paid to animal topics by postmodernist scholars and activists (although these two groups are often at ideological odds).[12] As Jacobs deftly encapsulates it: 'modernists display confidence in humans' ability to control nature', while postmodernists are convinced that humans construct it.' (Of course, they are not idealists in the manner of the redoubtable Bishop Berkeley; they are not contending that nature has no reality outside human minds; rather, that our capacity to understand the 'nature' of nature is limited by the nature of the minds that do the understanding.) At their extremes, however, they sometimes obscure the view that natural or biophysical forces act on human history.[13]

Internationally, processes are at work that challenge received wisdom – secularisation, urbanisation, diminishing family bonds, the refashioning of societies through globalisation, migrations – all precipitating a reconsideration of existing mental hierarchies and certainties. Some experience these changes as increasing alienation; some search space for aliens and anthropomorphise earth's animals to find echoes of our own humanity in a time of disaffection and social dislocation. Perhaps humans simply do not want to be alone in the cosmos.

Quite aside from human loneliness is the issue of the manner in which humans may be joined by other creatures within the axis of scholarly scrutiny. Some scholars contend that animals themselves cannot be discussed, only their representations.[14] Others concur: Chamberlin notes that '"[h]orse" is not a horse. It is the word for horse'.[15] Another contention is that what humans think they have learnt about animals remains simply a reflection of their own cultural preoccupations; thus, for example, Jane Goodall's 'discoveries are as much about humans as about chimpanzees'.[16] Some histories of animals thus

4

have adopted a more poststructural, 'textual' or 'linguistic' approach to their subjects on the grounds that such histories are necessarily representational, composed of past documents written by humans about animals, which are then doubly reinterpreted by humans.[17] When writing about animals, for example, Berger contends that he speaks of nothing more real than human imaginings,[18] and Baker and others have contended that animals themselves cannot be scrutinised, only their depictions.[19] Thus the 'curb' and 'snaffle' (as Campbell puts it) of critical discourse analysis is much in evidence, but the physical animal is missing.

Certainly, historians can benefit from the close reading technique of literary critics, and the emphasis on the genealogy and ambiguity of language. Close reading reminds historians that elements of concern about 'wild animals' or 'feral' animals or 'pets' or 'sacred animals' or 'dangerous animals' are a product of language and rhetoric. These categories are debatable and contextual, but they are certainly constructed with words.[20] Historical approaches to animals reveal the contextual specificity of any particular human–animal relationship and how categories, including those of 'human' and 'animal', are neither inevitable nor universal, but are forged in particular contexts by actors with often conflicting interests.

Of course, symbolic or rhetorical uses of the animal should indubitably receive the same critical attention from a historian as the real beast. That said, social history is perfectly able to contain ideology and materiality, textual discourse, and corporeality without recourse to postmodernist theory, as the final chapter will explore. Indeed, ironically (given the contention by Rothfels and Berger), it may well have been in reaction to the extreme rarefaction of the 'textual turn' within the discipline of history that made some (other) historians yearn for the possibilities of solid corporeality offered by the 'animal turn'. In this view, 'nature', and animals in particular, have a tangibility lacking in 'literary theory'. Animals cannot be just another cultural construction, because they have literal viscerality. They undeniably exist in a way that sits uneasily with postmodern insistence on textual primacy and, as Dr Johnson once did, we can use them to say 'I refute it thus'.[21]

Horses could reasonably have received Johnson's boot (although, unlike the stone, they might have kicked back). Horses are breathing beasts; they exist and live historical lives and impact on their own world and on the world of humans socio-politically and economically. Ironically – considering the pseudonymous

Phineas's parody of the kind of social history associated with E.P. Thompson, noted earlier – social history is well able to deal with both the material role of horses and their symbolic uses. Indeed, social history recognises the importance of exploring the linkages between both ideological and economic aspects of human–animal relationships.[22] Masters of social history, like Eugene Genovese, Eric Hobsbawm, Keith Thomas, Thompson and Charles van Onselen, customarily manage both discourse and ideology as equally integral to their study as material conditions, without needing to 'shift paradigms'. Writing in the early 1990s, both Hobsbawm and Thompson, for example, explicitly singled out the environment as a significant issue.[23] From the outset, environmental history has been influenced by a radical approach forged by social history, i.e. the idea of exploring history 'from below', although the concluding chapter will discuss the snaffle and curbs placed on such an approach.

While animals are generally still looked at by scholars in the humanities and social sciences with the goal of achieving a better understanding of humans, some have moved away from narrowly anthropocentric approaches of the past that depicted animals as passive objects of human agency. Preceding studies allowed little room for the agency of animals (or, indeed, some groups of humans, like women and the working class, for example), and this will be explored in the closing chapter.[24]

Horses and hyphenated historians

Environmental history (which includes the historical side of Animal Studies) and the new social history emerged in chorus as definable fields of study. To some extent, both academic projects stemmed from socio-political movements gathering impetus during the 1960s and 1970s: reacting respectively to the concerns of the ecology/animal rights lobby and the civil rights/feminist campaigns. They share fertile grounds for cross-pollination. The 'grassroots movement' could be quite literal: both learnt from the Annales school in calling for the grand bio-geographical context and both exhibit an Annaliste-inspired ambition to explore a totalising history. They espouse the creative use of source materials to tackle the previously neglected, particularly ordinary people over elites and everyday life over sensational events. They can both evoke the human face, as opposed to the aridities of statecraft and administrative development. Research in both fields can reflect a new scholarly egalitarianism, although there are limitations. They have both deployed particularity over generality, using case studies to examine larger issues. Both have faith in the possible political relevance of their work.[25]

The socio-environmental approach thus highlights new aspects of power, its sources and the motives behind its mobilisation. As Jacobs notes with wry irony, as both social and environmental historians claim to write 'from below', it is odd that they have not encountered each other more frequently.[26] While infrequent, their encounters have been significant. In 1972 Roderick Nash, an eminent pioneer in the field, commented: 'In a real sense environmental history fitted into the framework of New Left history. This would indeed be history "from the bottom up", except that here the exploited element would be the biota and the land itself.'[27] For social historians, 'the exploited element' is the human oppressed, those trampled underfoot, such as blacks, women, peasants and labourers. For environmental historians, it is that which is literally trampled underfoot: the small organisms, the soil, water and biophysical surroundings. Both approaches have sought not only examples of oppression, but agency, exercised by the ecological and social communities.

Animals can thus be seen as the latest beneficiaries of a 'democratising tendency' specifically within historical studies.[28] Some ethnographies now depict animals not merely as a vehicle with which to explore a particular human social facet. Anthropology thus offers a good model for other disciplines and historical writing has drawn on these perspectives. Nearly a half century ago Levi-Strauss urged anthropologists to acknowledge the ways in which animals afford humans an important conceptual resource (animals, he argued, are *bonnes à penser*, things with which to think), while more materialist anthropology considered how animals serve as sources and products of power and inequality (so they are good not just to think 'with' but also 'about').[29]

More specifically to South Africa, the seductive but dangerous simplicity of environmental determinism in earlier works, as Beinart has observed, conceivably rendered later historians uncomfortable with incorporating environmental issues into explanations of human change.[30] This was exacerbated by disciplinary insularity and a lack of familiarity with 'science'.[31] Also, as Steyn and Wessels suggest, the increasing political isolation of South Africa meant that the impact of the international environmental revolution was minimised locally.[32] Apartheid was the enemy that animated the vigorous radical or social history school, and many of the most capable historians focused their research on the deconstruction of racial consciousness and class formation. But the achievement of democracy in 1994 has allowed a growing historiographical diversity. Some of these approaches have been environmental, focusing on specific groups of people and their relations with the non-human living world, i.e. how communities related to the environment as they interacted with one another, emphasising issues of social power and identity. Thus, the end of apartheid has redirected some historians' attention to pastures new – literally in this case – prompting a 'move from red to green'.

Van Sittert has pointed out that environmental historical writing in South Africa is a 'broad church whose catechism has thus far defied the best efforts at scholarly synthesis', and certainly there are several divergent approaches to the subject matter.[33] For example, a pioneering intervention was made in 1932 by B.H. Dicke, writing on one of the first groups of Voortrekkers to trek, who were annihilated, purportedly by the Amatonga of the Makuleke and Mahlengwe clans.[34] But Dicke made the radical environmental argument that it was tsetse fly rather than the Amatonga that vanquished the trekkers.

Environmental themes have a long legacy in local historiography, with its roots in the strong agrarian social history of South Africa. Environmental history has run parallel with radical history because they both aspired to offer a corrective line that emphasised African agency in the face of European conquest and capitalist exploitation. This is clear in the writings of Beinart, Bundy, Delius, Keegan, Trapido and Van Onselen.[35] The radical or social history tradition made implicit use of the environment in explaining change over time, even though such writings were not self-classified as works of environmental history. Some historians consciously designate their work 'socio-environmental' history rather than purely 'environmental'.[36]

Hitherto, the label 'environmental' or 'socio-environmental' history has been preferred to the 'animal turn in history', which has not (yet) become a phrase in common parlance in South Africa. The term 'environmental' carries with it a portmanteau suggestion of social awareness, relevance and utility, and concomitant worthiness of state and institutional funding. In contrast, the adjective 'animal' in such a disciplinary concern appears the self-indulgent preserve of the feminine, middle class and white. (As one angrily amused reader of the *Mail & Guardian* put it: 'What is it with white people and animals?')[37]

Environmental history is more usually focused on the land than on animals per se.[38] The voices talking about the 'animal turn' in the southern African social sciences, however, and within the historical guild in particular, are still very few. Most recent international scholarship is still almost entirely Western, Eurocentric or neo-Eurocentric – about animals in Europe or in its settler societies in North America and Australia, for example. Exceptions with regard to the developing world include work on the camel in Islamic society; a study of tigers in the Malay world; and of horses in the Indian Ocean world.[39] In the southern African context, wildlife has received a great deal of historiographic attention, following MacKenzie's analysis of British imperialism and its hunting network and, specific to South Africa, Carruthers' intervention, which corrected public myths on wildlife protection.[40] Animal pests and diseases have received perhaps the most historiographic attention.[41] Colonial science (in this case, specifically ideas about animal management) operated in interaction with a 'vernacular science' – a hybrid of indigenous African, local settler and metropolitan knowledge systems, as Beinart and Musselman suggest.[42] There has been some scrutiny of historical ecological changes, particularly in Van Sittert's and Beinart's work, and human–nature relations in literary texts.[43] Historians have shown that just as they had done in other parts of the world, animal and plant 'colonisers' transformed their new habitats – both biophysical and social – in various ways.[44] Jacobs, for example, has offered a brilliant societal analysis (or an exposé of the politics of 'class and grass') through the lens of the 'Great Donkey Massacre' of the 1980s in Bophuthatswana, discussed in greater depth in Chapter 8. In the broader continental context, horses have been discussed by Robin Law, who wrote a pioneering study of horses in West Africa;[45] by Fisher on horses in the Sudan;[46] by Jim Webb in a skilful analysis of the equine role in western Sahara and Senegambia;[47] and Legassick on horses and firearms in the Samorian army of the late nineteenth century.[48] Research that uses animals as a window into understanding human society has, for example, been developed by research into wildlife and on domesticated creatures of southern Africa, including some pony tales.[49]

How does one look at animals?

One now need no longer ask, as Berger did in 1980: 'Why look at animals?'[50] Now one asks: '*How* does one look at animals?' The 'animal turn' (like so many other 'turns') is not founded on any one method or approach; instead, it remains elusive and diverse in terms of its methodology and *raison d'être*, mirroring the multiplicity of its object of study. It is defined more by its pluriform commitment to understanding animals within human society than by any one methodology or political agenda. Similarly, internationally, Animal Studies has meant different things to different people, and within the discipline there have been fissures and differences. Methodological and thematic ecumenism might be thought to satisfy everyone (except, as Peter Novick observed, in a very different context – those people who like short books).[51]

This book offers a history that tries to remain diverse in terms of its methodology, sources and ambitions. It also tries to speak to many audiences: those interested in animals and the past, certainly, but also those interested in southern Africa. Environmental change as the further fragmentation of history into sub-disciplines is not its intention. It was the fear of just such compartmentalisation and concomitant balkanisation that led Keith Thomas and E.P. Thompson to decline their support for the formation of the Social History Society in the 1970s because it was not another branch of history like 'postal history' or 'furniture history'; it was 'a way of doing any kind of history'.[52] Similarly, including other species in understanding the past may be just another 'way of doing history'. The animal turn encompasses a continuing process of inclusion, normalisation and gradual mainstream acceptance of the animal as subject, object and even agent. This process is already at work in the subtle shifting of vision, an ocular expansion that allows the creatures on the edge of vision into the disciplinary line of sight. In social history it happened first with workers, then with women, and now animals. The once invisible horse simply becomes visible.

The first aim of this book, therefore, is, on a very basic level, simply to scour the archives to try to find the 'bloody horse' – both the corporeal animal and the fictive beast – in order to reinsert the horse into the larger historical narrative. No guild historian has attempted a monograph devoted to horses in southern Africa.[53] Yet historically, horses existed, and they *mattered*.

Secondly, the book explores the material socio-economic effects and political ramifications of the introduction of horses as a non-native species. In some ways, it is simply an attempt to chronicle the effects of an inter-species relationship. The essays focus on key encounters between humans and horses and between different human groups over horses. In some ways, these stories are simply the adventures of a big, gentle herbivore and a small, rogue primate.

Thirdly, it considers the symbolic and ideological dimensions of this species in relation to human society. Horses offer a particularly potent symbol, linked with power and ethnic iconography. Narratives of breed were constructed in which conceptions of human difference (class, race, national character) were projected onto the horses and they were then used as vehicles to promote a sense of self-respect (through wealth, class and ethnicity).

Fourthly, because a historian is always in conversation with other historians, this book addresses the idea of ecological imperialism in order to draw southern African environmental history into a wider global dialogue on socio-environmental historiographical issues. The book is part of that conversation and begins with the long relationship between humans and horses that extends back for millennia.

Herds and hordes

Horses and humans have shared a long history: as predator and prey, as master and slave, as war comrades, and as allies. The equestrian age, which lasted for 6,000 years, has only been over for two (human) generations in the West and is not over everywhere else on the planet.[54] In human eyes, horses have changed from being edible meat, a means of mobility, a fearsome method of conquest and a way of tilling the soil to providing a leisure activity and a medium of therapy.

The horses able to perform these shifting roles can be traced back to multi-toed, dog-sized creatures that inhabited both the New and the Old World. About 50 million years later they had evolved into *Pliohippus* in North America, and after another ten million years an identifiable 'horse' evolved. This Ice Age, New World horse became threatened in this environment and was saved, as a species, by a vast migration, a diaspora to Siberia across a land bridge in the Bering Strait – a bridge humans would use to go the other way.

The steppe region of Central Asia, extending north-west from the Great Wall of China to the mountains of Outer Mongolia, was probably where nomad horse breeding began and was the epicentre from which hordes of horsemen emerged. Horses were the last of the common animals to be domesticated, from perhaps as early as 4,000 BCE, probably as a side effect of hunting horses for their flesh. The notion of controlling the herds and their breeding appears to have originated in eastern Europe or the Crimea.[55] The history of horses in human culture can be traced back as far as 30,000 BCE, when horses were depicted in

11

Paleolithic cave paintings.[56] Domestication was not solely a biological, but also a cultural process that affected both the human domesticator and the animal domesticate. Horses had the traits, limited to only a few animals, to make them domesticable in the first place.[57] They were large enough to be useful, but small enough to be manageable. Most importantly, they were herd animals, sociable and used to living within a hierarchy that translated easily into a new hierarchy under human custodianship. They could breed in captivity and were neither too panicky nor too aggressive when confronted by humans. Thus, the intersection of natural history and human history provided a favourable environment for domestication.

In order to be domesticated, animals had to be incorporated into the social structure of a human community and become objects of ownership, purchase and barter. This was the basis of the Neolithic revolution, when a fundamental change in human societies occurred and groups of hunter-gatherers became farmers and pastoralists. There was probably a succession first from generalised hunting in the Palaeolithic period at the end of the last Ice Age to specialised hunting and following herds. This was followed by taking ownership of a herd, then controlled breeding and ultimately human selection for favoured characteristics.

Artefacts unambiguously associated with riding or traction date to the start of the second millennium BCE.[58] Evidence from mitochondrial DNA studies suggests that the domestication of horses occurred in multiple locations and at various times, in eastern Europe and the south-west Russian steppes in Central Asia; in western Europe; in Iberia; and in North Africa.[59] Widespread utilisation occurred principally through the transfer of technology for capturing, taming and rearing free-born horses caught in the wild. Accordingly, the transmission of technology (rather than the selective breeding of horses) may have been the key leading to their wide-ranging use.[60] It was, therefore, probably not herds of domesticated horses that spread over the expanse of the Old World, but rather the *knowledge* that made their domestication possible, and this was slow to be disseminated. Arguably, the expansion of ur-horsemanship was restricted by an elite because this technology contained the secret of a new kind of power.

Newly created equestrian classes and communities had access to entirely new ways of life predicated on this novel access to dominance, commanding both fresh access to resources and a new mindset. Horses certainly transformed warfare, initially in the steppes north of the Black Sea.[61] By the middle of the second millennium BCE, horses were used to pull chariots – in Greece, Egypt and Mesopotamia, and in China by the fourteenth century BCE.[62] The horse allowed travel overland from the Atlantic to the Pacific coastlines, facilitating connections between centres of civilisation.[63] Mobility offered a new dimension of power: a human who could defeat distance could also defeat other humans. The first 'horse whisperer' or noted equestrian expert, Xenophon, himself commented on the conjunction of martial heroism, horsemanship and social privilege in the fourth century BCE. This historical dynamic was observed by Aristotle, who contended that cavalry states tended to be oligarchies, because horses were necessarily restricted to a wealthy minority.[64] An individual on horseback was seldom a slave; indeed, there appears to be a correlation between horse owning and human owning.

Horses have themselves changed because of the relationship they have had with humans. They have changed as a species in shape, size, variety, geographic distribution and demographics. As a consequence of their mutualism with humans, the geographic range of horses altered entirely: their northern and southern limits were transfigured. Ultimately, there was no area entirely off limits to equine colonisation. (Shackleton even managed to take Siberian ponies to the Antarctic.) In the southern African context, as the subsequent chapters will explore, the equine interlopers of the region were not only instruments of change, but in transforming the human socio-political and mental landscapes, the horse itself was transformed.

Animal history offers a way to cross literal and figurative borders.[65] Methodologically, horses are good for crossing boundaries. That their range (and therefore their study) is not limited by national borders helps break the constraints of area studies, particularly those bounded by the national historical imagination. Animals, and indeed 'nature' itself, are difficult to contain within the boundaries of the nation state (although states tried to do so and cross-border traffic, legal and illegal, generated a mountain of useful paperwork for historians). Environmental, ecological and biological processes work on transregional, transcontinental and global scales, defying, as environmental historians Donald Worster and Alfred Crosby note, 'a narrow view of political boundaries and nationality'.[66] Environmental history can thus offer a very useful tactic for escaping over-reliance on the nation state paradigm. In this way, horses can help us reach the synovial histories in the fluid spaces between the bones of the nation state.

This study tries to expand the geographical scope by including the former Basutoland, now Lesotho. The horses of empire are bound together, connected by blood, history and styles of horsemanship. South-east Asia and southern Africa are linked together by a common equine heritage. As the following three chapters will show, the horse of the Dutch empire in South-east Asia – the Sumbawan, 'Javanese' or 'oriental' stock – underwent a partial exodus to the Cape; the stock then spread into Basutoland; and horses from both Basutoland and the Cape were relocated to Australia and India within the imperial network, before receiving a massive infusion of genes from Russia, North and South America, England, Ireland, Hungary, even Burma, and also – ironically – from India and Australia.[67]

Global corporations and the nation state, in its control of horses in times of peace and war, were major consumers and producers of horseflesh. War and trade are great diffusers of genotypes. Imperial and, later, colonial concerns also had unintended effects on trends in demography and disease – both animal and human. They influenced the way in which people conceived of elements of nature, such as horses. Equids were pivotal in the economies and societies of the nineteenth-century Indian Ocean and South China Sea, crucial in war, trade, transport and leisure. Of course, horses, like guns and other imports, were not transferred seamlessly to the periphery from the core or from other nodes in the network.[68] The local contexts had an impact on the technology itself, as the chapters that follow will show.[69]

As Chapter 2, 'The Reins of Power', explains, the equine flotsam of empire was marooned in a hostile Africa of disease, scant forage, poisonous plants and dangerous predators – both animal and human. Yet they helped their fellow (human) invaders survive and take control, playing a central role in socio-political processes in the early settlement of the Cape and the interior.

In southern Africa, the Americas and South-east Asia, colonists created new breeds of horses to suit their needs, both deliberately and inadvertently.[70] These horses could differ markedly from those of the metropole, and after a while could come to be identified with the particular colonial culture, facilitating differentiation from the metropole. After independence, horses were often one of the symbols utilised in the development of national pride and self-definition.[71] Chapter 3, 'Blood Horses', offers a broad chronological investigation into changing ideas of 'blood' and 'breed purity' in horse breeding in the Cape from the introduction of horses in the mid-seventeenth century to the beginning of the twentieth century. The initial Dutch settler horse stock was set up with ponies from Sumbawa, and other working breeds were fused by the eighteenth century to form the hardy, utilitarian 'Cape Horse', which was exported to other parts of the global imperial network. The introduction of horse racing to southern Africa wrenched the breeding industry in a different direction, fostering the spread of English Thoroughbreds bred solely for speed and pedigree. The nineteenth-century wars of conquest and human migrations required the utilitarian Cape Horse, but the quality of these sturdy little horses was perceived to decline and various attempts were made to 'save' the breed. Breeding thus set up a fresh suite of debates in both state and popular arenas about the relationship between nurture and nature, ideas that both drew on and were then applied to notions surrounding race, class and gender.

However, attempts by settlers to cling to control of equine power were doomed. Horses were not a technology that could remain in the hands of just one community. Chapter 4, 'The Empire Rides Back', demonstrates how one indigenous group, under Moshoeshoe, came to wrest the technology free from the original group's grasp. Southern Sotho people scattered by the *lifaqane* were consolidated by Moshoeshoe within the territory that came to be known as Basutoland/Lesotho. From the time the Basotho first acquired horses from the 1830s, they deployed them variously in the processes of state building.

A major impetus towards mixing breeds and globalising phenotype came at the cusp of the twentieth century. Nothing globalises like an imperial war. In Chapter 5, 'The last of the old campaigners', the role of horses in the South African War (1899–1902) is considered. Aside from the human cost, the conflict exacted a heavy environmental toll, with massive animal mortality figures. The casualties suffered by these animals were on an enormous scale, contemporaneously understood as a form of 'holocaust'. The chapter analyses the reasons for such fatalities before discussing the human experience of equine mortality, in particular the civic memorialisation of the carnage and how combatants on both sides came to understand this intimate loss.

The immediate aftermath of this devastating war is discussed in Chapter 6: 'The Cinderella of the Livestock Industry', which begins with the devastated post-South African War rural economy and surveys the rise of the horse industry from the beginning of the twentieth century, when it seemed as if the horse era would last forever, to the 1940s, when its imminent end was palpable.

The horse industry had to recreate itself to survive. Thus, Chapter 7,

'High Horses', examines what happened to the horse trade after it began to cater to the high-end leisure market by focusing on an aspect of the growth of an Afrikaner bourgeoisie in the platteland through one of the 'things' they desired: a particular kind of horse. It explores the introduction of the exotic American Saddlebred horse from the United States to the agrarian sectors of the then Cape Province, Orange Free State and Transvaal, centred initially in the rural Karoo. The chapter analyses the elite – and, to an extent, internationalist – rhetorical space that these 'American' imports inhabited, by contrasting it with the self-consciously egalitarian and ethnically unifying discourse surrounding another horse used primarily by Afrikaans speakers, the Boerperd. The comparison between the supporters of American Saddlers and Boerperde, both factions within Afrikaans-speaking society, and an analysis of their quite different discourses reflect two ways of conceptualising identity, especially in the way they mobilised consumer hunger.

Thus, like the colonisers themselves, the equine 'invaders' were the instruments of extensive and long-term changes within both natural and social landscapes. The imperial exchange meant a reciprocal transformation. In abetting some humans in affecting change, the horse itself underwent a morphological transformation and its function within human society also altered significantly over time.

With the globalising spread of horses, the very sensory fabric of human life altered. The final chapter, 'The World the Horses Made', assesses the horse's impact on the human world of southern Africa from the mid-seventeenth century through an examination of the visceral – a way of offering a history that includes noise and smells. Secondly, the chapter debates the idea of historical agency of horses in human history. A debate is emerging over the issue of animal agency in historical processes, dealt with in Chapter 8, which explores the possibility of an animal-centred history. This is a tentative attempt to acknowledge the corporeality of animals and to argue that they have potentially their own history, entangled in that of humans to be sure, but their own nevertheless – as individuals, with memories and intentions and desires.[72]

'Ukukhahlelwa yihashi esifubeni'

A historian is '*ukukhahlelwa yihashi esifubeni*' – someone who has 'been kicked in the chest by a horse', i.e. a person who cannot keep secrets. The archives have yielded a wealth of historical detail and oral history opens up and probes the narratives of memory. Interviewing eyewitnesses to reconstruct past events is combined with recording popular history remembered in anecdote, poem, proverb and song. We have already discussed changes within socio-environmental history that might permit a transformed understanding of the horse as historical actor. Irrespective of whether one accepts a measure of equine agency in the horse's historical role, it is still possible to engage with the horse as a flesh-and-*blood* object. The textual understanding generated by analysing the discourse around them (their owners, the archives, magazines, poetry, songs, stories and myths) is coupled with the physicality of fieldwork (touching horses, watching them move, watching them being ridden, watching them eat and, of course, watching them defecate). Almost two decades ago, the pioneering environmental historian, Donald Worster, called for environmental historians to get mud on their shoes.[73] In my line of work, you step in a lot more than that.

Chapter 2

✳

The Reins of Power

Equine Ecological Imperialism in the Seventeenth and Eighteenth Centuries

ONE OF THE first European settlers in southern Africa was a horse. This creature was the sole survivor of a mid-seventeenth century shipwreck on the Cape of Storms. Wearing the decaying remnants of a rope halter, he was occasionally glimpsed by the sailors who arrived with the first wave of white settlement, but had become so wild he could not be caught.[1] He was the only 'wild' horse to exist in the Cape. Although species of the genus *Equus* – like the zebra and ass – have been present in Africa since earlier times, the horse (*Equus caballus*) is not indigenous, but was introduced into the continent. Although in regular use in North and West Africa from 600 CE, there were no horses in the southern tip prior to European colonisation.[2] African horse sickness and trypanosomiasis presented a pathogenic barrier to horses reaching the Cape overland. Indeed, sub-Saharan Africa had the worst disease environment for equids in the world.[3] The barrier presented to horses meant a barrier to certain groups of humans too.[4] So, it was with difficulty that *Equus* became an element of the 'portmanteau biota' that followed European settlement of southern Africa from the mid-seventeenth century.[5] Horses were the first domestic stock imported by the settlers; and the early modern colonial state that had emerged by the end of the eighteenth century – despite resistance from both indigenous groups and the metropole – was based, at least in part, on the power of the horse in the realm of agriculture, the military and communications.[6]

This chapter seeks to explore a particular facet of horse–human relationships, focusing on their introduction at the Cape and its consequent symbolic and practical ramifications. The growth of the colonial state and the rise of the Vereenigde Oost-Indische Compagnie (VOC, or Dutch East India

Company) from the seventeenth century had considerable consequences for the human and equine populations under its sway, linking far-flung South-east Asia and the southern tip of Africa. The 'invention' of new horse breeds meant the dissemination of equine genes and phenotypes from Europe, Asia and the Americas and their fusion through deliberate state intervention, idealistic individual efforts by groups of breeders and often by the everyday politics of economic pragmatism. The resultant breeds were thus partly a product of their adaptation to new environments and largely a corollary of their close connection to human society. Horses became integral to the settlers' identity as Europeans, used both symbolically and in a material sense to affirm white difference from the indigenous population. They were part of the twin technologies of conquest: the ability to dispossess people of their land and alienate water resources by means of horses and guns was at the very heart of South Africa's colonial history.[7] Horses endowed their owners with enhanced military capabilities, hunting prowess and transport capacity. Greater mobility in turn meant greater involvement in trade networks. Equine technology played pivotal material roles and concomitant cultural roles. From military display to the racing arena, horses meant not only the grasping of power, but the 'performance' of that power in key rituals of colonial society.

As necessary as bread?

The VOC, founded in 1602 and liquidated in 1795, was the largest of the early modern European trading companies, eclipsing all its competitors. It appointed local rulers, kept its own private army and concluded treaties in its own name. To entrench the company's mercantile interest in India and the Far East, the Cape's strategic positioning midway between Europe and the East Indies on contemporary maritime routes and the region's agreeable climate rendered it potentially useful as a site for European settlement. In the early seventeenth century the VOC, like several other European maritime powers, sought a reprovisioning station at the Cape to develop a meat supply from the Khoikhoi and to cultivate fresh produce.[8] By 1652 the decision was taken and the VOC directors, the Heeren XVII, commissioned Jan van Riebeeck[9] to establish a refreshment station to feed the scurvy-ridden and malnourished crews of the ships that passed the Cape en route to the East Indies. In 1657, one year before the first importation of slaves to the colony, the VOC released nine of its employees from their contracts, creating the first land-holding community at the Cape, the *vrijburgers* or free burghers.[10] It was intended that they would establish independent commercial farms that would provide the settlement with a steady food supply. The indigenous Khoikhoi/Khoekhoe and Bushmen[11] proved reluctant to enter the VOC-controlled wage labour economy, which both exasperated and mystified the colonists.[12] This added to the perceived necessity for equine draught power. The settlement initially faced carrying out construction with no draught animals. It was not part of the Dutch tradition to use oxen for draught.[13] Moreover, the cattle the VOC did manage to acquire from Khoikhoi were untrained to cart or plough. (As prey animals, horses and oxen have to be accustomed to the plough and cart. Otherwise, they sense that there is a large, close-following predator behind them who is unaccountably able to dog their every step. The results can be dramatic.)

Unhorsed?

Before the Dutch arrived, the pastoralist Khoikhoi herded cattle and sheep. Although they slaughtered cattle only on occasion, their livestock provided them with milk, meat and skins to make clothing and equipment. Prefiguring the horse's symbolic power, their cattle served, too, as transport and a means of warfare, and the source of status and power. Long before horses became the premier riding animals, oxen had filled this need.[14] At least 150 years previously there were Khoikhoi riders on cattle on the south coast, and on the lower Orange River by 1661. From them, the Xhosa had acquired riding skills by 1686. Other Nguni-speaking groups appear not to have ridden.[15] Trained oxen were ridden with saddles made of sheepskin fastened by a rope girth. They usually had a hole drilled through the cartilage of their noses and a wooden stick with a rope fastened to either end to enable the rider to direct the animal.[16] Only under the first wave of Dutch settlers were donkeys and mules introduced and produced, respectively.[17] Donkeys had been imported from the Cape Verde Islands by Van Riebeeck in 1656. Mules were produced after the 'mare with which the ass had been playing foaled a mule. Two or three more are in foal from the same ass, which is very welcome, as the female ass died [the previous] year whilst foaling'.[18]

The first white settlers attempted what is common to most settlers – to make themselves *at* home on the land by making it *like* 'home'. One aspect of this was the introduction of horses, which were not only an alien species brought in from the metropole, but had the potential to transform the physical environment with their draught power.[19] Van Riebeeck wished to reshape the land itself with horses; he wanted to remove the bushes, plough the soil, and cut down shrubs and trees, with that arboreal animosity common to settler societies, and encircle his settlement with a hedge of wild almonds.[20] He argued that horses would prove invaluable in transporting lumber, firewood, sand and clay to make bricks for construction, and for revolutionising agriculture at the settlement with ploughing and threshing.[21]

The VOC, however, only acceded to requests that delivered immediate material results, and Van Riebeeck's written requests were ignored by his superiors in Amsterdam.[22] Moreover, their original plan was not to create a colony, but rather a refreshment station at which to refuel and reprovision ships en route from Holland to the East. Horses and free burghers were entwined in Van Riebeeck's changing vision for the development of the country; with enough horses, he believed he could provide provisions for the Eastern settlements – and fashion a colony rather than a lowly provisioning station.[23] He attempted to persuade the VOC by insisting that only horses would allow for the exploration of the hinterland. In May 1653 he observed: 'I wish we had a dozen [horses], [then] we could ride armed to some distance in the interior, to see whether anything for the advantage of the Company is to be found there.'[24] He argued that it would accelerate the settling period, saving both time and human labour (particularly after he erected a horse mill in May 1657).[25] He further contended that horses would make the settlers independent of the Khoikhoi, enabling them to acquire their own construction materials and wood.[26] Accordingly, Van Riebeeck argued that his most insurmountable problem was the ongoing shortage of horses.

Horses and white settlers were first sent to the Cape in the same year, 1652; the horses however, were driven onto the island of St. Helena by a storm.[27] In 1653 four of these 'Javanese' (or more likely, Sumbawan) ponies were imported.[28] Van Riebeeck wrote in his journal that horses were *'soo nodigh als broot in den mont zyn'* ('as necessary as bread in our mouths').[29] This was to become a perpetual refrain. He recorded in November 1654:

it is to be wished that we had a few more horses than the [only] 2 we have at present [sent by a reluctant VOC], both of which are being used for brick-making. We should then be able to get from the forest everything we need, both timber and firewood, as the roads are quite suitable for wagons.

In April 1655 he wrote, 'we are therefore still urgently in need of another 6 or 8 horses'.[30] He judged horses to be his 'greatest and principal need', demanding: 'Horses! Give me more horses!'[31] His requests became petitions, which then became pleas, but remained largely ignored by Amsterdam.[32]

Equine settlement was more difficult than human settlement. Importation was perilous – in 1673, for example, most of a cargo of horses drowned and only two were saved, and in 1690 all the horses died on the arduous sea voyage. Simply getting the horses off the ship was hazardous. In 1664, as Van Riebeeck noted with exasperation, 'the old fool' of a skipper fired a salute while the horses were being disembarked, which startled them. One of them, a fawn-coloured male called Generael, was so distressed that he leapt overboard and (luckily) swam safely ashore.[33] Once on land, conditions were equally dangerous. African horse sickness (often dubbed 'distemper') was a perennial problem. An acute, febrile and infectious disease, it was the scourge of the wet season – a disease the settlers believed was carried by evening miasmas.

Disease

Animal afflictions contributed towards shaping human settlement patterns, land use, trade and military capacity (e.g. Bushmen soon learnt when the equines of settler forces were weakened by sickness and the settlers' defensive or offensive capacity was reduced).[34] Right from the beginning of the human movement from the coast to the interior travellers faced an invisible danger more formidable than human or animals and tried to ward it off with remedies that were little more than talismans.[35] This was because horses faced a barrage of dangerous afflictions. Southern Africa – even simply the area now known as South Africa – presents a range of topographies and environments, from temperate to tropical climates, and thus offers a diverse pathogenic and parasitic menu: glanders or '*droes*', farcy, strangles or '*nieuw ziekte*', *snotziekte*; *lampas*, *bota* or *papje*, biliary or gallsickness, roll-sickness or, simply, worms. More parasites were imported in successive waves by sheep-herding Khoikhoi and Bantu-speaking migrants with cattle, goats, dogs and chickens, and later by

Europeans with horses, donkeys and pigs. (No one knows exactly who brought the rat.)[36]

But the real scourges were sleeping sickness and horse sickness: the former lay in wait to the north and the latter inflicted devastating losses on the horse population.[37] They were both vector-borne diseases. (Particularly in the Lowveld and on the east coast in Zululand, trypanosomiasis – colloquially, sleeping sickness or nagana – was spread by tsetse flies.)[38] The result was muscle wastage, loss of energy, fever, anaemia, oedematous swelling, neurological problems and possibly death (the species that infected horses did not infect humans, although humans were affected by their own strain).

Similarly, the other scourge, African horse sickness, did not affect humans: it is a seasonal midge-borne viral disease of horses, donkeys and mules, and zebras, in decreasing order of susceptibility.[39] Endemic to the African continent, horse sickness is characterised by respiratory and circulatory damage, accompanied by fever and loss of appetite. It does not spread directly from one horse to another, but is transmitted by midges, which become infected when feeding on infected horses. It occurs mostly in the warm, rainy season when midges are plentiful, and disappears after the first frost, when the midges die. Most animals become infected in the period from sunset to sunrise, when the midges are most active.[40] At dusk, a horse could seem perfectly healthy and by dawn it could be dead. With froth pouring from its nose and mouth, it basically drowned in its own bodily fluids.

In dealing with these terrifying diseases and others, horse owners came to use idiosyncratic mixtures of local knowledge of disease management over time. Obviously, equine-specific disease had no local tradition of healing (and the first European settlers were not horse experts). Indeed, local knowledge came to be an amalgam, derived from various cultural sources.[41] From indigenous herdsmen who knew how to keep stock alive even in the tsetse belt, they learnt about using smoky fires to discourage the flies.[42] Travellers noticed how pastoralist Khoikhoi would relocate their cattle if they manifested illness.[43] Later, the horse-owning Khoikhoi, for example, kept the horses they acquired bordering the Zandveld. During the 'season of the paardeziekte horses are sent to the Roggeveld in January to avoid the horsesickness of the hotter months'. The first frosts of May provided the signal for the return of the horses.[44] Indeed, the only two useful ways of preventing horse sickness (although a legion of others were attempted) were determined by observational practice: removal to high ground and stabling.[45] By local observation it became clear that horses grazing on higher lands stayed free of horse sickness, so horse owners moved their stock strategically to higher elevation, and mountain ranges were often crown lands reserved at the insistence of *heemraden* and *landdrost* as sanctuaries for horses when 'distemper was abroad', infuriating farmers who coveted them for other livestock.[46] Many farmers had too few horses to be able to arrange transhumance around them, but those with larger herds routinely sent their horses to higher elevation to avoid the seasonal epidemics. From the seventeenth century and gathering impetus from the eighteenth century, the new settlers established themselves in places where their horses could survive. The desire to reach horse sickness-free zones determined the range of settlement. The disease made depredations every year, but after the first crippling outbreak in 1719 (which killed 1,700 horses), roughly every 20 years the disease became epidemic.[47] The degree of immunity in the high Hantam lured potential horse breeders.[48] Some towns, like Colesberg, were established with the *raison d'être* of keeping horses alive. In the northward movement of people, legal boundaries were crossed in order to reach safe horse country.

Yet nowhere was really safe. There was no natural fodder – hay or grain – and forage was often of low quality. Predation by lions and other wildlife played a minor role, killing some of the prime stock and necessitating constant vigilance.[49] In June 1656, when his best stallion was eaten by lions, Van Riebeeck anguished: 'This has greatly inconvenienced us, when one considers all the work done by horses – one alone does more than ten men in pulling the plough, in carrying clay, stone and timber from the forest.' Horses occasionally died from settler misuse (which underlines that these men were not horse owners in their home countries), and legislation was introduced to prohibit the premature use of colts and fillies, underscoring the importance of horses to the young settlement and how seriously the administration took them.[50]

Zebra crossing?

Initially, horse importation was hampered by two factors: the strict economy of the VOC and its desire to maintain the region as a refreshment station rather than develop it as a colony in its own right.[51] Instead, the company suggested that Van Riebeeck avail himself of the '*wilde paarden*', the 'indigenous horses' – zebras and quaggas. Three wild members of the horse family were local to the area – later classified as the mountain zebra (*Equus zebra*); Burchell's zebra (*Equus burchelli*); and the now-extinct quagga (*Equus quagga*).[52] Van Riebeeck initially planned to tame them, but found that he could not even catch them.[53] He recorded in 1660 that one of his explorers, Pieter Meerhoff, shot a 'wild horse' (zebra), and while it was down straddled it in order to sever its sinews, but 'the horse rose with him still astride, and immediately jumped a stream ... and [Meerhoff] received a kick in the face' for his trouble. Van Riebeeck went on to describe the 'horse' as a

> beautiful dapple grey, except that across the crupper and buttocks and along the legs it was ... strangely streaked with white, sky-blue and a brownish-red. It had small ears just like a horse's, a fine head and slender legs like the best horse one could wish for.[54]

He distinguished between quagga (an onomatopoeic word derived from *douqua*, the name the locals used because of its barking cough), which he likened to mules; and zebra, which he likened to horses (which the locals called *haqua*). He tried to capture living specimens of both – clearly hoping to tame them – but the Khoikhoi refused to assist, an indication of the dangerous, intractable nature of these equids, or, as Van Riebeeck argued, an indication that the Khoikhoi were 'beginning to realise more and more that we would thereby be the better able to keep them in submission'.[55] He felt that the 'Hottentoos [sic] [have] at present discovered too much already how these animals cause them injury, as by their means we can beautifully overtake them and be at their heels'.[56]

A later traveller speculated that if domestic stock had not been introduced so rapidly, a more determined and sustained attempt at taming the indigenous 'horses' might have been made.[57] Certainly, even after the introduction of horses and the founding of an embryo horse industry, indigenous equines with their apparent immunity to horse sickness (the first reported outbreak in 1719 killed 1,700 horses) proved an inviting proposition.[58] Anecdotal evidence has it that quagga were more tameable than zebra and only their extinction prevented their use as a viable alternative to horses.[59] In 1785 the Swedish explorer Anders Sparrman noted that it was indeed possible to tame zebras because they showed little fear; they could be turned out with the horses at night to protect them against predators. Furthermore:

Had the colonists tamed them and used them instead of horses, in all probability they would have been in no danger of losing them, either by the wolves or the epidemic disorder [African horse sickness] to which the horses here are subject.[60]

He argued that horses were weaker in the Cape than in Europe and quaggas or zebras would make better use of the dry pasture available.[61] Such cross breedings continued to occur.[62] In the Warm Bokkeveld, for example, in the early 1800s the traveller Lichtenstein encountered what he described in wonderment as 'a remarkable thing':

a tame quagga … feeding in the meadows with the horses, [who] suffered himself readily to be stroked and caressed by the people about. His spirit of freedom was, however, not yet so far subdued as that he would suffer himself to be rode. He was only kept by his owner for the purpose of making experiments in improving his breed of horses.[63]

But as a Cape Town chronicle noted with quiet resignation, 'the zebra is said to be wholly beyond the government of man'.

Invasive species?

Establishing an initial settler equine stock was difficult. The long journey between Holland and the Cape militated against sending Dutch horses, and the VOC resorted instead to sending stock from its base in Java, probably from Sumbawa. 'Javanese' imports were small, hardy creatures, 13.5 hands high.[64] They were also known as 'South East Asia ponies', an amalgam of Arab and Mongolian breeds, their ancestors having been purportedly acquired from Arab traders in the East Indies.[65] Van Riebeeck was unimpressed, criticising these first horses as too light, almost like English genets or insubstantial French horses. They were certainly not as sizeable, heavily built and solid as were the draught horses available in Holland.[66]

In 1659, a year that saw attacks on outlying farms, 16 more horses were permitted by the VOC to be imported from the East in order 'to put an end to theft by the [Khoikhoi]'.[67] Van Riebeeck argued the very 'preservation of the Cape establishment depends completely on our having horses'.[68]

These horses were intended as the seventeenth-century equivalent of 'shock and awe'. Together with a pack of hunting dogs, they were imported (to a certain extent at least) to inspire fear in the Khoikhoi, who were beginning to initiate raids on the settlement.[69] Van Riebeeck argued that a watch of 20 riders would prove a sufficient deterrent.[70] On 7 June 1660 the settler authorities used horses to display settler ascendancy: 'the Commander, galloping along the near bank towards the farms of the … Free Burghers, soon disappeared from their view. His purpose was also to demonstrate the speed of the horses, which caused great awe among them.'[71] Van Riebeeck noted with satisfaction that the local population were suitably astonished and impressed by horses because of the 'miracles' of speed he performed with them.

This laid the foundation for making horses key to a symbolic display of power that was to persist. Parallels can be drawn with the introduction of guns. Both introductions buttressed the perceived power of the owners and helped establish a social order in a time of flux.[72] As Storey has observed of guns, a 'new order is made out of a demonstration'.[73] The symbolic display went hand in hand with the practical deployment of horses in the pursuit and maintenance of material power.

The first commando was established in 1670, which initiated the horse's formal structured military role in South Africa, as opposed to draught, transport, guard duty and ad hoc armed expeditions.[74] The horse-based commando was a new institution for frontier policing actions (rather than defence against coastal attack from foreign powers). Essentially it was a 'mounted infantry', travelling as cavalry and attacking as infantry: the men dismounted to shoot, fired, retreated, reloaded and then charged again.[75] By this time there were over 50 horses at the Cape, all still owned by the VOC itself, which made a small unit possible. Over time, when both horses and some men ceased to be under direct company control, all burghers between 16 and 60 were liable for commando duty and were expected to provide their own horse and saddle and, frequently, their servants.[76] The commando developed as part of the social machinery in the construction of settler identity; and, as time passed, particularly of Boer masculine identity (discussed in Chapters 5 and 6), although the commandos relied on other groups too. Similarly, as Storey points out, although the right to own a firearm was integral to citizenship, the ironies and complexities of paternalism allowed servants to assist by bearing arms on commando. Horse-based commandos allowed Van Riebeeck to round up deserting slaves, something that would otherwise have been impossible.[77] Furthermore, horses were always brought home from raiding or punitive missions because they were considered more useful than the Bushmen, most of whom were perceived to be unenslavable.

There were – perhaps consequently – several attacks on horses. Two were killed by Khoikhoi in July 1672, for example. It is not certain whether these attacks were motivated with the intent of obliterating horse stock; out of a desire for food; or whether a horse acted as a proxy of white settlement, being perhaps one of its most visible and vulnerable manifestations.[78] The body of the horse was thus both a symbol of power and, perhaps because of this, a site of struggle. This supports a broader argument that 'animals and their bodies appear to be one site of struggle over the protection of (human) identity and the production of cultural difference'.[79]

Van Riebeeck was drawing on an entrenched tradition, because horses had long been associated in western Europe with the society of the elite and with the culture of hegemony. The horse distinguished the ruler from the ruled, with the rider a symbol of dominance.[80] The cost included not only the purchase price, but food, the transport of food and water, protection, structural shelter and space,[81] as well as accoutrements (tack, training devices and tack-cleaning materials), shoes or hoof trimming, labour (grooming, exercise and training), and medical attention.[82] In Europe, the nobility's focus on a range of equine activities (mounted games, dressage, ladies' riding, hunting, carriage or coach driving, or racetrack) and – as the Western/non-Western interface grew – an interest in exotic breeds like Arabians and Barbs[83] led to a marked and ever-increasing differentiation in varieties of horses bred for particular social niches. The complex, almost balletic, movements of what we would now call dressage, the style identified as *haute école*, swept Europe at the same time as Van Riebeeck used his riding horses as blunter instruments of power.[84] Practitioners were largely of the aristocracy, who had the leisure and financial resources to pursue the *art* – rather than the utilitarian dimension – of riding.

This 'art' was entirely absent in early settler society at the Cape and horses retained a utilitarian function until the beginning of the nineteenth century. Because most colonists came to South Africa in the service of the VOC, the majority of early settlers represented the lowest class of Holland's and Germany's hierarchical societies.[85] Company employment was both hazardous and poorly paid, thus attracting the most indigent elements of European society to its service – men unfamiliar with *haute école*.[86] In a different way, however, horses did become a symbol of status within the evolving southern African communities.

As the settlement developed, a hierarchical slave-owning landed gentry emerged in the Cape Colony predicated on a finely differentiated rank system signified to some extent by the social use of horses.[87] For example, in terms of the mid-eighteenth-century Tulbagh Code, slaves were not allowed passage through the streets of Cape Town on horseback or in a wagon.[88] There were also regulations on what rank of person could have horses with funeral furnishings. The sumptuary laws of 1755 dictated the number of horses permitted to draw a carriage; and coachmen and footmen could only wear livery if the owner was sufficiently well-to-do.[89] Differentials of wealth became more apparent over time.[90] The landed elite translated their wealth into local influence.[91] One of the key visible hallmarks of authority was riding. Indeed, a fundamental indicator of male *vrijburger* identity was the right to own a horse and gun. Thus, some subtle class distinctions were signified through horses: Shell has pointed out that the real difference between *knechts* and slaves was that *knechts* were permitted to carry arms and ride horses.[92] In a nuanced analysis, Worden has shown that as the eighteenth century came to an end, in an early nineteenth-century slave rebellion, for example, the rebel leaders dared to commandeer horses. In an almost saturnalian 'turning the world upside down', they performed their shift from slaves to free rebel leaders by their move from their hired wagon to horseback. It was highly symbolic when the rebels commanded the farmers to dismount and be carried in the wagons through the Zwartland. Even more tellingly, in their ensuing defence plea, one was actually more willing to admit his possession of a gun than a horse, while a number of slaves contended that they had 'been put' onto horses, as Worden observes, in 'a passive syntax that tried to minimize their active guilt in such a symbolic transgression of the social order'.[93] In other words, they were protesting their innocence of having literally got on their high horses.

Holding one's horses

Right from the beginning, despite the efforts of the authorities, horses were not contained by the ruling elite. Initially the VOC tried to monopolise both trade and ownership; neither attempts proved successful. There are parallels: the horse escaped settler control in other contexts, escaping from European settlements in the New World by 1680.[94] Horses were highly coveted by indigent whites, black communities, Khoikhoi and Bushmen. These groups frequently converted desire into possession. Technologies of power were adopted and adapted; but they could not be contained.

Just as with guns, the Khoikhoi were at first cautious, but quickly embraced the new technology insofar as they could gain access to it. Over time, asymmetric access to guns and horses drove the Khoikhoi into liminal areas or to join other groups like the Griqua or Tswana, discussed in Chapters 3 and 4. At first, this was done illegally. In the eighteenth century, when the Cape claimed jurisdiction over all Khoikhoi, they were forbidden to possess horses.[95] As previously discussed, because the indigenous population realised the extent to which horses formed the white power base, there were attacks on horses. Furthermore, as local communities realised the utilitarian value of the horse, stock theft became an increasing factor. But later such trade became more extensive and legitimate and the direction of acquisition was frequently reversed in the next century, as will be discussed in the following chapters.

Horse trading

The number of horses slowly grew. Although overworked, the horses initially imported bred successfully and by 1662 there was a herd of 40. They were now integral to the defence of the settlement, with 18 mounted men patrolling the border against cattle-raiding Khoisan. By 1667 50 horsemen were on watch duty. One of these guards and his mount drowned while drunkenly fording a river, and it is significant that the new settlement mourned the mare far more than the soldier.[96]

The original intention to confine the settlement to a slice of coastline had to be abandoned when not enough food was produced and the *vrijburgers* were liberated from VOC control to farm as individuals.[97] The *vrijburgers* engaged in small-scale farming, using unallocated areas as grazing commonage. Like their human counterparts, horses ceased to be under the sole control of the authorities in 1665, when a public auction was held and *vrijburgers* were granted the right to buy and breed horses.[98] However, they continued to be a public asset and were considered vital to the functioning of the settlement, so the authorities still exercised a controlling hand. In May 1674, for example, a man was prosecuted for shooting his own (rogue) horse.[99] The rising stock also saw an increase in quantity and a decrease in quality. Because the initial genetic pool was small, inbreeding affected the herds and certain birth defects such as weak hindquarters were becoming more obvious. In a 1686 *plakkaat*, the governor, Simon van der Stel, tried to prevent the deterioration of stock, imposing a fine of 40 rixdollars if colts were used under the age of three years; and decreeing that cruelty could be punished by a special magistrate. The administration also began importing stud stallions, apparently from Persia.[100]

The number of horses continued to increase. In 1673 two more Javanese ponies were introduced, and in 1676 two horses and four mules arrived from Europe. In 1683 four horses were imported from Persia via Mauritius; and 11 horses arrived from Persia in 1869. By 1681 the *vrijburgers* possessed 106 horses and the company 91. Along with the shifting of the settlement's borders, outposts were established at the front line of expansion. The frontier zone was uncontrollable and trade took place between *vrijburgers* and Khoikhoi who lived in the interior; the VOC was simply not equipped to control this illicit trade.[101] *Trekboeren* – quasi-nomadic stock farmers – moved further away, shifting the settlement from the south-western Cape to almost as far north as the Orange River and to the Great Fish River in the east. In 1700, when the trekboer lifestyle took off, there were 928 horses in the settlement. By 1715 the VOC had 396 horses and the *vrijburgers* 2,325. In 1719, when the first crippling epidemic of horse sickness hit, the horse population survived despite the loss of 1,700 horses. By 1744 the colonists had 5,749 horses. Other breeds, like Hackneys, were imported in 1792.[102] Horse breeding increased, albeit at an occasionally fluctuating rate. This resulted in a 'breed' or, more accurately, a broad morphological type of horse that came to be known as the 'Cape horse'.[103]

The Cape horse

It is a common trend that colonists create new breeds of horses to suit their needs. If a local horse existed (or if there were no indigenous horses, but various breeds were more readily available to import than those of the metropole), it could be utilised and often cross-bred with imported stock and deliberately shaped, ultimately resulting in a new form of horse. These horses could differ markedly from those of the metropole and in time could come to be identified with the particular colonial culture, facilitating differentiation from the metropolitan culture.

This general pattern was followed, but with slight variation, in the southern African context. There is little evidence to suggest an early identification of settler horse stock as superior to metropolitan breeds. As discussed, Van Riebeeck criticised the first horses as too light; they were not solid, like the draught horses available in Holland.[104] Correspondingly, there were ongoing but limited efforts by the authorities to alter the indigenising equine stock throughout the seventeenth and eighteenth centuries, chiefly by importing fresh breeding stock with a view to improving the various horse types in the Cape. 'Improvement' in this period meant simply making them hardier and larger (rather than faster, as in the nineteenth century, as the next chapter will discuss). Over time the distinguishing phenotypical type or 'breed' came to be spoken of as the 'Cape horse'.

Horses creolised as humans did. The Cape horse was the result of a globalised fusion of the original import (South-east Asian or 'Javanese' pony, itself arguably of Arab–Persian stock);[105] imported Persians (1689); South American stock (1778);[106] North American stock (1792); English Thoroughbreds (1792); and later Spanish Barbs (1807);[107] with a particularly significant Arabian genetic influence. In 1769 the first export of horses occurred ('small and ugly, but indubitably horses').[108] They were destined for Madras and initiated an interest in breed improvement, which in turn encouraged the importation of the new breeding stock. From 1769 it gained escalating renown as an army remount and was exported to India for use by the British over the next century. Increasingly after 1795, when VOC rule was temporarily replaced by imperial British administration (which became permanent in 1806), enthusiasm for horse racing proliferated and in 1769, the same year that the first horses were exported, the Cape-based horses diverged. One 'breed' was to meet the needs of the racing fraternity, which used Thoroughbreds (usually a Thoroughbred sire and a colonial dam), and the other 'breed' to be used for riding, transport and commandos (some descendants of which eventually became the 'Boerperd'). This Boerperd was variously known as the Cape pony;[109] the Caper (the name adopted in India for race horses exported from the Cape); and by English-speaking settlers as the 'Colonial', the 'South African' and the 'Boer horse'. Dutch speakers referred to these utilitarian horses as the Hantam (an area famous for horse breeding); Melck or Kotze horse (surnames of famous breeders); or even the Bossiekoppe (bushyheads or 'thick headed'/unrefined) by those less than delighted by its attributes.

By the end of the eighteenth century a visitor labelled the Cape horse admittedly small, but with 'a cross of the Arabian fire and are hardy in the greatest degree'.[110] The Cape horse was phenotypically very different from English Thoroughbreds. They were small, compact, short-legged horses of about 14.3 hands. They were distinctively hardy, with a famously strong constitution, and were disease resistant, due to natural selection of the most vulnerable to local ailments. As previously shown, for the first 100 years, the breeding stock was primarily South-east Asian, with admixture from Arabian and 'Persian' stock, and an injection of English Thoroughbred blood from the late eighteenth and early nineteenth centuries. This creature, a product of many 'breeds' from different continents, was increasingly stamped an indigenous horse 'belonging' to the Cape.

Moreover, settler riding styles replaced those of the metropole. This process developed during the eighteenth century, which was the period that the Cape ceased to be an extension of Europe and became instead a *colonial* society (due largely to a decrease in settler immigration and an increase in the birth of Dutch speakers). The trot, for example, considered 'unnatural', was replaced by an ambling jog called a tripple (or *trippel*) or slow gallop, making it easy to ride while carrying a whip or gun.[111] Lichtenstein commented on the 'short gallop' of the Cape horses, which was

> very agreeable to the rider as well as to the horse … This pace appears
> so natural to the race of horses in question that it is not without some
> difficulty the riders can ever get them into a trot or walk.[112]

Thus, the horse, like its human owners, had come to stay and had become a new force in the area, both adapting and being adapted to local conditions.

Making tracks

The world of the road is little explored by southern Africanist historians – but following horses allows one a better view.[113] Long before the horse's arrival, Khoikhoi transhumant pastoralists had created a network of hard-beaten paths through the Karoo. When the first Dutch expeditions ventured inland, they often traced the paths trodden by game. As time went by, the *vrijburgers* used pasture land beyond the settled areas, following the tracks of the Khoikhoi. In summer months they sent livestock inland (although initially they were supposed to keep them within a day's journey of the settlement). The roads became sand tracks, with maintenance of roads rudimentary.[114] As settlement expanded, existing paths connected key centres like Stellenbosch, Swellendam and Mossel Bay. Near Cape Town the farmers travelled in light carts or chaises, or rode horseback, but longer journeys were usually by ox wagon. In the early years of the eighteenth century horses roamed freely and grazed along sidewalks in Cape Town, and the streets of Cape Town were hazardous as pigs burrowed holes that uncannily attracted the hooves of vulnerable horses. The stench from uncollected animal dung was considerable. Thus, in 1724 authorities designated the Boeren Plein (later Riebeeck Square) the place to outspan. Further amendments were made to make traffic less disruptive and wagon drivers were discouraged from cracking their whips, which scared passers-by and even broke windowpanes.

As frontier conditions developed, the road network adjusted to suit changing traffic flow. The orientation of the roads in the early days of settlement was determined primarily by the needs of local farmers to migrate seasonally. Major roads to the north were straightened as the frontier shifted.[115]

A journey of 400–500 miles took six weeks. A trip between Cape Town and Swellendam took at least 60 hours or almost two weeks. Even in the vicinity of Cape Town roads were in bad repair. It took six hours to travel from Cape Town over the sandy Cape Flats to Stellenbosch. Each day's *skof* (journey) ranged from five to 15 hours, often during the night, so that the cattle could graze in the day. Travellers depended on their own food and fodder, and on the intermittent generosity of the farmers along the routes.[116] Riders on a long journey would ride one pony and lead two others, if they could afford to, riding for two hours and 'off-saddling' for half an hour near water and shade, if possible. At the end of a journey, the saddle and bridle would be removed and the horse knee haltered (by fastening its head to its leg just above the knee, with its leg lifted up and tied with a clove hitch); the horses then grazed until evening, before being driven into the kraal (or stable).[117] The horses of wealthier owners were fed on oats, barley or Indian corn, when available, and fodder had to be carried along with the human supplies.[118]

If the going was level and firm, the speed was about three miles an hour; by cart and horse, perhaps six miles an hour. But travellers often averaged only six hours a day because of the difficulties of crossing rivers, the crudeness of the tracks that passed for roads, and the frequent halts demanded by thirsty and tired oxen or horses.[119] There were no bridges, so larger rivers like the Breede were crossed by pontoons. The mountain ranges posed the biggest challenge, like those over the Outeniqua ranges or the Hottentots Holland Mountains. As Sparrman noted of crossing this range in 1775:

> The way up it was very steep, stony, winding ... Directly to the right of the road there was a perpendicular precipice, down which, it is said, that wagons and cattle together have sometimes the misfortune to fall headlong, and are dashed to pieces.

Horses left their imprint on the way the roads were negotiated. For example, the spacing of outspans (resting places) was dictated by how well horses or oxen would manage various topographical problems along the road. The average spacing was the distance the animals could travel in a day (the distance between water points was less, if possible).[120] On a more prosaic level, geography was further altered by horses when paths formed in the veld as vegetation was trampled, plant regeneration was hampered and root damage occurred. This damage was, however, minimal – particularly in comparison to comparative examples from the American West and Australian Outback, where equine impact on the environment was extensive.

The weeds of war

Horses were thus part of the rapacious biota of empire. The ecologically parvenu Europe was populated by invasive, dominating weeds: animals and plants that were pre-adapted to disturbed environments, a basic biota that dated only to the last Ice Age.[121] The European human weeds were successful imperialists because wherever they went indigenous populations and local ecosystems collapsed under their biological advance. As Crosby has described, Europeans established themselves in distant but temperate countries and often successfully shaped them into 'neo-Europes': the United States, Canada, Australia, New Zealand, Argentina and Uruguay.[122] These were the environments where Europeans rapidly became numerically dominant over the indigenous peoples, with the key backing of their allies – the domesticated animals, pests, pathogens and weeds that the humans carried with them. These adjuncts of auxiliary invasive species were sometimes consciously marshalled by settlers, but they often effected incidental imperialism.[123]

Similarly, at the Cape, the seventeenth-century power takeover and technologies of transfer included the horse. Yet, unlike in Crosby's 'lands of demographic takeover', in southern Africa the indigenous population remained demographically dominant, but power was nevertheless soon wrested into the hands of the settlers. Horses in the southern African context were not weeds, but rather delicate hothouse flowers. They failed to flourish, were easily eradicated by local disease, and had to be coaxed and nurtured into defending the white settlement.

The virgin soil epidemics of Crosby's model that decimated local populations worked the other way. Diseases, plant poisoning, predation and such challenges shaped the early cultural understanding and totemic resonance of the horses in southern Africa. Unlike the horse in other frontiers of settlement, like the nineteenth-century American West,[124] horses did not represent freedom or wildness to the white settlers; instead, they represented civilisation.[125] This was because there were no indigenous or escaped feral horses to be 'broken in'. Extremely difficult exercises in importation thus had to be undertaken and, even after arrival, equine existence in the colony remained precarious, threatened by lack of fodder,[126] disease and predators,[127] both human and animal. The frontier consequently did not develop rodeo or related equestrian games – there were no contests to see who could ride the wildest bronco. Horses were not wild creatures to be tamed; they were at first extensions of western civilisation to be nurtured and protected in order to serve the white expansionist project. Horses first meant (white) civilisation – both symbolically and physically. This was not to remain the case, however.

Horse in southern Africa

The equine weeds of empire found the soil of Africa difficult, and they remained delicate, requiring constant attention. Yet they helped their fellow (human) invaders to flourish, playing a key role in social and political processes in the early settlement of the Cape. After their hard-fought introduction, resisted by the metropole, horses were first used as draught animals to effect changes in the new environment. Between 1652 and 1662 the utility of the ox was eclipsed in the Cape, particularly in settler perceptions, by the value of the horse, which became a symbol of power and a useful draught animal.

The horse was also utilised by the VOC authorities as a signifier of difference and a marker of social status. It emphasised the difference between native and settler, to facilitate the psycho-social subduing of the indigenous population (and later, to a limited extent, to highlight the differences among white classes). Being such potent symbols, horses became victims of attack and, quite aside from human intimidation, remained vulnerable in their new environment, threatened by disease and natural hazards.

Thus, the role of the horse was predicated on *power* in both symbolic and material manifestations. Their iconographic role as status symbol served as evidence of wealth and power in individual transactions, as well as public spectacle. This helped entrench difference between those of higher and lower status. Equally, in a more material role, they advanced both economic and political ambitions.

From the last decade of the eighteenth century, two distinct horse cultures emerged – one embraced the British-led racing industry, the other a more utilitarian use of horses. There followed a conflict of horse cultures between those who clung to metropolitan fashions and those adopting 'indigenous' settler modes. As will be explored in the next chapter, moreover, the divergence led to a morphological difference between the race horses, which were of the English Thoroughbred type, and the utilitarian horses, which came to be considered a definite 'breed' known as the Cape horse, initially not accorded special status, but later invested with the pride of settler society. Indigenous and newly mixed, mobile groups took the horses' reins too. History was made with horse power; and equally the horses were shaped by human history, incorporating the environmental and shifting human needs into their very blood.

Chapter 3

Blood Horses

Equine Breeding, Lineage and Purity in Nineteenth-century South Africa

BLOOD HAS SATURATED the horse world. Its human inhabitants have deployed a vocabulary suffused with the sanguinary: 'bloodstock', 'blood heads', 'full bloods', 'warm bloods', 'cold bloods', 'hot bloods', 'bloodlines' and 'blood weeds'. Horse blood has played significant roles in human history; indeed, some humans have cared about equine blood for longer than they have about their own. Horse and human blood have even co-mingled.[1] This chapter explores ideas about blood in several different contexts in nineteenth-century South Africa, particularly in the Cape Colony. The emphasis is on how these ideas, partly permeating from the metropole and partly vernacular, influenced both people and horses in a range of ways from changes within colonial society to the genetic development of the horse itself. The focus is firstly on how breeding regimes, centred on blood, reflected shifting social preoccupations, both practical and ideological. Secondly, the chapter offers an analysis of the constant interplay between state officials and private breeders and between official discourse and popular ideas that helped shape this process. The expression superciliously used by those whose veins carried socially approved blood and who despised the ill-bred, both human and animal, was 'blood will tell' – and, indeed, it does. Blood tells a story about both the horses and humans of nineteenth-century South Africa.[2]

First blood

As we have seen, in sub-Saharan Africa there was no 'wild' horse blood. Breeding was never easy and, unlike in North and South America, significant feral populations did not arise. As the previous chapter explained, zebras – the 'blood brothers' of the horse – did not prove suitable for the settlers' needs. The various ruling elites were at pains to transform the indigenising equine stock throughout the seventeenth and eighteenth centuries. The initial Dutch settler horse stock was set up with ponies from Sumbawa, and by the later eighteenth century other working breeds were fused to form the hardy, utilitarian Cape horse, which was later exported through the global imperial network to India and Australia. Thus, the robust little Indonesian ponies received several injections of various bloodlines. As previously discussed, this Cape Horse was a mixture of the South-east Asian or 'Javanese' pony, Persians, South and North Americans, English Thoroughbreds and a few Spanish Andalusians.[3] Over time, one 'breed' (or, more correctly, phenotypical type) came to predominate and be regarded as the Cape horse.[4]

Khoikhoi Levies. Source: J. Carruthers, Thomas Baines, Eastern Cape Sketches (Houghton: The Brenthurst Press, 1990, p. 195)

This horse escaped its human provenance. In Cape Town and its surrounds, the management of horses did not remain in white hands. At first, specialised slaves took on the tasks of wagon makers, saddlers, blacksmiths, grooms, saddlers and coachmen. Grooms were 'coloured boys', 'Hottentot[s] or Cape boy[s]'.[5] A VOC official stationed at Stellenbosch noted of the Khoikhoi: 'some of them are very accomplished riders, and have learned to break horses and master them'.[6] Certain groups were perceived as particularly adept over time. In the eighteenth and nineteenth centuries, Malays became widely considered 'good drivers' and to 'thoroughly understand horses'.[7] The belief that Malays possessed an instinctive knowledge of horses became entrenched.[8] Malay men were considered 'excellent coachmen, their ability in the way of managing horses is proverbial, and it is a pretty sight to see them tooling a four-in-hand round an abrupt angle, or into a narrow courtyard, or passage'.[9] Many wealthier Malays also owned their own horses and carriages.[10]

Sir Charles D'Oyly, Malays Going to Town
Source: C. Pama, Regency Cape Town: Daily Life in the Early eighteen-thirties with
hitherto Unpublished Johannesburg Album of Sketches by Sir Charles D'Oyly
(Cape Town: Tafelberg, 1975), p. 32

As the previous chapter noted, the first imported horses were initially the property of the VOC and then of a small number of white settlers and officials. Swiftly, however, they were coveted by other groups: Khoikhoi, Bushmen, black communities, Griqua and indigent whites. These groups frequently converted desire into possession. At first this was done illegally; indeed, in the eighteenth century, when the Cape claimed jurisdiction over all Khoikhoi, they were forbidden to possess horses.[11] In the nineteenth century trade became more difficult for the authorities to control. In the early decades of the nineteenth century, horses were illegally traded along with guns in an arms race moving north and east among indigenous groups, as discussed in the previous chapter. Between 1833 and the mid-1840s horses accompanied the human diaspora in great numbers north of the Orange and Vaal Rivers and east over the Drakensberg mountain range.

The Griqua were the first people from the Cape to settle alongside or across the Orange River. Some Griqua raided or traded with local Setswana-speaking African communities for cattle, which they then traded with the Cape Colony for firearms and horses, as discussed in the following chapter. In the nineteenth century there were also major white resettlements: the Great Trek from 1836 to 1852 from the Cape Colony through the Orange Free State to the Transvaal and Natal. In 1874 the Dorsland Trekkers passed into the northern hinterland. Behind the trekking settlers in southern Africa and also among other groups, like the Griqua and Basotho, was an infrastructure based on animal-powered transport. The trekboers migrated in *kakebeen* ox wagons into the hinterland of the Cape in the seventeenth and eighteenth centuries, followed by traders, missionaries and settlers, who also used predominately ox wagons. The ox wagon became a necessity

of the South-African resident: it is his house, his ship, and in many cases his income. Until he builds a house, he lives in the wagon ... From the general suppleness of the vehicle, [owing to the small amount of iron used in its construction,] it is well adapted for the purposes of crossing the steep-banked rivers and stony roads.[12]

As the migrations of different groups escalated in the early nineteenth century, the hunter Chapman noted that the Boers were strictly forbidden to trade 'powder or horses' with neighbouring black groups, although, while they guarded against English traders handing over such bounty, they themselves did 'not all refrain from making a bargain now and then themselves'.[13] The direction of acquisition was often reversed. For example, the people coming to be considered part of the Basotho developed first into horse owners on an unprecedented scale and then into major horse sellers by the end of the nineteenth century, as discussed in the next chapter. Throughout the nineteenth century, travellers noted increasing encounters with horse-owning indigenous groups, worried white military officials recorded the accumulation of horses by potential adversaries, and Bushman rock art began to depict both black and white horsemen.[14] Some Bushmen incorporated the horses they themselves captured into their hunting practice, often riding them bareback, for example, to help run down eland. The notion of a massive 'Neolithic divide' between those of pastoralist inclination and hunter-gatherers has been exploded. The Bushmen leapt this gulf easily, acquiring (although not breeding) horses and becoming adroit riders. Domestic animals were easier for erstwhile hunter-gatherers to use than domesticated plants, as they were more easily incorporated into their lifestyle. Certainly, the last generations of Maloti-Drakensberg hunter-gatherers both rode and ate horses.[15] As an informant born in 1880 remembered:

> Early on, the Basotho were on good terms with the Bushmen, but later the Bushmen stole cattle and horses. They killed the horses and cattle – anything to eat. They used to catch young horses and ride them without ropes or anything. Even if a horse bucked and jumped, they could sit on it.[16]

Other bloods

The 'longing for other bloods', as C.S. Lewis described the human obsession with some animals, manifested in one group in particular – in the Maloti-Drakensberg mountains' rugged east-facing escarpment.[17] The AmaTola, a Creolised group of mounted raiders composed of Bushmen, Khoi, Africans and a miscellany of recruits from other groups assimilated horses into not only their new raiding existence, but into a belief system already replete with creatures.[18] The AmaTola initially brought horses to the Drakensberg from the eastern Cape frontier, raided cattle from Bantu speakers and white farmers below the escarpment, and proceeded to forge a fresh identity using a new combination of symbols and leaving a residue of their religious thought in rock paintings.[19] Challis points out a recurring pattern in the paintings of horses and their riders in connection with baboons and horses, and therianthropes.[20] Baboons and horses were key to the religious ideology of these riders. The baboon was a totem of protection believed to be able to raid crops and steal livestock with impunity, and horses were akin to baboons in their potency.[21] During ritual dances, such power could be harnessed: the dancing humans were depicted changing into baboons and horses. Thus, shamans literally became 'horsemen', shifting between human, horse and baboon and assuming their protective powers to keep the AmaTola safe on their mounted forays. Thus, the tools of colonialism and conquest were appropriated not only materially by the mounted raiders, but also symbolically in their new cosmology, Creolising around old and new beliefs merging in a changing world: men and horses became of one blood.

Horses in rock art. Source: P. Mitchell & B. Smith (Eds), The Eland's People
(Johannesburg: Wits University Press, 2009, p. 72).

However, Bushmen did not breed horses of their own, whereas the Kora, Griqua, Xhosa and Sotho, who were groups who had experience of stock breeding, began breeding horses as soon as they were acquired. For example, from the 1820s the colonial trade with the Xhosa ensured that horses and guns were transferred, although this was forbidden, and mounted Xhosa groups dispersed widely, even north of the Orange, amassing cattle and human capital (in the form of Khoikhoi, Bushmen and mixed-race supporters). They started breeding horses themselves and by the end of the 1830s an official noted: 'Not many years ago the Kaffir … looked upon a horse as a strange animal which few of them would venture to mount. Now they are becoming bold horsemen, are possessed of large numbers of horses.'[22]

In the main, their horses were of a mixed kind that could be loosely classified as Cape horses. As noted in the previous chapter, the tough little Cape horse was phenotypically very different from English Thoroughbreds. As George Thompson noted appreciatively, for example:

> I had travelled this day about 56 miles, the last 30 at full gallop on a hardy African pony, saddled for me fresh from the pasture. This would have killed almost any English horse, but the country breed of Cape horses is far more hardy than [that of the English].[23]

Nature and nurture both played a role. Natural selection had left them with a strong constitution and some immunity to local disease. Their early development was also a factor. As Heinrich Lichtenstein noted, local breeders' horses were 'so fine' and 'owing to their being accustomed from their youth to seek their nourishment upon dry mountains are easily satisfied, and grow so hard in the hoofs'.[24] By the end of the eighteenth century there were 47,436 horses in the Cape. These mixed-strain animals were to meet the growing colony's needs for riding, transport and cavalry horses. But another 'breed' was required to meet the needs of the racing fraternity, and their very name indicated the emphasis that their owners laid on their 'blood': Thoroughbreds.

Good blood

Pedigree had already begun to be considered seriously in the metropole, far from the young Cape Colony, a recent catch in the imperial net. From the late seventeenth century breeders had begun to show concern about ancestry; lineage began to matter in the realm of animal breeding in a way it had not done so previously, although some rudimentary notion of heredity had existed since the Tudor Acts were passed in the mid-sixteenth century requiring horse breeders to cull those of inferior size.[25] Intrinsic to these notions was the centrality of blood. Indeed, blood had long been important in the way reproduction was understood; it was considered the substance of heredity.[26] Even Aristotle was of the opinion that semen and menstrual blood were required to ensure procreation, with male input being active and the female contribution entirely passive. The thrust, as it were, of Aristotle's argument was taken up again by Italian experts in Henry VIII's court and prevailed until the end of the eighteenth century.

This came at the same time as British breeders were trying to improve livestock, with farming becoming more scientific in an attempt to feed the exploding population. Before the nineteenth century, 'breed' was usually loosely defined as a type of horse from a particular region, accompanied by the corollary that this specific environment actually shaped the type's characteristics. Over the century it changed in meaning: a breed came to be a biological group with specific shared traits. This was because breeders of livestock like Robert Bakewell (1725–95) used the principles governing heredity, carefully selecting both parents, inbreeding to those desirable individuals and then selecting for future breeding among the best of the progeny (especially the male progeny). Bakewell collected the 'best' animals he could find and then closed his herd to develop the desired 'type'. Through rigorous selection and inbreeding, he gradually made his herd 'breed true' for the required traits and his success led to widespread interest in 'pure breeds' that bred true for these particular traits. Such developments challenged the notion that livestock were valuable simply as a collective quantity, replacing it with the idea that some *breeds* were more valuable than others. (And, indeed, as, for example, in the horse racing arena, the idea that some *individuals* were more valuable still.) Eighteenth-century developments, particularly the ill-defined but widely believed notion of 'race constancy', contributed to the idea that good horses were bred from 'ancient lineage' and by preserving purity. By the late eighteenth century a public system of record was established to track the ancestry of Thoroughbreds.[27] There were differences between the two systems. Bakewell did not give as much credit to pedigree, whereas English Thoroughbred horse breeders used pedigree as a key selection device in the process of preserving genealogical 'purity'.

Hot blood

By the late seventeenth century the English had developed a keen interest in horse racing, a dramatic divergence from the *haute école* still embraced on the continent. This new pursuit required a new seat (or position in the saddle) and ultimately a changed equine physiognomy. The Thoroughbred came into being for galloping, adapted both conformationally and in terms of disposition.

The characteristic for which these horses were selectively bred was simply speed: they needed to be leaner, of lighter build and longer legged (almost a retention of neotenous traits) and were thus far more physically vulnerable and less suitable for farm or draught work than other horses. Thoroughbred breeders drew neither on the horses of the *haute école* nor on those of draught stock, but on the blood of the Barb, the Turk and the Arabian.[28]

As Russell observes, as early as the sixteenth century local mares considered worthy were bred to imported stallions.[29] The stallions were at first heavy Italian and Flemish stock; a century later, however, affluent breeders wanted Spanish or North African Barbs to provide the 'hot blood' believed to be lacking in English horses. Such heat and animation were considered inevitable casualties of the wet, chilly environment, so fresh blood was always sought. When racing began to capture the imagination of the aristocracy, native English mares were cross-bred with imported Barb stallions. As racehorses were frequently gelded, new racehorses had to be produced by crosses for each generation. From the late seventeenth century Arab and Turkish stallions supplemented the Barbs and with them came the Arab tradition of recording lineage over many generations of horses (focusing, in the Arab case, on the mares). Indeed, the very name 'Thoroughbred' comes from the Arabic *kuhaylan* (pure bred all through).[30] The belief in the hybrid vigour of crosses waned and, coupled with the growing realisation that it was untrue that hot blood would cool in the temperate climate, a new faith in 'pure blood' arose. These English-bred stallions replaced cross-bred geldings.

Just as for humans, equine potential had long been understood to be encoded as blood, representing innate qualities handed down from generation to generation. Thus, horses were homologous with humans in a hierarchy of rank according to their birth.[31] Explanations of pedigree were couched in the language of class. As Harriet Ritvo has noted, the growing interest in breed classifications became a way of managing and making sense of other problems of race and class distinctions.[32] The rise of interest in and celebration of prestigious progenitors paralleled (and encouraged) the codification of a genealogical guide to the metropolitan (human) aristocracy. In 1791 the Jockey Club published the *General Stud Book* a full decade before the first publication of *Debrett's Peerage* (1802) and almost a generation before *Burke's Peerage* (1826). The *Stud Book* was compiled simply to patrol the world of racing and ensure that mature horses were not run in races meant for youngsters. But, increasingly, age was replaced by 'blood' as the primary concern. Landry has shown that 'English' Thoroughbreds had their ancestry 'imaginatively anglicized'.[33] The 'massive mongrelisation', in Russell's words, of imported horse breeds came to be understood in terms of purity and autochthony.[34] So English-bred horses dominated the track and the English Thoroughbred, as it was baptised, came to represent the equine aristocrat.

Fresh blood

Blood only really began to matter in the Cape in the nineteenth century. This impetus came from two trajectories: increasing interest in local (human) settler pedigrees and the introduction of horse racing. Both were of particular concern to Lord Charles Somerset (1767–1831), who was governor of the Cape Colony from 1814 to 1826. The second son of the fifth Duke of Beaufort, he was the 'most determinedly aristocratic of colonial governors'.[35] He governed during a period when the Cape was making the transition from a tiny trading station run by the military and a few officials to a colony with a substantial settler population.[36] Somerset was reactionary, Tory, and inordinately fond of pageantry and public display, in keeping with the Regency set with whom he mingled in Brighton. He was obsessed with lineage – in both humans and horses – and his obsession proved infectious. After his governorship, middle-class life was entrenched in the colony; there was no large aristocracy to hinder the growth to power of the mercantile and agrarian middle class, and the racially restrictive employment pattern meant that even white workers could aspire to middle-class status.[37] This was not limited by language group, as the British colonial authorities found willing collaborators in the Dutch elite.[38] This symbiosis reached its peak under Somerset, and in return for acquiescence, the gentry secured affluence and even, in some cases, opulence.[39] This sector came to hold some sway over government decisions, especially in the rural regions. An incestuous circle arose – what Ross called an 'interpenetration' – of gentry and officials, linked by kinship and shared business interests.

Both Dutch and English colonists experiencing *embourgeoisement* began to take into account their own family trees. Belonging to the upper class or to 'good families' became important, something to which to aspire. 'All Cape snobs, however, shared a common respect for the English model.'[40] The similarities between the cultures of the colony and those of the metropole were reaffirmed anxiously.[41] Status was enhanced – just as it was in Britain – by land owning, however paltry; and because members of the aristocracy and powerful landowners were increasingly integral to the social endorsement and practical administration of horse racing in the metropole, horse racing similarly enhanced local social status among the upper echelons of Cape society.[42] Race meets saw the mixing of races, classes and genders (as spectators, jockeys, gamblers and grooms), while race horse ownership was limited to a stratum of wealthy English and Dutch men.

By the early decades of the nineteenth century socially ambitious colonists could claim status through their ownership of pedigreed animals, even if they were locked out of the bloodlines of human aristocracy. This led to increased willingness to support the breeding of 'pedigreed' horses. Already at the beginning of the nineteenth century, William Duckitt, who arrived to establish an Agricultural Department and an experimental farm at Klapmuts, noted in 1800: 'Here are some Spirited Breeders that don't mind giving 1,200 [rix] Dollars for a Horse … of an Improved Breed.'[43] By 1820 the colonial secretary, Lieutenant Colonel William Bird, noted that settlers that were unable to purchase a horse in England achieved an elevated local status because they could indeed afford one in the Cape.[44] Moreover, those who were in a position to afford one in any event gained an even more elevated status from the ownership of not just any horse, but one with certified blue blood. Immediately preceding and under Somerset, the wealthier settlers made (and in return received) further distinction predicated on the type of blood that ran through their horses' veins.

Thus, a growing coterie of elite breeders – encouraged by the racing boom – began importing pedigreed horses to the Cape.[45] A visitor noted:

[The horses of the Cape] are seen to best advantage in Cape Town, as, in order to create emulation, and induce the colonists to improve the breed, races were set on foot some years ago, and now take place twice a year in the months of April and October.[46]

Over a ten-year period Somerset himself imported 22 blood horses, while a further 36 English Thoroughbreds and Arabians were imported into the Cape by individual settlers. These men had 'become sensible of the advantages that the Inhabitants of the Colony might derive from an Improvement of the Breed of their horses', which then 'consisted of the Arabian, Javan, South American' and only 'a very few individuals of the European race'.[47] The introduction of horse racing to southern Africa and the ruling elite's mounting fixation with pedigreed Thoroughbreds set the breeding industry running on a new track, promoting the spread of English Thoroughbreds bred exclusively for speed and pedigree.

Fast blood

'Horse-racing will start sooner or later in any country occupied by the British', a later horse breeder, Hugh Archibald Wyndham (1877–1963), observed dryly.[48] The first English Thoroughbreds were imported to the Cape in 1792, immediately prior to both the British occupation and the institution of racing.[49] Although the Cape was not yet part of the British imperial web in 1792, an increasing interest was being taken in the English Thoroughbred, which was gaining international fame as racing gained popularity. Horses now assumed a leisure aspect, while remaining central to the military, being used for transport and even simply as a form of exercise.[50] In 1795, the year in which the first British occupation of the Cape took place, an agent for the British East India Company imported more bloodstock and the wealthy Dutch-speaking sector soon followed suit, particularly the horse breeders Jacobus, Sebastiaan and Dirk van Reenen.[51] A racing club, the African Turf Club, was organised and the first race meeting was held in Cape Town in 1797 – stray cattle grazing on the course were a distinct risk in the first few years.[52] By 1802 the Turf Club had ruled that race days would be Mondays, Wednesdays and Saturdays, with two races each day at Green Point.[53] Other turf clubs sprang up and in some towns racing became an obsession, even rivalling the Nachtmaal gatherings.

There were no bookmakers and each bet was an agreement between two independent parties. Initially, with the dearth of Thoroughbreds specifically used for racing and with race meetings being held only once every six months, any horse could participate as a race horse, even a hack, a hunter or a trap horse. There were disdainful references to the poor breeding of the available supply.[54] Because there were fewer horses, the race-going crowd had a greater personal knowledge of individual horses. The races became a diverse space, mixed in terms of gender, class, ethnicity and race. Bi-annual race meetings were significant social events, incorporating assemblies and theatre for the elite, and drawing a varied crowd at the meeting itself. At first, race meetings were held on open commonage, with no fence and consequently no gate money.

The jockeys were usually 'slave lads'.[55] Burchell commented in 1810 that it was 'amazing' to watch the 'gay scene' for the 'cape fashionables' and to observe

Sir Charles D'Oyly, Going to the Races, 1833
Source: Pama (1975, p. 49)

the motley crowd on foot: Malays and negroes mingled with whites, all crowding and elbowing, eager to get a sight of the momentous contest. But the patient Hottentot … seems to prefer a pipe of tobacco to that which affords such exquisite gratification to his superiors. Together with the art of making horses run fast, the science and mystery of betting has found its way to the farthest extremity of Africa; and on Green Point large sums are said to have been won and lost.[56]

A later visitor who had moved to the Cape for her health, Lady Duff Gordon, recorded:

[At the Greenpoint] races … a queer-looking little Cape farmer's horse, ridden by a Hottentot, beat the English crack racer, ridden by a first-rate English jockey, in an unaccountable way, twice over. The Malays are passionately fond of horse-racing, and the crowd was fully half Malay: there were dozens of carts crowded with the bright-eyed women, in petticoats of every most brilliant colour, white muslin jackets, and gold daggers in their great coils of shining black hair.[57]

There was a clash of horse cultures. Young subalterns, drawing on trends from the metropole, docked horses' tails. This infuriated Dutch locals, who observed that natural tails provided protection against flies.[58] There was no simple division between English and Dutch speakers over racing. More complicatedly, there was a seam of English-speaking colonial society that distanced itself from racing, principally because they disapproved of its ties to gambling. Governor Lord Macartney, for example, despised racing. Lady Anne Barnard attended the first race meeting in 1797 despite her scruples, while her husband absented himself on the spurious grounds of official business. She was aware of the ambiguities of her position – she personally disapproved, as did the governor, but she attended in the carriage of a Dutch speaker to emphasise her connection to the broader population and to show a lack of snobbery.[59] She was mortified by the behaviour of rambunctious young 'John Bulls' who galloped up to the carriage in which she was clearly the guest of Dutch hosts and disparaging the Dutch riders with 'Lord what a saddle', 'Christ what a bridle!'; and 'I would give twenty guineas to see that one thrown – ay, & his neck broke'.[60] She could not, however, restrain herself from noting with obvious disdain that the 'taste for *horseracing* [arose] … and as the horses of the Cape are totally unfit for it, having tho' a little Arabian blood no mixture of the English it must have been from idleness only the attempt arose'.[61] However, there is no evidence to suggest that Sir George Yonge, governor from December 1799, disapproved of racing; indeed, he joined the African Turf Club.

In 1810 the African Turf Club was revived and later, under Somerset, renamed the South African Turf Club. Having grown up in Badminton, a centre of English equestrian sports, Somerset was a well known figure at Newmarket. Nimrod, the famous sportswriter, called him 'the most scientific horseman of all the Somersets'.[62] From 1814 he reorganised the Turf Club, transforming it from an easygoing sportsmen's club holding two or three meetings annually to a vigorous organisation with a meeting as often as once a month on occasion.[63] In line with his preoccupation with refinement and gentility, he honed down the club from 150 to an exclusive 80 members. He also participated himself, running his own horses. In 1824 at the Stellenbosch Turf Club, the governor's colt – tellingly named 'Patrician' – romped home in first place.[64]

Racing initially depended heavily on the British garrison. The Turf Club had begun with 29 members, 20 of whom were officers in the army or navy, with only a sprinkling of wealthy Dutch-speaking horse breeders. There were efforts to encourage racing enthusiasm among the Dutch sector by organising a so-called Farmers' Race.[65]

During the period of Batavian Republic rule at the Cape (1803–06)[66] there is little evidence of racing, and the African Turf Club went into liquidation. However, after the second British occupation in 1806, Dutch speakers became increasingly active as spectators at race meetings. After 1807, although racing depended heavily on officers, the farming sector (particularly Duckitt, Melck and the Van Reenen brothers, who ran a 200-strong horse stud)[67] was progressively more involved. The Turf Club provided the social space for breeders to meet and trade. Racing became highly popular, with race clubs mushrooming in the interior.[68] Somerset was even able to counter imperial rumblings of a ban on racing (because of concerns about the encouragement of gambling) with his assertion that to do so would alienate the Dutch sector of the population.[69] (In 1822, for example, the Burgher Senate commented with approval on race meetings and even granted money towards a trophy, valued at 400 rixdollars [Rd].[70])

Somerset took control of the Groote Post Experimental Farm and redirected its focus to breeding horses, in part to foster the export trade to India. His plan was to use the racing industry as a means of improving the breed. He used the rationale that racing was simply a means to an end, a strategy towards improving local horses. This made little sense: draught and transport horses required no Thoroughbred pedigree; indeed, draught horses would have benefitted from warm blood infusions (from solid, weighty draught animals) rather than Thoroughbreds. Somerset's argument was likely a mere validation for his personal interest in both racing and breeding Thoroughbreds. As an acerbic observer contended in 1820:

A distinguished person at the Cape is thought to have conferred a singular benefit on the Colony by bringing over several Thoroughbred English horses, and disseminating a taste for racing. But it is difficult to imagine how the interests of an infant Colony can be advanced by the introduction of an animal perfectly useless for any purpose of trade or [agriculture], or by rendering fashionable an expensive and ruinous amusement.[71]

This 'ruinous amusement' meant that Thoroughbreds continued to be imported, adding to the older stock of Cape horses. Difference was apparent in the variety of horses available. As Alfred W. Cole noted of Cape Town in a mid-century poem:

> All sorts of steeds,
>   Of all sorts of breeds,
> From racers to funeral
>   Long-tailed ones, soon are all
> Saddled, careering,
>   Some kicking, some rearing ...[72]

Class division among the upper echelon was materially evident in the display of carriages at race meetings. Cowper Rose observed that one could see 'the regular gradation from the well-appointed English carriage to that curious piece of antiquity [Dutch cart] – the gig, the light wagon cart, and the long heavy wagon ... hired for the day'.[73] Burchell remarked that social display formed an important element of the events: 'Horsemen, without number ... exhibit their prancing steeds of half Arab or English blood; although some, indeed, of their noble animals refuse to prance without the incitement of the curb or spur'.[74] Similarly, class differentiation was marked with the vehicles acting as nuanced social signifiers, as indicated by this comment in 1822: 'lawyers in barouches; next in rank in curricles, and notaries [following] in a solitary gig. Doctors turned out in chariots drawn by four greys, surgeons in barouches or tilburies [delicate two wheeled vehicles], and an apothecary on a hack'.[75] Fashion fluctuated, as Wyndham observed, with fewer carriages at meetings in the 1840s, although they had regained popular appeal as a space for display by the 1880s.[76]

This was not limited to Cape society. A class-conscious visitor to Natal in the late nineteenth century noted the undeserved elevation that ownership of a horse might offer a man 'unworthy' of owning one:

The hobbledehoy on horseback who may espy them, conceives at once the sublime idea of showing off his proficiency as a horseman, and good appearance in the saddle. Accordingly he breaks into a full gallop, throwing up sand in boundless wealth – in fact, a veritable Sahara. I have seen many an inoffensive woman thus treated. As to slackening his pace for anyone, that is out of the question. Is this fair or gallant, and does it not merit the somewhat harsh remark, 'Put a beggar on horseback, and he will ride to the devil'? … To sum up [the tone] of the colony: their chief recreation is to be on horseback, or to be strutting about with an inferior cigar in their mouths.[77]

Such close encounters of the equine kind clearly allowed a public self-fashioning, a marker of social mobility. Quite aside from the obvious utility of 'strength and speed', as Lady Anne Barnard observed, a superior stamp of horse was 'flattering' to a man. Respectability and performance were integral to equine ownership. She went on to say of the forage shortage: 'If it was unpleasant and painful to ride or drive Horses that were ill-fed, & in bad condition, at least it was not *disgraceful*, as every one was under the same circumstances.'

There were regional differences with regard to equestrian social pursuits and their concomitant significance. Residents of Cape Town and even in the closer rural areas were more a driving than a riding people; they frequently used a Cape cart (or sometimes an ox wagon). Certainly, in the Cape, riding was less of a social marker than driving: 'The horseman is not the figure he is in Australia or the Western States of America.'[78] Driving became a prized skill and social accomplishment among the Malays of the Cape, as discussed above, but a visitor was dismissive of white Cape Town riders:

Very few of the owners of these animals rode, and those who went in traps preferred, as a rule, to entrust the reins to a black groom than to steer the conveyance themselves. To meet them at the City Club, they were a charming set of fellows … and always ready for a game of pool or poker; but horses were not much in their line.[79]

Full blooded

An important auxiliary to racing was hunting. While horse racing was frequented by all classes, fox hunting, or its local equivalent, was the preserve of the elite. After their arrival, officers initially hunted small buck, like the steenbok; when these became scarce, they turned to jackals. Needless to say, Somerset revelled in the pageantry of the hunt. He hailed, after all, from the 'greatest hunting family the world has seen' and subscribed to 'the fealty existing in feudal ties between the lords of territory and their retainers'.[80] He imported the propaganda and pageantry of English fox hunting, along with his Thoroughbreds, into the southern African veld. By the 1830s there were at least two regular packs riding to hounds, one under the control of the collector of customs and another under the wealthy Van Reenens. Hunts became of necessity somewhat modified, but retained their essence. After all:

> hounds run every whit as fast in the hot sun of Africa after jackal [*Canis mesomelas*] hunting and small buck as after the fox at home ... in South Africa, as at home, when the hounds mingle their wild melody, and the horn sounds, your nag reaches just as freely at his bit and strides just as keenly as an English-bred one.[81]

Hunting, the very epitome of blood sports, was itself plunged in sanguinary metaphor. For example, as a hunt devotee noted of a late nineteenth-century hunt on the veld, 'this was a capital run, and hounds well deserved blood'.[82] Even more telling was that some humans 'deserved blood'. 'Blooding' was a traditional celebration of a novice's first successful hunt by the master, who smeared some of the still-warm blood of the prey on his or her face. As people began to find this custom a trifle too earthy, 'blooding' fell into some disrepute during the nineteenth century, but it was nevertheless practised in some instances on the veld.[83]

Blue blood

The idea of aristocratic animals excited a great deal of attention not only from the British community, but, as noted, increasingly also from the elite Dutch farmers.[84] For example, Somerset placed this advertisement in the *Government Gazette*:

> English Stallions – To cover at the Government Farm at Groote Post, at five rix dollars each mare, and one rix dollar to the groom, the following famous English race horses: Walton, late property of His Royal Highness

the Duke of York; four years old, got by Walton, dam by Trafalgar out of Musidora. Vanguard, bred by His Grace the Duke of Grafton; six years old, got by Haphazard out of Vestal, by Walton out of Dabchick, the dam of Vandyke. Vanguard won the King's plate at Winchester in 1820, beating Euphrates and Merrymaker.[85]

As evident from this advertisement and its explicit mention of the horse once having been owned by the Duke of York, horses of 'good blood' were quite deliberately linked to their (in this case, erstwhile) human owners. Both were assumed to be possessed of similarly sanguinary superiority. A horse once owned by a duke was a more valuable creature – and the reverse was true too. An aristocratic horse, with an illustrious career on the track lent lustre to an otherwise lackluster human pedigree through the power of implied ancestry.

D. G. FOCK,
Dealer in all sorts of Grain,
BARLEY, OATS, HAY, BRAN,
OAT-SHEAVES, &c.
No. 49, LOOP-STREET,
(Lately occupied by AND. BRINK, Ds., *Esq.)*

Pleasure Wagons, Saddle Horses, &c., let on hire.
Horses taken in to Bait.
Good separate Stabling for the keep of
Race Horses.

Rytuigen en Paarden te huur.—Stalling en Voer voor
Paarden.—Handelaar in alle soorten van Graan.

Advertisement from Cape of Good Hope Almanac and Annual Register, *1850*

It is worth noting further correlation between notions of human society and their homologous animal counterparts. For example, Somerset did not limit his breed improvement scheme to horses. He also wished to import people of good British blood to improve the local supply. While the metropole wished to export the poverty stricken to ameliorate indigence on the streets of London, Somerset baulked at this and insisted instead on good yeoman stock. He consciously maintained a balance between imported women and men to prevent the mixing of blood between Europeans and local black women. Indeed, endogamous marriage helped sustain a 'pure' 1820 British settler identity.[86] Within this group, there was further differentiation into types, and class distinctions were rigidly patrolled, just as they were increasingly in the equine arena. This was not limited to the Cape: a visitor to Natal (admittedly later in the century) saw horses as a human analogue, noting,

> they partake of the nature of their superiors in the animal world. They are a very mixed lot. Some are underbred and stubborn. It is a common thing to see a riderless horse canter down the Berea. The brute has succeeded in bucking his master … There is much risk and loss attached to bringing horses from England. The colonists, however, have a penchant for good horseflesh.[87]

Noble blood

Horses of good blood consequently became luxury items. Concomitantly, Cape Town's elite and rich farmers from outlying districts began to have regard for select horses – arguably the most concerned they had been about their steeds since the mid-seventeenth century, when horses had been extremely rare and precious commodities. Somerset himself cosseted the new 'noble' imports, even at the expense of alienating sectors of the colony. An outraged critic of Somerset noted:

> the beautiful and extensive gardens round the government house [were] ploughed up in many parts, and sown with oats for Lord Charles Somerset's horses; this gave great offence to the Dutch. This garden is the pride of Cape Town, and the only place of resort for the people.[88]

Indeed, perhaps the elite owners cared too much about horses for the well-being of colonial society as a whole. In 1819, after a particularly bad harvest, Somerset was obliged to promulgate a ruling forbidding the feeding of wheat to horses, fearing the starvation of the (human) poor.[89]

This was because, economically, choice horses began to matter sufficiently to the elite consumers in Cape society to warrant almost as much state intervention as they did when horses were initially imported by Van Riebeeck. Horses and mules exported from 1826 to 1830 translated into income for the colony of £9,274 (out of a total of £218,412; but was eight times more significant than wool and twice that of ivory). This amount dropped, however, as other commodities became more valuable, and from 1831 to 1835 horses accounted for just £6,504 (of a total of £243,646; by comparison, wool, for example, was now significantly more valuable to the colony). But even so, while horse breeding did not make much money for most people, for a very small group it made a veritable fortune.

This was largely due to the growing trend towards valuing pedigree. Moreover, the export trade to India and Mauritius enriched breeders of the Dutch elite like Martin Melck, P.L. Cloete and Jacobus van Reenen.[90] The Van Reenens and Cloetes were influential families integral to the power structure; the Melcks, owners of 11 farms, were the only farmers rich enough to admit to having more than a hundred slaves.[91] As a prominent local horse breeder, Van Reenen noted that breeding Thoroughbreds rather than mixed-breed horses proved significantly more lucrative:

> my Family were known to have been the first breeders of Horses in the Colony ... But about nine years since we thought it expedient to purchase two English Stallions, since which our annual profit from breeding horses has been two thirds greater. In proof of the benefit derived by the introduction of English Blood Stallions, allow me to inform you that breeding of Horses is now a more lucrative employment than any other description of Agriculture, as will appear by my Father's giving it the preference, though his Estate enjoys every advantage which can render it eligible for the other kinds of produce.[92]

Evidence from his ledgers buttressed this testimony. Prior to the introduction of Thoroughbreds, his average for 36 horses had been 5,400 Rd, or 150 Rd each. After investing in bloodstock in 1824, his family sold six horses at 4,000 Rd;

two at 850 Rd; one at 850 Rd; one at 800 Rd; two at 1,000 Rd; one at 750 Rd; two at 900 Rd; and 21 at an average of 250 Rd each. In all, 36 horses were sold for 14,400 Rd.[93]

Another breeding family, the Kotzes, affirmed that after the importation of English stallions the prices for their horses were 'considerably higher than in former times'. For example, one of the English stallions had involved an investment of 6,000 Rd, but he had brought in 1,800 Rd in stud fees from other colonists and moreover had sired 30 foals from the Kotze's own mares. As yearlings, his progeny could fetch as much as 1,000 Rd.[94] William Duckitt concurred with this general sentiment and lamented his own lack of a Thoroughbred stallion. If he had the 'means to purchase an English stallion my profits would have been larger, as it is the Horse breeders alone who have during the last five years been able to make any profit of their Farms from the visitations that have befallen all other species of Farming'.[95]

The elite breeders all maintained that horse breeding was more profitable than both wine and wheat, with their respective uncertain and fluctuating markets.[96] They were at pains to emphasise that it was not random breeding, but rather a focus on that which Somerset fostered – a 'new species of property into the Colony', which is to say choice bloodlines 'from English stallions'.[97] This coterie had every reason to bolster Somerset's own claims on the usefulness of the imports in order to retain his continued favour. But their books tally with their claims about the economic value of good blood and the growing public's desire for it.

Nobles' blood

But the public was also thirsty for a very different kind of blood. The scandal hinted at in the previous section played a prominent role in early nineteenth-century Cape politics. From 1823 Somerset was accused of an increasing number of egregious acts, which included importing horses and selling them at exorbitant prices – in particular to the government-owned farms.[98] An outraged observer argued that the 'Boors being all ruined by the blight and storms, the public has been made … to supply the deficiency'.[99] The gossip was that the governor bought up teams of horses – keeping the best for himself and his son – then turned over the equine dross to the colonial cavalry. There was an increasingly obvious disjuncture between Somerset's vaulting ambition (his insistence on good blood) and the bad blood between him and a growing sector of the colony:

> There never was perhaps a man of such high birth as our Governor, holding such a situation, and receiving so great a salary, who could be found to debase himself by acts so low and disgusting to obtain money by horse-flesh.[100]

Public outrage was palpable. Somerset was accused of selling favours for horses, of selling inferior horses and of selling unsuitable horses – even once, memorably, of selling a dead horse.[101]

The central case against him pivoted on a particular case of alleged corruption. He was accused by D'Escury, the inspector of government lands and woods (an official recently disappointed in promotion) of

> having corruptly made a grant of land to [an individual colonist] in consideration of a sum of money amounting to 10,000 Rd ... under colour and pretence of a sale of a horse, a short time before he received a grant of 20,000 acres of land.[102]

Certainly, it was true that Somerset had sold a horse for a large price to the same individual who afterwards received an extensive grant of land.[103]

Six years previously, in 1817, Somerset had imported a shipment of valuable 'blood horses' – including an exceptionally fine specimen named Sorcerer Colt, who was to all accounts 'above all others that had ever been seen in the Colony for shape, bone, and muscular strength'.[104] The reputation of this horse soon reached the remoter districts of the colony, and especially the ears of colonists in the Hantam region (about 390 miles or nine days' journey from the Cape), which, as discussed before, had long been celebrated for its breed of horses. Somerset had reportedly heard that there were 'opulent Farmers either at the Hantam or in the neighbouring District of the Roggeveld who, if the opportunity offered, would be willing to give a large price for the purchase or use of a good Stallion'. At first, Somerset touted Sorcerer Colt around the outlying areas, trying to sell him for 10,000 Rd (about £750) (the price that had been asked for the horse, unsuccessfully, in Cape Town) and advertising his services to local mares for 100 Rd each.[105] But after two months no mares were sent to avail themselves of Sorcerer Colt's charms and he had meanwhile lost condition from his peripatetic state. A consortium of the Widow Louw and Willem Louw, her father, eventually purchased the colt for the full price of 9,600 Rd, including another horse that was valued at 400 Rd.[106]

There were many protestations about the value of such horses and the injection of good blood that they added to the colonial stock. In Somerset's defence, it was noted that it was

> scarcely possible for him to sell a horse to any Colonist who had not a petition in the public offices for land, loans, &c, or a cause in some of the Public Courts of Law, but it would be very hard if all his decisions as Governor were construed as having reference to the horses sold.[107]

For blood horses born and bred in England and sold in the colony there would be an actual loss unless the selling price in the colony exceeded 8,000 Rd.[108] The authorities decided that although 'it may be a subject of regret that he [Somerset] should have proceeded so hastily in some respects and so tardily in others', there was no conclusive evidence of 'undue favour, or his motives to that foul reproach which the passage extracted from Mr D'Escury's statement'. There was a widespread feeling in the colony that the governor would be protected by his own 'blood' – the powerful Beaufort influence.[109] In 1826, however, Somerset was recalled to England under a cloud, but his notions and those of the elite breeders remained entrenched.[110]

Pure blood

Such breeding ambitions remained influential and pervasive. Thus the sex life of horses came to matter to the state. Early nineteenth-century emphasis on pedigree meant that breeding became more controlled.[111] Fears spawned by widespread belief in telegony, discussed below, triggered further anxiety over indiscriminate mixing. Somerset had ruled that no

> entire Horse, exceeding two years of age, shall in future be turned out, either at the Outspan Places, or on Lands which are not enclosed, unless secured in such manner as to prevent access to Mares belonging to the

Owner of the neighbouring or other Place[,] subject to a 100 Rd fine in each case in the courts of *landdrosts* and *heemraden*.[112]

The lack of enclosures – and concomitant uncontrolled breeding – began to change in the early nineteenth century.[113] Furthermore, gelding became widespread to prevent indiscriminate mating. This process removed the testes, which caused sterilisation; this both prevented reproduction and also greatly reduced the production of testosterone, which in turn created a more compliant temperament.[114]

Popular appreciation of Thoroughbred bloodlines sometimes overlooked the virtues of the other horses, the hybrid collection of breeds discussed in the previous chapter, increasingly homogeneous enough to be recognised as a type, labelled the Cape horse. But the stock of other non-racing horses remained vital. Of course, many urban horses remained necessary for the prosaic transport needs of the growing colony. Formally regulated horse-drawn cabs were introduced to Cape in 1849, with a stand in Adderley Street. Within a generation visitors from the metropole noticed that cabs were 'patronised to an unprecedented extent' in Cape Town.[115] Omnibuses ran between Cape Town and all principal towns and villages. From 1852 the mail was carried along the main routes by carts with too often 'scarecrow ... steeds' that were whipped into moving at 7–12 miles an hour.[116] As the urban centre developed, transport became regulated and taxed.[117] As the nineteenth century progressed, with its numerous wars of conquest and steady human migrations out of the Cape Colony, utility horses – for transport, military, agricultural and everyday use – remained indispensable.[118] Closer to the urban centre, in the middle decades of the century, horses were more likely to carry some Thoroughbred blood. Within Cape Town and its immediate vicinity, the horses

> generally are like those of England, with a slight trace of the Arab in their head and hind-quarters; the breed, in fact, is a compound of the English Thoroughbred and the Arab. Several well-known English horses have found their way [here] ... when they were stale or broken down ... [and] acted as fountains for supplying a stream of pure blood through the equine veins of Africa.[119]

Those towards the periphery were more predominately of the older stock, the 'type' that came to be called 'the Caper' (although this term was slippery and the traits it was intended to convey largely depended on what the horse dealer thought would best sell his merchandise). The tough little Caper was unfailingly praised by travellers as hardy, willing and compliant; indeed, as 'worth his weight in gold … knows when he is spoken to, and obeys orders, fears nothing'. The Caper seemed to survive on just the veld, and its 'principal forage was fresh air and a roll in the sand'.[120]

A minor cult of fine horseflesh arose on both sides of the Orange River among some Free Staters, being 'fond of horses and pay[ing] a good deal of attention to breeding'.[121] Such Boers cast covetous eyes towards the Thoroughbred stock bred by Pienaar, the Van Zyls and the Von Maltitz brothers and imported some of their stock. For the most part, however, in the two Boer republics, it was observed 'the Boers do not believe much in blood'.[122] A traveller reminiscing about his journey in the later decades of the nineteenth century noted: 'in my day there were few well-bred horses in South Africa, except in the Cape Colony'.[123]

Ironically, this was perhaps the saving grace of the horses of the diaspora. Most horse owners to the north, like some Boers, Griqua and increasingly Basotho, as the next chapter discusses, focused on equine merits rather than pedigrees and their horses were concomitantly robust. Their horses literally moved through the veld differently from foreign imports. The Boers favoured the *trippel*, which was

> not exactly an amble, but a cousin to it, marvellously easy to the rider, whilst it enables the nag to get over a wonderful lot of ground without knocking up. It also allows the horse to pick his way amongst rocky ground, and so save his legs, where an English, Indian, or Australian horse would be apt to cripple himself in very short order.[124]

Indeed, '[o]ne of the very first things that strikes the wanderer in the … southern hemisphere is the strength and endurance of the horses'. Although they look the 'sorriest scrags [one] ever set eyes on, yet they appear to be possessed of a power of getting over the ground that is little short of miraculous'.[125]

Mother's blood

Efforts towards the improvement of horse breeding in the Cape were further hampered by a focus solely on the sire, to the exclusion of the dam. A mare was simply a 'womb with a view'. Breeders could thus produce English Thoroughbreds by crossing Thoroughbred stallions with Caper or 'half-bred' mares. Thus, gendered norms jumped the species barrier.

Overwhelmingly, in the world of work or war, riders were men, but there is some evidence that women rode for leisure or for short jaunts. For example, a widower, Rudolph de Salis, bought two horses in 1803, one for himself and one for his daughter, Netje. He recorded with paternal pride that Netje was able to ride just as her late mother had done. The delighted father noted both skill and pleasure in his daughter's riding, while Netje noted that the gift from her father was because she could ride independently.[126] Children rode horses for pleasure, mimicking adult pursuits. A later Irish traveller noted that, as

> children[,] all the colonists begin to practise riding. We have seen little boys … go at a dashing pace through the streets; and the same boys at home in Ireland would find themselves … mounted on a 'rocking horse' in the nursery.[127]

When Lichtenstein encountered families near Swellendam he noticed that their chief recreation was visiting friends and family within a few hours radius and that

> every member of the family, the wives and daughters not excepted, has a riding-horse, upon which they go a considerable distance in a short time. When one meets such a cavalcade, one is very doubtful whether most to admire the boldness of the riders, that of the women in particular, or the sure-footedness of the horses.

While in the wealthier areas families would travel in wagons, 'the younger part of the fair sex always prefer riding on horseback'.[128]

Interestingly (as a reflection on the gendered use of horses), particularly as good horsemanship was perceived to be a hallmark of masculinity, stallions received special treatment. This had long roots: the traveller Charles Thunberg noted in the late eighteenth century that while mares and colts were expected to forage for themselves, stallions were fed specially cultivated barley. Moreover, mares were perceived as having little importance and because the wealthy Cape classes considered it shameful to ride one, fillies were seldom broken or handled.[129] Certainly, by the nineteenth century, it was widely considered 'undignified to ride or drive [mares]. Only Hottentots did it'.[130] In 1858 a visitor noted: 'The stallion is all-in-all with Cape breeders, the mare being considered as quite a secondary item.' The consequence was that:

> from the frequent disproportion between the dam and sire, awkward-looking animals are common, more especially inland, where the science of breeding is less understood: a horse is frequently seen with fore-quarters equal to fifteen hands, and hind-quarters only large enough for a pony.[131]

Similarly, fillies were rarely deemed worth racing. Even by the end of the century, it was observed that Boers 'never ride or work mares, but use them as broodstock'.[132] The chief colonial veterinary officer, Duncan Hutcheon (1842–1907), campaigned for farmers to use fillies before breeding them.[133] He contended: 'Too much reliance is often placed on the sire without regard to the dam, and often the most worthless mares are put to a thoroughbred sire.'[134]

In similar vein, as it were, in efforts towards breed improvement, the infusion of 'good' blood was from the stallion, as 'any female equine was considered good enough to serve as a brood mare, and comparatively few were imported during the first half of the nineteenth century'.[135] Pervasive popular contempt for female horses was compounded by the widespread belief in the myth of pre-potency, the so-called ability to stamp the sire's own unique traits on a particular foal and then down through the generations, riding roughshod over the 'blood' (later understood as genes) of the mare and, indeed, of subsequent stallions. According to popular belief, pre-potency depended upon the presence of a high percentage of the blood of some particular individual. Pre-potency was assumed to be the result of a cumulative effect of ancestry, a supposed narrowing of the bloodlines, either through inbreeding, line breeding or some form of pedigree selection. Even incestuous blood was better than common blood.[136]

There was a general feeling that the strengths of the sires could overcome the flaws of the dams.[137] The myth arose firstly because in herd animals such as the horse there was only one creature in any particular season that could be compared to the mother, while there were many that bore a resemblance to the male. Clearly, it was a more sensible economic decision to buy a good stallion (as his good genes could be disseminated more widely than the good genes of a particular mare), and the female contribution was entirely disregarded. Secondly, patrilineal descent was paramount – the dam's lineage has historically been inconsequential.

This genetic denialism is found in several societies. The resort to quasi-mythical genealogies of shared 'pure blood' parallels, as anthropologists have shown, was the strategy mobilised to formulate the kinship classification in human societies. This led to the overemphasis on the importance of the male as far as hereditary influence is concerned, with the female understood as merely a mobile incubator. Consequently, it was almost always the males who were described as pre-potent. Occasionally, however, it was asserted that a pure-blood mare would override the genes of a common stallion, buttressed by the pervasive, though unarticulated, notion that the rules of genetics did not apply to the animals of the ruling classes.

Bastard blood

The notion of the mother's feebleness at influencing her progeny lent increased currency to the theory of telegony (from the Greek word meaning 'offspring at a distance') also known as 'infection of the germ' or 'paternal impression' – the supposed influence of a father on offspring subsequent to his own produced by the same mother by another sire. This was fairly ubiquitous in nineteenth-century thinking.[138] The assertion was later challenged by James Cossar Ewart, professor of Natural History at Edinburgh, who crossed a zebra stallion (*Equus burchelli*) with pony mares in order to disprove telegony. (Interestingly, as well as debunking paternal impression, he wanted to produce a more resilient draught animal for South Africa – one more immune to local diseases and more biddable than a mule.) It was an intensely controversial topic.[139] Further experiments by Ewart eroded support for telegony and helped explode such (mis)conceptions.

Among stock breeders, however, and even among many in the academe, belief in telegony remained strong. So tenacious was this belief that the accidental 'pollution' by a male of substandard blood meant the female would be considered permanently undesirable for breeding. Many accepted this idea that an infusion of bad blood would contaminate a race line forever or that 'bad blood drives out good, just as bad money displaces good money'.[140] The editor of the *Racing Calendar* warned breeders that in selecting mares, 'all those who have ever been mated with a donkey should be passed over, as asinine attributes will attach to their succeeding progeny even if [mated with] a thoroughbred horse'.[141] This helps explain the relative unpopularity of mules: the physical environment was appropriate, but the cultural environment was unsuitable.[142] They were never popular among the Cape elite, except on some wheat farms, perhaps because of the contamination (and subsequent loss in value) their horse mothers would face from mating with a male donkey, and certainly because they were more stubborn and less glamorous than horses. There was a porous boundary between the domain of animal and human breeding: the cordons sanitaires around the elite breeds and (white) families were both perceived as threatened by socio-sexual intercourse. Such hierarchical ideas about sexuality served as a 'graphic substantiation of who was, so to speak, on the bottom and who was on the top'.[143] Telegony was a powerful element of the socio-sexual world view as a widely and firmly held belief. As late as the early twentieth century, General Louis Botha refused to change his mind in the face of opposing scientific argument: 'If you cross an Afrikaner cow with a Friesland bull, you will never get pure red calves from her.'[144] At the same time, medical doctor and social commentator C. Louis Leipoldt noted that belief in telegony was widespread and not only in terms of animals. He had, for example, met a white farmer whose daughter had been raped by an African man. The farmer was convinced that his daughter had been 'ruined for life': 'Her children will always have that blood in them.'[145] Unsurprisingly, breeders who wished to produce Thoroughbred horses could not find buyers for foals produced by mares once polluted by ill-bred stallions or donkey jacks.

Cross-breeds remained a controversial and much discussed topic in South Africa. In a widely distributed article published in the last decade of the nineteenth century, Hutcheon, the colonial veterinary surgeon, noted the power of paternal impression, citing the case of Morton's mare.[146] Because he was an authoritative voice among Cape farmers, his views were widely circulated and the article was reprinted several times. He debated whether the 'vivid' impression on the female during conception or even gestation influences the foetus so that it resembles a 'male with which the mother may have been associated, but with which she never had any closer connection'. (He even went so far as to suggest that keeping the mother near freshly whitewashed homesteads might produce lighter coloured offspring.)[147] He was at pains to emphasise that these were not the views of the superstitious or ignorant. He cited James McGillivray (1849): 'when a pure female of any breed has been pregnant to a male of a different breed, such a female is a cross ever after, the purity of her blood being lost in consequence of her connection with the foreign animal.'[148] The message he promoted was that 'breeders ... cannot exercise too much care in the selection of sires for their breeding stock' as females' blood becomes 'vitiated'.[149] He cautioned sternly that this was all too common in the Cape, hence '[its] present mixed breeds' and even when using good sires, one should always mate the same mother and father together, unless the sire is of 'decidedly superior' stamp, as the more she is mated to the same sire, the more her blood would become 'imbued with the characters and constitutional qualities of that particular male at each impregnation' (although an impure-bred female is physically unable to 'taint' a pure-bred male). Hutcheon contended that Thoroughbreds were 'the most pre-potent breed of horses in the world'.[150] He urged colonial breeders not to trust half-breeds, 'however perfect in symmetry', as they needed the injection of 'several generations of pure blood'.[151] He felt that a particular danger was the practice of 'permitting a mongrel-bred male to serve the pure-bred females' as her purity is thus 'lost for life'.[152]

Blood weeds

Blood not only became 'impure' and 'diluted', but could also become 'contaminated'.[153] Horses faced a barrage of ailments or pollutants, but the primary scourge was horse sickness. As the previous chapter explained, since 1719, when the first epidemic of horse sickness struck, periodic outbreaks of the disease had wreaked devastating losses.[154] The disease was endemic and periodically became epidemic, and the really overwhelming epizootics spread intermittently from the disease's endemic base in the eastern Lowveld.[155] 'Salted' stock that had suffered and survived horse sickness were therefore much desired.[156] Especially for those travelling to the interior, it was an essential consideration in purchasing a horse to ask: 'Is he *gesout*?'[157] Donkeys (and hinnies,[158] for the most part) were purportedly immune, but mules and horses were vulnerable.[159]

The disease made depredations every year, but, after the first crippling outbreak in 1719, approximately every 20 years the disease became epidemic: 1780, 1801, 1819, 1839, 1854, 1870 and 1891.[160] Mortality was very high: the greatest proportional losses occurred in 1854, with 65,000 horses and mules out of 169,583 lost, which meant a loss of £525,000 to the colony.[161] (In 1870 a further 70,000 died[162] and in 1891–93, 100,000 horses died, almost 20 per cent of the total stock.)[163] The 1854 outbreak started in the eastern districts and spread rapidly throughout the region, leaving massive mortalities in its wake. Observers noted that it was

> dreadful work ... to witness favourite animals, old friends as it were, bred and reared by oneself, perishing miserably in this way, without the possibility of alleviating their sufferings, or averting their destruction ... One old riding horse of mine, a pensioner at grass, left one day the troop of mares he was running with, about two miles from the homestead, and deliberately walked up to the stable door, evidently stricken unto death, but as if to ask for assistance.[164]

There was, however, a small splinter school of thought that saw (in the long term) the infected blood actually improving the general population's blood. The eugenic effects of the outbreak were noted by a later commentator, Theal, who observed that the superior horses were sheltered and kept in their stables, while 'those that were swept off were the inferior ones'.[165] Even contemporaneously, T.B. Bayley, who owned a farm in the Caledon district, noted cheerfully that

> nine-tenths of the brood stock that disappeared were of the lowest caste, mostly used for the breeding of mules and common hackneys, and necessarily kept for farm work, because unsaleable elsewhere. To the unfortunate sufferer himself, the loss of such animals was undoubtedly a most serious disaster, and [brought him] ... to the brink of ruin; but when we consider the effects of the late epidemic in a national point of view, we need not regard the calamity as a mortal blow ... Almost all the breeders who had valuable mares and young horses found means of saving a large proportion of their best, and the epidemic never reached some of the most celebrated horse-breeding districts ... it is quite certain that a vast proportion of the defunct animals were mere rubbish, never likely to pay, and better cleared off, even by a process so summary, to make room for fine-woolled sheep, which *will* pay.[166]

Thus, Bayley called the disease a 'blessing in disguise'.[167] If so, it was a blessing exceedingly well camouflaged.

The disease meant wholesale death. The harrowing psycho-social effects and crippling economic consequences of this scourge have been briefly described above, as well as in the previous chapter. The effect was dramatic: the disease, 'which is almost always fatal, is characterised by the escape of immense quantities of watery fluid from the blood-vessels into various tissues', giving the impression that the horse 'drowned in his own blood serum'.[168]

Opinion was radically divided over the cause of the sickness. Some traced it to the 'deleterious influence of night air'. Others feared slow-running streams or stagnant pools, or soil that had been polluted by dead animals or buried carcasses.[169] Unusual levels of moisture on the veld and a fungus that grows on herbage were also blamed. Many medical men felt it was the 'peculiarly vitiated state of the atmosphere' acting as a 'poisonous agency in the system, destroying the vitality of the blood'. Some horses were bled as a precautionary measure and it was suggested that infected horses should be 'bled to exhaustion'. Bayley recommended that two quarts of blood be drained straight from the jugular.[170]

Thus, blood could be tainted as in the process described above or, it was believed, it could it even grow 'thinner', diluted or contaminated by the African heat.[171] Indeed, from the mid-nineteenth century a declensionist trajectory was widely believed and various attempts were made to 'save' the breed. It is significant that this notion was not confined to the Cape. Fear about degeneration was pervasive in the other colonies too. There was a sense that Europeans were maladapted to settlement in a warmer climate, which was blamed for the degeneration of imported European servants, both human and animal.[172] As Hayes noted of horses in the late nineteenth-century Cape:

Horses, however, are so greatly modified by the effects of climate, that each country, independently of the influence of selection, has its own particular type of animal, just as it has its own particular type of man. We see that European children born and bred in the tropics, acquire the small bones and delicate physique of the natives, in the same manner as the produce of imported stock loses to a great extent the characteristics of its sires and dams, even in the first generation. After three or four generations, almost all trace of the home blood will have disappeared.[173]

Bad blood

Thus, perhaps understandably, at the time more was written about the deterioration of the Cape horse than any other aspect of equine breeding.[174] From as early as 1800 there was growing concern about improving the equine stock. For example, in September 1800 Duckitt started a small stud of mares, went 'native' by becoming increasingly absorbed into the Dutch-speaking sector and became obsessed with improving the quality of the Capers.[175] Improving the 'quality' meant different things to different interest groups: race horse enthusiasts wanted to breed solely for speed; the British army wanted the hardiness of Capers, yet needed greater height for artillery horses; and for pedigree aficionados such physical considerations were secondary – they simply wished to keep the horses' blood 'pure'.

By the mid-nineteenth century horses were needed in India: the British army needed hardy horses that could survive a hot climate. The first exportation of horses from the Cape to India had occurred as early as 1769 and picked up after the British occupation of the Cape. However, the traffic had remained erratic, often limited to just one or two animals bought by individual British officers bound for India. Capers started winning more renown after a few exports started winning on Calcutta's racetracks.[176] At the same time there was a lively if limited trade to Mauritius. The Cape horse trade to India steadily gathered pace from the 1840s, as India began struggling to obtain enough horses from its inner Asian sources and north-western regions increased the cultivation of pasture at the expense of horse breeding.[177] The market boomed for five years between 1857 and 1861 as trouble erupted over the so-called Indian Mutiny. Colonel Apperley, the Indian remount officer at the Cape, consigned over 5,000 horses at average price of £30 each.[178] There was sudden affluence among horse breeders in the Hantam – with new pianos, jewels and a ready cash flow. Yet surprisingly, this boom was followed by a decline in the export trade.

It is important to note that it was not that horse numbers declined within southern Africa. Despite a devastating outbreak of African horse sickness in the mid-1850s, the number of horses actually exploded in both British colonies, Natal and the Cape, from 145,000 in 1855 to 446,000 in 1899. It was thus not a short supply horses that led to the decline in exports. Instead, there were three key reasons: one internal to the trade itself, one caused by a revolutionary discovery within South Africa and one triggered by broader global changes.

Firstly, there was a massive depletion of good equine stock. Pervasive injudicious breeding with inferior stallions took place to plump up the export trade. In addition, popular demand encouraged breeding from English Thoroughbreds, and pedigree became paramount, to the exclusion of merit.[179] Speculators imported the dregs of Tattersalls – broken-down horses with good pedigrees.[180] In one memorable incident a £5 broken-down horse was exported to the Cape and sold for £500. As the editor of the *Racing Calendar* conceded: 'numbers of the sorriest rips that ever escaped the knackers were imported.'[181] These so-called 'blood weeds' corrupted the gene pool, triggering a decline in stamina, height and healthy conformation.[182] (Efforts to remedy the 'weediness' by breeding with stout cart horses often led simply to awkward, unsymmetrical creatures.)

Moreover, particular horses were bred because of the vagaries of fashion – white socks, a blaze on the face and chestnut coats were all unpopular, for example. Horse owners preferred solid-coloured horses; this was supposedly a sign of purity. A traveller recorded how the 'qualities most esteemed' in the Cape were

> small head, small ears, large nostril, small muzzle, broad chest, large bone in the leg, short in the cannon and pastern, toes rather turned in than out; well ribbed home (many Dutchmen would not buy a horse that allowed more than four fingers to be placed between the last rib and the hip-bone).

The same visitor also noticed that 'several small peculiarities are esteemed at the Cape that are not even observed in England'; for instance, a local Dutch belief in stamina was signalled by 'the small size of the corns on the inside of the hindlegs'.[183] Thoroughbred breeding remained entrenched and mushroomed with the expanding racing industry, and the fashion grew during the early and middle nineteenth century for horses with a 'blood head', 'light neck' and a 'pedigree'.[184] See, for example, the illustration of Somerset below, with his docked tail (in accordance with metropolitan fashion), his curved 'Arab' neck and small 'blood head', all of which was considered desirable in an English Thoroughbred.

From the mid-nineteenth century breeding with inferior stallions was widespread enough to impact negatively on the high-end side of the export trade. Of the 500 English Thoroughbreds imported until 1892 not 'one half' was likely to improve the blood of the colony, the remainder having 'exactly the opposite effect'.[185] Thus, these 'blood weeds' and horses bred simply for fashion polluted the gene pool, precipitating a general decline in stamina, size, hardiness and sound conformation. The military authorities began noting with concern that the Cape horse was starting to suffer from 'want of size, smallness of bone under the knees, and drooping hindquarters'.

A View of Somerset
Source: Africana Museum 66/1909, signed C.B. Esqr,
published by Dighton, Spring Gardens, December 1811

The second reason for the decline in the export trade was simply that horses were needed within southern Africa. Minerals were discovered to the north, with the Kimberley diamond rush from 1867 and the discovery of gold on the Witwatersrand in 1886. As a result, more horses were needed than could be supplied by the coastal regions. Horses were needed in the booming transport industry and some were needed on the mines themselves, e.g. in the 'horse whims', which were large wooden wheels that raised ore from the pits in Kimberley. Consequently, domestic prices increased for Cape horses until it was no longer competitive to send them to India. The old-style Caper was more useful for the interior, which required not a fast horse, but a small, hardy horse.

Thirdly, in 1869 the Suez Canal was opened and the Cape lost its strategic position on the trade route between Europe and the East, losing much maritime traffic. Ironically, horses from the Cape had been sent to Australia in 1788 and they, together with successive imports from other regions, had flourished in the relatively disease- and predator-free environment. Australia began exporting horses (dubbed 'Walers') on a large scale in the mid-nineteenth century.[186] Australia gradually came to replace the Cape in dominating the trade in remounts destined for India, and after racing was stopped in Mauritius at mid-century, even that market dried up. The average for the Cape Colony of the market price of ordinary saddle horses decreased year by year from £16 14s in 1844, to £12 8s in 1894. The average price of draught horses decreased from £15 18s in 1884, to £12 4s in 1894.[187] By the end of the century, an expert noted that horses

> do not bring in much money to their breeders. The Cape horse of thirty years ago, was a strong serviceable animal that was well up to remount form, and was prized in cavalry regiments in India … His place is now taken by a weedy slave … The farmers have not alone to contend against scarcity of grass from want of water; but are menaced every season by that awful equine scourge, 'horse sickness', which slays an average of, probably, 20,000 horses a year. With the fear of this terrible plague over them, it is no wonder that the breeding of horses is neglected.[188]

Moreover, increasingly merino sheep farming took the place and pasturage that might previously have been relegated to breeding mares.[189] Wool farming did not suffer the same vulnerability to horse sickness nor the same fluctuations in the market as horse breeding. By the end of the nineteenth century the once redoubtable Cape horse was pronounced as being as 'extinct as the quagga'.[190] Thus, in part the Cape horse was sacrificed to the hunger for speed, to the dictates of pedigree and fashion, and to the instability of the export market.

In his final salute to the English Thoroughbred, Hutcheon bought stud stallions in England and Ireland to reinfuse colonial blood. But in some ways, practical on-the-ground knowledge was in advance of specialists. Public opinion had swung away from Thoroughbred horses by the final decade of the nineteenth century. Moreover, Hutcheon had to distribute his eight stallions over 50 districts. These peripatetic studs' fleeting visits were difficult to orchestrate with the mares' coming into season.[191] For example, the stallion named (with retrospective irony) Pride of the West was compelled to divide the season between two districts, with six weeks at Bredasdorp and then moving to Swellendam. However, to make the situation even more difficult, the drought made the mares come into season later. Owing to lack of exercise and public apathy, Pride of the West became grossly fat and subsequently impotent. Colonial mares were left disappointed and farmers demanded their money back.

Conclusions

A close scrutiny of the network of inter-linked equine and human families, careers and patronage affords the historian an almost Namierian prosopography of horses and people. The introduction of horse racing to southern Africa and the ruling oligarchy's growing preoccupation with pedigreed Thoroughbreds wrenched the horse-breeding industry in a different direction, moving away from focusing exclusively on utility horses and fostering the spread of English Thoroughbreds, bred solely for speed and pedigree. Once racing was entrenched under the second British occupation at the beginning of the nineteenth century, there was a concomitant recalibration among elite breeders of what 'good horseflesh' meant in the colony. The common herd of horses was leavened by the importation of Thoroughbred horses. In so doing, Somerset and the influential breeders tapped a social vein, feeding the public's growing hunger for pedigree. Blue-blooded horses were desirable commodities to settlers who were beginning to consider their own sanguinary consequence. Discourses of breeding were not hermetically sealed from political discourses. Breeding thus set up a fresh suite of debates in both state and popular arenas that drew on notions surrounding race, class and gender, and spread blood-based idiom more broadly. The ideas of animal breeders and their buying public became a synthesis of folk belief and fresh scientific advances. This combination, epitomised by faith in the pedigree beasts 'of pure race', drew on and sustained the popular vocabulary of race theory that was strongly evident in the colony. Although the Thoroughbreds imported to the Cape may have been granted some respite from the menial burdens borne by the other horses of the colony, perhaps they carried a heavier load still: the dreams and self-identity of the elite.

Horses were, however, more than just signifiers of elite status; they could contribute towards *creating* elite status. There was money to be made as a Thoroughbred breeder, which involved an elite group of male breeders from both the Dutch- and English-speaking sectors, not forgetting the governor. Ironically, the elitist insistence on the primacy of blood and populist fears about polluted and tainted blood actually contributed to the breed's downfall and the collapse of the export trade. Eyes enamoured of Thoroughbred bloodlines sometimes overlooked the virtues of the other horses, the hybrid pool homogeneous enough to be branded the so-called Caper or Cape horse, which was in decline by the end of the nineteenth century. Attempts to keep horses of one 'breed' were more successful than efforts to keep horse owners of one particular type. Horses could not be contained within the ownership of one group, and it is this theme that the next chapter explores.

So in the final analysis, 'blood did tell', but it revealed far more about the humans obsessed with it than it did about the horses in whose veins it flowed.

Chapter 4

✳

The Empire Rides Back

An African Response to the Horse in Southern Africa[1]

THE 1996 STATE funeral of King Moshoeshoe II of Lesotho was held at the foot of Thaba Bosiu Mountain.[2] Tradition holds that principal and paramount chiefs be buried on the mountain's summit and traditionally the coffin is supported by pallbearers to the top, escorted by a guard of horsemen. The king's own horse is led riderless to the place of interment with a Basotho hat, symbolising the king, resting on the saddle.[3] Much of the pageantry of citizenship in the mountain kingdom draws on horses.[4] The year before his death, for example, the king presented the then South African president, Nelson Mandela, with a dappled-grey stallion, among honours from other states.[5] Horses are still widely used (as many as 100,000 nationally) for general transport over the dramatic topography of Lesotho.[6] Aside from its still useful role in rural transport, particularly in the highlands, the horse has seeped into cultural references, as in idioms like 'Ho ja pere' ('eat the horse' – to do the forbidden) and folk tales.[7] They figure in praise poetry as men in seanamarenas[8] sing: 'Horses are the pride of Basotho men.' Horse races remain popular social events. And mare's milk, lebese la pere, may be used medicinally. The popular archetype of 'Mosotho, pony, blanket and gun' infuses the tourist literature and commodifies the romance of the rugged little mountain pony found only in Lesotho. The refrains (usually maintained by outsiders) 'the Basutos are naturally a horse loving people';[9] 'the Basotho are a nation of horsemen'; they are 'natural horsemen'; and their ponies are 'integral to the landscape' are entrenched – evident in the archival record; in the observations of foreigners; recurring in advertisements and travel literature; and even represented on stamps, coins, banknotes and the national coat of arms. This coat of arms (adopted post-independence in 1966) bears a shield, behind which are two nineteenth-century guns; the shield is supported on either side by Basotho horses. The long link with horses is acknowledged in the ironic identity *majapere* (the horse eaters) adopted in jest by Basotho themselves.[10]

Lesotho has produced more history than could be consumed locally.[11] As a small landlocked country completely surrounded by South Africa it has a history entwined with that of the larger country, and also with that of Britain, under whose control it was from 1868 until 1966. The capacity to dispossess land by means of the tools of conquest – horses and guns – was at the core of South Africa's history, which spilled across its borders into neighbouring states. Thus, as Chapter 2 explored, there were efforts to contain the horse within colonial grasp. Initial attempts by settlers to use horses to buttress their own power base pivoted first on retaining VOC and subsequently white settler control of equine power, as shown in previous chapters. However, these attempts failed.

Horses were to become pivotal in the defining processes of the nineteenth century, which saw societal convulsions, conflicts and reorganisations. Chiefdoms broke apart, migrated and merged. The human contours of the Highveld shifted, as smaller family-based communities were transformed into larger militarised proto-states. As discussed in the previous chapter, as the Khoi were pushed north and east by loss of land to Boers, many adopted the horses and guns of their enemies.[12] This dyad of conquest also moved east and north. By the first decades of the nineteenth century, Griqua, Bergenaar and Kora raiders became the most mobile groups on the Highveld, plundering those without guns and horses. After these attacks, communities to the north, like those in Kuruman, developed a loathing for men with horses, guns and light-coloured skins.[13] In fact, various chiefs, like Mzilikazi and Dingane, for example, found it difficult to distinguish among 'white' trekker, Griqua, Kora and other invaders: they all shared the defining traits of carrying guns, wearing European-style clothes and being mounted on horses. As Etherington notes, an escalating arms race ensued, with ever-increasing efficiency in killing. Key leaders like Mzilikazi, Sekonyela, Moshoeshoe, Dingane and Hintsa all turned their attention to ensuring that their combatants were mounted and armed as far as possible. There were also initiatives from ordinary people themselves to acquire horses and guns. Horse and gun ownership seeped through to the Caledon Valley, Highveld and eastern seaboard. The acquisition happened rapidly: in 1800, for example, Tswana were on foot fighting off mounted raiders, but a generation later they themselves had access to guns and horses. Similarly, in the 1820s Xhosa factions simply hungered after horses, but by 1846 they were able to mobilise as many as 7,000 armed mounted men.[14] But only one African group became a wholly mounted polity – the Basotho.

So this chapter looks at how horses, like guns – another key technology of conquest – were wrested from the grasp of white hands and how they were adopted in one case in particular – by the men of the people who came to call themselves the Basotho.[15] The chapter will show why and how horses were used to resist colonial incursions and threats by other indigenous groups by improving the Basotho's military capacity and integration into the regional cash economy, thereby creating conditions favourable to the complex processes of state building.[16]

Mid-Nineteenth Century Basutoland (highlighted)
Source: Rev. E. Casalis, The Basutos; or Twenty-Three Years in South Africa
(London: James Nisbet, 1861)

Horses for a kingdom

A brief chronological overview of the rise of Moshoeshoe's kingdom contextualises developments before more detailed thematic analysis can occur. By the sixteenth century people described much later as 'Sotho' began arriving in the region known now as Lesotho, intermingling with the San and Khoikhoi and establishing small chiefdoms. The area came to be characterised by groups of atomised, independent Sotho-speaking political units who had similar lifestyles. From the early nineteenth century widespread trade links were forged among the groups, as well as with external communities. By the late eighteenth and early nineteenth centuries, communities within this territory began to recognise both the external threat and the internal pressure on the environment presented by encroachment by white traders and Boer pioneers. Simultaneously, the *lifaqane* (or *mfecane/difaqane*) in the first quarters of the nineteenth century was a time of forced migration and social upheaval, with roots stretching back into the eighteenth century. Loosely organised, scattered southern Sotho groups were consolidated by King Moshoeshoe, who established a centralised mountain stronghold, Thaba Bosiu.[17]

By strategic use of this easily defended mountain headquarters and the use of guns and horses, as this chapter will demonstrate, the people who would become considered the Basotho were able to extend their rule into Transorangia to the west and defend their territory from external threat from variously Boers, Griqua and Kora in the 1840s and 1850s. In the 1860s, however, neighbouring Boers threatened to overcome the beleaguered Basotho. To prevent Basutoland's[18] absorption into the Boer Orange Free State, it was annexed by the British in 1868, staying a British protectorate until Moshoeshoe's death two years later. The very next year, Basutoland was annexed to the Cape Colony, which was granted self-government soon afterward. The former autonomous African kingdom lost a great deal of its fruitful land and political autonomy. In 1879 the chiefs of southern Basutoland resisted, which precipitated the invasion of Basutoland by Cape forces and the inflation of the already contentious hut tax. Cape authorities also attempted to enforce the 1879 Disarmament Act, ordering the Basotho to turn in their guns, prompting civil conflict between compliant and resistant Basotho chiefs and an uneasy peace with the Cape Colony in 1881. A year later, however, the Basotho began refusing to register their firearms and an attempt by the Cape Colony to enforce the gun tax proved ineffectual. The Cape Colony was confronted with the likelihood of never-ending insurgence made possible – as this chapter argues – at least partly by horses and relinquished control over the area to Britain in 1884 as a British High Commission Territory. By the end of the nineteenth century and the beginning of the twentieth, where this chapter ends, the powers of the Basotho chiefs remained relatively intact. But the roots of their power and the kingdom that came to be Lesotho lay a century earlier.

Men on horses

From the late eighteenth century significant new forces entered the territory. Boer frontiersmen mounted on horses entered the area from at least the 1780s. The second wave was variously identified by observers as 'Hottentot', 'Griqua' (Dutch speaking; often the progeny of Khoi women and white or slave fathers), 'Bastaard' (runaway slaves and renegade whites) and 'Kora' or 'Koranna'. They lived largely on plunder, particularly mounted stock theft and horse trading and raiding (a legacy is reflected in the popular Griqua surname 'Perderuiter' or 'horse rider').[19] The Griqua 'captaincy' of Philippolis had been set up in the mid-1820s, comprising a multiracial assortment of dispossessed men and women of arguably primarily Khoi descent (though in general they were prouder of the European admixture) who had congregated in the valley of the Gariep (Orange) River further to the west.[20] Casalis recorded that the Griqua in Philippolis were becoming increasingly equestrianised, 'breeding good horses' and using a miscellaneous stock of Cape horses.[21] Griqua commandos on the Highveld, like other trans-frontiersmen, often attacked as mounted infantry rather than cavalry. Witnesses reported that they used horses to supply mobility into battle and escape to safety if necessary. They used mounted charges, mindful of the fact that firing and then retreating to reload did not work in the mountains; their new mobility helped compensate for the protracted reloading of muskets.[22] Of course, this tactic was most effective against those who had not yet adopted it themselves.[23] The Kora and Bergenaar-Griqua groups to the west initiated horse-based raiding in the Langeberg Mountains, supported by white frontier settlers who provided ammunition and bought raided cattle and kidnapped children for labour. In one incident, for example, three stolen children were exchanged for a riding horse.[24]

Mountain fortresses were insufficient against this new threat posed by the organised and armed Kora. They had inhabited the region between the

Orange and Vaal Rivers from the late eighteenth century. After acquiring the twin technologies of horses and guns from the Griqua, they raided the Basotho. In the first clash between them and inhabitants of the Caledon Valley, only one Kora was mounted and armed;[25] but by 1824 there was a growing number of mounted Kora. (It was particularly difficult to halt their raids permanently because they had neither unified intent nor leadership.)[26] The recently acquired technology of the Kora made a significant impression on the Basotho. As Moshoeshoe observed: 'I was hardly established [at Thaba Bosiu, c.1824] when the Griqua-Bergenaars and the Koras began a regular system of depredation against my people. It was then for the first time we saw firearms and horses.'[27]

Basotho horseman in traditional military dress
Source: University of Kwa-Zulu Natal, Campbell Collections, D34/001-197.

Reports of weapons and horses had certainly already reached the leadership through Basotho who were working in the Cape under white and Griqua farmers.[28] Horses were not just a top-down acquisition spurred on by leaderships' vision. They were later acquired from white farmers in the Cape Colony or Transorangia, obtained in lieu of wages or plundered in border disputes. Old horses, like old guns, were sometimes exchanged for labour. (Horses could not become obsolete, but they could become old or lame. They were then exchanged, much as cartridge-based weaponry replaced old musketry.)

There is some dispute over when and how King Moshoeshoe himself acquired his first horse. There is anecdotal suggestion that the first horses were brought to the area by the Prussian botanist Zydensteicker (Seidenstecher) in 1829 or 1830.[29] This has commonalities with the origin myth of knowledge shared by the Promethean figure of a white man, familiar from the mythography of the Zulu chief Dingiswayo's acquisition of a gun and a horse from the whites. It is more likely that Moshoeshoe received his first horse from Moorosi, head of the neighbouring Baphuti, in 1829.[30] Moshoeshoe apparently learnt to ride by 'supporting himself with two sticks while an attendant led the horse'.[31] According to the missionary Thomas Arbousset, Moshoeshoe remained a poor rider (but became an expert shot); although this could refer to his lack of elegance in the saddle rather than his competence, as he was widely regarded by the Basotho as a great rider.[32]

Guns and horses

Moshoeshoe began to acquire more horses as he acquired more followers. Moreover, individual Basotho working across the border frequently returned with horses of their own. They had witnessed first hand the power of the horse as a creature of military might and mobility. They acquired their primary stock of horses on an ad hoc basis by raiding the predatory bands of both Kora and Griqua from the early 1830s.[33] (In a possibly apocryphal vignette, a wandering party of armed and mounted Griqua became intoxicated and were easily defeated by some Basotho. At first the Basotho purportedly watched the horses in trepidation to ascertain whether they, and not the guns, were the source of the lethal explosions.) There was a rumour that when the Basotho first captured horses and guns, they 'broke down the guns, and all the iron of the saddles and bridles to make hoes of the material'.[34] Eugene Casalis, a French missionary of the Paris Evangelical Mission, recorded that in the winter of 1833 the French missionaries on their way to Thaba Bosiu were met by a dozen Basotho riders who were still inexperienced horsemen.[35]

However, ten years later the horsemen were experienced enough to train their own horses. Indeed, regional 'horse culture' was so entrenched that when, for example, Arbousset wanted to use the standard South African method of 'knis alter' (knee halter, or *kniehalter* in Dutch), the locally trained horses 'started to frisk about and kick and bite' because in 'this region these noble animals want to know nothing but open spaces. During the day they carry us: at night they regain their freedom'.[36] The lively cross-border trade flattened any major local differences in horse training. By 1839 James Backhouse, a visiting English Quaker, found that the price of horses had increased to ten guineas (or six oxen for one horse) at Griqua Town because there was a ready buyer's market in the neighbouring Basotho chiefs.[37] Between 1833 and 1838 Moshoeshoe imported 200 horses and by 1842 was able to tour with a cavalry escort 200 strong.[38] By 1842 there were 500 armed horsemen.[39] Theal notes that men were under orders 'not to work [their] best horses but to keep them constantly prepared for war'.[40]

Systematically acquiring horses initially was a direct response to cattle losses. The Kora and Bergenaars (labelled at the time a 'mixed band of desperadoes' made up of Griqua, Kora and Boer outlaws)[41] appeared to harbour no centralised, territorially expansionist project, and smaller groups, even although armed and mounted, could make no substantial impact on the Basotho stronghold of Thaba Bosiu. They were, however, adept at raiding cattle, which, as discussed above, stimulated Basotho desire to share in their newly acquired technologies to use against them.

Horse stealing occurred from both sides of the Orange River.[42] Boers, Griqua and Basotho were all involved. The graph in figure 4.1, however, shows that while horse acquisition by the Basotho through theft was significant, their cattle rustling occurred on a much larger scale (and even goat theft was more extensive).[43] Of the horses that were stolen by Basotho, mares were most common, perhaps with the intention to set up brood stock, but most likely because they were the least protected by Free State farmers. As discussed in the previous chapter, mares were used for breeding rather than riding and were less valuable and thus more vulnerable to theft, standing in remote camps rather than close to camp, as were the cosseted stallions, and less likely to be in active use than geldings. (In fact, the still considerable number of geldings stolen arguably indicates that they were the most popular choice and Basotho may have recognised them as more immediately useful.)

At first, because of their scarcity, any horse was a precious and vulnerable commodity. Evidence of their social value lies in the fact that horses were not initially private property (just as in the mid-seventeenth century Cape under the VOC); their resale was controlled by chiefs and ultimate possession was technically vested in the people. Stray horses, as with cattle, were reported to the regional principal chief and eventually become his property.[44] The names of horses – Valiant Black (Ntšo-Seqhobane – or 'black of great strength') reflected the respect they could inspire. There was (in the early days of their acquisition) an almost totemic faith in the horse at times, as in a local belief that if a lion was approached on horseback it 'crouches from fear'.[45]

Just as the Basotho developed a shared identity from diverse beginnings, the so-called 'Basotho ponies' were originally of heterogeneous stock. The Orange River border was permeable and the type of horses acquired varied. The changing source of horses was reflected in the changing nomenclature. The earliest Sesotho phrase for horse was *khomo-ea-haka*, literally translated as 'cattle called *haka*' (*hacqua* being the Khoisan name for a horse) or 'ox that deceives'.[46] *Haka* was then replaced by the word *pere* from the Dutch/Afrikaans *perd*.[47] This arguably reflects that the first came from the Kora. This supply was then supplemented by trade with white farmers across the Gariep River. The widespread trading of cattle for horses continued and labourers in the Orange Free State were often paid in horses. From 1830 to 1850 imported stock was for the most part small 'Cape horses'. The 'good horses' were largely stock acquired from neighbouring white Cape farmers: the Cape horses (with much 'oriental' or, rather, 'South-east Asian' blood) discussed in the previous chapter.[48] In the second wave of acquisitions, from 1835 to 1840, there was predominately similar stock (with some English Thoroughbred blood from horses imported to the Cape Colony for the burgeoning racing industry), while from 1840 to 1870 there was a greater infusion of English Thoroughbred blood. In the first decades of acquisition, the horses they obtained were often of poor quality, because the Basotho were not only acquiring the necessary ready money or exchanging the required labour, but also learning the skill to judge good horseflesh.[49]

Consolidating power

Moshoeshoe consolidated his authority, centring on the Caledon Valley. By 1842 there was formal colonial recognition of his authority north of the Orange River.[50] The land itself was a tempting proposition for the white farmers because of its pasturage, while its absence of horse sickness was an added bonus.[51] Boers thus cast covetous eyes towards Basutoland. In 1842 a missionary leader, John Philip, noted that the 'part of the country actually under control of Moshesh is small' in comparison to that to

> the north and north-west of him, over which the Boers have spread themselves, but it is of vast importance in their eyes, as it is a fine country from its elevation for breeding horses in the only district of that Country in which the horsesickness is unknown.

As Philip observed: 'The Boers know that without their horses, which they cannot keep without the possession of this Country [Basutoland], they never can carry their ambitious designs into execution.' Philip urged British commitment to protecting this chiefdom, arguing that it would prove cheaper than having to expel the Boers once they 'exterminated these tribes and got possession of the country and horses of Moshesh'.[52] Moshoeshoe reciprocated by welcoming imperial interest – thus amplifying Boer bellicosity – and using his diplomatic skills to work towards British involvement in the buttressing of his authority over Transorangia.[53] He signed a statement welcoming the proposed imperial annexation of Transorangia (including Basutoland), accepting that the Basotho would be permitted basic self-government under British protection.[54]

Horse trading

An environment that could support equine life was clearly a prerequisite for their successful propagation. If Basutoland had been an inhospitable environment, horses might arguably have remained an elite status symbol, as they did in certain west African states.[55] Although the high elevation rendered the country relatively free of the scourges of the Lowveld – nagana and horse sickness – people and horses still lived dangerous lives in the late 1830s and early 1840s. There was the chronic danger of predators – either the imagined threat from recently reformed cannibals or the very real presence of lions.[56] Horses' lives were not much safer, as Arbousset's chronicle makes clear, except that in the early days they were often considered more worthy of protection from such dangers than were people (just as in the early VOC period, discussed in Chapter 2).[57]

The accoutrement of riding remained based on bought technology (e.g. no regional saddle type was developed in the mountains, but there were a few local saddle makers). In 1858, for example, a white trader sold 350 saddles, 500 bridles and 500 stirrups.[58] Over time, anthropogenic and natural selection led to a mixed collection of hardy ponies that were small (14–14.2 hands) and able to forage for themselves. Basutoland was a harsh environment. Protection from the extreme cold of the high plateau, natural vegetation for horse fodder, and equine-specific smithing and veterinary care were limited – only the tough could survive. The cold, the sparse forage and the steep, rugged terrain led through natural selection to the development of compact, sturdy ponies with legendary endurance and strong hooves. (A myth arose that these hardy little ponies must have been descended from Shetland ponies stolen from British settlers, which echoes the 'Promethean white knowledge giver' myth of origin discussed earlier.)[59] There were few specialised horse experts in the mountains; instead, there was a growing shared knowledge. For example, local knowledge promoted *papisi* (marijuana) to rid horses of parasitic worms.[60]

Jockeying for power

Getting rid of neighbouring human parasites was more difficult, so Moshoeshoe steadily continued to procure both firearms and horses to ensure security for his powerbase (see figure 4.1).[61] The twin technologies of horses and guns spread in tandem. Horses were used by the Basotho to transport mounted infantry or for cavalry action. There was increasing use of the musket in dismounted skirmishes, with *knobkierie* and assegai used during mounted strikes.[62] The 1830 defeat of the Griqua shows that Moshoeshoe's warriors had effectively made their enemy's weapons their own. Moshoeshoe continued to amass guns and horses over the subsequent decades – the adversaries changed over time, but the threat to security was constant.

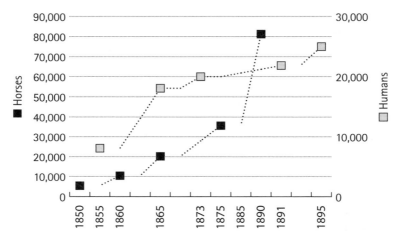

Figure 4.1: Analogous Basotho demographic trends:
Horse and human populations, c.1850–95
Source: Compiled from British Parliamentary Papers, Colonial Report, C.7944–4, 1895–96

Once the Griqua threat was defused, relative prosperity followed, with the fecund lowlands producing grain to trade with neighbouring white communities. This furthered the accumulation of firearms and horses, initially proving a seller's market and allowing cattle acquisition cheaply by the white border communities.[63] By 1850 British officials noted with concern that '[t]he Basuto people have within the last few years become exceedingly rich in cattle and horses, and possess more firearms than all the other tribes in the [Orange River] Sovereignty put together'.[64] By 1852 the Basotho had an estimated armed force of between 5,000 and 6,000, 'almost all clothed in European costumes and with saddles'.[65] An awed traveller, the Reverend Freeman, noted:

> Not more than thirty years ago he had not as much as a suspicion of the existence of white nations, and he had never seen either a gun or a horse; he is now perhaps possessed of the greatest number of firearms and horses of any chief in South Africa.[66]

The process of political consolidation was ongoing within the context of the changing environment in the Caledon Valley. For example, the threat from the neighbouring Batlokoa was only mitigated in 1852 after their final defeat by the Basotho.[67] Boers became the new key menace: settlers kept arriving in Transorangia and the rich Caledon Valley, setting up permanent dwellings and making claims of ownership. By the late 1850s Basutoland had become the 'granary of southern Africa' and its rich lands were an object of envy to neighbours. Ongoing boundary disputes between Boers and Basotho in the Caledon Valley continued. By 1858, prior to the War of Senekal (First Basotho–Boer War), a Basotho force of 10,000 was mustered and the Boers faced being overwhelmed until they received British aid.[68] A new boundary was established under the mediation of the Cape governor, who effected the feat of satisfying neither party. The Free State realised the power of the Basotho forces and were better equipped for the next conflict in 1865. When border tensions erupted again before the Seqiti War (Second Basotho–Boer War) there was an organised Basotho force of 20,000 that comprised almost the entire male population of military age.[69] Aided by Moroka's Rolong, the Free State won and a new treaty was signed the following year that reduced the kingdom to what is today Lesotho, with the loss of much arable land, pasturage and livestock. Yet by the 1860s the Boers had come to rely extensively on Basotho grain, and even after the loss of much arable land in the 1860s the Basotho kept supplying grain to the local market. There was also substantial trade between Basutoland and the Orange Free State. From the Boers the Basotho obtained a miscellany of necessities: soap, salt, guns and gunpowder.

The efforts of the Free State Boer republic to seize control of the Basotho grainlands and labour resources in the 1860s were thwarted by imperial intervention. Britain annexed the territory to the Crown as a dependency and renamed it Basutoland in 1868. After the annexation, the 1870 Aliwal North Convention laid out very circumscribed geographic parameters (Moshoeshoe died in the same year).[70] The loss of these lowlands intensified the urge to populate the highlands in tracts that had previously been used only as summer grazing ground.[71] Moreover, population growth had been an inevitable consequence of the success that the country knew in the mid-nineteenth century (see figure 4.1). There was a demographic surge, with more land brought under cultivation in the area along the western boundary and more villages being built in the mountains. Curtailed to the south or west, pressure could only be relieved by expansion to the east. Mountainous grazing ground was thus encroached upon, with larger-scale cultivation, with winter grazing permanently infringed. There was consequently over-stocking and, with ploughing, erosion on a large scale. Residents varied their food production by relying on a mixture of livelihood strategies, including pastoralism, livestock husbandry and cultivation, in a seasonal land usage pattern.[72] Horses became used not only in the military sphere, but also for everyday social interaction, including hunting and attending *pitsos* (all-male assemblies called by king or chief to confer over *molao*, the law, which allowed a measure of free speech). Horses facilitated governance of greater areas, by providing not only military defence, but a more effective communication system. Both the geographic distribution of horses and their primary use thus shifted over time. Their predominately lowlands distribution and military use changed with the utilisation of the highlands, which rendered horses key in rural transport.[73]

Horses and the state

Initially two socio-political processes were at work: external threat and internal unification/centralisation; the horse proved significant in both. In the 1820s Moshoeshoe had a personal following of 3,000; by 1848 this had mushroomed to 80,000;[74] and by 1869 it had reached 125,000 (see figure 4.1).[75] The external threat shifted over time from Bergenaar to Free State Boer, inspiring unity under Moshoeshoe because of the secure retreat he provided against these external dangers. Thompson has shown that Moshoeshoe created an ideological basis for uniting diverse people into a unit by defending Basotho land claims, thus legitimising 'king', 'nation' and the bonds between them. He was intent on an inclusionary project and was able to win over alien polyglot subjects with his fluency, for example, in Nguni languages.[76] He embraced attributes of the West, but on his own terms, espousing literacy and exhibiting what the missionary Arbousset called 'a deeper yearning for complete knowledge' as his 'horizons [were] not confined'.[77]

Taking a longer view, the period 1830–70 in Basutoland has been dubbed, perhaps Whiggishly, the 'Great Leap Forward', witnessing the consolidation of the tributary system, the reorganisation of the legal and economic powers of the patrilineage, and the reform of the organisational base of tributary power in the *motse* (village).[78] The services provided in turn by the subjects were military duty and the provision of agricultural labour. Chiefs had control of key items through the market – cattle, horses, guns – which were redistributed through relations of dependence, consolidating the new social order.[79] Of course, in state building, horses were not limited to military use. Stock exported to Kimberley fostered economic growth and was capitalised on by Moshoeshoe.[80] As Keegan has argued, Basutoland's rapid integration into the exchange economy was partly the result of Moshoeshoe's ability to direct the supply of cattle, uniting the scattered clans and lineages under his authority through clientship. His influence, as Keegan demonstrates, was also based on his controlling the supply of horses and guns for the protection of Basotho fields and cattle.[81] Moshoeshoe attracted support using the *mafisa* system, which was predicated on the tradition of lending cattle and which was modified to include guns, horses and saddles.[82] Loyalty was secured not simply by lineal connection, but by the ability of the chief to offer economic advantages and protection to his subjects. As a result, Moshoeshoe's new sort of roughly consensual central authority (and that of his lineage) was predicated on the protection and control of the large surpluses of grain produced in the Caledon River Valley. Thus, the need to win internal support necessitated the purchase of guns and horses to prevent external threats to the polity.[83] In his state building, Moshoeshoe thus strategised defensively – primarily against external pressure, but also against internal threats.

Horse soldiers

While central in new settlement patterns within the territory of Basutoland, horses remained important militarily. Just as in imperial and colonial societies, horse terminology became deployed in local metaphors of power. For example, the phrase '*bokhina pere*' meant literally 'to knee halter a horse', but it also referred to the practice of selecting new chiefs neither as permanent appointments nor outranking extant chiefs.[84] In 1872, for example, the governor's agent, Charles Duncan Griffin, clashed with Masopha's interpretation of the *matsema* (the chiefs' power of tribute exaction) as a symbol of political power.[85] Masopha had declared that this system was a 'bridle which the chiefs held in their people's mouths, by which they retained their authority over them … if this bridle was taken out of their mouths, they would no longer have … control over their people'. Griffin asked: 'are the chiefs to be allowed to keep the bridles … in the mouths of the people, or are the British Authorities to get the reins into their hands?'[86] Similarly, in 1871 Masopha likened the people to oxen and horses that must first be trained before [they] can obey [the government]. There are countries where horses and cattle may still be caught in a wild state, this is a country where wild men are still to be caught. You are the trainer who must catch and tame us.[87]

Horses provided mobility, but military structure remained loose. Just as for the Boers in the two republics, every man was a 'potential part-time warrior' and was expected to provide his own horse and weapons (although, of course, in both systems, indigence frequently prevented this ideal's materialisation).[88] Military units were formed on territorial lines: the followers of a chief formed a unit under his command, sometimes sub-divided by age. Both guns and horses became integral to the rites of masculine greeting: 'within a moderate distance of the camp, the royal attendants alighted from their steeds, fired a salute, then remounted and approached in the rear of their king.'[89] Military obligation was integrated into everyday social life. Just as in the Boer republics, military readiness reflected masculine values and men walked on foot only reluctantly.[90] The longevity of this militarised masculinity is illustrated by the oral testimony of an old man, born in 1896, who spoke of riding a horse and bearing arms in the early decades of the twentieth century even when it was not strictly speaking necessary, simply to exhibit a permanent preparedness for war.[91]

Basotho men developed a combatant component to their identity that was not uncoupled from their community identity (unlike in the Zulu military system, where there was a greater separation from non-military life). Consequently the horse, intended initially for military purposes, could be seamlessly incorporated into male domestic life. Cattle were relatively controllable and a secure source of nourishment; they remained integral to social transactions and of both utilitarian and social value. As noted earlier, the horse arrived in a context where cattle had figured for generations. Headmen could loan out horses in terms of the *mafisa* system (see above), and as strict control of horses waned, unmarried men still had access to horses and could possess their own. Paralleling the Boer commando system, as early as the 1850s it became expected that a militarily active Basotho man should possess a horse (although in both groups the indigent could of necessity not comply).[92] Moreover, because of Moshoeshoe's example and, as Thompson points out, increasing white pressure, every young Mosotho boy became ambitious to own a horse and gun.[93] Moshoeshoe promoted initial cautiousness with horses because of their scarcity, as Thompson argues, by 'being particularly sparing' in assigning horses in paying compensation, as opposed to cattle, with which he was more generous.[94]

This changed when horse breeding ensured equine sufficiency. It must be remembered, however, that unlike many other horse-owning societies like Native American groups (such as the Crow) that used horses as a primary signifier of status and central to the currency of exchange, the Basotho retained cattle as the primary status indicator.[95] Indeed, they were never as reliant on horses as some American Indian groups, for example, as they did not embrace a nomadic subsistence pattern. Horses were not a social or economic investment in the same way cattle were, but rather a depreciating asset, unless used for breeding. However, horses could be used in social transactions like *bohali* (bride price). Men usually received their first horse from their fathers and horses could be given as part of *bohali*.[96] One horse, the *molisana* horse, at least became a 'traditional' part of the bride price – if other horses were given, they were referred to as 'cattle'.[97] Aside from the part they played in such social transactions, women had little to do with horses.[98] Over time, women did occasionally ride astride, but only reluctantly.[99] Female riding proficiency came to correlate with the inaccessibility of a particular area and the absence of men.[100] Donkeys, which were introduced in significant numbers only at the beginning of the twentieth century, could be ridden by women and small boys, but men rode horses.[101]

There was considerable consumption of European-manufactured goods such as clothing, farming utensils (increasingly ploughs instead of hoes) and saddles. In the 1870s a population boom was precipitated by the Kimberley diamond discoveries.[102] Because of their earlier experience of cross-border commercial enterprise and labour migrancy, the Basotho were singularly well placed to benefit from these developments and thereby make good the destruction and stock losses caused by the wars of the 1860s.[103]

By the early 1870s Basutoland was a major foodstuff and horse supplier to the diamond fields, taking the gap earlier than the Free State Boers as far as supplying the market was concerned. Basotho ponies found a ready market in Kimberley, and the diamond fields helped monetise the market. By 1872, for example, the governor's agent reported that the hut tax had been paid entirely in cash. The Basotho used this trade boom to buy more guns and farm implements. Trading stations proliferated, with their numbers increasing from 20 in 1871 to

50 in 1873, for example. Consumers began to replace skins with blankets and rondavels (beehive huts) with rectangular homes. The previously European-owned commodity – the horse – once acquired, mastered, reproduced and sold by the Basotho, contributed to acquiring other European consumables. Horses thus played at least a part in helping to incorporate Basutoland into a cash economy and the wider southern African trade network.

The 1875 census reflected that the Basotho possessed 35,357 horses, and by 1891 this figure had increased to 81,194, even though it was a seller's market, with white farmers charging what they pleased.[104] Horses were considered so indispensable for military needs that the rapid acquisition of stock was supplemented with breeding their own.[105] In 1879 the chiefs of southern Basutoland resisted, which precipitated the invasion of Basutoland by Cape forces and the inflation of the already contentious hut tax. Cape authorities also attempted to enforce the 1879 Disarmament Act, ordering the Basotho to turn in their guns. This triggered civil war between accommodationist and rebellious Basotho chiefs. In September 1880 a Cape Colony armed force attacked Basotho breakaways. The Basotho horsemen resorted to the tactical defensive: dismounting and setting up ambushes, and then rapidly withdrawing to a series of positions on fortified hills to continue a guerrilla struggle. Mobility provided by their horses and their accumulated firepower was sufficient to defeat some enemy formations, most notably a column of British lancers at Qalabani.

Unwilling or unable to send sufficient troops, the Cape Colony effected a cantankerous peace with the Basotho in April 1881. Although having to pay tax on each gun, the Basotho were able to retain their weaponry. The Gun War was one of a small number of instances in southern African history of black Africans winning a conflict with colonial powers in the nineteenth century. A year later, however, the Basotho refused to register their guns or pay the compulsory tax. The Cape Colony faced the probability of interminable rebellion, made possible – as this chapter has shown – at least partly by horses. They thus handed over responsibility for Basutoland directly to the British government in 1884. Basutoland became a British High Commission Territory, and the powers of the Basotho chiefs remained comparatively unbroken – at least to some extent because of their strategic use of horses.

By the end of the nineteenth century virtually every male adult was mounted. Thus, there was a shift from a mounted body of combatants to a nation of mounted men. As an Australian war correspondent observed of

Basotho in the South African War, discussed in the next chapter: 'There are many things in this world that I know nothing at all about, but I do know a horseman when I see him … But nowhere have I seen a whole male population ride as these Basuto warriors ride.'[106]

Mounting population pressure

The outbreak of the South African War in October 1899 offered the Basotho a short-lived trade boom by stimulating a demand for high-paying labour and for produce and livestock.[107] There had been a dip in the economy: commerce had been stalled by the Gun War (1880–81), the drought, and civil disturbances between accommodationist and resistant chiefs. Moreover, the railway through the Cape to Kimberley helped undermine the Lesotho grain market. In the 1890s locust invasions and the ongoing drought affected the grain itself, and the 1898 rinderpest epizootic frustrated Basotho trade with neighbouring groups, with the border closed to stem the spread of the epidemic. When the South African War broke out, local traders and Basotho farmers experienced temporary but immediate relief.[108]

A war-time postcard, satirising the Basotho horse trade
Source: Robert Edgar Collection. Permission to use it is gratefully acknowledged

There was a boom in selling horses to both sides. The trading station entrepreneur, Donald Fraser, dubbed 'Ralipere' (father of horses), secured the contract to supply horses to the British army.[109] During the war, over 20,000 horses were sold legally at an average price of £16, but on the black market prices soared to £35 or even £40.[110] In 1900 alone the Basotho exported 4,419 horses worth £64,031.[111] Because of the upset in the grain market and the obstacles to trade in other commodities, the economy was thus briefly (and artificially) based on the equine export trade. Imports stopped and exportation began, so that by 1901 the export of horses accounted for 73 per cent of export market value.[112] The Basotho were divided during the war, and many supported the British, but some supported the Boers – indeed, during the war, several thousand Boers took refuge in Basutoland. The Basotho sold their ponies both to British remount officers and to the Boer forces and there was great competition for horses between British and Boers.[113] The postcard (see above) 'Greetings from Basutoland' depicts the British despair of acquiring stock, while Boers celebrate the covert trade in horseflesh – and the Basotho gets the best of the deal. The Basotho trader is depicted as manipulating a British remount officer, his shrug and outspread hands indicating that no horses are available, while clandestinely there are plenty of 'salted' (*gezouten*) horses available (at a premium, with their acquired immunity to local disease), as the Boers laughingly benefit.[114]

The Basotho ponies were particularly desired, because they were famously hardy and were already acclimatised to local conditions and diseases. The quality of these ponies was much praised by the imperial authorities and British press: 'They are all very square-built active animals, just the thing for campaigning, but the Basutos would not sell their own riding horses for love or money. All they would sell were the spare horses.'[115] A British remount officer noted that the Basotho dictated the terms of the market:

> The Basuto pony market is a very curious one … During the period of tension on the frontier, owing to the presence of the Boers round Wepener, not a pony could be got, and [after the relief of Wepener] … the supply flowed in, but not for gold.
>
> Instead, the preferred payment was cattle and 'another thousand horses were acquired thus'.[116]

This underlines a crucial point in the analysis of the Basotho acquisition of horses: the process was consistently secondary to acquiring cattle. Primarily, one must not fall into the trap of overestimating the horse's social centrality because of its anomalous position, especially because its pervasive and enduring use by an indigenous southern African group is so unusual. Culturally, cattle remained of much greater symbolic importance and cultural roles for horses were often prefigured by roles that cattle had played.[117] Cattle figured in more social transactions than horses, and the most significant transactions were based on the exchange of cattle (horses were valued – but would not do as sole items of exchange in bride price, for example). Simply put, more cattle were always desired (and acquired), but horses had a limited market once military needs were met. An Australian war correspondent writing about the South African War commented:

> All Basutos are mounted; never walk any distance … But there was evidently some subject that was interesting them, as they chattered away to each other, and at last it came out – their one object in life was cattle. They knew that the English had just captured thousands of Boer cattle, and … they would not take money if they could get cows. The cow is the currency of the place. … As one drives through the country crowds of horsemen are met along the roads, all sitting well upright, their ponies ambling at a great rate … and all the time they talked about cattle.[118]

The notion of an ethnic identity pivoting on horses has been fostered by nineteenth-century observers unused to seeing mounted African forces or being impressed by the horsemanship of the Basotho.[119] As one spectator noted, it 'takes a little time to get used to the shock of finding that the riders are all coal-black men'.[120] Moreover, a mystical notion of heroic horsemen or the 'centaur effect' clouded both contemporaneous and popular historiographical judgement, caused by the tendency of (in this case British) colonial administrations to admire equestrian societies over pedestrian ones.[121] Moreover, there is the risk of identifying Basotho horsemanship as an ethnic trait (observing, for example, that the Basotho are 'horsemen', whereas the Zulu are not). This unconscious ethnic essentialising ignores the socio-economic, political, and often primarily geographic and environmental exigencies for this 'trait'. Horses could thrive and form a breeding stock and, over time, a significant number of horses in the mountainous Basutoland became relatively free of nagana and horse sickness. They could not do so as successfully along the eastern seaboard among the Zulu, for example.

The biophysical environment played a significant role in establishing horses in Basutoland. Comparatively disease free and offering good pasturage, the country provided a context in which the processes of state formation could succeed. Clearly, Moshoeshoe was a singularly prescient leader and recognised the value of horses very early, but other African groups were similarly desirous of acquiring horses. Indeed, despite the control imperial officials applied to contacts with African trading partners, the Basotho themselves ran an underground trade to other African polities.[122] So it was not only Moshoeshoe's early identification of horses as a key technology that resulted in their successful establishment and deployment in the mountain kingdom. An important factor was the ready supply across the Caledon River of good horses. At first the supply was of the original 'Caper' stock and thus resilient – a necessary trait for horses acquired by first-time horse owners – and largely untainted by too much Thoroughbred blood, as discussed in the previous chapter.

The Basotho pony[123]

By the early years of the twentieth century there appears to have been widespread consensus that the hardy little Basotho pony had enough individuality to be classified as a distinct type (see illustration).[124] There were also repeated colonial attempts to improve the breed, as in the use of the government studs. As early as 1889 a stallion was imported to improve the Basotho pony.[125] After the South African War the Basutoland authorities instituted an interventionist policy, in association with white traders, to improve agricultural production – including breeding 'better' horses.

Lesotho stock returns in 1904 showed 63,677 horses (and 209,883 cattle). The authorities appointed a veterinary surgeon to improve stock, particularly the Basotho pony as a breed. Arab stallions were imported by the resident commissioner between 1903 and 1905, and a stud farm was set up offering free stud services.[126] The government hoped agricultural shows would improve stock.[127] There had been arguments for the introduction of agricultural shows as early as 1868.[128] But the belief lingered among the public that such shows were simply arenas for the display of freaks and deformed animals.[129] As the

Remount Commission, Basotho pony, c.1902
Source: Sessions (1903, p. 215)

environmental historian Alfred Crosby has suggested in another context, historically the horse has served largely as an instrument of ecological imperialism.[130] In the establishment of the mountain state, horses played not only this clear physical role, but they were used in the colonisation of the mind. Mental imperialism was effected – or, at least, attempted – by the horse improvement scheme. An official admitted the political agenda behind such agricultural programmes as inducement for the Basotho

> to see the sense of adopting modern methods; their health and their horseflesh – the latter, after their firearms, their most precious possessions – providing most suitable targets. People who had benefited by the white man's medicine, [and] had seen colts from the Government

stallions ... were, at any rate, not indisposed to listen to what white experts in other lines had to tell them.[131]

However, the horse performed not merely as an instrument of imperialism, but also as a symbol of resistance. There were problems in encouraging the local use of the government stud. There was a whisper of early twentieth-century resistance and identity politics played through the horse as traditionalism's totem, with so-called 'anti-progressive' Basotho opposing colonial breed improvement efforts: they rejected suggestions to castrate 'undesirable horses' and rebuffed attempts to draw them (i.e. the Basotho) into the breeding programme, challenging the notion that European imports were superior to 'indigenous' horses. [132]

Historical analysis affords one a more nuanced deconstruction of the romantic notion of the Basotho as simply a 'traditional nation of horsemen'. Other indigenous societies adopted this living technology of European conquest, used it to help reorganise their society and redeployed it as a form of resistance. For example, in many cases the subsistence patterns of the (American) Plains Indians were radically transformed over a single generation by the acquisition of horses.[133] Many primarily agricultural peoples abandoned hoes in favour of following the bison in a nomadic hunting lifestyle and engaging in predatory (and defensive) warfare. The south-eastern native Americans experienced the horse as a more gradual instrument of change. After the deerskin trade collapsed in the early nineteenth century, their horses went from an 'economic means' to an 'economic end' in themselves with the growth of an external trade in horses overseen by men and domestic exchange in equine-related products managed by women.[134] Just as in the Basotho case, guns and horses formed a nexus of exchange between white settlers and indigenous societies. The Basotho experienced the horse as a revolution in the military sense, a vital cog in the machinery of state formation. Horses also operated as a cohesive cultural force, continuing to be central in sports, festivals, social relationships (although secondary to cattle) and funerary rituals.[135] Competitions and other forms of recreation with horses replaced their traditional (male) activities of hunting and war.[136]

Conclusions

Like guns, horses were a key strategic resource adopted and then adapted by the Basotho in changing contexts. They acquired horses in response to cattle losses, then to fears of land incursion and later of annexation from a shifting range of neighbours. The threat came initially from white pioneer pressure; the Griqua, Bergenaars and Kora in the 1820s and 1930s; and the British and again from neighbouring white settlers in the 1850s.[137] The value of the horse as defensive asset shifted to a focus on its socio-economic utility over the century. From the late nineteenth century the role of the horse changed from military usage to general transport and retail purposes. If Moshoeshoe was the bridge between the pre-colonial and the modern colonial state, horses were among his technologies of transformation. Within the span of a mere two decades, horses had improved defence capability, switching from a technology in the hands of the Basotho's rivals for land and resources to the Basotho's own arsenal, aided by the uniquely favourable geographic features of the landscape.

A prevailing trope in environmental history has been how domestic animals aided their fellow (human) invaders in suppressing indigenous societies. The history of African reactions to the horse – even in this circumscribed telling – perhaps demonstrates a less imperialist side to 'invasive' species, or at least presents a much more complicated and shifting picture. Looking to imperial history and its ecological disruptions and focusing explicitly on the material contexts of the violence (both physical and figurative) that is connected to horses must not blind one to their role in resistance. This chapter has looked at how the 'empire rode back': how horses could not be kept in one group's hands, despite such efforts by colonial authorities. Horses bettered the Basotho's defensive (and to an extent offensive) capacity, thereby creating favourable conditions in which the processes of state building could occur. Horses helped incorporate the Basotho into the regional cash economy, along with labour, grain and other livestock, with horses becoming particularly important during the war-time boom of the South African War, discussed at greater length in the next chapter. Moreover, although a great deal of effort was thrown into scientific colonial breed improvement and there was ongoing concern over the 'deterioration' of type, there was also in several cases the rise of 'indigenous' varieties invested with the pride of settler or native society. Horses even served to represent an early attempt at symbolic resistance to the colonial metropole in resistance to foreign stallions being used as studs. Although never as significant as cattle, the Basotho pony became over time significant to the people who came to call themselves Basotho. This, taken with the undeniable military advantage it lent the emerging state that allowed it to take on encroaching neighbouring powers, including imperial Britain, leads one to ask: Was the horse not merely an instrument of ecological imperialism, as Crosby suggests, but also an instrument of resistance? Thus, in a sense, the Basotho showed how the empire rides back.

In a closing vignette, we return to the state funeral of King Moshoeshoe II in 1996. It was an event that reflects the use of horses in Lesotho national pageantry in common with other nations, and suggests both the horse's simultaneous ability to be an obedient part of the machinery of human social development, but at the same time exercise some agency of its own. Normally, as noted at the beginning of this chapter, the coffin is carried by pallbearers to the top of Thaba Bosiu, with a mounted guard in attendance. Because of the rain, however, the coffin was transported by helicopter, while the horsemen in black and scarlet blankets coiled their way up the mountain trail to the summit. The horsemen battled to rein in their mounts as three helicopters appeared (two from the Lesotho Defence Force and one from South Africa). The horses took extreme exception to these terrifying flying predators. As one observer noted dryly: 'Horses and helicopters do not mix well.'[138] But the funeral continued and the king was duly buried close to the grave of Moshoeshoe I. The crowd agreed it was the biggest assembly of horsemen in Lesotho for decades. But not all the horses returned.[139] For days afterwards, mourners were seen alongside the roads, cooking the meat from horses that had been unable to make the journey home.

Chapter 5

✳

'The last of the old campaigners'

Horses in the South African War, c.1899–1902[1]

The last of the old campaigners
Lined up for the last parade.
Weary they were and battered,
Shoeless, and knocked about
From under their ragged forelocks
Their hungry eyes looked out.

'Banjo' Paterson, 'The last parade'

THERE IS A strong measure of irony in the fact that horses, which have been such instruments of vast social, political and economic change in human society, can themselves be killed by change alone. Upset to their routine can precipitate enough anxiety to make them colic fatally. Horses are vulnerable creatures. An old *platteland* farmers' saying is that nearly all of God's creatures are perfect, but he should be given another chance to design the horse. Horses' systems are unusual in that their breathing and eating systems merge, making it impossible for them to vomit.[2] Simple indigestion can thus mean death. Horses need ritual and habit, and lack of these can further weaken their immune systems. In addition, horses are stoic. As prey animals, they reveal illness only if they cannot avoid it. They do not vocalise pain in the same way that other animals close to human society – like dogs – do, so it is difficult to tell when a horse is ill, at least in the early stages. All this is due to the evolution of their survival instincts so as not to appear as the weak animal in the herd, which would attract a predator's attention. (It would perhaps have made a difference to the way horses were used historically had they yelped like a dog when assailed with whips and spurs.) Eating unusual fodder, drinking too much water after hard work, a spell out in very hot or very cold weather, unfamiliar pathogens and alien plants can all lead to incapacitation and death – in short, all the changes one might expect a war in a foreign country to impose on a horse.

The changes offered by war were, of course, far greater than the small litany given above, but as this chapter will show, it was not direct combat that proved the greatest threat. In this chapter, the role of horses in this South African war is explored through the lens of their mortality. The focus is on the South African War (1899–1902), waged by the British to establish their hegemony in South Africa and by the Boers/Afrikaners to defend theirs in the South African Republic and Orange Free State.[3] Less than 90,000 Boers fought against a British army that eventually approached 500,000. The Boer forces, taking advantage of an initial advantage in numbers, won several victories early in the war. In 1900, however, British forces began to overwhelm the Boers. Resistance continued in the form of a guerrilla war in the countryside until 1902, by which time the British had prevailed by adopting a scorched earth policy. The signing of a peace treaty on 31 May 1902 brought an end to more than three years of devastating conflict. No British colonial war since 1815 had been so costly, both in terms of mortality and finances.[4] The War Office calculated that 22,000 of the 447,435 strong British force died.[5] For the Boers, the losses were proportionally even higher, with roughly 7,000 of the 87,365 Boer combatants killed and 27,000 Boer civilians dying in British-run concentration camps.[6] Africans' participation was on a substantial scale, with at least 100,000 in military employment on both sides, and the death toll for black combatants and refugees was between 16,000 and 20,000.[7] The South African War was the largest and most modern of the numerous pre-colonial and colonial wars that raged across the southern African subcontinent. Aside from the human cost, the theatre of war carried a heavy environmental toll, with the scorched earth policy shattering the rural economy of the two Boer republics and transforming the landscape itself. The environmental toll extended to animals. Both sides relied heavily on mounted troops, and the casualties suffered by horses were on a massive scale. On the British side, 326,073 horses and 51,399 mules died between October 1899 and May 1902, at the rate of 66.88 per cent and 35.37 per cent of the total head count, respectively.[8] This is widely regarded as proportionally the most devastating waste of horseflesh in military history up until that time; the slaughter was contemporaneously described as a 'holocaust' by an eye-witness, Frederick Smith.[9]

This chapter could thus simply, and certainly justifiably, take the form of an equine *Grand Guignol*, but this would mask other, hidden stories. Instead, the material context of equine casualties and the reasons behind them will be examined, before turning to a discussion of the cultural dimension of equine mortality, including human ideas on the death of horses. The public commemoration of the slaughter and how combatants on both sides were affected by this intimate loss will also be unravelled.

Horses in war

The horses in this war were among the last to engage in warfare in the way it had been fought for more than 2,000 years. The role of the military horse was changing and growing increasingly controversial. As an instrument of combat, it had already begun its slow and inexorable slide into obsolescence. Horses did not immediately become a military anachronism; the development of field artillery in fact rendered them vital for logistical purposes, as they hauled arms and ammunition to and from the field. Cavalry too remained tactically relevant by shedding their heavy armour plate, adding pistols and carbines to their weaponry, and working in concert with artillery and riflemen. But this change of tactics removed the mounted warrior from his pre-eminent position on the battlefield. Traditionally, the British cavalry had been trained to ride 'knee to knee' at a gallop and in so doing cut a swathe through the enemy (in contrast to the French, who charged *ventre à terre* or 'belly to earth' – each man at his fastest pace, so fast that the belly of the horse felt like it was touching the ground).[10] However, even before the South African War, there was growing debate over whether to preserve the use of blade weaponry, the *arme blanche* ('white arm' or steel-bladed weapon), or move to firearms in mounted warfare. Military traditionalists supported the continued use of the *arme blanche*, incorporated with the mass cavalry charge, believing that the cavalry charge still offered a heroic gesture, a romantic archetype woven into traditional cavalry principle that the best weapon is a man on a horse.[11]

This traditional approach was, however, to prove ineffective against Boer commandos made up of adaptable, experienced horsemen fighting in familiar environs.[12] By using their greater mobility, Boer commandos could simply circumvent old-fashioned large-scale mounted cavalry assaults. As the war correspondent and bush poet 'Banjo' Paterson wrote: 'Johnny Boer don't believe in front attacks or charging at the run/He fights you from a kopje with his little Maxim gun'.[13] He further observed, sardonically: 'Of all the puzzles of the war, there is no greater puzzle than to find out what was the real value of the cavalry. ... we have no less an authority than Conan Doyle saying that the lances and swords should be put in museums', adding '[o]f the few cavalry charges that took place in the war, it is safe to characterise 90 per cent as utter fiascos'.[14]

As noted, in the initial stages of the war, the Boer commandos held the advantage, because the British imperial forces suffered from inadequate combat preparation and were outnumbered by the Boers. Within months, the British under the overall command of General Sir Redvers Buller were besieged at Ladysmith, Mafeking and Kimberley, and had suffered defeats at Magersfontein, Stormberg and Colenso. In January 1900, however, Field-Marshal Lord Roberts assumed command. He believed that the 'knee to knee' cavalry charge was outdated and that all further mounted attacks should be carried out with the rifle rather than the steel blade. With the Boers driven back in the east and west, the imperial forces pressed northwards, capturing the two Boer capitals. From 1901 the war entered a new phase, with the Boers resorting to guerrilla tactics. The British response was to remove sources of food and shelter, implementing a devastating scorched earth policy. Farms were destroyed and large numbers of both the Boer and African civilian populations were relocated into concentration camps. This war reflected the shift to a new kind of warfare – modern technology was fused with the traditional use of the horse. Horses and mules (and even oxen) remained vital to mobility in the war and were utilised side by side with the tactical use of steam traction engines, telegraphs, telephones, searchlights and breechloaders.[15] As mounted infantry became favoured over traditional cavalry, the function of the horse concomitantly changed. But it continued to be the key solution to mobility, providing units of mounted infantry with fast, efficient transport.

The (re)mounting crisis

In terms of horseflesh, on the eve of war the British were utterly unprepared.[16] While the Boers and their *agterryers* simply had to provide their own horses on commando,[17] the British army had to muster a mounted force larger than any it had ever mobilised before and then transport it 10,000 kilometres to South Africa – further than it ever had to before. It soon became quite clear that pre-war remount estimations had been dangerously optimistic.[18] Predicting a speedy little victory in a 'teatime war', the imperial army entered the conflict with the idea that a mere 125 cavalry horses and 250 mules per month were enough and that the troops and their steeds would be home by Christmas. This prediction was to be wrong by a factor of ten. As one colonial combatant observed: 'I never knew there was a remount service before this war. It has its hands full now.'[19]

The Remount Department had been established over a decade earlier in 1887 to set up a register of horses that could be deployed in times of crisis.[20] This floating pool of owners (who thereby enjoyed a small but steady financial supplement by gambling against the outbreak of such a crisis) was composed of various horse owners: masters of hounds, omnibus companies and horse dealers. With war imminent, 6,000 horses were immediately enlisted in this way in 1899. The army needed three classes of horses: troop horses (including heavy cavalry, light cavalry and mounted infantry); heavy draught and artillery horses; and transport or pack animals.[21]

Horses were available locally from Rhodesia (which provided 3,220) and Basutoland, as discussed in the previous chapter, but as noted at the time, the Basuto pony market was 'a very curious one'. Payment was complicated, with cattle the preferred means of payment rather than cash (at times one could get five prime cattle for a horse, just as in the early VOC period, discussed in Chapter 2).[22] The total number of local British army horses and mules was under 1,000, and by October another 7,000 were purchased. Rapid estimates were made of the number of local horses in the British-controlled Natal and Cape Colony. It was estimated that there were 48,000 horses and 4,000 mules in Natal; as many as 201,535 to 357,000 horses and 40,000 mules in the Cape; and a further 248,000 horses and 20,000 mules in the Orange Free State.[23] This local stock would have been a practical solution to the immediate imperial equine requirements in that they were already in the theatre of operations and acclimatised to the environment, but they were owned by civilians. Writing in the immediate aftermath of the war, Frederick Smith argued that there were sufficient horses available in the Cape alone to permit the Remount Department to acclimatise all imported horses for the first year of the war; he cited a secret report compiled by the Intelligence Division of the War Office.[24] Perhaps the War Office initially feared provoking an uprising if local horses were simply commandeered.[25] It became inescapable that horses would have to be imported, and on a massive scale.

'There's another blessed horse fell down'[26]

Horace Hayes, an officer with experience of two remount voyages from England to South Africa, has drawn an evocative picture of conditions on board ship.[27] Horses were compelled to stand in stalls during their weeks at sea, being unable to roll or lie down. Those that lost their footing often could not get back up, and many were trampled. Aeration was inadequate and the stalls were poorly designed, which made it difficult to muck out the decaying dung and excoriating urine.[28] Occasionally, insufficient fodder was packed and horses simply starved to death. For example, the *Monterey* left New Orleans for Durban on 7 August 1900 with 1,168 horses on board. By the time it docked in Durban, 39 days later, 25 horses had died of starvation, while three-quarters of the remaining horses were so weak that they were unfit for duty for two months. As a contemporary noted with dry understatement: 'Horses and mules do not make good sailors.'[29]

Troops and horses embarking at Bombay

Source: KAB, Leica, L543

108

On many of the ships no one with any veterinary experience was available. In one case an inexperienced staff threw 200 to 300 horses overboard, erroneously thinking they had contracted the infectious disease glanders.[30] Every crew was meant to include a remount officer and a veterinary surgeon, but the staff officers were not of the first rank. Indeed a pre-war report lamented the 'third-rate men' who applied, because the army paid too little to get the best candidates.[31] Wasserman has shown that of their number, many were dismissed for alcohol abuse, larceny, gross insubordination and soliciting illegal commissions on the horses they bought. Critical observations were even made in the House of Commons about the behaviour of British officers based at a remount centre. The men under these officers, who were supposed to offer everyday care to the animals, were even more ill-suited. Muleteers, who facilitated the equine importations from North America, were a motley crowd of drifters and grifters, petty felons and ex-convicts (one random search of the freshly appointed horse custodians, for example, yielded a heap of firearms, blades and straight razors).[32] Caring for horses was simply their free ticket to another part of the world.

Yet of the 352,353 horses that embarked for South Africa from all ports, only 13,144 failed to survive the voyage – a loss rate of only 3.73 per cent.[33] It was not so much the voyage that killed them, but its aftermath – its debilitating effects coupled with the absence of an acclimatisation period. It is still uncertain whether the lack of acclimatisation was because of ignorance or simply a desperate measure because of the pressing need for horses. Certainly, as the war progressed, the need for such a process became glaringly obvious. In the absence of acclimatisation depots, horses would arrive incapacitated – dehydrated, malnourished and with their immune systems severely compromised – and instead of the weeks or months needed to revive, they would be transported to the front almost at once. For the first eight months, the remount command was at Stellenbosch.[34] The rest mainly went through Port Elizabeth. The central remount command was near Johannesburg and as the war progressed, Durban became preferred because the Natal government's railway offered a discounted deal.[35] Insufficient numbers of carriages were available to the British, meaning that iron coal trucks had to be modified for this purpose. These carriages were overloaded with seven to ten horses in a truck, resulting in injuries and deaths when the animals lost their footing in the hastily modified trucks. The transportation of animals by train from the depot in Stellenbosch was usually a journey lasting three full days. Most of the horses could not be provided with water and there was an absence of trained officers to oversee their transport, so many of these horses died en route.

Furthermore, there were insufficient supplies, which entrenched constant low-level malnutrition. As Smith maintained in outrage: 'We actually allowed to the horses in this campaign 2 lbs less of grain than is given to animals during peace manoeuvres!' The intended daily horse ration for the British was 12 lbs (5.5 kg) of oats and 12 lbs of hay for horses over 15 hands and 6 lbs (2.7 kg) of oats and 20 lbs (9 kg) of hay for mounted infantry horses. However, within the first months of the war, forage rations had been reduced to 12 lbs of grain per animal. A witness declared that it 'was not the severity of the work they had to do which killed them; but it was the wretched conditions under which they did their work'. For example, in July 1900, Lieutenant Colonel Lewis received a complement of 500 remounts that had been in transit for 11 days with only seven men allocated to care for them. While only three died en route, the rest were so exhausted that they could scarcely stand when they reached their destination. After a couple of days of recuperation they were deployed. Predictably, within three weeks, 60 per cent of them were dead.[36]

With statistics like these, the Remount Commission was increasingly condemned – Lord Rosebery calling it a 'gross scandal' – but its remit was extremely difficult from the very outset.[37] The remount depot itself was seen as a kind of exile – a 'Siberia' for incompetent officers. This resulted in the depot providing the world a new verb and the expression 'to be Stellenbosched' came into use: officers who had not distinguished themselves at the front were sent by Lord Roberts to Stellenbosch, because to serve in a remount depot was a humiliating punishment.[38] Castigated officers were said to be 'Stellenbosched' even if they were sent to some other place. Indeed, the director of remounts at Stellenbosch sank into a depression and eventually shot himself.[39]

The remit was almost impossible. Remount officers were required to find healthy young stock at the low prices mandated by the government. During the war, the maximum purchase price was only £50. Even without the limiting financial constraints it was a difficult job. The officers of the Remount Commission also faced the delicate task of fine calibration: while any fool could tell if a horse were really good or really bad, these officers needed to be able to judge a horse of 'medium quality': was the horse 'good enough to take' or 'bad enough to reject'?[40] With 336 horses lost daily, the remount depots resorted to the dangerous solution of bringing in unbroken (untrained to saddle) horses from around the world. The Remount Commission's stipulations that the horses had to be between 14 and 15 hands, between five and nine years of age, and had to be 'broken-in' were of necessity increasingly loosely interpreted. Some horses were not even 'halter broken' (trained to walk obediently with a handler). After the nightmarish sea voyages, they were then broken in upon arrival. Sometimes, to shatter its spirit, the horse was tied head to tail, or head to girth, with a foreleg strapped up. The British cavalry's manual of horsemanship suggested a ten-week minimum for the breaking in of troop horses, but there often was insufficient time. The method of throwing the horse down violently in order to reinforce notions of human dominance was standard. Backing, or first sitting on the horse's back, often took place in a high-sided breaking pen until the horse (or the fence) gave in.

Horses were acquired on a global level with much variation in suitability for the veld. In the first 15 months of war, England and Ireland supplied 87,000 horses, considered by the troops as the best quality available. However, many of these horses were large, unwieldy animals requiring better forage than the sparse veld could provide. As a Boer general noted acerbically: 'The British cavalryman might have used elephants with almost as much advantage as their colossal horses.'[41] Slightly smaller, hardier stock came from the United States, which provided about as many horses as England, Ireland, Australia and New Zealand combined, with a total of 109,878 animals. By the end of 1901 as many as 6,000 horses were being imported from the United States per month (including many mustangs).[42] A total of 14,621 horses were sourced from Canada, widely considered hardy animals, but they were more suitable for draught than for saddle. Similarly, the 26,544 South American horses were more suited to draught work and most were deemed obstinate and ungainly. From the South American contingent, only the Argentinean stock had any reasonable reputation.[43] Horses bred in Russia were small and unable to work hard; nor could they survive on little food. In contrast, the Austro-Hungarian stock, of which there were 64,157, were collectively damned as 'bad do'ers'.[44] A total of 8,000 horses from New Zealand, 23,028 from Australia and 5,611 from India were imported, both the latter gene pools having a strong South African ancestry from earlier exportations, as discussed in Chapter 3, and thus were able to adapt and survive slightly better than the other stock brought into South Africa from around the world.[45]

With globalised stock, basic but significant adaptations were needed. Some horses had come from another hemisphere and needed weeks to grow or shed their winter coats, depending on when they arrived in South Africa. For example, horses arrived in South Africa from England in the southern summer of December 1899 with their heavy winter coats of fur and were immediately sent to the front line, suffering inordinately in the heat of an African summer.

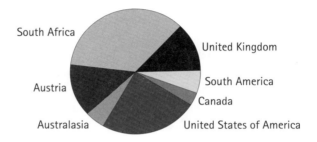

Figure 5.1: Sources of horses for British army
Source: Statistics from Royal Commission on the War in South Africa (1903, p. 258)

With global variation came unanticipated difficulties. As commented on at the time, regional variation in the horses' own lived experiences had tremendous knock-on effects: 'The manners, habits, and paces of the horses bred in the wilder parts of the world are so very different from those of horses bred in thickly populated countries.'[46] Multinational horses under British command each demanded different types of forage. South African horses would eat both oats and mealies; New Zealand horses would eat oats, but would not touch mealies; while Australian horses would eat mealies, but not oats.[47] Regional variation in training and horsemanship had a damaging effect. All horses had to become accustomed to the British manner of bridling horses, a practice that the previous experiences of the various horses found foreign and 'unnatural'. In some cultures, the horses were 'seldom groomed or handled, not used to corn or hay, seldom shod'. The Remount Department had initially little notion of the sheer complexity and diversity of 'horse cultures' and 'horsemanship'. In Argentina, for example, many mares were not broken in; instead, the horses would live in free-roaming little herds of riding horses. Each man-made herd had one matriarch whom the others trusted. When separated for remount work, the scattered horses would miss the guidance of the senior mare and could grow emaciated, pining for their erstwhile companions – a phenomenon unforeseen by bureaucrats in London.[48]

Cause of death

It was the role of the remount services not only to provide the horses, but also to work in the field to prepare both fresh and sick horses for action on the front. Disease, physical privation and combat itself, coupled with the sheer inability to care for their horses on the part of the military, all contributed to the massive casualty figures. Of course, it must be remembered that even in peace, few British-owned horses lived long and very few died natural deaths.[49] Horses that collapsed in the streets of London, for example, were the province of the licensed horse slaughterer. In effect, no horse that entered his yard could come out alive again or as a horse. Horses were dispatched rapidly: in a half hour it would be axed, skinned and dissected; its bones boiled for oil for leather dressing and lubrication; some bones mixed with sulphuric acid to make fertiliser; some bones sent to button makers; the skin and hooves sent to glue makers; old shoes removed and sent to farriers; tails and manes used to stuff sofas; and their meat used for pets' food. Less is known about the South African experience of horse death, but what sketchy evidence there is suggests varied potential demises, dependent on the wealth and sentiment of the owner. Owners usually buried their horses or occasionally kept the skin of a favourite horse.[50]

Disease was rife, particularly contagious ailments, because the debility camps and remount depots were often merged in the same facility. Strange ailments, like a mysterious 'tongue illness' (probably vesicular stomatitis) spread from the American imports to local stock, who had little resistance to it. Mange, a highly communicable disease, affected more equines than any other disease. In 1901 alone 12,000 head infected with glanders had to be put down. Biliary or 'tick-bite fever' (caused by a parasite in the red blood cells and carried by the red tick, which was picked up during grazing), to which South African horses were partially immune, affected most of the imported horses.[51] Strangles (an infectious disease of the respiratory system) and equine influenza were triggered by the stress induced by transportation and became more widespread as large numbers of animals were suddenly brought together, compounded by the conditions of poor hygiene in which they were kept. Pneumonia was yet another disease that levied a high toll and was especially dangerous for horses after gruelling sea voyages and extended overland transportation. Certainly, local horses had more immunity to local diseases and were usually more robust because they had not suffered the rigours of maritime transportation, which weakened these imported horses' immune systems.

Compromised immunity rendered horses more vulnerable to endemic diseases. For example, in the second and third year of the war horse sickness resulted in 5,700 fatal cases.[52] On the Boer side, General Viljoen's commando alone lost 40 horses to this 'dreaded horse-sickness' while passing through the 'bush country'.[53] Horses also suffered from trypanosomiasis or sleeping sickness. Riders grew inured to 'the giggling calls of the gray and brown jackals, the doleful howl of the slinking hyena, even the deep breathing sough of the lurking lion'. But they still feared the tiny organism: the settler's 'only haunting dread was the crippling of his march by the deadly tsetse fly or the wasting diseases' that made his horses the 'prey of the vulture'.[54] One could purchase 'salted' horses, which had recovered from the sickness and were believed to have a measure of immunity, but as Randolph Churchill observed, such horses were 'sorry, wretched steeds, without spirit, with very inferior strength'. A 'salted' horse was said to have a 'sleepy kind of look' and was 'often very lazy'.[55] Moreover, it was largely unaffordable, from £50 upwards.[56] In any case, such horses did not enjoy perfect immunity from further bouts of sickness – and desperate measures were deployed to treat those who suffered. (A common dose for horse sickness, for example, was half a bottle of gin and quinine. As one owner noted with a certain grim stoicism: 'The animal died.')[57]

Improvised precautions were taken on an ad hoc basis as preventative measures against disease. Vernacular knowledge of local disease and local lore were more useful than the international equine dogma, and this gave Boer horses yet another advantage over those owned by the imperial forces. One of the regulations of Viljoen's commando, for example, forbade spending the night near water or basins, to avoid fever.[58] Combatants on the front lines were expected to supplement fodder through grazing, rendering their horses vulnerable to poisonous plants. In South Africa, there were numerous types of poisonous plants, many with digestive irritants, such as tulp, ink-brash and oleander. *Senecio* poisoning of horses unaccustomed to the veld, for example, was a major difficulty for the British (more than the Boers). There was often a 'kill or cure' mentality in veterinary treatment, arguably born out of sheer desperation, particularly in the face of such dramatic symptoms. For tsetse fly, 'an injection prepared of carbolic acid' was suggested as an antidote.[59]

Fodder was scarce due to the lack of transport and the generally ad hoc nature of commando bureaucracy. Indeed, by 1901 the Boer republics were run by a mobile 'government on horseback'. General Viljoen noted that '[i]t was a very strange sight to see the whole Transvaal Government on horseback'. (He added that some 'had not yet got used to this method of governing, and they had great trouble with their luggage, which was continually being dropped on the road'.)[60] Boer horses thus had to rely in large part on the veld for food. On the southern and western fronts, visible evidence of overgrazing by commando livestock appeared. By early 1900 the horse fodder scarcity reached critical proportions. Provisions ran low and the veld often proved insufficient. The eastern Orange Free State had managed to supply fodder to the commandos in the guerrilla phase, but by the end of 1900 the scorched earth policy impeded the flow of food. Some commandos contrived to grow their fodder in liminal areas or pillaged it from African communities.[61] When Boer commandos passed through the bushveld of the Transvaal Lowveld in September 1900, the late rains meant there was very little grass for the 'poor creatures'. Water was scarce and Viljoen records that they came to rely heavily on African communities, 'from whom we obtained handfuls of salt or sugar, or a pailful of mealies, and by these means we managed to save our ... horses'.[62] Combatants were often helpless to assuage the thirst of their horses[63] and sometimes they were compelled to leave them behind, 'emaciated and exhausted'.[64]

Even when equine casualties suggested an epidemiological factor as primary cause, the vectors operated synergistically: those enfeebled by malnutrition were more prone to disease, which in turn hampered calorie absorption and further weakened them. Horses' propensity for ritual further undermined their condition. As a British eyewitness recorded:

> one of the most pitiful things I have seen in all the war was the astonishment and terror of the cavalry horses at being turned loose on the hills and not allowed to come back to their accustomed lines at night. All afternoon one met parties of them strolling aimlessly about the roads or up the rocky footpaths – poor anatomies of death, with skeleton ribs and drooping eyes. At about seven o'clock two or three hundred of them

gathered on the road ... and tried to rush past the Naval Brigade to the cavalry camp, where they supposed their food and grooming and cheerful society were waiting for them as usual. They had to be driven back by mounted Basutos with long whips, till at last they turned wearily away to spend the night upon the bare hillside.[65]

Boer combatant and his emaciated horse
Source: Used with the kind permission of the War Museum of the Boer
Republics, Bloemfontein

In addition to the large-scale dramatic epidemics and wide-ranging malnutrition, there were barely remembered incidental casualties. Even in wartime, a semblance of ordinary life continued for humans and horses. Horses were often not strictly controlled, even by the imposed discipline of military life, and some mares bred and gave birth to foals. Over-stressed and half starved, they sometimes delivered stillborn foals and by first light would have to be on the move again, leaving the small, forgotten casualty of war behind.

'They shoot horses, don't they?'

Of course, aside from deaths caused by disease, environmental hazards and deprivation was the effect of combat itself. Ironically, the likelihood of dying

Birth in wartime
Source: KAB, AG2600

in battle was far less than that of succumbing to an illness. Just as for humans, the casualty rate as a result of disease was far higher than that of wounds and injuries incurred during battle. As the horse's primary role was mobility, not cavalry charges any longer, it allowed some distance between horses and the firing line, keeping horses relatively safe. Yet combat casualties among horses were still commonplace during the war.

An evocative description captures the sense of such combat. In an early engagement in the war, a Transvaal Artillery Creusot gun opened fire and the 'very first shell stampeded all the troop horses. The poor maddened brutes came tearing past us, and we leaped on our horses to head them off, but had to retreat, to avoid being trampled down as they thundered by'.[66] General de Wet recalled that a 'young burgher, while riding behind a ridge and thus quite hidden from the enemy, was hit by a bomb, and both he and his horse were blown to atoms'.[67] One pony was shot through the body 'from saddle-flap to saddle-flap, but the plucky little animal carried [his rider] a thousand yards before he fell dead'. Decomposing horses were left behind as grisly remnants after battles. Reitz noted grimly: 'Rifle-fire at point-blank range is unpleasant at the best of times, but when one is on a maddened horse staggering amid wire loops, it is infinitely more so.'[68]

On the British side, the Army Veterinary Department (AVD) was widely damned as inadequate in dealing with equine casualties. 'The waste in horseflesh … has been little short of appalling, and for that waste the inadequacy of the AVD has been largely to blame.'[69] The AVD was just a loose bundle of units, with no veterinarians or farriers of its own (as these were regimental) and was stretched beyond capacity, with no executive control. Untrained personnel – indeed, men 'entirely new to the intimate needs of a horse' – were detached to the AVD. By the end of the war there were 322 veterinary surgeons working in South Africa, which, although a small number in the context of the war, represented more than 10 per cent of the entire British profession.[70] Moreover, requests for additional personnel, equipment and facilities for the veterinary service fell on deaf ears, because soldiers received priority over animals. The lack of qualified equine-care personnel led to elementary errors of judgement, which had dire consequences for the animal populations. For example, contagious diseased horses were penned with exhausted and malnourished horses out of the inability to discern between the symptoms of these ailments, which thus triggered unnecessary epidemics. Furthermore, it was 'generally a "stiff-un" who took charge of the hospital – and a cavalry officer selected for his incapacity can be "stiffer" than any of the horses he is ever asked to handle'.[71] There was a widespread feeling that the 'men who were employed to look after the animals were amongst the roughest, the most dissolute on the face of the earth'.[72]

A less-documented cause of equine mortality was simply bad horsemanship on the part of the soldiers. Inexperience on both the human and equine side played a role. On the Boer side, Viljoen noted that:

quite one-third of the horses we had taken with us were untrained for the serious business of fighting, and also that many of the new burghers of foreign nationality had not the slightest idea how to ride. Our first parade, or 'Wapenschouwing', gave food for much hilarity. Here one saw horses waltzing and jumping, while over there a rider was biting the sand, and towards evening the doctors had several patients.[73]

On the British side, Lord Rimington put it bluntly when he said that many mounted men 'did not know whether to feed [their horses] on beef or mutton'.[74]

Another commentator noted grimly: 'There is more than a substratum of truth in the remark once made by a caustic foreign critic, that an Englishman talks more and knows less about horses and their management than any other man.'[75] For example, during the relief of Kimberley, two new infantry brigades were hastily assembled using regular troops, some of whom had apparently never ridden a horse. During the relief of Kimberley alone 15,000 horses were lost. Merely galloping a few miles in ignorance killed many British cavalry horses, and their bodies littered the relief's path. The British-owned horse was burdened with an average weight of 22 stone (140 kg).[76] As Pakenham remarked, 'their masters ... had yet to learn that they could not gallop across the veld as though hunting with the Quorn.'[77] The horse casualties were due to want of water, forced marches and ignorance of horse mastership on the part of all ranks, who were inclined to regard cavalry work in the light of a steeplechase.[78] For example, Roberts' army arrived with its horses (like its men) on half rations. Forty-hour forced rides sometimes occurred with no rest, the result being '[s]ore backs, the outcome of long-continued pressure on shrunken muscle, collapse from exhaustion and want of water, the various diseases of the blood which come from over-heating food'.[79] In the early stages of the war in particular 'the horses were ridden to the end as long as they could carry a man, and directly they fell they were left to die on the veld'.[80] Cavalry horses were difficult to replace (the exhausted, depleted horses destroyed the effectiveness of the division). As one American observer noted dryly: 'I really believe the English cavalry would do well if so many of them did not fall off.'[81] However, a Boer general noted that 'British horsemanship improved during the war: in the beginning any sudden shock or surprise always unseated a number, whereas later in the war they stuck to their saddles'.[82]

Both the British and Boers believed themselves quintessential horsemen. Ironically, styles and equipment perceived to be particularly characteristic of either were commonly used by both sides, e.g. the Boer *rysambokkie* was akin to a British crop. In fact, the two sets of equipment and styles were very similar, with only small differences, e.g. the Boer *trippel*, a comfortable rambling trot, was not favoured by the British.[83] Both sides disparaged the other's equestrian skills. The British horse trainer Horace Hayes, referred to earlier as a serving on remount voyages, held a series of horse-breaking demonstrations throughout South Africa prior to the war. He noted that he had to fight hard to win the good opinion of the Boers, whose hatred of the English is equalled only by their contempt for us as horsemen. These farmers, I need hardly say, judge Englishmen only by the specimens who go out to South Africa, few of whom have had any previous experience among horses.[84]

At one of the shows, Hendrik Truter, who had served with the Boers at Majuba, brought an unrideable horse that Hayes broke in and 'instead of being pleased, he seemed rather annoyed that a "Rooinek" should be a better breaker than any Boer'. Boers, in turn, frequently cited an organic archetypal horsemanship – as Reitz observed: 'We learned to ride, shoot and swim as soon as we could walk.'[85] Horses and identity became increasingly wrapped up in each other, particularly in terms of Boer masculine identity.[86] The manner in which a Boer acquitted himself while on commando would affect his status as a man in the community, while his status in the social realm would in turn decide his authority in the commando. Horsemanship was one of the marks of manhood and thus a frequent target by the other side. Both sides felt the other groups did not love horses, merely used them. A war correspondent noted that the African 'is not fond of horses … A horse is to him merely something to get about upon, and he cannot understand our fondness for our equine friends. I have noticed the same trait in the Boer character'.[87] Further, a British observer noted witheringly:

A horse broken in by Boers was a horse spoilt. They must be the very worst horsemen in the world … this applies especially to the Transvaal Boers; some of the younger Natal Boers, who had mixed more with English, had much better seats.[88]

The idea among the British that good horsemanship was contagious – the Boers could catch it from prolonged proximity to English speakers – endured because British equestrianism had become integral to the national identity. As one commentator averred, '[t]he English may undoubtedly claim to be the most equestrian nation on the face of the earth'.[89] Superior horsemanship and the pre-eminence of English horses seemed to substantiate the glory of empire.

Horse–human relationships

A point that may otherwise be lost in the analysis of the war's devastating effect on horses is that the war helped both accelerate and highlight a time of changing association between human and horse. Of course, there was a strongly economic interest in this change of relations. There was an obvious pecuniary incentive to treat horses well: the average imperial mounted soldier in South Africa went through seven remounts during the course of the war. The general rate of wastage for the war was 25 per cent per month, which meant that on average, each horse had to be replaced once every four months. Roberts eerily echoed Van Riebeeck's pleas of two-and-a-half centuries previously in his urgent and neglected pleas to the metropole for more horsepower. Appeals for horses by generals in the field, especially Roberts, were met with refusals from the War Office, especially Lord Lansdowne (the war secretary in 1900). After Pretoria was captured and in the following year the same dynamic was replicated by both Kitchener and Brodrick (the next war secretary). Equally, on the Boer side '[t]he burgher knows perfectly well how valuable to him is his horse, and he is thus constrained to use his knowledge in carefully tending it, moreover, considerable

British soldiers horsing about
Source: KAB, Jeffreys Collection, J3408

affection exists ... between the master and his beast'.[90] The rare moments of a soldier's happiness in this devastating war were often connected with his horse. In the all too brief periods between battles, horses were used in leisure pursuits, strengthening still further their bond with their riders.

Economic self-interest was not the sole issue. Visceral experience of the combat slaughter evoked powerful personal and public emotions and changed minds about what was an acceptable casualty of war. Of course, morale was affected by the devastating loss, and this in turn affected the course of the war itself. But it was not a simple equation – both sides seemed emotionally affected by loss. After the capture of Bloemfontein in early 1900, a British officer, with obvious empathy, described the horrific state of the horses:

> From side to side this living skeleton swayed and crossed its hind legs if compelled to move. When tied up in batches they leant against each other, and the centres collapsed under the pressure ... These wrecks of war, this flotsam and jetsam of human passions and strife, these helpless victims of a policy of the grossest cruelty and gravest injustice, were dying by hundreds.[91]

Certainly, the rotting carcasses of horses and mules left psychological scars.[92] Death shadowed the horses, as a war correspondent observed:

> overhead, betwixt the smoking earth and smiling sky, flocks of vultures come and go, to them the sound of guns is merriest music; it is their summons to the banquet board ... A horse drops wearily upon its knees, looks round dumbly ... then turns its piteous eyes upward towards the skies ... with a sob which is almost human in the intensity of its pathos ... and one wonders, if the Eternal mocked that silent appeal from those great sad eyes, eyes that had neither part nor lot in the sin and sorrow of war, how shall a man dare look upwards for help when the bitterness of death draws nigh unto him?[93]

On the British side the peculiarly Victorian emphasis on 'sentimentality' was increasingly visible in the relationship, especially following the 1877 publication of Anna Sewell's *Black Beauty: The Autobiography of a Horse*. Sewell's novel had chronicled the rise and fall of a Thoroughbred gelding, Black Beauty, from

Carcasses of horses after the Battle of Magersfontein
Source: KAB, AG Collection, AG6074. In the Battle of Magersfontein in December 1899
Boer forces defeated British troops sent to relieve the siege of Kimberley.

the pastoral pre-lapsarian bliss of his foalhood on a landed estate to his final misery as a cab horse working the streets of London. Drawing on her Quaker background, Sewell wished 'to induce kindness, sympathy, and an understanding treatment of horses'. Although earning her a mere £20 on first publication, the novel became a sensation. It offered more than a simple inventory of the brutality suffered by horses at the hands of humans: it mobilised the language of slavery to invoke calls for compassionate management,[94] and Sewell's effective use of anthropomorphism (advanced by the novel's first-'person' narration by the eponymous Black Beauty) permeated popular consciousness. It was certainly influential in extending the very idea of the humane treatment of animals.[95]

It arguably also helped propagate the idea of seeing and talking about the horse as a 'person' with a personality and agency of its own. In earlier periods there was little anthropomorphism surrounding the horse as 'personality'. In one particularly revealing incident over a century before, an official in the service of the VOC, Wolraad Woltemade (1700–73), endeavoured to rescue sailors going down with a storm-damaged VOC ship. Woltemade made seven trips to the ship, riding his horse 300 metres into the sea, saving 14 sailors.

On his last attempt the remaining sailors panicked and too many clutched at the horse, dragging them all down. Significantly, the horse was not accorded hero status (indeed, initially neither was Woltemade),[96] and the horse's name is lost to posterity. Correspondingly, there appear to be few contemporaneous equine luminaries globally.[97] However, by the time Dick King and Ndongeni Ka Xoki made their famous 1842 ride from Durban to Grahamstown (taking a full ten days and covering no less than 600 miles), the name of King's horse, Somerset – who is said to have died the day after the epic ride – grew to be well known to the public.[98] And by the late nineteenth century, certainly, various southern African horses were accorded celebrity status. However, it was arguably only with the advent of the racing industry from the beginning of the nineteenth century that horses began to acquire individual public persona in southern Africa. Race favourites became known and adored by the crowds. This was further stimulated by the rise of popular media, available more cheaply to an increasingly – albeit slowly – literate public, and further fostered by military campaigns (e.g. the First Anglo-Boer War of 1880–81 and the Second of 1899–1902), which facilitated the popularisation of heroes, both human and equine. A similar argument may be made for Britain and, gradually, the global context.[99] This reached an increasingly widespread audience with the publication of Sewell's *Black Beauty*, which served as an indicator and further promoter of the anthropomorphised horse as personality.[100]

In South Africa impetus came both from the racing industry, as discussed in Chapter 3, and the arena of war itself. Leaders had iconic horses that became war-time celebrities in their own right: General de Wet's famous grey Fleur and General de la Rey's 'famous little white-faced pony' Starlight; General Malan's Very Nice; and General Smuts's Charlie.[101] Lord Roberts's Arabian Vonolel, who had carried him in campaigns in India, Afghanistan and Burma, actually won service medals from Queen Victoria.[102] Moreover, the period had seen a greatly increased discourse on caring for horses, which included references to horses' own agency and individuality. For example, a contemporary veterinary surgeon, George Fleming, noted:

> Physical fitness is closely related to mental fitness; for that horses have minds, affections, and memories, no one can deny, and all who have studied them will bear testimony to the effects of ill-treatment and

kindness upon them, not only in the performance of their work, but upon their durability.[103]

'Banjo' Paterson declared more simply: 'There are more capacities in horses ... Horatio, than are dreamt of in your philosophy.'[104]

'Of horses and men'

Horses mattered as individuals in a way that other animals did not. Certainly, one of the seminal war narratives from the Boer side was originally entitled 'Of horses and men', which reflects that the position of the horse was not only pivotal, but contemporaneously *understood* to be pivotal. Indeed, so vital were horses that initially Milner had wished to concentrate on removing only all the horses rather than to impose the scorched earth policy.[105] The primary sources offer suggestive descriptions of the horse–human bond and new ways of articulating it. An affinity and even a tentative analogy were observed between common combatant and horse. Smith likened the English horses to 'the townbred soldier' – both were 'newly arrived' foreigners, 'ignorant of the country'. On the Boer side, Reitz observed, as the war wore on, that the Boers presented 'long columns of shaggy men on shaggy horses'. On the other hand, he noted, the officers at General Smuts's headquarters in friendly derision referred to the staff officer equivalents as '*kripvreters*' (stall-fed horses who did not have to scavenge their food from the veld like ordinary horses). Equally, there are sub-textual suggestions of contemporary understandings of animal agency and evidence of a clear belief in equine agency. Reitz, for example, describes his horse, who was baptised Malpert (crazy horse) by the police at the government laager. Malpert was 'possessed of the devil'. His methods of work evasion relied heavily on 'kicking and lashing' until he left men somewhere 'between cursing and laughing'. But Reitz maintained that Malpert came to respect only his brother and himself, because he had once clung to Malpert during one of his bucking paroxysms until the horse was 'bested'. His brother had once doctored Malpert's ulcerated back and the horse 'showed his gratitude by obeying him'.[106] Thus, a measure of agency was granted to the equine fellow combatants.

Significantly, this was one of the first wars in which ordinary soldiers were commemorated. Perhaps a related point is that it was also one of the first wars in which animals were celebrated, both as individuals and as a group. Reitz even freed another of his horses, a little roan mare, as a reward when he felt she could no longer serve effectively, as he felt that she had shown 'the mettle of her Free State pasture, and the marvellous endurance of the South African horse'.[107] In another example, A.G. Visser composed a post-war poem dedicated to the eponymous 'Voorslag', his war pony:[108]

I was a youngster and he a young horse,
  Ek was 'n penkop en hy was 'n jong perd,
When with De la Rey the two of us charged;
  Met De la Rey het ons storm geja;
Under a rain of bullets Voorslag
  Onder 'n bui van kartetse het Voorslag
Carried me and my comrade from the battlefield.
  My en my maat van die slagveld gedra.
Give me my mount, a musket, a buck,
  Gee my 'n ryperd, 'n roer en 'n wildsbok,
And I won't envy the richest his gold;
  En ek beny nie die rykste sy geld;
A King on his throne is neither as happy nor free
  Vryer en blyer as Vors op die troon is
As Voorslag and me in the endless veld.
  Voorslag en ek op die eind'lose veld.
Arriving in the land of the Great Beyond
  Aangeland in die Hiernamaalse Velde
I have but one earthly desire:
  Sou 'k van die Aare net een ding begeer:
Give me the best, most loyal of friends,
  Gee my die beste, die trouste van Vrinde,
Voorslag, my mount, give him back to me.
  Voorslag, my ryperd, gee hom vir my weer.

This poem captures the sense of affection – indeed, comradeship – felt at least from the combatant's side towards his horse. There is a great deal of evidence for such sentiment being widespread among the men. A Boer general noted of his men: 'No doubt the burghers were very kind to their animals ... [they]

126

sometimes carried it too far, and the superior officers had often to interfere.'[109] Some Boers granted their horses almost mystical powers, feeling that they would warn them of danger ahead.[110] Viljoen noted of yet another of his horses, a 'sturdy little Boer pony, Blesman', that:

> he remained my faithful friend long after he had got me out of [trouble]; he was shot, poor little chap, the day when they made me prisoner. Poor Blesman, to you I owe my life! Blesman was plainly in league against all that was British; from the first he displayed Anglophobia of a most acute character. He has served me in good stead, and now lies buried, faithful little heart, in a Lydenburg ditch.[111]

Reitz poignantly describes the loss of his commando pony:

> One morning he came staggering and swaying up to me from the grazing ground, and I saw at once from his heaving flanks and glassy eyes that he was stricken with the dreaded horse-sickness, from which scarcely one animal in a hundred recovers. Nosing against me he seemed to appeal for help, but he was beyond hope, and in less than an hour, with a final plunge, he fell dead at my feet. This was a great sorrow, for a close bond had grown up between us in the long months since the war started.[112]

When conditions permitted, the corpses of horses were treated as bodies rather than meat. When Reitz's Malpert died, the commando 'climbed down to pay a last visit to his poor emaciated carcass'.[113]

Tellingly, one war correspondent noted that British soldiers would try to prevent the vultures from feeding on fallen horses. He describes how the birds swooped down:

> in a revolting mass of beaks and feathers above the fallen steed, as devils flock around the deathbed of a defaulting deacon. A soldier on the outer edge of the extended line swings his rifle with swift, backhanded motion over his shoulder, and brings the butt amidst the crowd of carrion. The vultures hop with grotesque, ungainly motions from their prey … their necks outstretched and curved heads dripping slime and blood, a fitting

setting amidst the black ruin of war. The charger now looks upward from eyeless sockets.[114]

In a particularly revealing reflection, a British combatant described how his horse, Peter, had:

> learnt most of the philosophy that soldiering teaches; learnt to like ration biscuit, and to lick his lips when he was thirsty. [W]e had shared many a meal …, and slept together, hungry and uncovered, on the veld. Only by such companionship does one come to know a horse. Not his paces and his vices and his powers, but his interests, his understandings, his capacity for self-effacement … [the] horse with which one has lived happily for long hours, day after day, on lone and dreary marches, is bound up, unawares, with all the dreaming sympathies which such days breed. He is an unaccounted confidant; his spirit and courage have lifted the flight of reflections, and in the rhythm of his paces our vague thoughts have trod. One learns from the parting how close has been the comradeship, and feels, too … a sharp reproof for [having kept] in a place of danger one innocent of all share in the quarrel from which came his end.[115]

Lonely soldiers chatted to their horses; they spent more time together than with any other living entity and experienced shared dangers that forged close bonds.[116] In the case of the Boers, this took a literal form: near the enemy, the men slept with their 'unsaddled horses by their sides, and the bridles in their hands'[117] or even tethered to their feet. This was true of *agterryers* too. The latter were pivotal on commando, caring for the horses, maintaining tack, ensuring they were fed and guarding the horses at night.[118]

There was an uneasy friction between the growing view of horses as comrades and their official designation as military property. This was played out in the arena of death. For example, both sides used euthanasia on terminal cases. However, when a British combatant 'ended his [wounded horse's] South African career with [his] revolver', instead of waiting for the farrier sergeant to do so, he faced arrest for destroying government property.[119] This was true only for the British, because the Boers rode their own horses on commando.

Because every Boer was his own ordnance, supply and remount department, as the war progressed horse ownership gained a certain fluidity derived from necessity; however, ownership was sacrosanct and if a good case could be made out for ownership, the horse had to be returned to its original owner. Reitz records his loss of a captured remount horse after a young man claimed the pony as belonging to his father, who had been killed that morning. The young man brought both Reitz and the horse to General Beyers, to whom he proved his father's ownership; Reitz promptly 'handed over the pony', unable to refute the justice of the boy's case. Nevertheless, since horses were indispensable, theft of horse and tack was rife. Saddlebags, horse shoes and nails were all in short supply. Horses' appearance could be altered with the strategic docking of a tail or cutting of a mane. Sometimes a ward number was branded on a horse's haunch to thwart theft. Being so valuable, horses came to be well known as individuals – when looking at some hoof prints, Reitz recognised the 'slightly malformed marks of Michael du Preez's pony'.[120] Certainly, there were prosecutions for horse theft in the guerrilla phase where, quite literally, one's horse could mean life or death.[121]

There was perhaps understandable tension between mounted burghers and those on foot.[122] A commando member observed that without a horse, a man did not really 'belong in the Boer army'; instead, one is simply thrown together with 'lower-class Afrikaners'.[123] To be a horseless man meant almost certain capture – or worse. A combatant noted: 'the burghers without horses were suffering terribly from the killing heat, and many were attacked by typhoid and malarial fever through having to drink a lot of bad water.'[124] In a telling example, which reflects the desperation for horses of any kind, 300 horseless men drew lots for remounts – mainly unbroken mares: 'those of us … unsuccessful in the drawings had at least the fun of seeing the winners break in their mounts, a diverting spectacle.' In another case, Boer soldiers stumbled onto a herd of feral horses in the upper reaches of the Caledon River. They managed to break them to bit and rein in a few days, and then freed their own badly run-down horses, 'hoping they would pick up condition and be recaptured and used'. Rapidly broken-in quasi-feral horses provided occasional Boer remounts – until the British became wise to this strategy and peppered them with machine gun fire, rendering them uncatchable.[125]

The value of horses was such that their loss brought combatants to utter despair. Reitz, for example, shared his worst experience of the war: being caught in a hard winter downpour, with 50 or 60 ponies dying from exposure, rendering a quarter of the commando horseless, on foot in the freezing rain, carrying their saddles and stumbling over the carcasses.[126] The night was so psychologically damaging that the little group that survived felt a shared traumatised identity, calling themselves the '*Groot Reent Kerels*' (the 'Big Rain Men'). On the British side, an equally poignant vignette captures the close bond forged between man and horse:

> Two troopers had been shot, one fatally, as the men cantered back to cover. The horse of the other stopped when its master fell, and, after standing by him for some time, walked over and took a look at the dead man. Then it came back to the other, rubbing him with his nose, and pretending to go away without him. At last, as if realizing the wounded man's condition, it knelt down beside him, the trooper making several ineffectual attempts to scramble into the saddle. The enemy, with a marksmanship on a par with his humanity, tried to knock over the horse, which started to its feet at each near whistle of the bullet, and at last scampered off as if hit by one. [T]he whistle of the Mauser following his every movement. There, raising himself on one arm, [the trooper] waved the other to his horse, which cantered back at the signal to the rest of the troop.[127]

This anecdote, with its emphasis on the lack of humanity on the part of the enemy towards the horse, also reflects how growing public humaneness could be mobilised as effective propaganda.

Death and the gentleman

As propaganda it was successful because the treatment of horses was increasingly mobilised as a trope of distinction – indeed, as a hallmark of civility. Viljoen, for example, was at pains to record in a memoir written during the war that while Boers made boots out of the hides of horses that had died of disease, 'no horse was specially slaughtered for this purpose or for the purpose of food'. He then went on to emphasise, however, that the British killed horses for food and openly indulged in hippophagy: 'It was only General Baden-Powell and General White who slaughtered their horses to make sausages.'[128]

There was a long tradition among both Britons and South Africans (of different races) of aversion to horsemeat. Up until the war, as South Africa's first black novelist, Sol Plaatje, wrote, eating horsemeat was unthinkable and he only 'saw horseflesh for the first time being treated as a human foodstuff' during the Mafeking siege.[129] In the British context, an earlier commentator noted: 'With a liking for the sausage ... there has always been present to the mind of the consumer an uncomfortable suspicion respecting the bona fides of the veiled delicacy.'[130] In a shocking counterpoint, in the siege of Ladysmith (where some horses were indeed slaughtered for food), White fed his cavalry horses the mealies that could have been used to feed his garrison.[131] In the siege of Mafeking, Baden-Powell slightly reduced the horses' provisions, although they still received ten times the rations given to the men.[132] However, in the sieges of Mafeking, Ladysmith and Kimberley, as food began to grow scarce after a few weeks, horses were added to the menu.[133] As one veterinary surgeon who survived the Ladysmith siege observed:

> A horse ... had died on the veld, and as I rode in among the thorn trees I came across two poor Tommies hacking off pieces of its flesh with their clasp-knives. They looked very guilty and confused ... but I had nothing but commiseration in my heart for poor fellows driven to such straits.[134]

Certainly, public shock was evident at 'Kimberley, eating her horses'.[135] A besieged resident of Kimberley, in a chapter entitled 'Horse for dinner', rationalised the hippophagy that was clearly provoking anxiety: 'Somehow one does not quite relish the idea of eating horse, but it must be simply because one has not been used to doing so. The horse is a clean enough feeder.'[136] A civilian in the siege of Kimberley noted that horseflesh tasted like beef, but 'all the same it took some pushing down'.[137] Another source claims that day after the relief of the town:

> horses that had collapsed through heat and overwork are being shot in all directions. The people here have been living on horseflesh and ... [when] a horse is shot, [Africans] fling themselves on it like a crowd of vultures, and in ten minutes there is not a scrap left.[138]

Horses made up a third of available meat and often Africans were not even allowed to buy horsemeat.[139] Arguably, the eating of horses broke the intimacy taboo that had been increasingly reinforced by sentimentalising the horse–human bond. In a social environment where horses and men relied on each other, it was a shocking act, tantamount almost to cannibalism, an act that became stamped in popular memory.

Horses being shot to provide food for the garrison, siege of Mafeking
Source: KAB, Leica, L912

Death and memory

The manner of memorialisation of the South African war offers a lens into contemporary rituals of sorrow. The monuments raised in Britain after the war were the first mass raising of war memorials.[140] Before this war, military memorials were almost exclusively to men of commissioned rank.[141] The South African War, however, was one of the first wars to show recognition not only for the generals and upper echelons, but also for common soldiers and, perhaps because of the growing emphasis on the role of the subordinate strata, it was also one of the first to show recognition for the ordinary horses. Nostalgia played a large part in any social understanding of war and much reminiscence included reference to horses. Reitz's memoir, for example, written in self-imposed exile after the war, talked of the 'long road we had travelled, of camp-fires on mountains and plains, and of the good men and splendid horses that were dead'.[142]

After the war, among the other cenotaphs, a statue was erected by public subscription (largely among English speakers) to the dead horses in Port Elizabeth. A pro-British women's committee had initiated the subscription during the war, when community sympathies were elicited by the dejected remounts that disembarked at Port Elizabeth.[143] There was some public opposition to the memorial by those who felt it may be anti-religious to raise an idol to a beast and by some who simply felt it self-indulgent while the country was still at war. Afterwards, in the difficult reconstruction period, some thought it was an unjustified expense at £800. The statue was not politically neutral. Three years after the war it was made in England by Joseph Whitehead, shipped to Port Elizabeth and swung onto the docks, much as the remounts themselves had been. The three-ton bronze gelding did not stand alone; he was accompanied by a one-ton British Tommy. They were both draped in a union jack and then unveiled by the mayor to a rousing chorus of 'God Save the King!'[144]

Port Elizabeth Horse Memorial (courtesy Claudio Velasquez)

International interest was aroused in the horse memorial in South Africa and postcards of it sold in great numbers.[145] Simultaneously, in Britain similar memorials were raised. For example, in 1903 in Surrey a memorial was raised in memory of the 'mute fidelity of the 400,000 horses killed and wounded at the call of their masters during the South African War 1899–1902 in a cause of which they knew nothing. This fountain is erected by a reverent fellow creature'. A few years later a granite memorial at Winchester was erected simply 'in memory of the horses killed in the South African War 1899–1902'. The war museum in Bloemfontein features statues of Boers and their horses, erected nearly two generations after the war.[146] Revealingly, however, there was no monument erected to *agterryers*.[147] The public consciousness of the equine fatalities was to save lives in the far greater conflict that followed a decade later in the First World War.

The war in South Africa, as Rudyard Kipling observed, taught the British 'no end of a lesson'.[148] One of the lessons was remount management on a massive scale. Questions over the remounts lost to the wastage of war engaged the attention of a military court of inquiry and two committees. Reforms were instituted after public outrage, particularly after the Royal Commission on the War in South African forced an overhaul of the Remount Department. There was widespread contemporary understanding of the significance of slaughter through military error and administrative incompetence.[149] The post-war commission of inquiry concluded that the 'great loss of horses during the campaign is no doubt chiefly due to the rawness of condition when brought into the field, but must also be attributed in part to the inexperience of great numbers among the men who used them'.[150]

Certainly, both Kitchener and Roberts agreed that poor horse mastership rather than horsemanship had been the problem. Indeed, Roberts felt it was not enough that cavalry or mounted infantry troops should know how to ride, they should also know 'how to get the utmost out of their horses ... by never-failing consideration of their wants'. Interestingly, as a reflection on the discussion above of animal agency and the agency of ordinary soldiers, Roberts believed the 'discouragement of individuality and the practice of training men ... to follow precise rules [was] to blame. A man should be taught to ride as an individual ... and the same with horse management'.[151] Following the commission of inquiry, there was pressure to reform of the Army Veterinary Service from the Royal College of Veterinary Surgeons, politicians and the public. In the immediate aftermath of the war in 1903, the Army Veterinary Corps was created, and four years later the most outraged commentator of all, who dubbed the equine wastage a 'holocaust', Major General Sir Frederick Smith, became its director general.

The bitter end

Both the strengths and vulnerabilities of horses were significant in the war, underlining the point that including horses in human history does more than simply complete the story – it changes it.[152] The history of the horses in this war has offered a useful way into understanding changing human–animal relations as emotions and actions were heightened in combat, which caused subterranean social currents to rise to the surface. Tens of thousands of the newly arrived equine combatants became part of what Lord Kitchener described as 'the great wastage of animals'. The material context of and reasons for equine casualties have offered a foundation for discussing the human cultural dimension: particularly the public commemoration and the personal experience of combatants on both sides. Like the veterans themselves, the equine warriors were agents of lasting change, and the imperial exchange meant a two-way transformation: in modifying the human socio-political landscape, the 'horse' itself underwent a morphological transformation. Almost no horses returned to their home countries with their fellow veterans after the war. This precipitated a public outcry. Indeed, 'Banjo' Paterson assumed the voice of an Australian army horse left behind in South Africa, asking:

> *Over the sea you brought us,*
> *Over the leagues of foam:*
> *Now we have served you fairly*
> *Will you not take us home?*
>
> *This is a small thing, surely!*
> *Will not you give command*
> *That the last of the old campaigners*
> *Go back to their native land?*[153]

By the end of the war there were still over 131,000 horses on the books of the War Office, with an additional 28,700 sick horses recovering in remount camps. The Repatriation Department faced the Herculean task of restoring the devastated country and dealing with remaining combat animals – a logistical cleaning of the Augean stables. About 9,500 horses suspected of infection were simply destroyed to forestall epidemics. But that still left 120,500 horses from all over the world. These remnants of empire were sold to local farmers between 1 June 1902 and 28 February 1903, and their fates are discussed in the following chapter.[154]

So the horses accustomed to the fields of England and Ireland, the steppes of central Europe and Asia, and the pampas and plains of the Americas found a new home and new herds on the *platteland* and Highveld. The war thus transformed the equine gene pool of South Africa. In closing, we end as we began, with irony. The animal that hated change was itself transformed utterly.

Chapter 6

✳

'The Cinderella of the livestock industry'

The Changing Role of Horses in the First Half of the Twentieth Century[1]

THIS CHAPTER BEGINS where so many stories have ended, with the conclusion of the South African War and the signing of the Treaty of Vereeniging in 1902. Post-bellum, the horse industry was in chaos. Horses had been both central to the war and its worst casualties, with almost half a million killed. The national herds were destroyed: in the Transvaal, 75 per cent of the horses were dead.[2] As the previous chapter explained, the war had necessitated the introduction of a massive number of horses from a range of countries and this flood of exotic stock had smuggled in foreign pathogens. The Repatriation Department faced the Herculean task of restoring the devastated country and dealing with the remaining combat animals. This chapter traces the horse's role up to and following Union in 1910 and through the first two decades of the twentieth century, which saw the horse's position undergo a transformation with the development of the modern state. The chapter then discusses how, as horses were rendered increasingly obsolete in a mechanising economy, they were nostalgically redeployed in literature in the 1930s. The chapter ends with another war, the Second World War, by which time the role of horses – constant for almost three millennia in human history and for three centuries in southern Africa – had been transformed within a single (human) generation.

Aftermath of war

The 'scorched earth' anti-guerrilla policy and three years of war had left a shattered rural economy, particularly in the Orange Free State and Transvaal. The effects of war were catastrophic.[3] Locally adapted horses had been increasingly destroyed or commandeered by the British. As the war progressed, there were anxious estimates that only 10,000 mares and foals remained alive in the Orange River Colony and perhaps half that number in the Transvaal.[4] Among the livestock that had survived, disease was rampant. As the previous chapter discussed, the war had been responsible, for importing poorly inspected stock from all over the world and then moving the animals throughout the sub-region in defiance of basic veterinary precautions. Thus, to the endemic diseases of biliary, horse sickness, gall sickness, blue tongue, rinderpest and heart water were added the fresh horrors of glanders, redwater, mange, scab and infectious pneumonia. By the end of the war there were still more than 131,000 horses on the books of the War Office, with an additional 28,700 sick horses recovering in remount camps. About 9,500 horses suspected of infection were simply destroyed to forestall epidemics, but that still left 120,500 of them. This equine flotsam of empire was sold to local farmers and the first halting steps were taken to revive the industry.

The inhabitants began picking up the pieces of the shattered rural economy.[5] Farmers were anxious to start production again. The War Office was keen to set up stud farms to breed military horses.[6] Similarly, the constabularies hoped to buttress their equine numbers. The best horse-breeding areas remained the western Orange River Colony districts (Boshof, Petrusberg, Bloemfontein); the Kimberley area; the Old Hantam (Colesberg, Middelburg, Hanover, Richmond, Steynsburg); the Cape south-western districts (Malmesbury, Worcester, Robertson, Heidelberg, Bredasdorp); and, in the Transvaal, the Standerton, Ermelo, Wakkerstroom, Heidelberg and Middelburg districts. Almost every sector within the new authority was agreed on one thing: the fundamental need for more horses. (The sole exception was the magistrate of Hoopstad, who sternly cautioned against the introduction of more horses, 'since they would tend to induce the Boer, who is too much a social man, to neglect his farm for the purpose of visiting his neighbours and towns'.)[7]

A measure of bleak optimism existed among farmers and some administrators at having survived the apocalypse. 'Native stock' seemed unlikely to recover without intervention. Among farmers, there seemed to be a general feeling that horse breeding should occur on a massive scale and that a bold, experimental approach was to be adopted. Repeated flirtations took place with the notion of breeding horses and zebras to create nagana- and horse sickness-resistant hybrids.[8] A long tradition of blinkered gendered thinking, discussed in Chapter 3, was broken with the radical suggestion that the breeding of the mare, rather than solely the stallion, also be taken into consideration.[9] There was initial flexibility about what breeds should be propagated, a concession that one could not breed 'like from like' if there were no fixed known 'types' with which to begin. Increasingly, however, as post-war reconstruction was implemented, emphasis was placed on using British breeds, like the Thoroughbred and Hackney, to improve the stock. This belied the lived experience of the war, where the 'native stock' had received glowing praise for its endurance, hardiness and temperament. There was a drift towards considering the imported, by definition, as superior to local livestock.

The large-scale importation of stock was not sensible until disease was brought under control. Moreover, Alfred Milner, British high commissioner for South Africa, did not consider it a priority to pour massive state funding into importation and felt that this could be devolved to private enterprise.[10] Milner subscribed to the idea that the empire should pay for itself and was wedded to the notion of 'constructive imperialism' by which science and modern bureaucracies should encourage economic growth.[11] On the new regime's part there was a forthright acknowledgement that '[g]overnment stud farms do not pay' and a concomitant need for reliance on the 'South African capitalist'.[12] The administration noted bluntly that the military authorities were labouring under a 'mistaken impression' if they believed that Milner's government had any intention of inaugurating horse-breeding establishments on an 'extensive scale'. In fact, all Milner intended to do was allocate grazing for a few horses that needed it and offer 'one or two of the smaller and most suitable farms now in [government] possession, for the accommodation of stallions purchased by Government … [to serve] mares belonging to local farmers'.[13]

Thus, the new administration tested the water to see which would be the most efficient – and, most importantly, cost-effective – method of restocking: the repatriation boards or private enterprise. Their focus was not on large-scale state breeding. The new authorities felt that the 'miscellaneous collection of mares which have survived the campaign will, if suitable sires are used, produce in course of time stock well adapted to the requirements of the country:

but these mares ought to be very carefully selected'.[14] Milner's focus was on modernisation and education, with a few stud farms and a skeleton staff of veterinary officers 'with experience of the world … whose opinions would carry weight'.[15]

The programme of reform was predictably loaded with political criticism of the previous regime, partly in order to emphasise the innovation of reconstruction. The director of agriculture, for example, felt that the Transvaal could become a Mecca for livestock breeding. He argued that the previous government had done little to develop animal husbandry, other than their (indifferently applied) contagious diseases acts. Although the state had provided £15,000 per annum to the agricultural societies, they had not educated farmers. He noted caustically that pre-war Boer methods of horse breeding were 'primitive in the extreme', with 'their one idea being to increase the number of their animals with as little trouble and expense to themselves as possible'. Instead, he wished to introduce an active programme of breed selection, new feeding regimes, different types of shelter and the improvement of the carrying capacity of the veld.[16] He wanted to introduce veterinary services – made so obviously necessary by the war – and damned the 'ignorant Boers' who had, he maintained, considered disease an inevitable visitation from Providence.

There was a strong sense from the regime's side that breeding should be regulated and breeds defined. They wanted pure-bred stock for the purpose of 'grading up' the national herd. Accordingly, a small stud comprising 53 pedigreed stallions and mares was purchased in the UK for £6,000 for the Agricultural Department.[17] Inspectors could admit offspring of local mares of 'Welsh or English type' and imported sires into the Stud Book.[18] Although there had been much praise for the 'clever and quick', 'wiry and enduring' Boer horses, even from the British side, the post-war authorities were incongruously dismissive not only of Boer horsemanship (given its recent renown in the war), but also of Boer equines, considering the evidence of their hardiness, discussed in the previous chapter.[19] Discussions over pedigreed versus unpedigreed stock were fissured through with other issues. Milner and the new administrators considered Boers ignorant of high-quality animals.[20] Perhaps inevitably in the aftermath of a bruising war, the ostensibly neutral taxonomic discourse drifted into a chauvinistic nationalist vein. Milner, for example, was strongly in favour of breed improvement via a 'class of stout … English thoroughbreds'.[21] Indeed, there seemed an elision of human and equine stock:

> The State wants to raise a healthy British Race in Africa. The human sires and dams of future generations cannot be imported like Cossacks, but it must be made worth their while to immigrate, not to the goldfields, but to the veldt! How better can this be effected than by wisely spending money with open hand to … encourage the Multiplication of the best stock of all kinds.[22]

Yet on the ground there was an evident desire for local stock and suspicion of imported stock, particularly in places like Vredefort, Vrede and Wepener. Post-war nativism among locals in the two former republics was strong, not only because of regional loyalties, but because of the very recent experience of the war in which indigenous horses fared incomparably better than imported stock.[23] As Milner himself conceded, 'there was [p]robably no country in the world in which it [w]as more difficult to acclimatize imported stock'. Either way, restocking was beset by problems. Importation was difficult as there was a new drive to control disease through putting a stop to the incessant movement during the war. There was confusion over which stock to import even if it were permitted; and then who would receive the stock? In the Orange River Colony the farmers were still waiting for their compensation claims and lacked the cash and security to restock.[24]

Moreover, there was red tape among the administrative sub-regions and even among different units.[25] For example, horses were imported in mid-1902 for the constabulary. Although the horses were sturdy useful stock, when disembarked at Durban they were herded with the military horses from North and South America, Russia, and Belgium and contracted foreign diseases in their weakened condition. So the military simply branded the best for themselves and it was 'a standing joke in Durban … how the Military Authorities passed the rubbish of all countries over to the Constabulary'. Then, before relocation, the horses spent weeks in yards, 'above their hocks in mud and filth, reeking with disease', in the Durban 'feverbed'.[26]

Even mere rumours of the call to restock unleashed a commercial feeding frenzy.[27] 'All the stock exporting countries of the world [were] striving to obtain a footing in [South African] markets.'[28] Opinion, both solicited and unsolicited, poured in from abroad.[29] More organised groups clamoured to be part of the project: national bodies like the National Live Stock Association of America; local clubs like the Welsh Pony and Cob Society; private companies like the

141

British and South American Steam Navigation Company; and other colonial authorities like those in Brisbane all attempted to win contracts.[30] There was even a deluge of hopeful missives to Colonial Secretary Chamberlain himself from 'old friends' and from 'Good Englishmen'.[31] Only a few farmers situated in a low-risk area for diseases and who were successful in breeding horses received brood mares with which to breed.[32] In any event, in 1903 there was no big market for horses, and so a few horses were imported and distributed in a small way,[33] but – as with many state reconstruction projects – the sheer volume of paperwork was considerably more impressive than its consequence.

State control?

Bureaucracy became the early twentieth century's equivalent of the nineteenth century's barbed wire fences.[34] A defensive barrage of paperwork was thrown up to guard against disease. As noted, among the remnants of the exotic horses imported by the British and sold off to local farmers and increasingly also among local horses, disease was rife. There had been large-scale culling of infected stock. Before the war, there had been some tentative measures towards horse disease management, but the crash course in administration provided by the war allowed for a more ambitious approach, particularly in the controlling of animal movement.[35] Indeed, Sol Plaatje suggested that the oppressive 1913 pass laws for black Africans had their antecedents in passes for animals.[36] By the 1930s and in the decades that followed, the perception of environmental degradation in the cramped designated African areas added impetus and justification to livestock-limitation policies as part of rural control.

The sub-regions became heavily policed in terms of quarantine measures administered by the commissioner of lands through a network of resident magistrates, district commandants and principal veterinary surgeons. While equine disease was progressively under state control, breeding was still in individual farmers' hands, aside from a few ill-defined legal guidelines. The desire for state intervention was frequently mooted at rural meetings.[37] From the farmers' side, at the very least the intervention of the government was expected to identify the proper class of horses to offer the best returns.[38]

At a meeting at military headquarters at Roberts Heights on the eve of Union, Lord Methuen, commander of the British army in South Africa, concluded that 'horse breeding should become a great industry in South

Africa'. He was the 'more anxious that this should be so ... since horses were ... becoming dangerously few in [England] and ... the whole Empire'.[39] Accordingly horses were considered a key enterprise for imperial defence. Furthermore, as farmers had resorted to using oxen for ploughing, agricultural officials, echoing Duckitt's nineteenth-century entreaty, wanted farmers to be more 'progressive' and use horses, thus saving oxen for their 'proper end' – beef.[40] In the run-up to and immediately after Union, the state was pressed to intervene to control private breeding initiatives. Some legal regulations were indeed put in place, stipulating, '[t]hat any farmer who has received a mare shall not dispose of her in the ordinary way of business until he has proved that she is unsuitable for breeding purposes'.[41] After 1910 there were repeated calls from the agricultural unions for a state subsidy for good horses and the wider availability of government studs.[42] This was to become a refrain, echoed for the next generation.

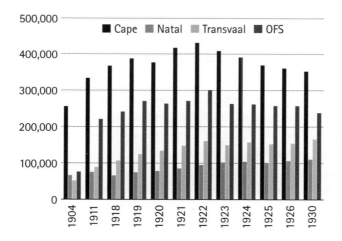

Figure 6.1: Horse numbers in South Africa, 1904–30

Source: Derived from Department of Agriculture, Handbook of Agricultural Statistics, 1904–50 (Pretoria: Department of Agriculture, 1960–61); and Official Yearbook of the Union of South Africa and of Basutoland, Bechuanland Protectorate and Swaziland, 1931–1932, vol. 14 (Pretoria: Government Printer, 1933)

The stock of horses increased by an impressive 60 per cent between 1904 and 1911, (from 449,539 to 719,414).[43] As figure 6.1 indicates, the four provinces followed similar trajectories: there was a rise immediately after the South African War to Union (less visible in the Transvaal and significantly less in Natal, where disease precluded serious breeding programmes). Then an approximate plateau was reached, with a steady decline in the Cape and Orange Free State, the critical breeding regions.

Yet horse-breeding remained a minor industry in relation to other livestock, let alone in relation to agricultural endeavour more broadly; horses always remained a scarce commodity compared to other livestock, particularly sheep and cattle, and compared to their ratio in other colonial settlements. At the beginning of the twentieth century, even prior to the automobile revolution, the Cape, for example, carried a small number of horses: just 0.92 per square mile.[44]

Arguably, there was never any point in heavily investing in breeding (except for small, highly pedigreed studs catering for local elite or racing markets at specific points in time, as explored in Chapters 3 and 7). Large-scale farming or breeding for the export market was unlikely to make a profit for commercial breeders. Firstly, as observed by the equine authority and showman Horace Hayes, who toured South Africa at the turn of the century, although there was no significant feral population, throughout South Africa there were

> horses raised in a semi-wild state on the various farms. Very few of these animals would be from an English, Australian, or Indian point of view, worth breaking; for the privations they have to undergo from want of grass, make them weak and listless.[45]

Such horses, he continued, 'even if they could be obtained for nothing, would not be worth exporting to India or to any other country'. Moreover, the relatively long period it took to raise and train a horse from foal to rideable adult (or even to break in a recalcitrant semi-feral mature beast from the veld) gnawed away at what small profits could be garnered.

The returns on ordinary utility horses certainly remained meagre. Breeders argued that 'one of the biggest sinners' in stifling the industry was the Union government itself, as it offered fixed, low prices for remounts and police horses (a horse worth £30 would sell for £18).[46] Increased land prices further eroded profits.[47]

Secondly, exportation of horses would not work until a prophylactic for horse sickness was discovered. Farmers were reluctant to invest in a stud, never knowing when African horse sickness would strike; once it did, they were largely unable to effect a cure. In some regions, the seasonal incidence of the sickness was particularly unpredictable. A Natal visitor noted that horses' 'value at this period is purely nominal; for a man may go to bed at night with a dozen healthy horses in his stables, and awaken in the morning to find that he has not one'.[48] By 1914 mortality simply from the rudimentary vaccine offered by the state was 10–12 per cent (in the Transvaal, of 870 horses immunised in the first four years, 109 died).[49] Even without horse sickness, there was a very high percentage breeding loss – up to 50 per cent aborted in the first few months of gestation, unlike other livestock. The opportunity costs were thus high and sheep farming, for example, was a much safer investment.[50] In 1914 wool was the chief pastoral product: followed by mealies, then ostrich feathers, so while even the 'ostrich breeders have a right royal time like the birds themselves', as Du Toit noted, horse breeders, deserving 'coddling', felt the cold.[51]

Thus, the industry remained speculative, only profitable on a large scale during short-lived booms generated by an external crises (as in the mid-nineteenth century Cape for the imperial export trade; and during the South African War, when Basutoland's export of horses accounted for 73 per cent of export market value; respectively discussed in Chapters 3 and 4).[52] The state was thus reluctant to invest heavily or offer protection: a few experimental programmes were put in place and a few years into Union, farmers could choose to access one of 90 stallions at state stud farms.[53] Yet the desire for state cost-cutting measures ensured that breeding remained largely in the hands (or, more importantly, out of the pockets) of the breeders.[54]

Experts and breeders both argued that horses were necessary for national defence and the police services and a few even hoped for a renaissance of the once-significant export trade. Horses remained in demand for the flourishing racing industry, but this was small-scale elite breeding that severed most ties with the state and followed a self-directed trajectory.[55] Certainly, it was accepted that horse breeding was still an important project in a modern state. Yet at the same time there was already an undercurrent challenge to this official policy, posed neither by a desire to privatise breeding nor by economic measures, but rather by the forces of modernisation itself.

Transport and agricultural mechanisation

With a certain irony, the first car had been transported by horse and cart from Pretoria to Johannesburg in January 1897. This development was suspended by the war, but by Union competition with equines was recorded from increasing motor traffic, first from harbour trains and trams and then motor cars.[56] These worlds would at times quite literally collide, as in the road accidents recorded between motor cars and horse-drawn Scotch carts.[57] Effective mechanical competition to the horse was evident in the first decades of the twentieth century. The first railway was constructed in 1863 from Cape Town to Wellington. But by 1875 there were only 115 miles of line in Cape Colony. This accelerated with the diamond discoveries, so by 1885 the mileage was 1,498 (and 116 in Natal). Following the opening of the gold mines, connection was made to Johannesburg in 1892, and a connection between Johannesburg and Natal in 1895. Bicycles were also a popular, adaptable and inexpensive means of transport.[58] In 1901 there were only a dozen cars at the Cape; by 1912 there were 250 cars and 40 motor cabs, and commentators noted (rather prematurely) that 'horsed vehicles for hire' would 'soon be a thing of the past'. At the same time, Johannesburg had about 1,000 cars and about half the vehicles in the Union were being driven on the Rand.[59] In Natal, with its mere 70 private motor cars, the speed limit in 1905 was 8 miles/hour (m/h), increasing to a heady 10 m/h in 1910, and a frankly reckless 15 m/h in some outer reaches.[60] In 1912 the motor car was described as 'increasingly used in this country by business and professional men' and the medical fraternity in particular, but it was still a luxury.[61] In 1920 there were 22,957 cars and 40,008 vehicles in total; a decade later there were 135,177 cars and 186,073 vehicles in total. The vast majority were for private use and were chiefly imported from North America. By mid-century there were 474,417 cars and 634,978 vehicles in total. Thereafter, vehicle numbers started doubling every decade.[62] In the urban centres like Johannesburg, electric trams, cars and bicycles were increasingly common sights and cab driving became a profession of 'last resort'.[63] Animal traction, however, remained predominant into the twentieth century and stayed central in some sectors. Gradually, however, alongside the usual discussions of horse disease and equine management in the farmers' *Landbou Weekblad*, articles on 'Die outomobiel' began to appear.[64]

As the century progressed, mechanical power became ever more central in transport, mining and large-scale agriculture. Already by the late nineteenth century the 'tramp floor', where grain was trodden by horses, had started yielding to machine power. By the turn of the century the latest time-saving mechanical reaping machines were in use among wealthier farmers in wheat-farming Cape districts like Malmesbury.[65] A dual agricultural economy developed. Horse power became increasingly obsolete in commercial agriculture, although it remained significant in small-scale agriculture (albeit entirely secondary to the ox and, in some places, the donkey).[66] Even though in South African urban areas work horses were no longer widespread, they were – and still are – used for neighbourhood deliveries and collections (like coal and scrap), e.g. in Soweto, Thaba Nchu and the Cape Flats. Urban workhorses, often in sun bonnets, remained a common sight until the latter part of the twentieth century (the headgear was not just a whimsical anthropomorphic sartorial affectation, but a useful device to keep off flies).

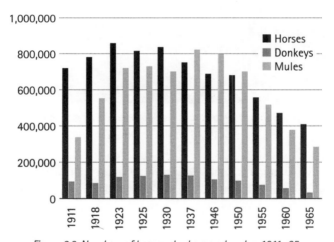

Figure 6.2: Numbers of horses, donkeys and mules, 1911–65

By 1994, when the first democratic elections were held, it was estimated that in the more liminal rural areas of South Africa, 40–80 per cent of families engaged in smallholder farming used animal power for transport or crop growing, usually oxen, but often horses. Urban and peri-urban animal traction declined, but animal power stayed significant in rural smallholder farming systems.[67] Oxen continued to be most significant in some areas, e.g. along the east coast, the Eastern Cape and Mpumalanga. Donkeys were more popular with smallholder farmers in the northern districts. Horses remained prevalent in highland areas (like Lesotho) where horse sickness was less virulent) and in the Western Cape. Small numbers of mules were used, but did not become very significant, except on some sugar cane plantations along the east coast.[68] Though equine draft power moved increasingly to the periphery, the decline of the horse was neither immediate nor linear and followed different trajectories in different areas.[69]

White boys arriving at school on horseback in Namaqualand
Source: KAB, AG Collection, AG14374, 1922

So, while animal traction remained central to small-scale farming, the middle decades of the twentieth century saw the large-scale farming sector move from almost total reliance on animal power to reliance on tractors. Just after Union, whites owned 563,000 out of 719,000 horses. This increased briefly to a high point of 767,000 in 1922 and then declined steadily to 480,000 in 1926; 404,000 in 1937; 347,000 in 1947; and just 303,000 by 1950. Black ownership (which, given the racialised nature of South Africa's agricultural sector, was usually for small-scale production and transport needs) remained more or less constant (205,000 horses in 1926; 170,000 a decade later; 190,000 ten years thereafter and 223,000 by mid-century.[70]

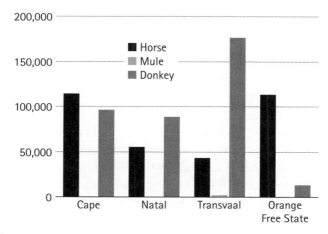

Figure 6.3: Black ownership of horses, mules and donkeys by province, 1946

The mechanisation of farms and horse ownership were understandably inversely correlated, as figure 6.4 shows.

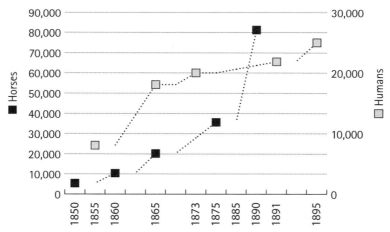

Figure 6.4: The mechanisation of farms in relation to horse ownership, 1918–60
Source: Central Statistics Office, Pretoria, Official Year Book, various, 1917–60

Commercial horse breeders (and the industries that coalesced around horses: farriers, cart makers and furnishers, harness makers, horse traders, grooms and stable hands) worried increasingly, agonising that 'the farmers have become mechanically minded with a vengeance'.[71] By mid-century there were 33,925 tractors on commercial farms. The process was not uncontested and farm mechanisation provoked furious debate, with 'machine versus horse' endlessly disputed in the popular press. By the end of the twentieth century there were approximately 60,000 large-scale (mainly white) farmers that used tractors and 1.2 million smallholder farmers who combined human, animal and tractor power.[72]

This debate was played out in microcosm in Graaff-Reinet in the third decade of the twentieth century. Horses were still used for essential services, like refuse and 'slop water' removal, and for health services. Determined to modernise the town, the town clerk found it 'difficult to get local authorities to depart from ancient methods which are quite out of the question in modern times'.[73] In 1927 two Chevrolet motor lorries were purchased. His calculations showed that 'a motor vehicle can do in two hours what any horsedrawn vehicle would take a whole day to do'.[74] Comparative costs were as follows:

Cost of two Chevrolet lorries at £225 each: £450
Wages of two drivers @6/- per diem: £198
Wages of two labourers @2/6 per diem: £78
Repairs (nil because of one-year guarantee)
Petrol – 8 gals per diem @2/3 per gallon: £282
Total cost: £1,008

Cost of six Scotch carts @£25: £150
Cost of six sets of harnesses @£10 each: £60
Wages of six drivers @2/6 per diem: £234
Wages of labourers to assist with loading: £150
Repairs: £10
Feeding, stabling of six horses @2/- per diem: £219
Total cost: £823

But that was only the first year; in the second year the lorries apparently became more economical (see below). This might well have been too optimistic an estimation, as more repairs might have proved necessary, but it does indicate the growing preference of small-town civil servants.

Depreciation and repairs on two motor lorries: £100
Wages of two drivers: £198
Wages of labourers: £78
Petrol, oil, etc.: £240
Total cost: £616

Whereas, for the equine traction:

Repairs to carts, shoeing: £60
Wages of six drivers @2/6 per diem: £234
Wages of labourers to assist with loading: £200
Feeding, stabling of six horses @2/- per diem: £219
Total cost: £713

Similarly, in other small towns, the savings in investing in a truck seemed clear to those motivating to make the shift to motorisation.[75] Yet the road to mechanisation was bumpy and had its own stumbling blocks, and each area had its own story.

Mid-twentieth-century horse transport in Cape Town
Source: KAB, AG Collection, AG13614

Of course, those interested in purveying (rather than purchasing) horses met mechanisation with delaying tactics, and the outbreak of the Second World War deferred it further. Restricted use of mechanical power during the war facilitated a revived use of horses by fruit and flower growers on smallholdings, in cartage contracting and in some municipalities.[76] Indeed, draught equines became briefly so valuable that a temporary export embargo was placed on them.[77] Yet the replacement of horse by engine continued, with the banning of leisure horses from various urban centres.[78] The social incursion of motor vehicles was evinced on a small individual scale by adverts like: 'I am selling the horse because I have a motor bicycle and I have not much work for him to do.'[79] On the state level, in 1928 the minister of agriculture, General Jan Kemp, simply dismissed horse breeding as 'obviously a waning industry'.[80]

A further illustrative case study is offered by the South African Police Force. When the force was established in 1913, it was based chiefly on horse power; in fact, at the end of the nineteenth century policing was described as the perfect job for a man who 'likes horse, dog and gun'.[81] In 1915 the force had only 12 motor vehicles and 56 motorcycles. By 1920 it was increasingly mechanised – but still required 3,679 horses. A decade later its number of recruits had expanded, but it required still fewer horses (3,202) than ten years before, because mechanisation had increased significantly.[82] This was intended to allow police patrols cover more ground per day: in 1927 the average mounted policeman covered 13.4 miles per day (which was only 0.8 of a mile more than the foot patrols), but by 1945 the average police car was able to cover 33 miles per day.[83] This trend extended inexorably so that by 1946 the force had only 2,320 horses, with 250 new ones required to replace casualties annually.[84] By the 1950s mechanisation was virtually absolute, with a concomitant redundancy of horses, so the 1,290 horses at the start of the decade dropped to 660 and finally to just 200. The breeding farms were sold. Horses were, however, retained for ceremonial parades like the opening of parliament.[85] This hints at a widespread trend, explored in greater depth below – as post-mechanisation horses played a shrinking role in the economy, they played a far greater one in the social imagination.

Horse as symbol

Horses had long been enveloped in a particular way of understanding oneself in terms of masculine identity; e.g. as a Boer or – as the terminology changed – Afrikaner man, as discussed in the previous chapter. So when the freshly minted Union abolished the horse-based commando system in terms of the

1912 Defence Act, it was an especially public and emotional trumpeting of the end of the previous regime and the beginning of the modern bureaucratic state. The response was so emotional that it helped trigger a social rebellion that was predicated on profound socio-political disillusionment and economic alienation. At least in part, the 1914 rebellion was based on nostalgia for a past only recently faded and already romantically reimagined.[86] Afrikaans-speaking men sidelined by the industrialising economy began to convey their alienation to their erstwhile leaders, themselves estranged from the new locus of central state power. In the south-western Transvaal and the northern Free State particularly, poorer farmers and bywoners (share croppers) turned to their old commando leaders. Images of commando may have tallied little with the lived experience of combat, but the rebel leaders helped fuel the republican nostalgia that revolved on a seductive reimagining of mounted manhood. An observer noted that the majority of rebels were men to whom being on commando 'meant a happy time of riding around on horseback from town to town, living on the country as they proceed'.[87] Just as in other parts of the world, as new forms of transport triumphed, the horse was already a sign to some of regret and nostalgia.[88] After all, as the rebel leader General de Wet once famously maintained, a 'Boer without a horse is only half a man'.

Near the end of the 1914 rebellion, with the rebels in confusion and the leadership on the run, De Wet launched an attempt to escape on horseback to the remaining free rebel leader across the Kalahari, in German territory. However, violent rains turned the sand into mud, into which the horses' hooves sank.[89] Close on his trail was a petrol-driven government fleet. These cars converged on the trapped commando and defeat was utter and final. De Wet's resigned lament perhaps epitomised the modernising state's undermining of an identity predicated on mounted manhood. He said with a sigh: 'It was the motor-cars that beat me.'[90]

The unrelenting motorcar

This notion of the relentless mechanised offensive against the old equine-based way of life manifested in various contexts. Testimony before the Senate Select Committee in 1928 turned into a eulogy: 'The motor-car of course has been the greatest means of murdering the horse breeding industry throughout South Africa.'[91] Later, C.R. Swart[92] offered this tribute:

153

If, in the past years, there was war or rioting, we called the able men to arms with the well known command: 'with horse, saddle and bridle, rifle and provisions for eight days.' Yes, and Boereseuns of today still think back with pride and loving memory to our own loved and indispensable riding horses on the farm – old Spotty, Prince … and all the rest. But the machine is unrelenting.[93]

This impulse to deploy the horse metonymically as one of the ways of remembering the past was to gain much impetus, particularly among the post-war writers like Mikro, or in the *rit-rympies* (riding verses) of Toon van den Heever. By the 1930s there were two main points of cultural and historical reference for a growing Afrikaner nationalism, the so-called Great Trek and the South African War. Horses (as pivotal in both) were drawn into this broader myth-making process. One of the richest seams of such material is the magazine *De* (later *Die*) *Huisgenoot* (Home Companion), which reached 20 per cent of Afrikaner families by the early 1930s.[94] In that capacity it echoed and also shaped the views of its readers. It ran many stories about the role of horses in the war,[95] after which readers would write in to say that their horses or their father's horses deserved special mention.[96] As one reader of the *Die Huisgenoot* noted:

No other horse in the world could do what the Voortrekker horse did – the authentic Boer horse. Today we can smile about the old muzzle-loader, but we know that just as far as the modern [M]auser is before the old muzzle-loader, thus far is the riding horse in South Africa today behind the riding horse that entered the wilderness with the Voortrekkers. The Voortrekker era was the golden era in the history of the horse in South Africa.[97]

Horses were especially significant in the construction of identity as the 1930s progressed. As poet and medical doctor A.G. Visser observed: '*Ryperd en ruiter en roer is 'n drieling/Tuis al van ouds in die land van die Boer.*'[98] Equestrian skill was used as a measure of authentic character: as in the observation on a *volksheld* (a national hero): '*Hy het altyd Boer gebly … tuis op 'n perd.*'[99] The role of their horses was accorded a special role in the memory landscape. In novels based on war experiences, one of the characters was frequently a horse. This theme permeated the literature, and prize-winning author Hans Jurie Vermaas published a series of equine-themed novels, like his *Sy Perd Staan Gereed* (1954) about a horse tamer and his 'fiery Arab stallion'.[100] In his *Die Perdedief* (1960) the eponymous hero is a horse thief who simply cannot resist the temptation of a good horse. Nevertheless, he joins up to fight the British and is killed. His black horse, Satan, refuses to abandon his fallen owner. The author wonders about the hero's last thoughts … were they perhaps about his woman or about his horse?[101]

Some of the most popular war novels for both children and adults were written from the 1930s by C.H. Kühn, a prize-winning author who worked under the pseudonym 'Mikro'.[102] His novels, which include *Die Jongste Ruiter* (1954), *Die Kleingeld-Kommando* (1956), *Die Jongste Veldkornet* (1963) and *Die Ruiter in die Nag* (1936), followed a pattern of the courageous (Boer male) war hero on a stallion that inspired respect in both the English and Boers camps.[103] His most famous heroes, first debuted in 1936 (the same year as the Great Trek centenary) were the mysterious 'rider in the night' and his horse Vonk (Spark).[104] In the sequel, published the following year,[105] Vonk perished in a dramatic getaway from the English forces:

> Now Sarel is totally alone and he feels it doubly so because not even his old friend Vonk is with him. That day at the ruin, Vonk was killed … Maybe it is better so, the English took all their horses and sent them home by train. He would not have been able to cope with losing Vonk that way. Then it is better that Vonk died, he does not want to see him in someone else's hands.[106]

Later, when speaking to his fiancée about the war, he found that the only thing he was unable to talk about was Vonk's death.

Another of Mikro's human heroes, known as 'Boerseun' had a special relationship with his horse. The young man's nickname is significant in its evocation of an autochthonous male identity. His relationship with the horse was described in detail, forming part of the character description a real Boer hero:

> There is no other horse as loyal as Aandblom; mild-mannered, but with endless stamina. It is wonderful, the love between him and Nico. Day or night, Nico will not eat a morsel before taking care of Aandblom. He frequently chats with him. When he dismounts and orders Aandblom

Book covers of Mikro, Die Ruiter in die Nag *and Hans Jurie Vermaas,* Die Perdedief

not to move, he will stay absolutely still, even if the bullets whistle past him.[107]

'Boerseun' has frequent conversations with his horse: "'Aandblom, shall we tear into the Tommies [British soldiers]? Do you agree?" … Aandblom, almost as if he understands his companion, plays his head up and down.'[108] As discussed in the previous chapter, the participation of horses in the war as agents in their own right was sometimes conflated with perceptions about the way in which the Boers fought. This was especially so with regard to the skills necessary for the speed and thrust of guerrilla tactics, with the presence of horses being emphasised in reminiscences of the war.[109] Indeed, the horses were seen as so integral to the Boer war effort that fear was even expressed that when the authentic 'Boerperd' died out, so too would the Boer:

> We do not want to detract from the courage and mettle of the Boers in the Second War of Independence, but they will be the first to acknowledge that their famous exploits would have been impossible

were it not for their exceptional horses. In that conflict many an Afrikanerboer went to his grave. It was also the grave of the Boerperd. Today, we can count the number of authentic old Boer mares on our plains on the fingers of our hands. Does she, like the Voortrekker, now belong only to the past?[110]

Horses were part of a discourse of masculinity, and not simply in the sense that a good horse was the prerequisite of a strong male hero. Coming-of-age stories frequently involved a boy and a horse. In Mikro's *Die Jongste Ruiter*, a 13-year-old boy dreams of becoming a scout under General de Wet, who rides a white horse to show his lack of fear for the British.[111] His dream comes true; he wins his spurs and his place on commando as part of becoming a man, with a horse that turns out to be, of course, equally 'manly'. It became a common literary device to signal a stock weak character by depicting him as unable to control (or win the loyalty of) a horse (or a woman, for that matter). Some characteristics common to a horse, especially stubbornness and a display of self-will, were described as particularly 'female', often in a way that was seen as tongue-in-cheek or humorous:

> Uncle Moustache bought a chestnut horse with a blaze that he kept stabled. You can plainly see that she can run, and she could, but it is always very difficult to foresee what a chestnut horse or a woman will do.[112]

Similarly, in the context of the growing urbanisation of young women and the concomitant debate in the letter columns on '*boerenooiens* vs town girls', it was advised: 'I would just like to whisper one thing in the ears of men and it is that a smart woman and a difficult horse must be handled with care otherwise they can escape control and become spoiled.'[113] Perhaps it became all the more necessary, if horses were to remain integral to an iconic masculinity, to reinforce ideas of a kinship between horses and women and their shared deference towards men, because as the twentieth century progressed, ownership of (leisure and sport) horses by women increased.

The key usage of horses moved from the spheres of mainstream agriculture and transport in two chief directions: to small-scale transport and agriculture and to sport and pleasure. Horses acquired different owners in the process. The latter trajectory saw the rise of other new horse communities – like the dressage,

Gonda (Butters) Betrix on Gunga Din, Rand Show, 1958[114]
Source: Gonda (Butters) Betrix with J. Attwood-Wheeler,
Gonda Betrix: Jumping to Success *(Cape Town: Southern Book Publishers, 1991), p. 8*

THE CAPE ARGUS, WEDNESDAY, JUNE 18, 1958

'Let's face it, chaps; this girl on Gunga Din is a better man than we are!'

Source: Cape Argus, 18 June 1958

equitation, endurance, show-jumping and eventing enthusiasts. The most iconic was Gonda (Butters) Betrix. This was largely by middle-class white, not African, women. Exceptions existed, as in the case of the powerful social figure of the (female) traditional healer, depicted below.

Traditional healers and horsewomen in Pondoland
Sources: University of KwaZulu-Natal, Campbell Collections, C52-270,
Album C52/001-396, 'Native life in western Pondoland'; University of
KwaZulu-Natal, Campbell Collections, C52-279

As in other parts of Africa, work animals do not only physical, but also socio-cultural labour. Most have been and continue to be controlled by men – with the exception of donkeys.[115] Donkeys were used by African women: they were cheaper to buy, more economical to maintain and less culturally loaded.[116] In the leisure sector, the gendered disproportion lay in the opposite direction, with disciplines like dressage and show jumping dominated by women competitors. Women and horses were both emancipated in the same century: the former by entering the work force *en masse* and the latter by leaving it.

It was not just women as a group over whom hegemony in the equine

159

realm was sought, but also other races. This was sometimes portrayed in Afrikaans coming-of-age narratives where the 'Kleinbasie' became the 'Baas'. Die Huisgenoot published a story in which a Boer boy gets a new saddle for his birthday and he is then required to break in a horse without the help of the 'strong black men' and in full view of his family.[117] Just like white women, African men increased their ownership of horses, which sat uneasily with the growing symbolic link between horses and 'Boer' identity. A racist sub-text was clear in discussions of horse care and ownership,[118] as in this example from an agricultural journal, Boerdery in Suid-Afrika:

> Another serious problem with regard to horse breeding is the lack of people, including farm workers, who have knowledge and experience with horses. The average native who frequently, in a criminal way, forces the last grain of strength from a patient ox, often has less intelligence than the horse at his mercy. Our youth must look back a bit at the history of their stalwart forefathers, and cultivate the same love for, and experience with one of the noblest animals in our service.[119]

Just as decades later black drivers behind the wheels of expensive cars would be pulled over as profiled criminals, in the first decades of the twentieth century there were stories of 'natives being shot for riding nice horses'. A witness remembered:

> [T]here was a[n] [African] man who had a very nice horse – a black stallion – and he wanted £40 for it … One day … a Dutchman stopped him and asked him what he wanted for the horse. He said £40. The Dutchman said, you dont [sic] mean that you want my farm for a horse. The man said if you dont [sic] want it leave it. The Dutchman shot him almost dead at the spot, and the horse ran away … The Dutchman was arrested, and his native servant gave evidence and said, he shot him because he stole a sheep … All that shows is that we will be shot down as dogs.[120]

Ownership of a horse became a way to try to patrol the social border between Africans and Afrikaans 'poor whites', the socio-economic proximity of whom increasingly worried Afrikaner culture brokers. An example is provided in

160

Pondoland rural transport
Source: *University of Kwa-Zulu Natal, Campbell Collections, C52-272*

Afrikaans author Jochem van Bruggen's prize-winning *Sprinkaanbeampte van Sluis* (1933), which revolves around the central character Lambertus Bredenhamp's rise from white poverty and his search for status in his community.[121] Bredenhamp is appointed as a locust officer, which saves him from destitution and concomitant social disgrace. When he is told by the Jewish storekeeper that he should buy a horse for his work, he responded tellingly:

A Horse! ... The Jew is right ... To get to all the farms he will need a horse ... a horse, a saddle and bridle! A suffocating feeling of self worth wells up in his heart, and his mind's eye sparkles at the thought of a locust officer riding a horse along the roads in the vicinity of Sluis.[122]

Nor was the link between wealth, status and horse ownership described as unique to the main character; it was recognised by the whole community. When Bredenhamp arrived home, his daughter greeted him joyously, shouting: 'Father has a horse! ... We are becoming rich!'[123] Interestingly, the horse's original name,

Rusland (Russia) was taken to be a '*kaffernaam*' (a derogative, 'kaffir name') and therefore less worthy. To take ownership, Bredenhamp preferred to baptise the horse Poon (Pony), an Afrikaans name.[124] Thus, as the horse became less materially significant and more iconic, it became a powerful symbol, integral to a particular sense of gendered ethnic identity mobilised by culture brokers.

'To save our horses from the motor'

Yet at the same time, from the 1930s there was a small body of men comprising a few state officials and a group of commercial (largely Afrikaans, male, wealthy) farmers who were determined to wrest the horse firmly out of the novel and back into the real world. Horse breeding, they argued, had to be retained as a serious economic endeavour. They utilised the forums of the *Farmer's Weekly* and *Landbou Weekblad*, much as the writers had used *Die Huisgenoot*. Indeed, sitting uneasily with the novelists' symbolic insistence on an organic horsemanship inherent to Afrikaner men, this group's enduring refrain was how difficult it was 'to educate these people'.[125] These men were certainly not averse to exploiting the growing symbolic status of horses, but their prime efforts were directed towards the practical. They maintained a dogged counter-narrative that horses were still – and, indeed, would always be – essential to the state.[126] They used the vocabulary of nativism and long termism:

> if our forefathers entertained the same pessimistic ideas of starting a new breed [as the nay-sayers] would we today have all the established and beautiful breeds of cattle, sheep and horses? ... I am quite certain that none of the originators of the Friesland, Afrikander, Merino or Percheron breeds ... knew them as we know them today ... They were ambitious enough to leave their children a heritage in the animal world, and so can we. We can only endeavour to lay some sort of a foundation, so that they can do the actual breeding.[127]

However, far from subscribing to the popular quasi-mythological notion of a Boer's innate horsemanship propagated in novels, the group took more seriously modern British literature (like Captain Horace Hayes's *Points of the Horse* of 1897 and Harry Sharpe's *The Practical Stud Groom* of 1913) and subsequently wrote their own texts to educate local farmers.[128] P.J. Schreuder and F.B. Wright (officers in the division of Agricultural Education and Research) then published the Union's first textbook on the 'modern principles of horse breeding'.[129]

Schreuder played a particularly pivotal part in developing the horse industry.[130] Born in 1885 in Boshof, a renowned horse-breeding district, he had served on commando and became a prisoner of war. After Vereeniging, he studied at Victoria College (later Stellenbosch University), winning a scholarship to Leipzig University and finally producing his 1915 Cornell University doctorate on 'The Cape horse: Its origin, breeding and development in the Union of South Africa'. He then studied economics and political science at Kings College London before returning to South Africa as technical assistant in the Education Section of the Department of Agriculture in Pretoria. Then for a decade he lectured and managed departments of animal husbandry at Potchefstroom and Glen Colleges of Agriculture.

The government still maintained a few studs and provided equine extension training at agricultural colleges. Schreuder was the driving force behind a series of articles in the mid-1930s published in tandem with the novels and short stories centring on horses in the popular Afrikaans press. These resonated with broader social concerns, being couched in terms usually used to discuss the poor white problem, focusing on the dangers of 'agteruitgang' and the 'herstelling van die Ras' (regression and the rehabilitation of the race).[131] Schreuder called for the prevention of uncontrolled breeding; instead, the union of good mares of the 'old type' to the right stallions was recommended. Just as for the solution to the poor white problem, he declared, '[d]ie heropbouing van ons perdestapel is 'n nasionale plig' (the restoration of the horse stock is a duty of national concern).[132] He mobilised practical economic issues too, contending that in the severe depression of the early 1930s and the devastating drought that accompanied it, the horse was the only livestock that retained its original value. He urged: 'Ons wil elke vooruitstrewende boer in die saal sien' (we want to see every progressive farmer in the saddle);[133] and even more hopefully: 'Elke Boer in die saal' (every farmer in the saddle).[134]

By 1928 the Senate Select Committee on Horse Breeding noted with concern that the 'utility horse for military purposes' was verging on extinction and the stock of utility brood mares had disappeared. The oft-repeated exhortation for state-sponsored studs was reiterated, as it was each time the industry was discussed (regardless of the fact that they already existed and were poorly patronised).[135] There were some mercantilist calls for state protectionism and state control, as was the case in the sheep, cattle and ostrich industries.[136] The only serious intervention was to impose an import tax of £100 on imported race horses (except those for breeding purposes to raise bloodlines), which had the immediate effect of encouraging the importation of top-quality horses for breeding.[137] Such a protectionist tariff was designed to both protect and encourage local breeding of Thoroughbreds, mainly for the racing industry.[138] This reflected the late 1920s and early 1930s fear of speculators, dubbed 'harpies and ghouls without conscience', importing the dregs of Tattersalls, just as they had done in the mid-nineteenth century.[139] This 'avalanche of low-class thoroughbreds' would then swamp the unfortunate 'colonial thoroughbred breeders'.[140] The Jockey Club protested, arguing that 'new blood' was necessary to prevent 'deterioration' because it had 'been proved over and over again that sires bred here from imported stock are unable to transmit their inherited high sire qualities to the next … generations'.[141] Senator George Munnik's bill dealt with race horses rather than the general utility horse, except for a minor clause, which allowed the state to offer some financial assistance to private breeders and agricultural societies to maintain studs.[142] In contrast, in neighbouring Basutoland, the state had a much greater proportional interest in horse breeding.[143] Frank Arthur Verney, chief veterinary officer for Basutoland, observed that while South Africa should privatise its breeding entirely into the hands of white commercial breeders, his own country required exclusively state-funded studs, because, after all: 'We are dealing entirely with natives.'[144]

Ironically, it was actually successful horse (and particularly donkey) breeding by black farmers that triggered anxiety in South Africa in the mid-1930s. Some 20 years before, the 1913 Natives' Land Act had shattered African agricultural initiatives, producing a landless proletariat, forcing Africans into the mines and thwarting successful black competition in farming. As Sol Plaatje noted, this Act had a direct impact not only on the humans it alienated, but on their animals, as it debarred Africans from pasturage. Seeing the landless 'roving pariahs', Plaatje had wondered 'if the animals were not more deserving of pity than their owners'. He observed wryly that animals 'have no choice in the selection of a colour for their owners'.[145] By the 1930s, however, among some commercial lobby groups it was felt that while horse numbers were increasing, protective legislation was needed to geld 'worthless' horses, which – since the horses had been 'left largely in the hands of natives – had multiplied alarmingly'.[146] The move from oxen to donkeys was farmer led generally and actively opposed by state officials.

Horses were also controlled, particularly in African areas, due to perceived overstocking. Instead of dealing with scarce pasture and erosion by granting more land to Africans, authorities curtailed stock numbers. The importation of horses into Transkei, for example, was heavily controlled and subject to local magistrates' approval. Migrant labourers who invested in equine assets to send home found their horses impounded at the railway stations. The state had legislated to develop the cattle industry with the Livestock and Meat Industries Act (Act 48 of 1934), which triggered proposals from farmers' organisations for similar initiatives for the horse industry. Farmers urged the equine enforcement of the example set by cattle improvement schemes – eliminate the 'scrub entires' (uncastrated stallions) who 'roam at large'.[147]

There was subsequently a 1938 initiative by A.M. Bosman, chief of the division of Agricultural Education and Extension, to stop 'retrogression' and set up 'permanent rehabilitation'. Even Bosman acknowledged that the race horse industry, which received no state assistance, was thriving, but utility horses 'received little or no attention'.[148] Nevertheless, some farmers continued to militate for strong state intervention to centralise breeding and patrol breed purity, even suggesting that owners of registered mares who bred from non-registered males should face a punitive fine.[149] The inspectors were given 'the power to guard against indiscriminate and incorrect breeding', with breed standards promulgated and with an 'examiner-committee' to police the 'legal status' of some breeds.[150] Some breeders even tried to work out a mathematical 'equation for purity'.[151] There were occasionally proposals for more vigorous eugenic interventions, like the suggestion to simply 'shoot the worst' to improve the quality of horses,[152] and sending the unused and unusable to 'bone and meat meal factories'.[153] But no legal measures were enacted, let alone enforced, in policing horse breeding, because it remained such a minor industry.[154]

Reiterating the recurring chorus, breeders contended that horse breeding had been neglected by the government for the preceding 20 years.[155] Certainly, the state was intent on privatising the risk. Instead of using government stallions, it would simply compensate farmers for keeping good stud stallions. The state offered them a £25 annual premium, with the proviso that the stallion had to serve 12 mares per season. Moreover, approved mares would earn their owners a further £1 subvention if they managed to fall pregnant. The mare would also receive a free state-funded railway trip to reach her intended. The state provided just £2,000 and two inspectors to oversee this initiative.[156] This reflected the state's sentiment that the stallions at the government institutions were a waste of money and no longer warranted. This was because, as even Schreuder conceded, no farmer could survive by breeding horses alone and few made use of the breeding stations.[157] Indeed, the state wanted to reduce their number to just three stallions.[158] So forlorn government studs stood alone at agricultural colleges, waiting for mares that never came.[159]

These stallions at stud were not a large-scale initiative; in the first decade after the horse improvement scheme introduced in 1938 only 1,600 mares were served.[160] Perhaps more significantly, equine extension courses were introduced into the growing network of agricultural colleges.[161] Colleges such as Glen, Grootfontein, Potchefstroom and Elsenburg embraced the scientific courses with an enthusiasm that occasionally bordered on the extreme. In one example, some Free State college students celebrated the new courses with 'happy rowdiness'. The students' chairman assured the principal that it was not the two bottles of wine that intoxicated the students, but rather the 'pure enthusiasm' of horsemen 'gathered for the first time in history to study their subject'. They were nevertheless chastised – particularly the one drunkenly playing the concertina.[162]

This 'pure enthusiasm' was driven by the Horse and Mule Breeders Association, with concerted efforts towards improved scientific knowledge of horses and horse breeding.[163] There were four private breeding societies: the Horse and Mule Breeders Association (founded 1938, parent of the others); the Percheron Horse Breeders Society (founded in 1939); the Saddle Horse Breeders Society (founded 1941) and the Clydesdale Breeders Society (founded in 1945). Furthermore, in fruit- and grain-growing areas like Ceres, Tulbagh, Worcester and Robertson, more studs were established.[164] In the Western Province, for example, a network was forged among the Stellenbosch-Elsenburg College of Agriculture, the stud breeders, farmers and societies exhibiting at the agricultural show.[165] Diseases, breeding, stable management, feeding, types and judging were taught.[166] Through organisations like the Agricultural Union, white commercial farmers put pressure on the state to finance veterinary research.[167] Karen Brown has argued that the considerable stretches between farms, as well as the under-capitalisation of many farmers, weighed against the rise of a significant private veterinary service until the 1940s. In a bid to increase pastoral yields, the state (and the racing industry) bore the cost of discovering equine remedies. There were other state-driven developments in understanding and controlling disease, like the invention of an effective inoculation against horse sickness in 1934, which opened up new areas of the country to horse breeding, namely in the Transvaal Lowveld and the littoral regions of Natal and the Eastern Cape – ironically, precisely at the time when horse breeding had ceased to be a matter of national importance.[168]

Finale

The utility horse on commercial farms and in public transport became an issue of national importance one last time, during the Second World War, when there was a short-lived revival of optimism among horse breeders. There was brief interest in draught horses, because motor supplies and fuel ran low in wartime and its immediate aftermath.[169] Schreuder was brought out of retirement. The war gave him fresh hope: he jauntily anticipated reviving his old plans for a world that seemed to need horses again. Having studied at Cornell, he had implicit faith in the US model; he was eager for South Africa to export horses to the 'devastated European countries' and 'also export many thousands of tons of salted and tinned horse meat – prepared from lower and unwanted classes of horses, thus making room for the best types'.[170] He injected energy into arranging 'horse days', judged horses at horse shows and propagated breed societies.[171] The maize and Merino belt in the south-western districts of the Cape, for example, held community horse sports days, with one in 1949 drawing a 900-strong crowd, including the US consul general, Willard Stanton.[172] Within the limitations of Schreuder's perennially modest funding, his shoe-string office gallantly propagated a sense of the power of technology and urged embracing the global arena. Schreuder's central platform was education as the solution.[173] He was in communication with tertiary education facilities internationally and in the United States in particular, institutions like the Texas Agricultural and Mechanical College.[174] In dialogue with key farmers, Schreuder noted: 'Am very glad to find we are slowly catching the American spirit and ways to save our horses from the motor'.[175]

One of these 'ways' was to mobilise history to buttress his claims of the value of horses. Horses were, after all, among the first domesticated animals imported by the white settlers and the first exported. Schreuder was particularly keen to use modern technology to promote his agenda. He established a library of 16 mm films such as *The American Horse* and *The Horse America Made*[176] before producing a film of his own: *The Horse on the Farm*, the first colour film on a livestock theme.[177] This film was made on a trifling budget, using amateur volunteers instead of professional actors. Schreuder strategically mobilised a sentimental association between horse and 'white civilisation'. As he wrote to a senator, the film was on 'Van Riebeek's [sic] arrival in the Cape when Javanese ponies had just arrived to help him establish the cradle of Afrikaner people'.[178] His film included the subtitles: *The Horse Came with the First Settlers and with Us He Will Stay* and *The Horse Came with Van Riebeek* [sic] *to Help Establish the First White Settlement at the Southern Point of Darkest Africa*. It called for scenes of 'van Riebeek [sic] and few orphans and men in dress of period, lovely Arabs in spot with no houses only Table Mountain in background'. Then there was the commando scene, subtitled: 'All through the cradle days of our nation the horse was a most reliable and indispensable source of civilising power and expansion.' Schreuder thus tactically linked the equine past with the nation's future: showing horses on the farm, horses at shows, different breeds, at gymkhanas, racing and on government improvement schemes, '[s]aving imported traction using imported fuel'.[179] It concluded with lines from iconic Afrikaans poet A.G. Visser's '*My ryperd*'.

Schreuder, drawing on a sentiment popularised in the novels of the 1930s, was thus eager to underscore the notion that horses were key to a particular ethnic understanding of South Africa's history that was gaining popularity: 'As you will remember horses came with van Riebeek [sic] and the opening scene must for a few seconds pin the public's mind on this historical event.'[180] With the National Party campaign, notions that had proved so popular in the mid-1930s of the 'burgher and his horse' were revived in the Afrikaans popular press.[181] In 1948, under the new apartheid government, Schreuder launched a last, defensive strike in a war that it was increasingly clear he would lose. He attended an international conference where he tried to demonstrate that modern nation states needed horses.[182] He still argued that mechanisation had been 'too rapid' and that horses would be as useful after the Second World War as they had been after the South African War almost five decades earlier.[183] But even Schreuder accepted that despite these renewed efforts, 'as never before, the threat of mechanisation [hung] like the sword of Damocles – to damp the ardour of enthusiasts and true horse economists'.[184]

Yet on behalf of the few farmers that were interested, the chairman of the Horse and Mule Breeders Association continuously pleaded that 'the

Department would not lose interest in the improvement of the horse stock of the country'.[185] There were doomed attempts to slow the inexorable mechanisation of state transport. Frantic petitions to the minister for railways and transport were made to use animal transport instead of mechanical power.[186] Fruitless efforts were attempted to redirect the industry towards slaughtering horses for 'native consumption'.[187] The armed forces acknowledged equine superfluity to the modern military, allowing their transfer to the Department of Agriculture.[188] In the aftermath of the war, the South African horse industry faced the undeniable reality of an overproduction of horses and a distinct lack of a popular need or desire for them.[189]

There was a certain irony in the faith Schreuder put in North America as it precipitated the final nail in the local industry's coffin. Post-war Canada and the United States reduced their stock of surplus equines by slaughter, sent thousands to the United Nations Relief and Rehabilitation Administration and exported tinned horsemeat to post-war Europe, thus streamlining the gene pool to suit agricultural needs, while importing the cream of stud stock from impoverished Europe. South Africa also had a war-stimulated surplus of which to dispose post-bellum. Foreign states such as Greece did approach South Africa for small mares from the south-western Cape,[190] but US aid rules stipulated that only American equines could be purchased by states (like Greece) receiving aid and furthermore undercut everyone else's bid to assist with their own domestic surplus. Thus, the South African market floundered.[191] By 1949 even Schreuder openly conceded that the state would never again fund the industry. His concession was couched in typically sanguine rhetoric, declaring that the industry was sufficiently developed to be in the hands of the farmers now and no longer under state support, although the state's input had never been overwhelming.[192] Having handed over the responsibility to breed utility stock from state to farmers, the Department of Agriculture assumed the flimsy mantle of merely offering 'critical guidance' for equine stock for the 'new type of farm economy'. Increasingly, Schreuder and his circle accepted that the industry had to reinvent itself utterly or face collapse. Concomitantly, they recognised the obsolescence of the utilitarian equine to large-scale agriculture, industry, transport and policing. As the next chapter explores, they turned their attention more and more to the future of the leisure and show horse in South Africa, a future they helped shape.

Conclusions

After a brief resurgence following the South African War, it became increasingly clear that horses were becoming obsolete on large-scale commercial farms and for public transport, the military and police forces. The 'relentless machines' of the modernising state, commercialising agriculture and the increasing momentum of mechanisation meant an end to the utilitarian role of the horse. This was despite the dogged efforts of a group of private breeders and a few dedicated government officials, in particular Schreuder. Essentially, there were five decades of grand plans and small triumphs. The desire for particular reforms shifted over time, specific initiatives waxed and waned, but there was one constant from 1902 to after the Second World War: a feeling that the horse industry had been the unwanted step-child of the state.[193] Their enduring refrain was, as Schreuder had it, that the '[h]orsebreeding industry is still given too much cindarella [sic] attention by promotors [sic] as well as users'.[194]

The decline of the horse in the large-scale commercial sphere was not linear. Even though effective mechanical competition for horses existed, there were complex local stories and an uneven shift to mechanisation. As elsewhere in sub-Saharan Africa, the transport role of horses did not diminish in many communities. Animal-drawn carts continued to be used for trade and haulage, and within communities to drop off the goods transported there by motorised vehicles. A two-tier system persisted, paralleled elsewhere in Africa, of animal transport and mechanised transport co-existing.

A final florescence of optimism among commercial white breeders blossomed with the Second World War – the horse seemed suddenly, but, as it transpired, only momentarily in the ascendant. The coterie's anxieties were dispelled by the war's hunger for horsemeat. But the end was nigh, and by mid-century horses were rendered redundant on a large scale. As they moved out of the commercial realm, horses were mobilised as potent symbols in a growing class-based, gendered identity configuration, evident in the growing Afrikaans press, in popular novels and in everyday discourse. As a farmer noted of his own district, all the farmers increasingly bought tractors to do the work and a pair of well-bred horses about which to boast.[195] Thus, the so-called 'Cinderella of the livestock industry' reinvented itself in order to survive.[196] This dramatic reinvention is the subject of the following chapter. By mid-century, the utility horse had galloped out of the South African economy and into the fields of the imagination. As in the story of Cinderella, a bleak and grim reality was romantically reshaped into an equine fairytale.

Chapter 7

High Horses
Horses, Class and Socio-economic Change in South Africa[1]

'Things are in the Saddle and ride mankind.'[2]

IN THE FIRST half of the twentieth century there was a seismic shift in the relationship between horses and humans in commercial South Africa as 'horsepower' stopped implying equine military-agricultural potential and came to mean 746 watts of power.[3] By the 1940s the South African horse industry faced a crisis. There was an over-production of horses, exacerbated by restrictions imposed by the Second World War, which rendered export to international markets difficult.[4] Farm mechanisation was proceeding apace and vehicle numbers were doubling every decade.[5] As the previous chapter has shown, there were doomed attempts to slow the relentless mechanisation of state transport. As late as 1949 the Horse and Mule Breeders Association issued a desperate appeal to the minister of railways and transport to stall mechanisation and use animal transport wherever possible.[6] Futile efforts were made to reorientate the industry towards slaughtering horses for 'native consumption' or sending chilled equine meat to Belgium.[7] Remount Services had been transferred to the Department of Agriculture, a significant bureaucratic step reflecting the final acknowledgement of equine superfluity to the modern military. As the previous chapter discussed, the so-called 'Cinderella of the livestock industry' had to reinvent itself to survive.[8]

A new breed of horses thus entered the landscape of the platteland: the American Saddlebred.[9] Unlike the horses that had preceded them, these creatures were show horses. The breed was noted for its showy action in all paces, its swanlike neck with 'aristocratic arch' and its uplifted tail. These horses could not be used for ordinary farm work; they were largely stable based in the show season and taken out of their stalls only for exercise and shows. A Saddlebred was the consummate leisure horse. It was the 'ultimate showhorse' – the 'peacock of the show ring' – and a highly visible marker of disposable income.[10] As a conspicuous signifier, the Saddlebred provides a useful method of tracing and understanding social transformation in a rapidly changing South Africa. This chapter offers an interpretation of the socio-cultural symbolic role of this animal in the South African platteland milieu. It explores the introduction of the Saddlebred to South Africa from the United States and the rise of the Saddle horse 'industry', predominately in the Afrikaans-speaking, agrarian sectors of the then Cape Province and Orange Free State. Analysis of breed discourse provides insights into the role of status symbols, and the reasons for and manner of their acquisition in upwardly mobile Afrikaans-speaking rural communities in South Africa, particularly from the late 1940s and through the 1950s.[11] The discussion includes the material socio-economic context of their acquisition and the cultural impetus for their rise in popularity and wide geographic diffusion. Oral history provides evidence in which Saddlebreds were conspicuous in the narratives of rural success[12] as significant signifiers of status in a group of upwardly mobile rural whites, who were predominately male and Afrikaans speaking.[13] In addition to the material context, the elite – and, to an extent, internationalist – rhetorical space that the American Saddle horse inhabited is analysed by contrasting it with the self-consciously egalitarian and ethnically unifying discourse surrounding another horse, also used by primarily Afrikaans speakers, the Boerperd.[14]

This chapter in the history of horses seeks to contribute to an area that is perhaps neglected in southern African historiography: the 'cultural web of consumption', with an emphasis on 'things' and their meanings. Just as Schlereth contended in his study of American rural consumption in the period of rapid capitalist transformation before the First World War, historians of rural life usually neglect material accumulation and particularly the display of that which Mumford called 'the good life'.[15] Insights drawn from international scholars of consumption patterns, particularly in their focus on consumption as a social category, are useful in writing this part of South African history. Of course, there was not only a linear, top-down model of cultural influences.[16] Equally, it would be incorrect to see only one cause for consumption – 'status striving'

– and ignore the multivalent forms of meanings inherent in the process of consumption.[17] To do so would be ungenerous to the complexity of human desire and our ability to appreciate new forms of beauty.

Creating the community

One result of historical shifts in labour on consumption patterns has been the reorganisation of human–animal relationships so evident in the previous chapters. While some have intensified and some disappeared, other new forms of associations have developed as a result of structural societal changes. This chapter traces the development of a new breed of horse valued for its show form rather than its productive capacity. Indeed, the training methods imposed on this new type of horse could be highly complex and technical. Most Saddlebreds are born with the usual equine gaits: the walk, trot and canter, and an inherent ability to learn the special gaits (stepping pace and 'rack'). To prepare the Saddlebreds for the show ring, a specialised regimen of 'fetlock chains', 'side reins' and 'overchecks' could be imposed. Highly technical corrective shoeing was often utilised to modify pacing, altering the geometry of equine form.[18] These processes entailed considerable purchase costs and necessitated substantial financial investment and technical skill, even a special farrier and a trainer (both for horse and rider). Tails were washed and underwent a monthly 'set'. But to initially 'set' the tail, the lateral ventral sacrocaudal muscle could be cut to create an arched, liberated tail. False tail wigs might also be added for show purposes.[19]

As will be discussed, stratification within the horse industry was reflected by the symbolic status (and symbolic 'identity') attached to different breeds, with the differential value attached to breeds reflected by several economic markers (like sales prices and stud fees), as well as the value attributed by different sectors of society. As Clatworthy has shown in the North American context, the Saddlebreds are valued for aesthetic reasons, with 26 per cent of respondents mentioning the 'love of beautiful horses' and only 3 per cent mentioning money or profit.[20] They have differed from racehorses – which have also been, of course, symbols of affluence – as these have been notionally an investment and often generated income, while even the best show Saddlers did not 'make money' for their owners. The Saddlebreds were thus arguably used to demonstrate and enjoy wealth, rather than to acquire it. A sardonic joke circulated in Saddler circles: 'How do you make a small fortune from these horses? Well, you start with a large fortune.'

The American Saddlebred horse can be traced to horses shipped to North America from the British Isles in the seventeenth century. By the time the first horse shows were held in Kentucky, Virginia and Missouri in the early 1800s, horses called 'American Saddlebreds' were exhibited. In 1891 the American Saddle Horse Breeders' Association and a Saddle horse registry were established. Horses became a major commercial commodity in Kentucky in the mid-nineteenth century, with Kentucky Saddlers shipped to the eastern market, throughout the south of the United States and, finally, the international market, including South Africa. The American Saddlebred horse was first imported into South Africa in 1916 by Claude Orpen, an upwardly mobile sheep farmer from Barkly East.[21] Orpen became known as the father of the 'high class saddle horse breeders in this country'.[22] Following Orpen, Stephanus Phillipus 'Fanie' Fouché from Rouxville became known as the other 'father' of the Saddle horse in South Africa,[23] importing his first stallion in 1934.[24] The Second World War temporarily halted the importation of such horses.

After the war, however, a growing network of rural notables connected by kin or business began to import American stock and buy them from one another. As one breeder argued, the 'purely working horse' was becoming 'something of the past'.[25] With the expanding use of motor vehicles, a niche was necessary for a different kind of horse, suitable for showing rather than basic transportation and farm work.[26] Horse breeding would have to reinvent itself to stay financially viable in a mechanising world. Commentators argued that horse breeding could only be considered an economic proposition if it began to cater 'for the luxury and sporting market of the show ring'.[27] Equally, as horses were thus no longer utilitarian, they could be mobilised as status symbols. Certainly, the big studs appear to have become increasingly well known to the public.[28] When imported horses arrived, excited rural crowds gathered.[29] In 1948, when Fouché imported the stallion Edgeview King, an enthusiastic throng gathered at the railway station to see 'The King' arrive. Over the month after his arrival, 300 people visited the famous 'Edgeview King' and would watch the novel training process.[30]

Pioneers such as Fouché and Taillefer Retief imported stock even during the difficult years following the Second World War.[31] Simply importing from America, as opposed to Europe and the United Kingdom, was evidence in itself of conspicuous consumption. For example, importing a horse from America cost one buyer £500, whereas Thoroughbred stallions could be imported from England freight free in terms of a government agreement with the Union Castle Mail Steamship Company.[32] There was much more bureaucracy involved in American imports, with strict disease control measures that relaxed only gradually.[33] From the late 1940s there was intense discussion in the rural press, precipitating what one observer dubbed the 'Cult of the Saddle horse'.[34] By 1947 generally high prices (progeny of imported American sires varied from £150 to £800; with imports at £500–£2,000 for a stallion and £250–£1,000 for a mare)[35] and occasional freakishly expensive horses (like Retief's £3,000 import)[36] won publicity at agricultural shows.[37] Early 1940s discourse on the Saddle horses had still emphasised the 'usefulness' and 'hardiness' of the creature,[38] but such qualifiers were rapidly abandoned and by the late 1940s these horses came to represent a clear demarcation between 'productive' and purely 'consumptive' activities. Two opposing camps formed between largely Afrikaans-speaking male proponents and critics of the Saddler. Thus from the late 1940s there ensued a vigorous debate in the agricultural press, the content of which offers a window into deeper currents of ideology.[39]

In the early 1940s a few breeders had called for state-controlled, centralised horse breeding to take the process out of the hands of amateur farmer breeders who experimented on 'alchemistic' lines. There were even suggestions that punitive fines be levied against owners of registered mares who bred from non-registered males.[40] But these were largely unheeded and programmes proceeded under the private control of a few wealthy farmers.[41] By 1942 there were six (male Afrikaans-speaking) breeders who had pure registered American Saddlers.[42] This small but growing number of aficionados, reacting to critics, reiterated that importations were privately and not publicly funded. As noted earlier, changes in the post-war horse breeding industry meant that breeding could only be considered an economic proposition when it supplied the 'luxury' market of the show ring.[43]

In 1942 local notables established a (non-breed-specific) society, the Saddle Horse Breeders Society of South Africa.[44] The society was not intended to promote a particular breed,[45] but rather for 'any European breeder or owner of high class saddle horses'.[46] The idea was to recover the 'good name' that South African horses used for riding purposes 'held 60 years ago in India and other Countries' in order to boost the export industry.[47] With the enormous loss of equine life in the immediate aftermath of the war (a million were lost in France, three million in Russia, and one-and-a-half million in Poland)[48], the idea was not to promote show horses, but to capture a slice of the international draught, military and transport market.[49] The initial notion was to use government support, particularly the Department of Agriculture, to smooth the bureaucratic path.[50] Government assistance in importation was militated for and received.[51]

The American Saddle Horse Breeders Society of South Africa that formed seven years later in 1949, although a subsidiary of the Saddle Horse Breeders Society of South Africa, had quite a different motive and modus operandi. Its members were from the wealthy rural elite, predominately wool-farming Afrikaners, with a few English-speaking rural notables, who formed the association with the specific purpose of promoting this show breed.[52] The society established inspectors, judges, horse shows and ultimately a 'World Cup', initially between South Africa and America. The association also made gestures towards genteel philanthropy, with funds for polio and other 'deserving funds'.[53] Members used individual capital investment to promote their cause. There was a drive to avoid state control and establish strictly private ownership of the breeding process.[54] There was an initial attempt to form the society without affiliation to the state-sanctioned Stud Book Association (Act 22 of 1920).[55] In 1952 Philip Myburgh, after a six-month international tour to study the breeding of Saddle horses – the first South African farmer to go abroad for this purpose – suggested annual horse shows on American lines.[56] Central to his argument was the idea that America was 'a century ahead of the rest of the world' and South Africa was 'the second greatest saddle-horse breeding country in the world', while Britain had 'low' breeding standards. Myburgh maintained, with some truth, that post-Second World War horse values had plummeted; 'pessimists raised the cry that the horse was a thing of the past' and would soon vanish from the platteland. The declining interest in the horse during the next few years had resulted in 'the disappearance of the mediocre and poorer class of horse, and there was a limited demand only for the very best the market could offer'. As a result only 'top-line breeders' could survive financially. Supporters agreed on the need for a centralised national annual show and wanted to let spectators and readers of the rural press in on 'the intensity of the struggle between, say, the winner and the runner-up of the five-gaited championship ... or that the third horse may have been the favourite of the crowds, drawing all the applause'.[57] In 1954 the first American Saddle Horse Championship was held at Middelburg in the Cape. The show attracted 7,000 rural spectators and an elite group of breeders and owners.[58]

In this changing rural milieu the first horse textbook for the South African market was published in 1949. It was written by P.J. Schreuder and F.B. Wright, both in the state's Agricultural Education and Research division.[59] As discussed in the previous chapter, Schreuder was a recognised expert, vocal in the discursive space provided by the growing rural press. As director of Agricultural Education and Research, he facilitated the importation process[60] and actively advised investment in American Saddlebreds, plugging both the American and show horse angle.[61] It was Schreuder in particular who urged showing horses as a solution to the crisis in the horse industry.[62] He noted that it was 'quite obvious that a breed with such a high status in the livestock economy and the social and agricultural life of the great American nation can certainly contribute [to the South African context]'.[63] He celebrated it as a 'distinct and exclusive American breed', with 'beauty, fineness, good manners'. Simultaneously, he gave a cursory nod to the politics of autochthony by suggesting that these horses' ancestors' blood flowed in the South African Hantam, or Cape horse. Schreuder further urged that the 'SA American Saddler Society' take advantage of the Pedigree Livestock Act by urging compulsory affiliation to the national Stud Book to maintain breed purity.[64]

Localists erupted, demanding to know why South Africans should simply be 'copy-cats' of America, and whether Dr Schreuder was 'employed by the Union government or by the government of the United States'.[65] The impassioned nativist defence contended that many unadulterated South African horses with 'not a drop of American blood' were five-paced (i.e. exhibited the special 'show' gaits).[66] One critic even suggested that an 'indigenous' horse of his who had pacing ability had been owned previously by Claude Orpen and had covertly contributed to Orpen's purportedly 'pure' American Saddlers:

> We had the riding blood in this country, but the Americans hypnotised us with motor cars in 1912, and while we were still under the effects of Uncle Sam [they] built up, perfected and sold us an article, the ingredients of which we had had for years.[67]

Sceptics dismissed these animals with their 'beautiful names' and specialised equipment in favour of local Boer stock.[68] A debate on gaits[69] ensued, with some critics contending that the fifth gait was 'nothing new', that riders of so-called *strykloopers* of the Sandveld area near Piquetberg (Piketberg) 'beat the American Saddlers at their own game'.[70] Others defended local horses by taking the entirely opposite tack and damned the fifth gait as 'artificial and distinctly American'.[71] Detractors likened saddlers to 'wooden toy horses seen in shop windows to amuse children' and their high tail action was compared to baboons' bottoms. Localists asked: 'Why cannot we breed a South African saddle horse distinct from any other country?'[72] 'A true South African type, South African bred and South African reared horse is the only horse for the future South Africa.'[73] They urged a shift away from expensive American importations and a return to public interest in the 'indigenous' 'Hantam' breed, which 'could be created into a distinct South African breed', using the ways of our 'forefathers'.[74]

Antithetically, the opposing clique emphasised both internationalism and modernity, defending the 'proud' American Saddler for the 'modern horseman'.[75] Promoters argued that 'America lives today in an age of mechanization, of radar and television, of jet propulsion and the atom bomb, but in spite of that the pet interest of the average American is still the horse'.[76] Breeding horses and embracing modernity were thus, they argued, compatible ideals. They defended the 'world-famous breed' from base attack by the 'ignorant' and uncultured.[77] Moreover, to escape the parvenu stigma, this group eschewed the vulgarity of mere usefulness. Aficionados affirmed that it was 'undoubtedly a pleasure horse for the rich man',[78] and because a 'show-horse is not a work-horse', what was required was a 'perfection of paces, not hardiness'.[79] Supporters mooted the idea of ambitious breeding schemes.[80] They celebrated the fact that for 'sheer spectacle no other breed touches it',[81] that it was 'flashy';[82] that it was, in fact, an equine 'film star'.[83] Others described it as the 'epitome of elegance and refinement ... it displays breeding and brilliance in every line'.[84] This was also summed up in the metaphor of carriages: 'Having owned [other breeds], the difference between them and the American Saddler ... is almost the same as that between a springless Scotch-cart and a light rubber-wheeled well-sprung buggy.'[85]

The cult of the Saddlebred

By the early 1950s saddlers had won 'tremendous popularity in South Africa',[86] with public followings for famous Saddlers.[87] They were popular crowd pleasers

A 'show-horse is not a work-horse'
Source: Kaplan (1974, pp. 4, 8)

in pageants and parades.[88] By 1956 South Africa was the largest importer of American Saddlers.[89] Prices soared.[90] As noted, breeders and owners had established a registered Saddle Horse Breeders Society of South Africa and Rhodesia, and by the late 1950s there was a widening dispersion of Saddler blood in South African riding horses.[91] There were requests in the press for recommended literature on judging and training American Saddlers.[92] Reflective of this new focus on equine theatre, farmers were being advised by the rural press on how to show their horses and how to 'take better horse photographs' rather than on mundane issues of drought or transport.[93]

This notion of display had been discussed by Veblen, who was among the first to recognise (and offer social satire on) both the consumptive ethic and the social transformation in which the symbolisms attached to consumption began to take centre stage. He noted that in the United States, Saddle horses 'at their best serve the purpose of wasteful display'[94] and described the importance of acquiring the 'correct' taste, which 'is a taste for the reputably correct, not for the aesthetically true'. This explains the need for trainers and inspectors to teach (and then patrol) what was 'reputably true'. The trainers and judges, set up by the society, worked directly with the farmers to teach them to appreciate this new equine aesthetic – what in the American context Veblen dubbed, sardonically, the 'pecuniary canon of beauty'.[95] The correct form – for both horse and rider – had not only to be taught, but, moreover, had to be taught to be appreciated. As Veblen noted in another context, 'the canons of taste have been colored by the canons of pecuniary reputability'.[96] The Saddle horse suited this aim: the slow gait and rack, for example, could take a horse over two years to master under guidance from a trainer.[97] In similar vein, films like *The Horse America Made* and *The American Horse* were shown at farmers' associations and by the American Saddle Horse Breeders Society.[98] Platteland eyes needed to be schooled in the appreciation of a new form of equine beauty and to be taught to read this new morphological language.

Gaited communities?

The simple explanation for the 'cult of the Saddle horse' was the wider availability of greater disposable income. This, however, offers us a simple facilitatory model: they did it because they could do it. However, there were secondary causes that warrant attention. The 'wool boom' of the 1950s, triggered by the Korean War, when wool sold for 'a £ for a pound', had two significant effects in this context.[99] Firstly, it led to the accelerated creation of wealth among rural Afrikaners. Per capita income among Afrikaners was less than 50 per cent of English speakers in 1946, but rose to 80 per cent by the late 1970s, while the gross value of all farm products rose by 67 per cent in the decades between the 1935 and the 1960s.[100] Secondly, it turned some elite Afrikaner eyes to the United States (in that country's role of Britain's replacement on the world stage) as part of their consumer revolution. Dubow and others have described how, although there was perhaps a Malanite nationalist narrowing of outlook, there was in the same period among other sectors a sense of internationalism – of a more confident looking outward.[101] As O'Meara points out, with Smuts signing the UN Charter in San Francisco, 'many white South Africans felt an almost American sense of boundless possibilities in 1945'.[102] As F.E.J. Malherbe, professor of Afrikaans at Stellenbosch, noted: 'The city Afrikaners have taken off their velskoens [sic] for good … and take their fashion cue from London and New York – even Paris.'[103] One observer noted: 'Afrikaners have become a hamburger-eating and cola-imbibing people':[104]

> we are already four-square in the American era in South Africa … In some ways the most shameless habits, first popularised in America, are slavishly followed by South Africans, and no less by Afrikaners … South Africa, previously culturally attached to Western Europe, is becoming more and more a protégé of America.[105]

In the post-war landscape, the United States had adopted the new symbolic role of world leadership[106] and the realm of the everyday in some South African circles was becoming Americanised:

> When a former President of the United States, Mr Harry Truman, had himself photographed in a gaudy picture shirt … it did not take long to be become *de rigueur* in the country of the Voortrekkers. Every day we see Afrikaans children with these piccanin shirts, abounding with American place names or pictures, which seem to familiarise the wearers more with these names than with the names of places, plants and animals of their own country.[107]

By the late 1940s and early 1950s the 'countryside' was arguably more a state of mind than a place – and it could be bought. In a series of *Huisgenoot* articles, Wim Hartman depicted the 'new [urban] Afrikaner' with only a thin connection through nostalgia to platteland life.[108] Afrikaners involved in agricultural occupations dropped from about 30 per cent in 1946 to only 8 per cent in 1977, while those in white collar employment increased from 29 per cent to 65 per cent.[109] This process of urbanisation, often equated contemporaneously with modernisation, was ameliorated by shrouding it in traditionalism, a nostalgic *ubi sunt* motif.[110] While the urbanised poor struggled to keep their identification with a rural golden age, the more affluent could simply purchase a reconnection with the land.[111]

For those still connected (either emotionally or materially) to farming, the popular rural press was growing and facilitating an expanding communication network. The *Farmer's Weekly* (started in 1911) and *Landbou Weekblad* (1919) created a virtual community and helped disseminate the idea that the American Saddler horses were symbols of cosmopolitanism and living emblems of a newly arrived class.[112] Moreover, regular shows and the show circuit itself acted as an agency of change, much as they did – although far earlier – in rural America in the last decades of the nineteenth century. For example, in 1938 and 1940 the Colesberg Agricultural Show was used as an occasion for breeders to come together. These agricultural shows certainly afforded opportunities for commercial exchange, but additionally they created both the sense of a 'community' and the space for spectacle. The district show became the major event of the year in rural areas, with the horse displays perhaps the greatest attraction for spectators.[113] Shows provided this opportunity for theatre and thus for public self-aggrandisement, which created, in turn, a market for status symbols, which was pivotal in the production of desire.

A brief demographic analysis of key members of the 'Saddlebred community' reveals the interconnectedness and profile of that community, which explains why the trend successfully reached the tipping point. The core elite were mainly Afrikaans-speaking wool farmers, men of influence and upwardly mobile. There is some indication to suggest that many were United Party supporters and they were open to the inclusion of a few wealthy English-speaking neighbours.[114] There was a close relationship between the coterie of early breeders, with most – individuals such as Orpen, Fouché and Retief – engaged in large-scale sheep farming. Such men usually had some local influence. Claude Orpen from Barkly

East, for example, whom we have already met as a key figure and opinion shaper in the early process of American Saddle horse acquisitions, was also a member of the International Wool Secretariat and chairman of the Cape Woolgrowers' Association. William Maré 'Pouerra' Moolman from Somerset East was a member of the executive committee of the Somerset East/Cradock Agricultural Shows.

The intimate web of linkages stretched even further. 'Fanie' Fouché (from Rouxville in the south-eastern Orange Free State) knew Orpen and noticed his horses while moving sheep through his land. Johannes Hendrikus Viljoen van der Merwe (from Richmond in the Cape) used Orpen and Fouché stock. Taillefer Retief (from De Aar on the Richmond road) knew of Fouché's stock and first bought stock from Orpen. Bert Wyer Henderson bought stock from Fouché; P.J.A. van der Merwe (from Richmond) bought stock from Fouché and Retief. Retief purchased from Fouché, and then imported from the United States. From 1944 onwards J.H. van der Merwe (West Front, Britstown) bought from Fouché and used a dam bred from stock owned by Claude Orpen.[115]

Little serious attempt had been made by these affluent men to revive 'traditional' pre-industrial Afrikaner sports and leisure pursuits.[116] For this wealthy sub-group, the Saddler movement provided a space where man, horse and power formed an axis that pivoted on display, predicated on upward mobility and competitiveness. In recreational activities identified with male social status, it afforded an arena for the display of individuals' power while remaining reliant on elite networks and kinship patterns and the rural 'virtual community'. Women were arguably equally competitive, but in a gender-stratified society sought to impress in other networks, particularly through the transformation of the domestic realm.[117] Thus, conspicuous leisure was effective as a social strategy in small, highly personalised reference groups such as the rural communities described here. They converged at nodal events such as district shows and in sharing an imagined community created by the rural press.[118]

'History' vs 'modernity'

The upsurge in this kind of spending by upwardly mobile Afrikaners was arguably driven by the need to clarify social difference. Consumer culture is more than the 'leisure ethic': it is an 'ethic, a standard of living, and a power structure'.[119] Oral history shows that Saddlers were seen popularly from the

1950s as a mark of success, of having 'arrived'. As Giliomee notes, '[i]f Afrikaners were beginning to capture capitalism, capitalism was also capturing more and more Afrikaners'.[120] Identity was shifting with the changing material context and was to manifest two distinct ideological approaches to 'history', as opposed to 'modernity', which are discussed below.

By the 1930s Afrikaners were still predominantly working class, with very few wealthy businessmen.[121] By 1935 Afrikaner income was only 60 per cent of that of English-speaking whites and there was not yet a robust middle class.[122] In this context, the *petit bourgeois* culture brokers wished to win workers away from the incipient left wing and incorporate them into the volk to mitigate dangers of international labour solidarity.[123] There had long been economic differentiation in the Boer population, yet there was a strong sense of community predicated on what O'Meara dubbed a 'Calvinist, petty-commodity-producer *Weltanschauung*'.[124] Growing socio-economic differentiation could be papered over by nostalgic affirmation of a shared rural past, which was, as O'Meara and others point out, validated by appeals to the symbols of this 'shared' history.[125] There was, as a result, an intensification of a long-standing trend from the 1930s onwards towards embracing history in order to validate identity.[126]

Analyses of the culture of (Afrikaner and other) nationalism have largely focused on this more familiar process, i.e. on the ways in which memory and 'history' constructed community/ethnic/national identity.[127] Yet, as illustrated by the American Saddler aficionados, identity could also be focused on 'modernity' and consumerism. Identity could be as much coupled to current gratification and future dreams as it could be rooted in recollections of the past.[128] This was because 'modernity' made the quest for 'quality of life' a central one for the new *bourgeoisie*. On a larger, national scale, modernity came to be judged by the consumptive capabilities of a nation.[129] As in the United States, the post-Second World War middle class was the backbone of this consumer revolution. Household durables and consumable items improved in quality and exploded in variety, with household success represented by amassing these products – and, more than success, their 'identity' as well.[130] As Marcuse noted of the rising elite in the American context: 'The people recognize themselves in their commodities; they find their soul in their automobile, hi-fi set, split level home, kitchen equipment.'[131] Consumerism revolutionised desire and brought new cultural influences. Although the United States was not South Africa's chief trading partner or source of investment capital, post-war American consumer icons had growing appeal to South Africans of various classes and ethnic groups. White children played 'cowboys and Indians' (rather than 'Boers and Zulus'), and country 'n western styles percolated into local Afrikaans music.[132] '[A]lmost every Afrikaans magazine ... found it indispensable to incorporate a film column, largely devoted to the caprices of Hollywood stars.'[133] Even the agricultural press was saturated with advertisements for brands like Electrolux, Chevrolet and Ford; with Hollywood gossip[134] and with trips to America for trade or pleasure.[135]

Consumption patterns in the developing Afrikaner middle class were in transition and the changing social order meant new theatres for consumption. Conventionally, Afrikaners had seen commerce as unsavoury – the realm either of the low-status *smous* [travelling trader][136] or of the exploitative 'Hoggenheimer',[137] and social commentators, like those serving on the Carnegie Commission, had noted – and even lamented – the widespread lack of 'acquisitive spirit' shown by Afrikaner farmers in the 1920s and 1930s.[138] Now, however, there was a revolutionary transformation in public mentality: consumption is good. Just as in America, consumption became linked to the notion of 'freedom'.[139] Van Onselen has shown that the boom of 1939–49 precipitated changes in the Afrikaner 'economic metabolism', manifested in a more aggressive political stance when farmers who had been dependent on 'English' banks, grain traders and property speculators found 'themselves able to transcend the constraints of populist politics and in a position to embrace a new and far more ambitious vision of Afrikaner nationalism'.[140] This political and psychological change – a new appreciation of commerce – was so palpable that within decades the Afrikaans press commented on the new generation of Afrikaner Hoggenheimers.[141] Increasing links with the international business world during the emergence of Afrikaner capitalism provided the major globalising impetus in Afrikaner society in this era[142] and, as Du Pisani has argued, the mood of sectors of Afrikaner elite capitalism had turned from its early impetus of saving the volk towards the consumer pleasures of individual success.[143] With increasing political dominance and economic might, anti-capitalist elements of nationalist rhetoric were increasingly discarded. One critic noted bluntly: '[Afrikaners] tend to be snobbish as soon as material wealth is accumulated'[144] and 'I am noticing that the inferiority complex which bedevilled Afrikaner actions for so long is fast disappearing.'[145]

Evidence of the pervasive and revolutionary nature of this injection of materialism may be found in widespread discussion of the nature of luxury and whether consumerism compromised the national character with its seductive appeal. There was much soul searching in magazines like *Die Huisgenoot* by *sedebewakers* (supporters of traditional values) into the social implications of prosperity for Afrikaner identity, with jeremiads against consumerism: '*Word ons Afrikaners te ryk?*' (Are we Afrikaners becoming too rich?).[146] One commentator noted hyperbolically of the 1950s:

> The farmer plays billiards, 'does' Europe on a Cook's tour, buys a new car when the ash-tray of the old one is full, goes deep-sea fishing and puts stinkwood parquet flooring in his shearing pen. There is the barbarism of super-duper parsonages, the expensive, vulgar modern church buildings in a beautiful platteland dorp, the struggle to surpass last year's tithes with another thousand.[147]

A growing consumer secularism was very visible by the 1970s, predicated on sport, leisure, travel and increasingly fractured Afrikaner ethnic unity.[148] The papering over the cracks between the classes and the deliberate cross-class mobilisation evident in the 1930s (through events like the Eeufees – centenary festival – for example)[149] had changed. Equally, racial intrusions into the sport were patrolled. Evidence of exclusion is found anecdotally: in 1976, Gerrit van Schalkwyk, for example, wanted his senior groom, Willem Tieties, to ride a particularly spirited horse at the Tulbagh Show. Tieties was asked by the organisers to leave the ring as no coloured exhibitors were allowed. Van Schalkwyk's daughter records, with irony: 'the fact that hand classes [in which horses were led rather than ridden] were almost always showed by "Coloured" exhibitors seemed not to register.'[150]

Developments (like the saddler movement) provide evidence of the way identity could be predicated on class, not to include but rather to exclude. While many culture brokers reclaimed the poor whites for the volk, others distanced themselves.[151] Thus, an upsurge in consumption was arguably driven by the need to clarify definitively uncertain social status by the accumulation and display of material things.[152]

This fits a Veblenian model of the need of the leisure class to spend money in a way that 'serves the purpose of a favorable invidious comparison with other consumers' – i.e. to spend money in a way that makes other people feel poor. This 'growth of punctilious discrimination' as to 'qualitative excellence' shows off not only capital accumulation, but is also designed to demonstrate knowledge, discrimination and taste. There is a fine but significant distinction between feeling rich and feeling upper class. The 'specialised consumption of goods' as evidence of 'pecuniary strength' had begun to work out in a more or less elaborate system, '[s]ince the consumption of these more excellent goods is an evidence of wealth, it becomes honorific; and conversely, the failure to consume in due quantity and quality becomes a mark of inferiority and demerit'. Simply put, status and money were connoted by close proximity.[153]

Money and modernity met in a nexus of this new identity. South Africa could enter the competitive realm of an imagined America acting as metonym for modernity. During the 1956 National American Saddle Horse Championship in Beaufort West it was widely reported that a visiting American judge said 'emphatically and persistently that the American Saddlers in South Africa could hold their heads high in the company of the best which America could put on show'.[154] Local observers argued that 'horse-breeding was not only of agricultural but also cultural value; it is not only a national industry but a link of international relationship' and 'can often succeed where diplomats and politicians fail'.[155] An important part of the symbolism of consumption was to signify success in furthering the aims of the modernising project. In other words, consumption could be used as a yardstick for the 'modern' nation's success; it represented the reality that the nation had attained greater control over its fate by improving productivity'.[156] This is vividly demonstrated in the Saddle Horse milieu by inviting Americans to judge shows and devoting a great deal of press space to their affirming commentary on South Africa's own domestic-bred horses as validation. There was particular emphasis on celebrating that 'our' horses are 'as good' as America's and, later, much celebration at actually being able to export American Saddle horses to America itself.

Horses for dis/courses

It was precisely against this 'Americanisation' that a very different group of Afrikaner breeders initially reacted.[157] The realm of 'everyday life' provides evidence of popular nationalist politics, where 'ordinary pursuits' were given a 'distinctly ethnic character'.[158] Localists started asking: 'Nevertheless … if the

American nation were able to create [the Saddler] out of the basic Oriental and thoroughbred blood ... why should [South Africa] ... not be able to create an equally magnificent South African horse – the Boerperd?'[159] There was an assertion of the need for breed status:

> Is the name [Boerperd] only the *nom de plume* used for all horses that cannot be called American Saddlers, Arabians, Thoroughbreds or Hackneys? Are the Boerperd classes at agricultural shows meant to contain all the part-bred American Saddlers who fear they may be outclassed in their own division ... [?][160]

From the 1940s, and gathering momentum thereafter, the 'Boerperd' (literally either 'farm horse' or farmer's horse or 'horse of the Boers [or Afrikaans speakers]', a significant but lost etymological distinction) was not seen as simply a category for any animal rejected from other breeds. There was a new desire to use a 'breeding policy' to fix the 'conformation and stamina' which made the 'Boerperd' renowned during the South African War. So in 1949, a year after the National Party victory, breed societies were created and breed management centralised.[161] The Saddle Horse Breeders Society of South Africa and Rhodesia used the term 'Boerperd' to mean simply 'farmhorse' or even the 'cross-bred section', but at other times discuss it as a 'breed' (although not a 'pure' breed) in its own right.[162] The first Boerperd trials were held in 1955 and the movement gained quiet momentum and emergent popularity. By 1973 the Boerperd Society was formed, codifying for the first time the 'breed standard' of the heterogeneous mixture of breeds, mingled over three centuries: 'Javanese' (Sumbawan) stock, American stock, Arabians, Persians, Barbs and English Thoroughbreds that had shaped the 'Boerperd' over time. Programmes were initiated to cross the affordable 'Boerperd' with the expensive American Saddler (in particular the showy five-gaited saddlers from Kentucky and Tennessee).

But in the same year, a faction, uneasy about adding more American blood, initiated schism and started breeding 'pure horses like those introduced into the two Boer Republics by the Great Trek'.[163] These 'Historical Boerperd' breeders insisted on breed purity and emphasised the quality of indigeneity. Consequently, in 1977 the society renamed the breed the 'Historical Boerperd'.[164] Meanwhile, a splinter group made a case for the use of more American Saddler blood, developing what came to be known as the Cape Boerperd.

Several themes were emphasised in the definition and marketing of the Boerperd. Firstly, history and nativist heritage were underscored (with, for example, assertions that General de Wet's famous grey Arab was a Boerperd; and slogans like 'The Horse from the Past for the Future'); they included the idea of an organic, ethnically essentialist notion that the 'Boers were good and natural horsemen'. This included efforts towards establishing the Boer commando riding style as a judgeable event for shows. For Afrikaans horse names, military victories and the names of Boer generals' horses were often used; the claims used in marketing these horses included such things as 'their ancestors carried the Voortrekkers' and they provide a link to "white" civilisation' and '[t]he SA Boerperd is as old as civilisation in South Africa'.[165] Secondly, there was an elite group patrolling the borders of the breed, an aristocracy (like the Burgers, Conradies and Grimbeecks) acting as breeders, judges and inspectors – often in overlapping roles.[166] Thirdly, there were six distinct pure bloodlines, and the register was closed to 'outside' horses. Fourthly, the horses were promoted as autochthonous and 'authentic', with the slogan *'Geselekteer en Aangepas vir Afrika'* (Selected and Adapted for Africa). The second and third traits contain a measure of irony, as they are at odds with the fifth trait, which comprised the simultaneous insistence on the hardiness, ordinariness the everyday quality, and the naturalness of the Boerperd's ancestry – the antithesis of a horse kept chiefly for showing, like the Saddler. Even the breed standard stated that the Boerperd had to be able to 'survive on the veld'. Thus boerperd with a small 'b' became Boerperd with a capital letter, because of a particular kind of identity politics.[167]

This antagonism to class stratification is illustrated by the example of a breeder/inspector who had a book printed at his own expense and recorded with relish every time a Boerperd beat a Saddlebred at a show.[168] It was the discourse of the foreign, effete aristocrat being defeated by the local, indigenous breed. He observed in his notes to the breed standard that the Boerperd is a 'racially pure horse that holds its head high'. He contended that the South African war had led to the 'mongrelisation' of most of our breeds, so 'we must take off our hats to those Boers who kept their boerperde pure'.[169] He further noted that as a judge and inspector, one must look 'first and foremost for racial purity'. Clearly, there is identification anxiety and resultant compensation, as he goes on to say:

The Boerperd is just as genuinely South African as we are ourselves, because his ancestors also date back to the seventeenth century and like us grew famous for his hardiness, utility and independence. This is the heritage our ancestors left us.[170]

It is also significant that Eugène Ney Terre'Blanche – who established the right-wing commando-based *Afrikaner Weerstandsbeweging* (Afrikaner Resistance Movement) at the same time as the Boerperd breeders broke away – has used the Boerperd as a symbol not only of power, but of the equine-oriented Boer *volksgeskiedenis* (people's history) and organic masculine Afrikaner horsemanship.[171] In a letter he wrote to me from prison, he noted that the horses of General de la Rey and Manie Maritz (heroes of the South African War and both rebel leaders in the 1914 Boer rebellion) were both Boerperde. He also claimed that he did not really fall from his horse (referring to a much-televised shot of his horse slipping as he led an AWB march), contending that the South African Broadcasting Corporation had simply used it as propaganda, knowing that to ridicule his horsemanship was to undermine his masculine and ethnic power.[172] He – and the breeders and inspectors – emphasise the accessibility of the Boerperd. Not only has it shared an intimate history with the Afrikaner, but it can be afforded by every Afrikaner: it needs no trainer, no special farrier and no special knowledge, and can be ridden using the old Boer riding style. Horse-based commando mythology has saturated the politico-cultural realm. For example, '*Opsaal*' or 'Saddle Up! The Republic Is Coming' was a National Party slogan for its campaign for the republic.

Nooitgedacht horses

A further illustration of the complexities of breed creation is provided by another 'indigenous' breed. In 1950 a committee was set up by the secretary for agriculture, Dr C.H. Neveling, to investigate indigenous breeds of sheep, cattle, goats and so on that were of interest to Afrikaner culture brokers. This was catalysed by a letter from an extension officer, A.W. Lategan, on a distant, isolated station in the Northern Cape, who pointed out that while there was much effort towards soil conservation, indigenous animals well adapted to local conditions were disappearing. He stimulated interest in preserving livestock like the Basotho pony, Boer horses and Boesmanland donkeys.[173] The Standing Committee on Indigenous Livestock of the Department of Agriculture in 1951 bought a nucleus herd of 12 typical Basotho-type ponies. The representative horses hailed, interestingly, not from Lesotho, but from the Orange Free State. A breeding station was established at Nooitgedacht in Ermelo (Eastern Transvaal, now Mpumalanga) to 'preserve the Basotho pony' and to develop a utility riding horse.[174] It was called the 'Nooitgedacht' pony rather than Basotho pony, ostensibly because of the breeders' admixture of Cape horse/Boerperd and Arab blood to the Basotho base.[175] Breeders prized the type for its amiability, sturdiness and resistance to disease. The ideal Nooitgedacht was a hardy, strongly built pony with intelligence and a sweet nature. A studbook was kept open for females who passed a phenotypic inspection (small Boerperd or Arab). Interestingly, the breeders permitted admixture from Afrikaner breeds, but specifically no British pony breeds were allowed. In 1967 eight subsidiary studs were set up and two years later a breed society was established in terms of the Registration of Pedigree Livestock Act (Act 28 of 1957). The society changed the name from 'pony' to 'horse' for commercial reasons.[176] In 1976 the state-controlled South African Stud Book recognised the Nooitgedacht (invented a mere 24 years before) as its first indigenous horse breed and sold it at public auctions and gave stock to preserve to the Universities of Pretoria and Stellenbosch. The horses were celebrated as indigenous and autochthonous.[177] This reflects the difficulties of defining 'breed', understood as a group of animals that through selection have come to resemble one another and pass their qualities to their offspring. The point at which a collection of animals becomes a 'breed' is a human decision, not a genetic event, and their identity is at least as historical as it is biological.

Conclusions

The story of the American Saddler is more than the story of a horse; it is the story of how horses continued to find a niche in a changing South Africa. It is also a story about how horses came to mean something new in the chronicle of desire for a standard of living representative of a newly arrived Afrikaans-speaking social echelon. By the 1940s South African horse breeders faced a crisis and the industry had to reinvent itself to endure. In a time of mechanisation, when the utility horse was becoming obsolete and the horse-breeding industry had to be redesigned or face collapse, the American Saddle horse filled a new commercial niche.[178] But more than that: the Saddler filled a niche in the imagination of a people who were coming to conceive of themselves differently.

The Saddlers were symbols of a newly desired cosmopolitanism – particularly Americanism – modernity, taste, skill and wealth. Significant expense – on the right things – established a conspicuous imprimateur of class.

The increase in discretionary income in this sub-sector of Afrikaner, mainly male networks was pivotal, but there were also secondary factors. The expanding communication network played a role, with the popular rural press assisting in the creation of a community.[179] Regular agricultural shows afforded opportunities for spectacle and, of course, provided entertainment to entice customers to this arena of countryside commercial exchange, both vital elements in the process of competition, of which the Saddlebred was simultaneously icon and subject. Equally, shows were helpful in reflecting a hierarchy of expertise in an (initially) masculine rural art form.

Historians have shown how consumer items and sports, for example, were invested with ethnic identity; the 'cult of the Saddler' reflects the role of class. Past historiography on the culture of national identity has largely focused on the ways in which shared understanding of 'history' was mobilised to produce group (ethnic/national) identity, but identity could also be predicated in part on the embrace of 'modernity' and consumerism. The comparison between the supporters of the Saddle horse and Boerperde, both factions within Afrikaans-speaking society, and an analysis of their quite different discourses reflect two ways of conceptualising identity, especially in the way they mobilised consumer hunger.

Genetically, the horses were close, separated by lineages, training regimes, diet, usage and the imagination. The ways in which they were imagined were tempered by changes over time, various political currents, various agents of change and different commercial niches. The Saddle horse discourse reflects the development of a new class, with fresh manifestations of desire and a need to demarcate social boundaries. It moreover indicates a different way of thinking about Afrikaner self-identity: confident, internationalist, pro-American, elite – above all, embracing of 'modernity', the future, and not invested in the past. There is some evidence to suggest that owners were largely United Party supporters and they were clearly open to the inclusion of a few wealthy English-speaking neighbours in the project. Instead of 'Afrikanerising' the American horse, it remained more prestigious to maintain a foreign link. Saddler representations distanced themselves from history – both Afrikaner and South African – with a focus on modernity, internationalism, display and spectacle, whereas Boerperd breeders revelled in history, classlessness, usefulness and autochthony. Boerperd discourse offered a demotic *Weltanschauung* and the Boerperd breeders refuted the notion of a horse as a *fainéant* relic of a higher class. Instead, they represented an animal that was vigorous, robust, useful, ordinary and egalitarian (within ethnic parameters). Ethnic nationalism was a good marketing tool and the Boerperd was invested with the politics of 'everyday nationalism', with a distinctly ethnic character that pivoted on cohesive, inclusive – and often nostalgic – ethnicity. Antithetically, the American Saddle horse movement was used historically not to bind the volk closer, but (quite conversely) to designate difference; to underscore not only wealth, but exclusivity. Identity needed to be packaged just like any other commodity; and, in turn, it was used to package other commodities – in this case, horses.

The chronology of breed recognition was significant: the recognition of the Boerperd followed that of the Saddle horse, rather than preceding it. The Boerperd movement and its celebration of nativism from the early 1970s was a particular intra-ethnic, class-based reaction to the elite dynamics displayed by the Saddle horse movement. The Boerperd, which required a much diminished financial outlay than Saddlers, was embraced by the economic class who championed an explicitly unifying and self-consciously classless ethnic nationalism. This suited the vision propagated by the *petit bourgeois* culture brokers, who had promoted the idea of a seamless rural Afrikaner identity unfissured by class distinction. This was resisted by some in the rising elite, who (quite literally) 'got on their high horses'.

Finally, there was an undeniably sensual side to the Saddle horse movement that should be recognised. Oral narratives evoke the remembered pleasure generated by the learned appreciation of the horses' movement, by the physical and mental skill required to ride them correctly, and by their sheer beauty.

Chapter 8

✳

The World the Horses Made

I T IS UNLIKELY that there are any truly wild horses anywhere in the world today. During the Pleistocene era, right up until ten thousand years ago – when the human experiment in agriculture first began – wild equids proliferated in Asia, the Americas and Africa. In the modern world, however, only seven of these species survive: the African wild ass (*Equus africanus*), Asiatic wild ass (*Equus hemionus*), Kiang (*Equus kiang*), Grevy's zebra (*Equus grevyi*), mountain zebra (*Equus zebra*), plains zebra (*Equus burchellii*) and Przewalski's horse (*Equus ferus przewalskii*).[1] Yet a new one has come into being: the domestic horse (*Equus caballus*). While this recent arrival flourishes, five of the eight surviving species are 'vulnerable', 'endangered' or even 'extinct in the wild'. Przewalski's horse, which was once found in the remoteness of the Altai Mountains in the Dzungarian Basin and Chinese Turkestan, probably no longer exists in its pure state, having been diluted with herds of semi-feral horses. It exists nowhere in the wild; the last was a solitary stallion spotted in the Mongolian Desert in 1969. The immense herds of ostensibly 'wild horses' of the western United States, Australian desert, and South American llanos and pampas are really the feral descendants of sometime domestic stock.[2] The 'wild horse' nomenclature is revealing: 'mustang' is from the Castilian *mesteño*, meaning belonging to 'everyone or nobody'.[3] The worth of such 'wild horses' in the Americas fluctuated from very valuable to utterly valueless, as human needs varied over time. This offers a sharp contrast to the history of horses in southern Africa, where horses have never thrived as a feral population and, equally, were never without considerable worth. In southern Africa, generally speaking, a horse had an owner: there were no vast 'wild horse' herds able to live freely on their own terms.[4]

Tellingly, even mustangs imported during the South African War (1899–1902) were immediately tamed for military use and later sold to South African farmers. Indeed, in vivid contrast to the herds of the American West, wild horses in southern Africa are anomalous – small, isolated groups which, because of their scarcity, have inspired local myths and followings.[5] For example, in the 1920s there were wild, shaggy horses with 'long, flowing manes and tails' on the islands at the mouth of the Orange River. A traveller noted that to evade capture these horses would plunge into the water and swim to 'refuge in the extensive island labyrinth'.[6] The palaeontologist Robert Broom thought them the descendants of a fossil horse, the long extinct *Equus capensis*, and the young Union of South African hoped they might prove a 'horsesickness-proof horse'.[7]

In a similarly water-logged example, the so-called 'mutant horses' of Bot River in the estuary between Kleinmond and Hermanus on the south-western Cape coast are said to graze on vlei or marsh grass and have hooves the size of plates. This group is believed to have roamed the salty marshland for a century, part of a herd hidden from soldiers during the South African War. Its numbers were reputedly swollen by horses released by farmers following mechanisation in the agricultural sector after the Second World War and added to by other escapees over the years. The tiny herd has engendered a localist folklore of salt-water drinking, webbed-footed horses, seldom seen by humans, as they roam behind the Kogelberg, an area once demarcated as a restricted military area for missile tests.[8]

In another southern African milieu, but in an antithetical environment to the small, damp habitat of the Bot River herd, a very different feral group has endured – in the arid vastness of Namibia. A couple of hundred so-called Namib Desert horses have survived in an area of about 350 square kilometres around Garub, 20 km west of Aus, a barren zone where rainfall is erratic and unpredictable – barely sufficient for succulents and a ragged stubble of Bushman grass growing in the hot sand. They are rumoured to be the descendants of horses that belonged to an eccentric German nobleman, Baron Hansheinrich von Wolf, who built a castle in the desert and died in action in France in 1916. Legend has it that his wife, maddened by grief at hearing the news, released his 300 prized horses into the desert. But they are more likely to be the progeny of horses left by soldiers during the First World War; those of the

South African Expeditionary Force and the retreating German colonial forces, with an admixture from a stud owned by the one-time mayor of Lüderitz.[9] Under Namibia's South African occupation their range fell under the control of a subsidiary of the Anglo American Corporation. The area was off limits to humans as a restricted diamond-mining area. Through the 1970s and 1980s, a mine security officer who developed a fondness for the herd made sure they always had water.[10]

Another ex-mining community, the nearly forgotten village of Kaapsehoop on a buttress of the Mpumalanga escarpment, nurtures its own feral population of about 200 horses. Community legend suggests that their ancestors were miners' horses dating back to the discovery of gold in the late nineteenth century. Locals are fiercely protective of the horses and warn visitors to slow down as the horses loom out of the perennial mist unexpectedly on the little-travelled roads.

Some feral herds exist today only in the imagination and memory. A feral herd was said to have come into existence after the 1852 shipwreck of HMS *Birkenhead* en route to deliver soldiers for the war in the Eastern Cape. At the eastern tip of Walker Bay on the Cape south-west coast, the ship struck an uncharted reef. The *Birkenhead* became famous as the first shipwreck where the 'women-and-children-first' rule was applied. The horses ignored this gendered directive and simply swam ashore. They were said to be the ancestors of a free roving band that roamed the *strandveld* plains east of Gansbaai until late in the twentieth century.

Such small runaway *droster* equine communities (and the occasional lone rogue) were fugitives from human society, while most horses have been captive within the human social order.[11] The 'world the horses made' was built in close conjunction with humans.

This book has talked about the horse as a commodity and as a device used by humans to effect change or to wield or display power. But, as the previous chapters have also shown, in another sense the horse has been the quintessential migrant labourer in southern Africa and moved about as the human economy dictated. In the subcontinent, the human and horse species have become entangled in a range of relationships from slavery, to partnership, to fellow combatant, and to a mutualistic alliance of sorts. They have also moved in different labour arenas: horses have filled the roles of urban slave and rural serf. Both the strengths and vulnerabilities of horses acted as an historiographic 'unseen hand', radically affecting human history, from the outcomes of battles to patterns of human movement, both extending and imposing limits on human activity. This underlines the point that including horses in human history does more than simply complete the story – it changes it.[12]

Thus, the preceding chapters have discussed the material difference horses made to human settlement, transport networks and military capacity; social life; and even the human sensory experience. It is clear that horses have changed history. What is much less clear is how best to write that history. Undoubtedly, horses were more than simply depreciable capital goods or data for a statistical series. This leads us to questions of how to write history that engages with animals as subjects. This chapter explores ideas suggested by the previous chapters, particularly Chapter 1, with a particular focus on social history's long-time concern with agency and with understanding socio-cultural experiences from the perspective of those who actually lived them. Building on this basis, the chapter probes the constraints and possibilities of writing history that takes animals seriously.[13]

Making horsetory?

Their story might thus be told in ways suggested by the rise of the 'new social history', which encouraged studying the past not from the perspective of the elite, but from the viewpoint of such previously neglected groups.[14] Yet including horses in (human) social history exposes important contradictions. As this chapter will show, the history of horses can be to some extent compared to that of oppressed social groups/the subaltern, but at the same time, horses have been the adored animals of the colonising elite and certainly instrumental, if not critical, in the process of colonisation and oppression. Thus, to locate horses at the centre of the narrative, one has had to extend the directions suggested by social history radically while accepting that the parallels are analogous but not interchangeable. In examining 'the world the horses made', this chapter draws on the example set by classic studies of 'worlds' made by the oppressed – like Genovese's *World the Slaves Made*; Sobel's *World They Made Together* or Hill's *World Turned Upside Down*.[15] As Nash suggested, and as discussed in Chapter 1, some working in environmental history (the usual home of Animal

Studies, or the animal turn[16]) have embraced social history's notion of exploring history from below, while others consciously fuse the approaches to write 'socio-environmental' history.[17]

Horses share similarities with other under-represented groups: marginality from the centres of power and record keeping. As Chapter 1 has argued, social history has long offered ways of discussing the oppressed and the silenced. From this tradition one can learn from the ways in which other under-represented groups received historiographic recognition. Of course, to make the parallel between animal and human oppressed is neither to conflate nor to trivialise the suffering of any subaltern.[18] Simply, one draws on what the new social historians of the 1960s called the worm's-eye view of history, which was liberating to a generation frustrated by the conventional histories of the elites.

Over the next two decades, historians began to focus on women's history, black history, gay history, and the histories of colonised peoples and the working class. An illuminating case study is offered by women's history (which shares many similarities with Animal Studies, because both their stables comprise practitioners from a liberal, middle-class tradition). The first wave of feminist interventions into historiography countered exclusively male narratives with a gynaecentric variant of 'big man' history focused exclusively on the powerful women of the past. This tradition of 'herstory' was progressively succeeded by a second groundswell that studied less-powerful women, first as passive victims of patriarchy (just as the Fabian orthodoxy insisted the working class were just inert victims of *laissez-faire*). Then followed a third wave acknowledgement that even under oppressive patriarchies, ordinary women possessed, albeit in limited circumstances, agency of their own (as Thompson and others did for the working class). The parallels between writing the histories of both groups are striking. Horses and women have much in common historically: both were socially integral but subordinated groups that were not always conveniently tractable. Some characteristics of a horse, especially a display of self-will, were described as particularly female, as in an Afrikaans narrative from the third decade of the twentieth century, which translates to 'it is always very difficult to foresee what a chestnut horse or a woman will do'.[19]

Drawing on the gendered or women's history paradigm, perhaps historians' first step could be simply to demonstrate that animals have a history in the first place. Just as first 'great women' were 'reclaimed', historians claimed the animal equivalents like the famous racehorse Horse Chestnut and military leaders' magnificent chargers. Secondly, historians could find the ordinary horses, victims of society's oppression, like the nameless horse owned by Wolraad Woltemade, who was compelled to rescue drowning sailors from a wreck until he drowned himself; or the over 300,000 horses that died in the South African War.[20] Historians could ask whether an animal has a history that can be traced and expressed. Firstly, clearly each animal has an individual history, a history often written on their bodies. The scarred knees of a Cape carthorse, saddle sore scars of a Maluti Mountains pack horse and the steroid-based bone problems of a racehorse all bear testimony to how horses have endured human needs. Their history is reflected in their behaviour too. The cordite-inured police horse, the dead-mouthed school master and the bolting ex-racehorse all reflect their individual past experiences through their reactions to current experience.

Indeed, the focus on narratives and life stories became a significant part of writing women's history, which required the documentation of women's ordinary lives. Social history has uncovered the value of life history research, with many of the most complex and detailed explorations of women's history incorporating extensive life history and personal narratives.[21] Narrative forms are infused with specific notions of causality; they link the individual life and the sense of agency. Thus, one could start to write the biography of a horse called Somerset. In Chapter 5, this horse was alluded to as simply 'Dick King's horse'. Yet Somerset had more varied experiences and a more interesting life than such anthropocentric labels allow. Somerset, a brown (bay or chestnut) gelding (named after Lord Charles) was first owned by an English officer, then bought at great expense by a prospective Voortrekker for his journey into the interior. Somerset experienced the Great Trek and saw active service – he was purportedly even ridden in combat by Boer notable Andries Pretorius. Later, in Port Natal, Somerset was allegedly stolen and sold to the British garrison. The British were then besieged by the Boers near Congella in 1842. Dick King, a member of the Port Natal Volunteers, and an African volunteer, Ndongeni Ka Xoki, volunteered to ride to Grahamstown to obtain relief for the beleaguered troops. King and Ndongeni (who accompanied King for part of the way, but suffered due to a lack of stirrups) alternated between riding Somerset and an unnamed white horse. Somerset won renown as the horse that made this incredible journey of 600 miles or 960 km in ten days, fording over a hundred rivers. In his later years, Ndongeni remembered Somerset as a horse who leapt where other horses could only walk or wade.[22] Ndongeni and King received farms for their services. Somerset was widely rumoured to have died the day after the epic ride. A counter-narrative has him growing old and fatly happy on King's sugar farm.

Similarly, another way to approach writing history that takes animals seriously could be simple: capturing the lived experience of particular creatures in the past. Static snapshots of the daily lives of horses in the past could be combined and run chronologically to create a picture of how an average day in the life of a horse changed over time, much as the first works on social history on women and the working class did. For example, an everyday picture of horses in the 1730s could be derived from Otto Mentzel, a German expatriate who lived at the Cape, who described such a day as follows:

> At six o'clock, or if it rains hard, a little earlier, the … [horses are brought in with the other animals]. Each kind [of animal] is driven into its own kraal, but the saddle-horses are put in a stable. But unless they are wanted for riding the next morning, they are not on that account given forage at home.[23]

Contrasting snapshots like this with others underscores the twin points that horse's lives can be discovered and that these ways of life changed over time.[24]

But were these lifeways affected by the horses themselves? This brings us back to the key question of agency, which occupies most discussions of oppressed groups by historians. 'Agency' has been the principal element of the third way of writing the history of the oppressed, which accepts that such groups are not passive victims, but acted in their own right, albeit not in circumstances of their own choosing. In other words, as Marx said of humans, they 'make their own history, but they do not make it as they please; they do not make it under self-selected circumstances'.[25] This notion of agency is now explored in the context of multiple possible ways of writing horses into history.

Previously, agency has not been a salient feature in historical analyses of animals. Robin Law, for example, who wrote a pioneering study of horses in West Africa, was at pains to point out that he himself had no particular enthusiasm for horses *per se* nor treated them as subjects in their own right.[26] Equally, McShane and Tarr sculpt an able biography of the horse, but their focus was not on the horse as an animal possessed of agency; instead, they discuss it as a 'living machine' in an urbanising society. A similar approach is observable in

Africa, from Fisher's ground-breaking work on horses in the Sudan[27] to Webb's research of the equine role in western Sahara and Senegambia[28] and Legassick's study of horses in the Samorian army.[29]

Efforts to locate agency in human groups are often seen as an act of redress. Equally, an approach to inserting animals into history might take the form of reparation, drawing on the approaches, for example, of feminist historians and historians of slavery, who emphasise what has been termed 'compensatory' history. A fissure lies in the division between researchers working from an academic activist position conducted in a spirit of commitment to praxis and a camp more deliberately non-partisan. The first faction contends that Animal Studies should provide the representative voices for non-human animals in an institutional structure that considers them voiceless. This faction contends that because animals do not speak for themselves and leave no texts, Marx's formula on French peasants in *The Eighteenth Brumaire* is uncannily applicable to animals, who cannot create their own documents, oral or written, or author their own historical accounts: 'They cannot represent themselves, they must be represented.'[30]

The unseen hoof

Another way to address animal agency is to reassess the idea of agency itself. Some have argued that the failure to question agency in the telling of history actually reproduces familiar forms of power.[31] Efforts to reassess the histories of labour, girls, the subaltern, childhood and so on attack prevailing hegemonic notions of agency predicated on the idea of an autonomous individual who follows the imperatives of rational choice, fully aware of how the world works. Instead, some historians search for more subversive tradition, although they still tend to structure narratives around political rebellions in public spaces. Yet 'agency' and public resistance are not synonymous and a search for agency should not be indexed necessarily by the presence of heroic acts of conscious self-determination.

Compellingly, on the issue of agency, historically humans involved with horses *recognised* their horses' efforts as resistance; i.e. there was contemporaneous identification of (animal) agency.[32] For equine insurgence deemed incorrigible there remained capital punishment, as in the case of rogue horses that were executed. On a very obvious level, animal agency might also be seen as surfacing, at one remove, in the very constraints that humans have had to apply to them. The instruments of control – reins, stables, whips, bits, chains, curbs – tell their own story about the *need* for control. Horses exhibited what James Scott called the 'weapons of the weak'.[33] Building on Thompson and Bourdieu, Scott argued that the displays of public domination by the elite differ from the camouflaged protest of the weak – for humans, millennial visions, gossip (or horse maiming)[34] and for horses, even less conspicuous acts. Acts of rebellion might be quotidian, like the horse's flattened ears and bared teeth as the girth of the saddle was done up. As Hobsbawm observed, after all, most subordinate classes are less focused on transforming society than in 'working the system … to their minimum disadvantage'.[35] Such everyday insurgency might be reflected in the refusal of the marooned horses to be recaptured and the fawn-coloured male called Generael who jumped ship, referred to in Chapter 2; the 'underbred and stubborn' horses in Chapter 3 who cantered riderless down the road after bucking off their masters; the horses scattered by helicopters who disrupted the funeral referred to in Chapter 4; or Malpert's 'kicking and lashing' in displeasure at a stranger's attempt to ride him in Chapter 5. Even the restrictive practice of knee haltering could not always curb Cape horses, who often still cantered away 'nimbly' on 'three legs'.[36] Such rebellions are found in the throwaway and incidental, as in the half-humorous story jotted down by Lady Anne Barnard, a late eighteenth-century observer of the Cape milieu and a self-confessed 'coward of Horses standing at their own discretion without a governor', who nearly suffered the 'ugly accident of being killd [sic] after her carriage horses bolted and left her with injuries that needed two days in bed for her to recover from.[37] The illustration below from the South African War elegantly depicts an almost unobserved rebellion: the British officer's horse in the foreground displays an obediently lowered head and a body controlled in the approved manner. In the background, however, a horse reacts in his own way, defying his rider's attempts to rein him in.

These small, private protests can be overlooked easily by historians. Like other powerless groups historically, horses were exploited, they laboured, they produced, they followed human orders and they were a force in social change.[38] In the final analysis, it is difficult to refute their agency.

THE CAPE MOUNTED RIFLES.

An almost unobserved rebellion. Cape Mounted Rifles.
Source: From the author's collection

Horsepower

To move to another kind of agency, historically the reasons for successful conquest and colonisation have been honed down to three advantages: superior weaponry, inadvertently imported diseases and material technology (animal power, in this case) – 'guns, germs and steel', to use Diamond's phrase – brought in by settlers and their stock.[39] On the various frontiers, new technologies opened up fresh routes to the accumulation of wealth and the acquisition of power. As Storey has shown in southern Africa, environment, technology and politics shaped and co-created each other. What made it different in this case was that the technology in question was sentient.[40]

Ownership of the means of production by the powerful was foreshadowed by ownership of the means of destruction.[41] Simply put: horses were mobile, breathing armaments. Indeed, as the *Union of South Africa Yearbook* baldly phrased it in several editions: the horse 'played an important part in establishing the supremacy of the white race'.[42]

Yet, horses did not stay in solely elite hands and neither can their effects be understood in declensionist terms alone. Certainly, horses were agents for marking and defending social borders, as Chapters 2 and 3 have shown, but also for shifting them, as Chapters 4 and 7 demonstrate. Neither did horses remain under white control. Race, class, gender and geography played significant roles in horse ownership and use over time. The disparities of power between these categories were (and remain) fundamental to the ways people relate not only to each other, but to the environment, including, of course, to particular animals. Of course, the agro-pastoralism that preceded colonial capitalism was not a prelapsarian state and should not be romanticised: unequal power relations and environmental injustice existed then too. With colonial incursion, racial classification and the new classes it created further limited the ways blacks interacted with the environment and animals, as Chapters 3, 4 and 6 have shown. Although race was not the only salient characteristic of that power – gender, class, ethnicity and geography all played a role.

The power achieved through cooperation across species was more complex than that of germs or guns. It was made up of three parts: it was partly the power over the horse; and chiefly the power over other humans that having a horse gave to its owner. But there was a third dimension to consider: the agency of horses themselves in acknowledging and understanding power that made human power (over them and therefore over other humans) possible in the first place.

Horses were able to be used in human power plays because the horses themselves understood power only too well. For example, horses thrown together in a camp for the first time will quickly sort out a new hierarchy, with demonstrations of dominance, both symbolic (like teeth baring and squealing) and physical (like kicking and biting). One of the key reasons why horses could be domesticated and successfully deployed within human societies was because, in their wild state, they had herd hierarchies that translated to human direction. Their own suite of behaviours thus made them (and a very few other animals) capable of being domesticated. As discussed in Chapter 1, they accepted human direction because they understood the idea of a chain of command. The emphasis horses put on hierarchy made them valuable: horse and human were able to function as co-workers, with the driver or rider acting as the proxy dominant horse.

Equally, horses form strong individual bonds, grazing together, grooming each other and standing head to tail for hours to swat the flies off one another. Grooming by humans, necessary to remove dirt and parasites, replicated herd behaviour and encouraged the horse to understand himself as part of a horse–human herd of two. The horse's ability to form individual bonds with other horses and the transferability of this trait to humans were significant. Horses put their trust in herd leaders so, for example, in the cacophony of war a scared horse would listen to his rider.

Horse sense and human senses

The past is mysteriously silent. Historians have long neglected noise, mainly because of its ephemerality and lack of an archive. The story of sound in human history includes both how aural landscapes change over time and how humans relate differently over time to sounds. Noise is sound with emotions attached to it. Thus, not only sound, but noise is historically contingent, varying over time.[43] Aural landscapes – or soundscapes – are created by configurations of physical ecology (in South Africa, east coast dune forests replete with reflective surfaces, for example, resonate differently from the Karoo or the Highveld). Certainly, even without changes to the vegetation, the rural and urban soundscapes of southern Africa are significantly different because of horses and were characterised by the sounds of hammer on anvil; the jingle of bits; the creak of leather saddlery; the crack of whips; the whinny of horses; and, as a contemporary observed, 'the muffled beat of hoofs, the dull champ on bridles, the ring of a stirrup'.[44] Travellers' nights, sleeping around the fire, were disturbed not only by snoring men, but also snorting horses.[45] Perhaps above all, the absence of the noise of that by which they were replaced – the machine – made the horse era world a different place from either the pre-colonial period or the present. Sometimes the sounds would have been grisly, but familiar at particular periods, e.g. as a combatant reminisced about a particularly vivid visceral memory of 1900: 'the unmistakable thud which a heavy bullet makes on horseflesh'.[46]

Horses changed human history not only on the macro level discussed in the other chapters, but in the small, intimate arena of the sensory and visceral, and, for some, on the personal level of belief. In the shadow of the big stories about horses – conquest and colonisation – exist small slices of personal, intimate history. These are the secret histories of how contact with horses changed the way in which humans experienced the world physically and changed how some thought about the world and their own place in it. The sensory fabric of human life in southern Africa has been shaped by the coexistence of humans and horses since the mid-seventeenth century.[47]

Hearing (and smelling) horses

Human understanding of sound is historical and cultural, with the ability to interpret noise (and experience it as melodious or jarring) changing over time. As Coates points out, noise is to sound as stench is to smell – something dissonant and unwanted. It is tempting to assume that noise is noisier now. However, in much of the urbanised West this simple linear model of noise pollution growing worse over time is flawed, because while the ascendancy of the engine has meant a noisier world, it is worth remembering that opposition to horses in urban centres (and support for the horseless vehicles) was the perceived need for the reduction of racket.[48]

In South Africa, as horses were replaced by machines in the twentieth century, discussed in Chapter 6, and where horses were increasingly kept out of towns in the mid-century, it was for reasons of economy, disease and waste rather than noise. Southern Africa saw the rise of 'imperialistic spread of more and larger sounds' in urban settings as horses replaced feet, carts replaced horses and cars replaced carts.

As recently as 1900 it would not be unusual for a human in some groups – like some men within the so-called Cape 'Malay' Muslim community, and a majority of Boer and Basotho men in southern Africa (as Chapters 2, 3 and 4 have shown) – to be able to decipher the equine lexicon.[49] Many humans would have spoken a rudimentary horse–human patois. A local equine vernacular was in evidence by at least the nineteenth century and probably much earlier, e.g. 'the chirp, psp, used in the United States to urge horses forward, is used to stop them in South Africa'.[50] While some domesticated animals, like dogs, for example, could be taught highly idiosyncratic signals from their human owners, horses could not. This was because horses typically were used by different riders or drivers concurrently and often had more than one owner in their lifetime. A horse that could not comprehend the signals was of little value. Thus, humans had to teach horses common signals. Equally, humans had to learn horse signals. They would have been able to understand that squeals and grunts indicated excitement; snorts signified interest or possible danger; a soft whicker was meant to reassure a foal or express anticipation of food; and a whinny meant the horse was all alone. Some (mostly male) humans were particularly familiar with the subtle nuances of the idiom – those engaged in the horse industry itself, like grooms, stable boys and jockeys; those who used horses as part of their jobs, like itinerant *smouse* (peddlers); transport riders; or communities that imposed horsemanship as a condition of manhood, like Boers in the eighteenth and Basotho men in the mid-nineteenth century. They were able to understand the non-verbal vernacular, e.g. the v-shaped tightening of the muscles behind the nostrils revealing tension or the curled lips conveying a stallion's interest in a mare in heat. The non-verbal language included a horse swishing a tail, or shaking a head to indicate irritation, or moving its ears to convey its moods.[51] Such humans were able to interpret the flared nostrils of an excited or frightened horse, or the thunderous farting of a startled – or triumphant – horse. The horse in a stable or kraal with an *afdakkie* (small lean-to) would have generated a cosy, familiar flatulence. Our history tends to come deodorised, as Roy Porter has pointed out.[52] But a history of the sensory reminds one that the smell generated by horses was an everyday part of the life of a significant proportion of people.[53]

Unconstricted spaces were also affected. The sensory experience that was altered with the introduction of the horse age in South Africa included the human experience of speed and the meaning of distance. This was, in fact, one of the reasons they were imported. Chapter 2 explored in depth the reasons for horse importation from 1652 onwards, but a central motive was to utilise their capacity for short bursts of speed to intimidate local communities. The ability to travel at less intense but more sustained speeds proved useful too. A horse could cover six miles an hour or well over 30 miles a day if not too heavily loaded.[54] For example, on the eastern frontier, for the Xhosa campaigns, the British army, for example, bought Hantam ponies that were expected to be able to do 230 miles in four days, if pushed to their extreme limit. With the physical elements of increased speed (and, concomitantly, decreased relative distance), human geography itself changed. Distances between places started to be understood by those with access to horses in the number of days' travel on horseback.

Thus, horse riders or drivers or passengers in horse-drawn conveyances could experience the world in fresh terms of speed and distance. Yet they were undeniably circumscribed by the horses' own vulnerabilities. Just as human sensory experience of the southern African world changed with the arrival of horses, it changed with their passing from centrality. In a world without horses, humans no longer heard or made certain sounds. Human ears no longer heard the heartbeat thud of hooves on ground. Conversely, the very sounds humans make changed with the transition to mechanisation. Humans still make certain sounds, but in a horseless world they have forgotten the reason why they do it: the traditional tuneless whistle through their teeth as they clean their cars was once necessary during grooming to keep out the dust that arose as they brushed the horse down.

This chapter has explored some subaltern histories in the shade of the big story of horses as instruments of conquest. The acquisition of horses also introduced individual people and small groups to new experiences of the world in the intimate, personal realms. Humans were lent speed and a fresh sense of distance by riding or driving horses. In borrowing the power of horses, humans also fell victim to their vulnerabilities, particularly to disease, which imposed a suite of opportunities and limitations on human experience. Moreover, as Chapter 3 discussed, some humans could acquire equine power: physically, through riding or driving them and mentally, through connecting with them spiritually. Through rituals and trances, AmaTola shamans could even become horses.

Environmental agency

Thus, the history of the relationship between the two species is made up not only of the grand narrative of human development buttressed by the labour of horses, but also by small stories and curious connections.[55] Perhaps the epitome of the grand narrative has been the act of domestication itself, popularly understood as the epitome of human agency over a passive, agentless cipher, as noted in Chapter 1. Generally, 'domestication' has been seen anthropogenically as a process whereby succeeding generations of submissive, tamed animals gradually became absorbed into human societies, were increasingly exploited and eventually lost all contact with their wild ancestral species.[56] However, an argument could be made that some (albeit perhaps limited) agency was exercised on the part of the animal, that the process may have begun as a symbiosis, in which certain species of animals 'chose' to become associated with human societies as a survival strategy at the end of the Ice Age.[57] They challenged the popular Manichean understanding of domestication as either a heroic act of human 'triumph over nature' or a tragic act of human 'domination and debasement of nature'.[58] At the end of the Pleistocene era, rapid climatic changes that disrupted habitats and food supplies favoured animals that were the animal equivalent of 'weeds' – opportunistic, adaptive generalists. Crudely put, in the ensuing extinction spasm, evolution favoured some animals with juvenile traits that made them appealing to *Homo sapiens*. The rapidly changing environment created a natural selective pressure that favoured neoteny (the retention of juvenile traits into adulthood). Humans would have selected animals with paedomorphic or neotenic variations because they were more tractable. Those animals who became adult enough to breed, but remained neotenous enough to cower and play and to tolerate human beings and other strange species, contrived to carve a niche for themselves. Humans helped these forever-young animals succeed by feeding, sheltering and even breeding them. Thus, so-called 'artificial' selection by humans was arguably 'natural', or at least exhibited some animal agency.[59]

Horse domestication took a comparatively lengthy period to develop and probably depended on chance genetic changes that would have predisposed some horses to breed in captivity. Horse domestication could thus, in a sense, have been initiated (at least genotypically) by the horses *themselves*.[60] The most credible hypothesis is that both the human and equine parts of the equation would have evolved together in a mutually dependent relationship. Arguably, the equine species' nomadism could have lured human societies into a nomadic lifestyle – perhaps the ultimate evidence of agency.

Environmental historians have challenged common assumptions about human agency in other ways too.[61] One way to breach the divide between evolution and history is to think about an organism by placing it firmly in its environment rather than seeing it as a self-contained individual confronting an external world.[62] So another possible way to tell the story is to couch it in terms of the natural history of an invasive species. An ecological reading of history could couch the horse's history as the invasion of a non-native species and the impact of this alien, allied in an influential symbiotic relationship to another invader, on local biotic communities.[63] From the fifteenth to the twentieth centuries, European nations dominated the earth and, as a result, Europeans and their organisms made an appearance nearly everywhere.[64] Some aliens arrived by predictable accident (like rats jumping ship and emigrating secretly to the mainland), some by slightly less predictable accident or small errors of judgement (like the rabbits on Robben Island) and some by a frankly weird twist of fate.[65]

Others arrived by design. The horses introduced to the Cape from the mid-seventeenth century (and then on the cusp of the twentieth century), as Chapters 2 and 5 explained, were deliberately brought in as part of a bigger plan for an invading sub-set of *Homo sapiens* trying to expand their home ranges. Strictly speaking, there had been an earlier version – the giant prehistoric Cape horse or zebra (*Equus capensis*) discovered by Broom that roamed the *fynbos* (sclerophyllous heath) – wiped out by climate change or by early human predation 12,000–10,000 BP.[66] But this creature's younger cousin, a non-native species, arrived as late as 350 BP. Introduction of a non-native species – like this youthful equine cousin – occurred when 'propagules' arrived in a new area outside their previous geographic range and established a viable population. Strictly speaking, 'colonisation' by a species occurs when a 'founding population' is able to reproduce and 'increase sufficiently to become self-perpetuating'.[67] In southern Africa, this has not happened for horses, outside of the few isolated examples already discussed (and even those had human assistance in droughts). A species is said to be 'naturalised' in its new environment when it successfully establishes a new self-perpetuating population that is incorporated into the resident ecosystem. Without the mutualism of another species (*Homo sapiens*), the horse could not be said to be naturalised. Indeed, this is a narrative of not one (mid-eighteenth century) equine invasion, but rather three (mid-eighteenth century; mid-nineteenth century and early twentieth century; and, finally, a smaller American invasion in the mid-twentieth century), as the earlier chapters argued.

Yet, even so, as the preceding chapters have shown, horses were undeniably both vectors and recipients of environmental forces, which is another way of interpreting 'agency'. As vectors, horses precipitated environmental change: there even appear to be signs of active resource management among some horses.[68]

There was certainly evidence of indirect impact, particularly at specific flashpoints. For example, immediately after the Anglo-Boer War/South African War, new diseases were introduced and epidemics raged, as explored in Chapter 5. The introduction of the horse thus altered the environment, changing the flora of the new territory. Foreign weeds were noticed in the remount and repatriation camps. The one million tons of fodder – chiefly hay and oats – imported to support the horses needed by the imperial troops inadvertently imported a number of fellow travellers. The seeds of foreign plants survived the digestive process and were excreted in the horses' faeces.[69] The nomenclature of the weeds of war reflected their origin: 'langkakiebos', 'kleinkakiebos' and 'kakiedubbeltjie', 'kakieduwweltjie'[70] – with the 'kakie' referring to the British soldiers. 'Nassella-polgras' arrived from hay imported from Argentina, polluting grass and lowering the carrying capacity of pasturage. Little sweet-toothed Argentine 'sugar ants' (*Linepithema humile*) arrived with the horse fodder and were distributed with fodder for the army's horses. These small, fast, competitive ants, who milk other insects for 'honeydew', spread into the interior and are now themselves marching on Pretoria.

Of course, horses wrought other kinds of ecological change. Horse tracks can contribute to erosion – unsurprisingly, as the impact force of a galloping hoof is 8.89 kN – six times greater than that of the human foot.[71] Along very localised paths in the veld, galloping changed indigenous flora to more mesic composition – literally, squashing – and thereby reducing the number of invertebrate fauna in the soil.[72] Compared to other ungulates, horses possess a unique evolutionary history that makes them disturb the environment in a very different way. As noted in Chapter 2, distinct from ruminants, horses are cecal digesters and, together with their large body size, this kind of digestion adds extra time-energy constraints.[73] This means that the free-roaming horse is one of the least discriminating grazers, leaving fewer plant species unscathed. Moreover, this kind of diet means that horses have to consume 20–65 per cent more than would a cow. Coupled to this, horses have elongated heads and supple lips, and, unlike cattle, possess upper front incisors. As a result, they can nibble plants more closely to the ground, setting back plant regrowth further.[74] In South Africa, horses were an ecological disaster waiting to happen as soon as their number reached a tipping point or their population became feral.

But this disaster never struck. While certainly harbouring the potential to wreak environmental havoc, the horses of South Africa never did – unlike the vast herds of the American West and Outback Australia, and even on a very minor scale, Namibia.[75] There was much soil erosion in southern African landscapes, but little of it was attributable directly to horses.[76] This was essentially since they did not become feral because of ecosystem constraints, particularly local diseases, and the consequent high (human) value placed on the horse. Any 'feral' population or escapees were appropriated by humans for use or as trade goods. Basically, a living horse was an owned horse and horses did not roam in large herds. Therefore, as a species, they never inflicted substantial environmental damage: there was never a 'plague of horses'.[77] Where they wrought destruction it was through the actions of their riders and the power lent by horse ownership.

Plundering and pondering power

This power was coveted. So a new crime came into being: horse theft. For example, James Backhouse, a travelling Quaker, noted that by the mid-nineteenth century horse stealing had become a serious social crime. Such crime was not restricted ethnically and occurred between different groups and crossed national borders.[78] It even produced its own celebrities (like Scotty Smith, who won renown as the 'Robin Hood of horse thieves').[79] The nature of crime changed too: speed could now be an element of a quick getaway. Horses whose riders were victims of robbery were sometimes killed pre-emptively to prevent hot pursuit. In 1807, for example, a band of Bushmen stole 300 head of sheep belonging to a Hantam farmer, murdering the shepherd (a slave) and killing nine horses in order to stall the chase.[80]

This power also affected human ways of imagining, as illustrated by the changing cosmology of the AmaTola Bushmen in Chapter 3 and expressed in changing metaphors of dominance. Horse terminology became integral to metaphors of power, for example, in Basutoland by the late nineteenth century in a place where a mere generation previously horses had been unknown. As discussed in Chapter 4, a son of Moshoeshoe likened the people to a horse that:

> must first be trained before it can obey; [t]here are countries where horses and cattle may still be caught in a wild state, this is a country where wild men are still to be caught. You are the trainer who must catch and tame us.[81]

The state's relationship to the people was couched in equestrian terms, as was the role of masculine identity for specific ethnic groups, discussed in Chapter 6, as in De Wet's famous dictum: 'A Boer without a horse is only half a man.' Thinking 'with' horses, as Levi-Strauss had it, was far more widespread in southern Africa – and simpler – than thinking 'like' them.

The view from the saddle

This brings one to the final way of approaching writing the history of the horse: from the perspective of the horses themselves. Just as Gutman suggested of Genovese's *World the Slaves Made* (he compared it to an imagined history of steelworkers that began with a 150-page biography of Andrew Carnegie),[82] 'the world the horses made' is still too much a history of their riders. It is still too much the 'world the horses were *made* to make' (by humans) rather than 'the world they made'. Equally, it is perhaps also too much *by* their riders. Simply studying the unrepresented is not the same as seeing through their eyes; social history is not a synonym for 'bottom-up history'.[83] The view from 'below' is not presented; rather, it is the view from 'above' – literally, from those sitting on its back. Thus, one gets a view of (and largely 'from') the elite, not 'of' or 'from' powerless people, nor of the animals themselves.

After all, most individuals in the history of southern Africa neither owned horses nor had access to their use. Asymmetric access to the technologies of power, of which horses were one, buttressed elites. Horsemen had to have some power to even possess horses and once they did, they could seize more power and deploy it more effectively by using horses in a military capacity or in utilising trade networks more lucratively.

Thus, unless one accepts the notion that animals, or at least domestic animals, are themselves marginalised or oppressed groups, using horses as a subject precludes much that is valued by social historians, which is the ability to tell the story of the marginalised and down-trodden. If one really wanted to tell a 'bottom-up' social history story of the (human) marginalised, donkeys would be a better vehicle than horses. In the twentieth century, horse power became increasingly obsolete in commercial agriculture, although it remained significant in small-scale agriculture (albeit entirely secondary to the ox and, in some places, the donkey).[84] Even though in South African urban areas workhorses are no longer widespread, horses are still used for neighbourhood deliveries and collections and are a key form of transport in Lesotho. Donkeys are low maintenance and low cost, are more resistant to disease, and are able to survive even on drought-shrivelled grasses. Similarly, donkeys were particularly used by women, since horses were the instruments only of the men in some societies, like in gerontocratic Basutoland (which began as an innovative borrowing by a vulnerable group, but helped to improve military capacity, which bolstered the group's power).[85] As Epprecht and others have commented, on account of the donkeys' perceived destructive grazing habits, they were the focus of a punitive campaign by the government in the 1920s and 1930s in Basutoland. The chiefs (at least ostensibly) supported the Basotho women against the state on this issue, preserving donkeys, which became a symbol of this gendered resistance.[86]

In focusing on a different vulnerable group, Nancy Jacobs has carried out an extraordinary class-based analysis of 'the Great Donkey Massacre' of the 1980s in the homeland of Bophuthatswana. From the 1940s the South African Native Affairs Department, followed by the puppet regime in Bophutatswana, imposed authoritarian conservationist regulations. Only the rich could afford to accumulate cattle for status or commercial production or keep horses, but the poor were able to afford and maintain donkeys. Anti-donkey propensities transcended race and remained entrenched in class: affluent cattle ranchers and officials attacked the widespread agro-pastoralism of commoners, blaming their donkeys for precipitating erosion by first greedily devouring and then trampling the veld. Periodic small-scale donkey culls exploded during a severe drought into the arbitrary and savage slaughter of thousands in the so-called Donkey Massacre of 1983 – a silent massacre, hidden from the official archival record.[87] Soldiers from inside their armoured vehicles shot and killed donkeys. Some people tried to flee with the donkeys or even hide them in their houses: bloodied carcasses piled up, traumatising residents. As a distraught woman mourned in the aftermath of the massacre, '[i]t was like they were people'.[88] Jacobs speculates that the killing was politically driven, designed to remind the commoners of the futility of opposition. It was in effect a demonstration of the power of the state over poor and disenfranchised people. Afterwards, the carnage became politicised – a cause against the Bophuthatswana puppet government and apartheid. A protest song was later written about the slain donkeys haunting the puppet leader and urging listeners to join *Umkhonto we Sizwe*, the armed wing of the African National Congress.[89]

One could also use a focus on donkeys to tell the story of people perhaps even more liminal than the Thornveld agro-pastoralist – the itinerant sheep-shearing '*karretjie mense*' (donkey-cart people) of the arid Karoo, who represent a rural under-class, 'the poorest of the poor', tracing descent from Khoikhoi and /Xam-speaking San ancestors. Their nomadic '*karretjie*' lifestyle emerged only in the modern era in response to the wool industry's changing needs. With fencing, the farmers' needs for full-time shepherds lessened and labour was required really only in the shearing season, so a floating excess labour force arose. At the end of the nineteenth century the shearers moved on foot, but within a few decades in the early twentieth century they adopted the donkey cart, constructed from defunct horse carriages and, later, car parts.[90] Numbering an estimated 5,000 by 1994, the '*karretjie mense*' received scant poverty relief measures with the coming of democracy; they were technically classified as coloured under apartheid, although as one woman observed: 'We are too poor to be brown. We are the yellow people.'[91]

Poor whites, an indigent group that excited much more public and state attention than the '*karretjie mense*', were linked to donkeys too. As ownership of the beasts was racialised, there was concern from middle-class reformers and politicians about the reliance of indigent whites on donkey transport. For example, in the first decades of the twentieth century in the Cape the state provided donkey transport for impoverished white school children who lived more than three miles from a school. The Carnegie Commission into the Poor White Problem, however, raised a widespread concern: 'Donkeys are most generally used for this purpose, and many teachers are of the opinion that the intimate association for many hours each day with this type of animal has an adverse influence on the child!'[92]

From the horse's mouth

Thus, as a lens solely into the history of marginalised humans in southern Africa, horses are not as good a choice as donkeys. However, horses were (and still are) used on small-scale farms and in urban settings, like itinerant coal merchants and cart drivers of the Cape Flats and some urban settlements like Soweto. They were and remain in widespread use in the Lesotho Highlands. Yet even in those cases, horse owners (almost all men) represented an upper strata among the poor. If, however, one were to try to embrace the teachings of social history to write through the perspective of 'the silenced' in a very different way, one would have to offer an equine history of the world 'from the horse's mouth'. Aldo Leopold famously urged us to 'think like a mountain', but, as mentioned above, even thinking like another mammalian species has proved challenging to historians.[93]

Horses and humans would write different histories. Both cultural and biological differences between the species would shape very different kinds of stories about their pasts. There are some similarities. Like some southern African human communities, feral equid societies are large and polygamous, and, like many humans, individual horses live in long-term, non-territorial reproductive associations.[94] Just as in most human societies, incest is avoided. In the herd, everyday decisions about where to eat are made by an older mare. Horses, like humans, have few physical defence mechanisms: both use flight, but humans use tools and both groups' survival strategies centre on the formation of strong social bonds. Social isolation is always highly correlated with extreme stress. Unlike humans, however, horses are not obsessed with territory. Horses do not – in Scott's term – 'see like a state'. Moreover, with different obsessions, histories and ecological niches, horses and humans fear different enemies. For example, horses and humans would tell very different stories about the South African War. As a Boer combatant observed, horses that had coolly withstood enemy rifle fire could be stampeded simply by a 'night-roving porcupine'.[95] The nature of horses 'cultures' varied geographically, depending on acquired knowledge of local conditions, e.g. in the wide-open veld of the Free State 'if a horse [saw] a tree it shie[d] at it'.[96]

The second difference in the history narrated by horses would be the chronological and temporal structuring. The human horological obsession provides no template for how horses structure time. Furthermore, horses' nasal acuity allows them a broader temporal understanding than humans possess; their 'nasal vision' allows them to see not only through space, but also time. Thus, thirdly, our worlds look and feel different and so, concomitantly, would our historiographies. Our biological constraints show us a very different world: horses' hearing is far more sensitive than that of humans. A horse's own sense of smell is acute – like hearing, it has evolved as a vital part of its defence system. There is ongoing production and receiving of pheromone signals (smell messages produced by skin glands). Horses have an olfactory experience different from that of humans; they can smell emotions and sexuality, allies, enemies, and places. Members of a group are identified by a corporate odour.

Particular smells – like those of fire and blood – resonate sharply and rapidly, generating understandable alarm in a predator-fearing herbivore species that evolved while roaming highly combustible grasslands.

Historians and other humans tend to dwell in the realm of the visual. Equine sight is very different to that of humans. Their eyes are large in comparison to other mammals, suggesting a reliance on that sense, with the size giving them good night vision. Unlike humans, horses focus by raising and lowering the head rather than altering the shape of the lens. Their eyes are on the side of the head with monocular vision so they can see separate objects with each eye at the same time, permitting wide lateral vision and curtailing only immediate frontal vision. This allows a grazing horse almost panoptic vision, even at night, essential for wary herbivores. Seeing like a horse is well nigh impossible for a human, but many have tried to think like a horse, which was essential in the processes of domesticating and taming them.

An experiment in blurring the genres of *history* and *natural history* with an exploratory 'horsetory' of the world is possible. This hippomorphic story would be suffused in the horses' physical pleasure, memory, intense fear and cyclical seasonality, and strongest traits (as grass-eating prey herbivores with a fatal tendency towards over-eating and over-heating). It might be a story of grass, foals, blood, sex, pain, fear and food – perhaps mainly food. It is an interesting and helpful exercise to write history through the eyes of the horse, forcing the human historian to adopt a new and sympathetically imaginative perspective. But it remains a Rorschach test, revealing more about the historian (and her/his own epoch) than about horses. Similarly, social historians have received analogous critique for 'ventriloquising' their subjects, silencing the authentic voice 'from below' and allowing only the narrative voice of the historian to be heard.[97] Furthermore, how useful would a history of horses without humans be? As Thompson observed: 'We cannot have love without lovers, nor deference without squires and labourers.'[98]

Yet historically, humans have put more effort into trying to understand the world from the horse's point of view than that of any other animal. It was necessary for humans to think like a horse – to a certain extent – in domesticating, training and riding them – dangerous and intimate processes that historically have compelled humans to see the world through horses' eyes far more than, say, the eyes of a cat or a snake. There have been South African horse trainers who specialised and made it their sole profession, particularly

In training a horse in western Pondoland in the twentieth century, a small boy, known as the ' inkawu', or 'monkey', was the first to sit on the horse's back.
Source: Campbell Collections, University of KwaZulu-Natal, C52-281

in the twentieth century, as discussed in Chapter 7. But in southern Africa, the bulk of the population has 'trained' (or 'tamed' or 'broken in' or 'brought on') its own horses over time by merely soliciting advice from those who are experienced.

At first this advice was simply given over the fence post or transmitted from homestead to homestead, and later, particularly in the twentieth century, in the popular agricultural press.[99] A vernacular lore, coupled to a more international equine body of knowledge, was arising, fuelled by the mixing of horse cultures precipitated by the war. As discussed in Chapter 5, there is evidence of contemporaneous acceptance of the notion of equine agency among combatants in the South African War. This was in accordance with the contemporary climate, with Darwin arguing for a real continuity between the emotional lives

218

of humans and those of animals, with differences being of degree rather than kind.[100]

Like other vulnerable groups, horses were exploited. They laboured, they produced, they followed human orders, they were a force in social change. Perhaps more than any other animals (except dogs), horses were treated as human. Compellingly, on the issue of agency, historically, humans involved with horses *recognised* their horses' efforts as resistance, i.e. there was contemporaneous identification of (animal) agency.[101] For insurgence deemed incorrigible there remained capital punishment, as in the case of the executed rogue horse referred to in Chapter 2. Horses also displayed the 'weapons of the weak'.[102] They disobeyed commands; destroyed equipment; escaped; and resisted by, literally, 'bucking the system' or 'kicking over the traces' (albeit very rarely successfully). Horses were a great cause of untimely (human) death. Not only were they frequently (albeit passively) embroiled in metaphorical downfalls, as discussed in Chapter 3 – like that of Somerset and Branford[103] – but they were commonly the active and direct cause of physical downfalls. In the end, it is difficult to deny their agency.

Conclusion

This chapter has explored alternative ways to write history that tries to engage with the lives of animals. The social history of the horse–human relationship reveals how its experiences alter in time and space, as does (concomitantly) the social experience of that relationship. This kind of history could run the gamut between models of the labile and contingent versus the innate, or the social versus the biological. Nature and nurture are inescapably important – the two are locked together and both need to be understood in writing social history. Looking at the real breathing animal points the historian back to the material, while not ignoring the symbolic resonance of the horse. Of course, it is not a fundamental rewriting of southern Africa's past, but it changes, however slightly, how historians might write the social history of the South African War, for example. There are real, undeniable differences in the way humans and non-human animals inhabit the world. But perhaps the anthropocentric notion of agency, like its inverse environmental determinism, is too simple to describe what takes place. Hard technological determinists might see a kind of 'agency' even in iron horses and spinning mules, let alone in living, breathing horses and mules.[104] A different lens perceives the origin of agency in human action, with the horse a vector subject to human actions and desires, and also to many factors beyond human control. In that sense, this book has discussed the world horses were '*made* to make' (by humans) and, to a small but real extent, *made* themselves. It was a very different world from the one they first entered, in which the only equids were quaggas and zebras.

To conclude by returning to one of the herds that escaped human society: the feral horses of the Namib attract thousands of tourists each year and when they faced starvation during droughts in the 1990s, public relief efforts were overwhelming. Why is it that these runaway horses touch a chord in some human societies? They have something that not only fascinates particular humans, but for which we actually envy them: evidence of agency. These horses seemed to have gained the freedom to live according to their own rules and their own social order. The chapters that preceded this have surveyed the horse and its connection to social power, from its pre-history in a horseless pre-colonial state where the equids were wild, to the history of the horse in the two and a half centuries of horse-powered state, to a post-history of the horse as a memory – an icon of nostalgia and identity, discussed in Chapter 7. Something about the horses triggers a human reaction in the modern urbanising world. Wildness is not a trait that horses have usually had in southern Africa. Chapter 2 explored the difference between the identity attached to susceptible equine imports of southern Africa compared to that attached to the feral herds of the Americas. In the latter, the horses were themselves a frontier to be conquered, but in southern Africa they were a tool in the conquest of the frontier and remained vulnerable. So some humans latch onto the very tiny populations of 'feral horses' in their little pockets of wilderness in a way that is disproportionate to their number, everyday lived reality and history. This is because such animals are not only biological creatures, nor solely technologies of change, but also totems to which humans can attach their dreams and desires, in ways the previous chapter has explored. With the horses of Bot River, the Namibian Desert, the Kaapsehoop and the Sandveld of Gansbaai, it is a yearning not for the wilderness, but for wildness – and perhaps for agency.

✳

Endnotes

Preface

1   Indeed, it is a work in progress on its own, with specific focus on African horse
     racing.
2   R. Law, *The Horse in West Africa* (Oxford: Oxford University Press, 1980), p. vii.
3   The lowest geographical point in Lesotho is higher than that of any other state.
4   James Boswell, *The Life of Samuel Johnson LL.D*, ed. George Birkbeck Hill, vol. I
     (London: 1897, repr. Echo Library, 2006), p. 424.
5   Derek Freeman, *The Fateful Hoaxing of Margaret Mead: A Historical Analysis of
     Her Samoan Research* (Boulder: Westview Press, 1999).
6   J. Edward Chamberlin, *Horse: How the Horse Has Shaped Civilizations* (New
     York: Blue Bridge, 2006), p. 30.
7   The evidence supporting the divisive nature of the exchange vastly outweighs
     the cohesive view. For example there follows a consequently rare episode from
     1946, at the end of a bibulous discussion of the equine: 'a Natal man said he
     had no idea Free State men could be so companionable and such enthusiastic
     horsemen'; South African National Archives Repository (hereafter SAB): LON,
     221, A120/57, 'Short course in horse husbandry', Glen College, principal's letter,
     5 November 1946.
8   'Banjo' Paterson was a journalist, poet, soldier and renowned horseman. During
     the South African War, he worked as a war correspondent. Further discussed in
     Chapter 5.
9   B. Bozzoli, *Women of Phokeng: Consciousness, Life Strategy and Migrancy in
     South Africa, 1900–1983* (Portsmouth: Heinemann, 1991).
10   As Terry Jones said of the *Life of Brian*.
11   See Daniel Roche, '*Montaigne cavalier: Un témoin de la culture équestre dans la
     France du XVIe siècle*', in Bernard Barbiche & Yves-Marie Bercé, eds, *Études sur
     l'ancienne France offertes en hommage à Michel Antoine* (Paris: École des Chartes,

2003). Actually, in the works of Montaigne, there are the many references to the equestrian culture of a nobleman. He always maintained that he wanted to die while on horseback. (Or possibly, more correctly, he meant immediately afterwards.) A fall from his horse, in fact, led him to conquer his fear of death. I find this somewhat surprising, as it has each time only served to reinforce mine.

12   Tellingly, Herodotus, our first professional practising in the fifth century BCE, was dubbed the 'father of history' and also the 'father of lies'. Interestingly, this earliest historian wrote about horses too – the white savage horses of Scythia; Herodotus, *The Histories*, bk IV (London: Penguin, 2003), p. 257.

13   Andrew Barton 'Banjo' Paterson, *Happy Dispatches* ([1934], Sydney: University of Sydney, 1998).

Chapter 1

1   *Debates of the House of Assembly*, 1 (Pretoria: State Printer, 17 May 1916).

2   Some sections of this chapter appeared as Sandra Swart, ' "But where's the Bloody Horse?": Textuality and corporeality in the "animal turn" ', *Journal of Literary Studies*, 23, (3), June 2007.

3   Alfred Crosby, *Ecological Imperialism: The Biological Expansion of Europe, 900–1900* (Cambridge: Cambridge University Press, 2004), p. 194.

4   For an ovine comparison or the 'ungulate irruption', see Elinor Melville, *A Plague of Sheep: Environmental Consequences of the Conquest of Mexico* (Cambridge: Cambridge University Press, 1994).

5   Charles Phineas, 'Household pets and urban alienation', *Journal of Social History*, 7, 1973/74, pp. 338–43.

6   For some classic texts that set the current parameters of the field, see Donald Worster, *Nature's Economy: A History of Ecological Ideas* (Cambridge: Cambridge University Press, 1985); William Cronon, ed., *Uncommon Ground: Rethinking the Human Place in Nature* (New York: W.W. Norton, 1996a); and Donald Worster & Alfred W. Crosby, eds, *The Ends of the Earth: Perspectives on Modern Environmental History* (Cambridge: Cambridge University Press, 1988).

7   See, for example, conferences like Animals in History and Culture, Bath Spa University College, 2000; also Representing Animals, University of Wisconsin-Milwaukee, 2000.

8   Harriet Ritvo, 'Animal planet', *Environmental History*, 9(2), 2004, p. 204; see also Juliet Clutton-Brock, *A Natural History of Domesticated Mammals* (Cambridge: Cambridge University Press, 1989a); and Nicholas Russell, *Like Engend'ring Like: Heredity and Animal Breeding in Early Modern England* (London: Cambridge University Press, 1986).

9   See, for example, Nigel Rothfels, ed., *Representing Animals* (Bloomington: University of Indiana Press, 2003); and Chris Philo & Chris Wilbert, eds, *Animal*

Spaces, Beastly Places: New Geographies of Human–Animal Relations (London: Routledge, 2000).

10 J. Wolch & J. Emel, *Animal Geographies: Place, Politics, and Identity in the Nature–Culture Borderlands* (London & New York: Verso, 1998), p. xi. See also, on the state of the field, 'Ruminations', H-Animal discussion network, <http://www.h-net.org/~animal/>.

11 In 1959 Snow delivered the annual Rede Lecture, subsequently published as *The Two Cultures*, arguing that the failure to communicate between the sciences and humanities was a barrier to solving the modern world's ills.

12 See Neil Smith, 'The production of nature', in George Robertson et al., eds, *Future Natural Nature/Science/Culture* (London & New York: Routledge, 1996), pp. 35–54; and Wolch & Emel (1998, p. xii). Equally, many of those on the political left fear that the concern may in fact be premised on a return to pre-modern 'animistic' beliefs.

13 Nancy Jacobs, *Environment, Power, and Injustice: A South African History* (Cambridge: Cambridge University Press, 2003), p. 19.

14 Steve Baker, *Picturing the Beast: Animals, Identity, and Representation* (Chicago: University of Illinois Press, 2001), p. xvi.

15 Chamberlin (2006, p. 43).

16 Cited in Baker (2001, p. xi).

17 Erica Fudge, 'A left-handed blow: Writing the history of animals', in Nigel Rothfels, ed., *Representing Animals* (Bloomington: University of Indiana Press, 2003), p. 6.

18 John Berger, 'Why look at animals?', in *About Looking* (London: Writers & Readers, 1980), p. 2.

19 Baker (2001, p. xvi).

20 For fine examples on other themes, see William Cronon, 'The trouble with wilderness, or, getting back to the wrong nature', in William Cronon, ed., *Uncommon Ground* (New York: W.W. Norton, 1996b), pp. 69–90; Simon Schama, *Landscape and Memory* (New York: Alfred A. Knopf, 1995); and William Cronon, 'A place for stories: Nature, history, and narrative', *Journal of American History*, 78, 1992, pp. 1347–76.

21 Dr Samuel Johnson (1709–1784) once famously became infuriated at the suggestion that Bishop Berkeley's idealism could not be refuted. Johnson kicked a nearby stone and proclaimed, of Berkeley's theory, 'I refute it *thus!*'

22 Molly Mullin, 'Animals and anthropology', *Society and Animals*, 10(4), 2002, pp. 387–93.

23 Eric Hobsbawm, *The Age of Extremes, 1914–1991* (London: Michael Joseph, 1994), pp. 568–70; E.P. Thompson, *Customs in Common: Studies in Traditional Popular Culture* (New York: New Press, 1993), pp. 14–15.

24 Clifford Geertz, *The Interpretation of Cultures* (New York: Basic Books, 1973); Tim Ingold, 'The animal in the study of humanity', in Tim Ingold, ed., *What Is an*

Animal? (London: Routledge, 1988), pp. 84–99; Claude Levi-Strauss, *Totemism* (Boston: Beacon, 1963); Molly Mullin, 'Mirrors and windows: Sociocultural studies of human–animal relationships', *Annual Review of Anthropology*, 28, 1999, pp. 201–24.

25 See Alan Taylor, 'Unnatural inequalities: Social and environmental histories', *Environmental History*, 1(4), 1996, pp. 6–19.

26 Jacobs (2003, p. 16).

27 Roderick Nash, 'American environmental history: A new teaching frontier', *Pacific History Review*, 41, 1972, p. 363.

28 Changes in socio-political ideas are usually echoed in the themes explored by historians. Just as the field of labour history followed the rise of the labour movement and the sub-disciplines of women's history and African-American history followed the women's movement and the civil rights movement, animal-related causes have gained increasing support in the West; see Harriet Ritvo, 'History and Animal Studies', *Society & Animals*, 10(4), 2002, pp. 403–6.

29 Mullin (2002, pp. 207–8).

30 This section appeared in an earlier incarnation in Sandra Swart, Albert Grundlingh, Christopher Saunders and Howard Phillips, 'Environment, Heritage, Resistance and Health: Newer Historiographical Directions', in Robert Ross, Anne Mager and Bill Nasson (eds.), *The Cambridge History of South Africa, Vol. 2: From 1886 to the End of Apartheid* (Cambridge University Press, New York, 2011).

31 William Beinart, 'African history and environmental history', *African Affairs*, 99, 2000, pp. 269–302.

32 Phia Steyn & André Wessels, 'The roots of contemporary governmental and non-governmental environmental activities in South Africa, 1654–1972', *New Contree*, 45, 1999, pp. 77–80.

33 Lance van Sittert, 'Writing and teaching the history of the land and environment in Africa in the twenty-first century', report on conference session, *South African Historical Journal*, 50, 2004, pp. 223–24. For the best discussion of developments, see Beinart (2000); and W. Beinart & J. McGregor, 'Introduction', in W. Beinart & J. McGregor, eds, *Social History and African Environments* (Oxford, Athens & Cape Town: James Currey, Ohio University Press & David Philip, 2003).

34 B.H. Dicke, 'The tsetse-fly's influence on South African history', *South African Journal of Science*, 29, October 1932, pp. 792–96.

35 W. Beinart, P. Delius & S. Trapido, eds, *Putting a Plough to the Ground: Accumulation and Dispossession in Rural South Africa, 1850–1930* (Johannesburg: Ravan Press, 1986); Colin Bundy, *The Rise and Fall of the South African Peasantry* (London: Heinemann, 1979); Timothy Keegan, *Rural Transformations in Industrializing South Africa: The Southern Highveld to 1914* (Basingstoke: Macmillan, 1986a); Charles van Onselen, *The Seed Is Mine: The Life*

of Kas Maine, a South African Sharecropper 1894–1985 (New York: Hill & Wang, 1996).

36   Jacobs (2003); Swart (2007).

37   'Q and A', *Mail & Guardian*, 15–21 August 2003.

38   This is probably because of the already extant strong bedrock of work on agrarian history, as historical writing is often generated dialogically, in conversation with other historians who have gone before.

39   Greg Bankoff & Sandra Swart, *Breeds of Empire: The 'Invention' of the Horse in the Philippines and Southern Africa, 1500–1950* (Uppsala: Nordic Institute of Asian Studies, 2007); Peter Boomgaard, *Frontiers of Fear: Tigers and People in the Malay World, 1600–1950* (New Haven: Yale University Press, 2001); Richard Bulliet, *The Camel and the Wheel* (Cambridge: Harvard University Press, 1975).

40   D. Anderson & R. Grove, eds, *Conservation in Africa* (Cambridge: Cambridge University Press, 1989); Jonathan Adams & Thomas O. McShane, *The Myth of Wild Africa: Conservation without Illusions* (New York: W.W. Norton, 1992); E.J. Carruthers, 'The Pongola Game Reserve: An eco-political study', *Koedoe*, 28, 1985, pp. 1–16; E.J. Carruthers, 'Game protection in the Transvaal, 1846 to 1926', *Archives Year Book for South African History* (Pretoria: Government Printer, 1995); J. Carruthers, *The Kruger National Park: A Social and Political History* (Pietermaritzburg: University of Natal Press, 1995); E.J. Carruthers, 'Nationhood and national parks: Comparative examples from the post-imperial experience', in T. Griffiths & L. Robin, eds, *Ecology and Empire: Environmental History of Settler Societies* (Edinburgh: Keele University Press, 1997), pp. 125–38; A.E. Cubbin, 'An outline of game legislation in Natal, 1866–1912', *Journal of Natal and Zulu History*, 14, 1992, pp. 37–47; Stephen Ellis, 'Of elephants and men: Politics and nature conservation in South Africa', *Journal of Southern African Studies*, 20(1), 1994, pp. 53–69; John MacKenzie, *The Empire of Nature: Hunting, Conservation and British Imperialism* (Manchester: Manchester University Press, 1988).

41   Karen Brown, 'Political entomology: The insectile challenge to agricultural development in the Cape Colony 1895–1910', *Journal of Southern African Studies*, 29(2), 2003, pp. 529–49; K. Brown, 'Frontiers of disease: Human desire and environmental realities in the rearing of horses in nineteenth- and twentieth-century South Africa', *African Historical Review*, 40(1), 2008a, pp. 30–57; Karen Brown, 'From Ubombo to Mkhuzi: Disease, colonial science, and the control of nagana (livestock trypanosomiasis) in Zululand, South Africa, c.1894–1953', *Journal of the History of Medicine and Allied Sciences*, 63(3), 2008b, pp. 285–322; D. Gilfoyle, 'Veterinary immunology as colonial science: Method and quantification in the investigation of horsesickness in South Africa, c.1905–1945', *Journal of the History of Medicine and Allied Sciences*, 61, 2005, pp. 26–65; W. Beinart, 'Transhumance, animal disease and environment in the Cape, South Africa', *South African Historical Journal*, 58(1), 2007, pp. 17–41;

S.J.E. Vandenbergh, 'The story of a disease: A social history of African horsesickness, c.1850–1920', MA diss., University of Stellenbosch, 2009.

42   See, for example, William Beinart & E. Green Musselman, 'Scientific travellers, colonists, and Africans: Chains of knowledge and the Cape vernacular, 1770–1850', in William Beinart, ed., *The Rise of Conservation in South Africa: Settlers, Livestock, and the Environment 1770–1950* (Oxford: Oxford University Press, 2003); Malcolm Draper, 'Zen and the art of garden province maintenance: The soft intimacy of hard men in the wilderness of Kwa-Zulu-Natal, South Africa, 1952–1997', *Journal of Southern African Studies*, 24(4), 1998, pp. 801–28; E. Green Musselman, 'Plant knowledge at the Cape: A study in African and European collaboration', *International Journal of African Historical Studies*, 36, 2003, pp. 367–92.

43   For example, see Wendy Woodward, 'Social subjects: Representations of dogs in South African fiction in English', in L. van Sittert & Sandra Swart, eds, *Canis Familiaris: A Dog History of Southern Africa* (Leiden: Brill, 2008).

44   See Sandra Swart, '"Race" horses: Horses and social dynamics in post-apartheid southern Africa', in N. Distiller & M. Steyn, eds, *Under Construction: Race and Identity in South Africa Today* (London: Heinemann, 2004), pp. 13–24.

45   Law (1980). For literature beyond Africa, see Peter Edwards, who offers the best synopsis of the early English arena of the inter-species relationship that transformed the history of transportation, commerce, leisure, warfare, agriculture, art and diplomacy; Peter Edwards, *Horse and Man in Early Modern England* (London: Hambledon Continuum, 2007). For a ground-breaking wider European perspective, see Karen Raber & Treva J. Tucker, eds, *The Culture of the Horse: Status, Discipline, and Identity in the Early Modern World* (New York: Palgrave Macmillan, 2005). In the Americas, McShane and Tarr, Derry and Greene offer recent careful, nuanced studies; see Clay McShane & Joel A. Tarr, *The Horse in the City: Living Machines in the Nineteenth Century* (Baltimore: Johns Hopkins University Press, 2007); and Margaret Derry, *Horses in Society: A Story of Animal Breeding and Marketing Culture, 1800–1920* (Buffalo: University of Toronto Press, 2006); also Ann Greene, *Horses at Work: Harnessing Power in Industrial America* (Cambridge, MA: Harvard University Press, 2008).

46   Humphrey J. Fisher, '"He swalloweth the ground with fierceness and rage": The horse in the central Sudan, II: Its use', *Journal of African History*, 14(3), 1973, pp. 355–79.

47   James Webb, 'The horse and slave trade between the western Sahara and Senegambia', *Journal of African History*, 34(2), 1993, pp. 221–46.

48   Martin Legassick, 'Firearms, horses and Samorian army organization, 1870–1898', *Journal of African History*, 7(1), 1966, pp. 95–115.

49   See Bankoff & Swart (2007); Malcolm Draper, 'Going native? Trout and settling identity in a Rainbow Nation', *Historia*, 48, 2003, pp. 55–94; C. Roche, 'Ornaments of the desert: Springbok treks in the Cape Colony, 1774–1908',

MA diss., University of Cape Town, 2004; and L. van Sittert & S. Swart, eds, *Canis Familiaris: A Dog History of Southern Africa* (Leiden: Brill, 2008).

50   Berger (1980), pp. 1–26.

51   Peter Novick, *Noble Dream: The 'Objectivity Question' and the American Historical Profession* (Cambridge: Cambridge University Press, 1988), p. 9.

52   Keith Thomas, 'We are all cultural historians now', *Times Literary Supplement*, 14 October 1994. For an up-to-date position, see Keith Thomas, 'New ways revisited: How history's borders have expanded in the past forty years', *Times Literary Supplement*, 13 October 2006. For the shifting trajectory of their thoughts, see Keith Thomas, 'The tools and the job', *Times Literary Supplement*, 7 April 1966, pp. 275–6; and E.P. Thompson, 'History from below', *Times Literary Supplement*, 7 April 1966, pp. 279–80. Both historians championed subjects that would now be labelled 'interdisciplinary' approaches. In his piece, Thompson proposed that it might be better for Social History if it stayed liminal, fighting from the fringes of academe. 'Perhaps it will prove most healthy for it if it remains somewhat disestablished', he contended, lest it 'become successful: grow fat: and adopt Norman habits in its turn'.

53   There has been a growing body of journal articles and valuable – if scattered – references in books. For book references, see Beinart, 2003); William Storey, *Guns, Race, and Power in Colonial South Africa* (Cambridge: Cambridge University Press, 2008); Sandra Swart, '"High horses": Horses, class and socio-economic change in South Africa', *Journal of Southern African Studies*, 33(4), 2008, pp. 193–213; Bankoff & Swart (2007); Sandra Swart '"Horses! Give me more horses!": White settler society and the role of horses in the making of early modern South Africa', in Karen Raber & Treva J. Tucker, eds, *The Culture of the Horse: Discipline, and Identity in the Early Modern World* (New York: Palgrave Macmillan, 2005); Swart (2007); and Vandenbergh (2009). For the early South African period, see P.J. Schreuder, 'The Cape horse: Its origin, breeding and development in the Union of South Africa', Ph.D. thesis, Cornell University, 1915; H.A. Wyndham, *The Early History of the Thoroughbred Horse in South Africa* (London: Humphrey Milford & Oxford University Press, 1924); and J.J. Nel, 'Perdeteelt in Suid-Afrika, 1652–1752', MA diss., University of Stellenbosch, 1930. For an analysis of the equine dimension of the period leading up to and during the South African War, Harold Sessions, *Two Years with the Remount Commission* (London: Chapman & Hall, 1903) is a useful primary source. For popular reading, see Kobus du Toit, *Die Geskiedenis van die S.A. Boerperd*, some chapters of a draft manuscript, <http://www.boerperd.net/tuisblad.php>; a memoir by Arabian breeder Charmaine Grobbelaar, *The Arabian Horse and Its Influence in South Africa* (Pretoria: Protea Book House, 2007); Jose Burman, *To Horse and Away* (Cape Town: Human & Rousseau, 1993); Daphne Child, *Saga of the South African Horse* (Cape Town: Howard Timmins, 1967); and F.J. van der

Merwe's delightful *Perde van die Anglo-Boereoorlog/Horses of the Anglo Boer War* (Kleinmond: self-published, 2000).

54   As in Lesotho, discussed in Chapter 4.

55   Juliet Clutton-Brock, ed., *The Walking Larder: Patterns of Domestication, Pastorialism and Predation* (London: Unwin Hyman, 1989b).

56   It is thought that the horses depicted in Paleolithic cave paintings were simply hunted for their meat by humans.

57   For discussion, see Jared Diamond, *Guns, Germs and Steel: The Fates of Human Societies* (London & New York: W.W. Norton, 1999), chap. 9.

58   S. Piggott, *Wagon, Chariot and Carriage* (London: Thames & Hudson, 1992); C. Renfrew, *Archaeology and Language: The Puzzle of Indo-European Origins* (London: Jonathan Cape, 1987).

59   Thomas Jansen et al., 'Mitochondrial DNA and the origins of the domestic horse', *Proceedings of the National Academy of Sciences of the United States of America*, 99(16), 2002, pp. 10905–10.

60   Carles Vilà et al., 'Widespread origins of domestic horse lineages', *Science*, 291(5503), 2001, pp. 474–77.

61   D.W. Anthony & D.R. Brown 'The origins of horseback riding', *Antiquity*, 246, 1991, pp. 22–38; L. Boyd & K.A. Houpt, eds, *Przewalski's Horse: The History and Biology of an Endangered Species* (New York: State University of New York Press, 1994); M.A. Levine et al., 'Palaeopathology and horse domestication', in G. Bailey & Charles R. Winder, eds, *Human Ecodynamics and Environmental Archaeology* (Oxford: Oxbow, 2000).

62   I. Shaw, 'Egyptians, Hyksos and military technology: Causes, effects or catalysts?', in A.J. Shortland, ed., *The Social Context of Technological Change: Egypt and the Near East, 1650–1550 BC* (Oxford: Oxbow, 2001).

63   Miklós Jankovich, *They Rode into Europe: The Fruitful Exchange in the Arts of Horsemanship between East and West*, trans. Anthony Dent (London: Long Riders' Guild Press, 1971).

64   Aristotle, *Politics*, rev. Trevor J. Saunders; trans. T.A. Sinclair (London: Penguin, 1981), 1321a.

65   Horses can provide a way of self-consciously avoiding pitfalls of area studies; see Bankoff & Swart (2007); Boomgaard (2001); Brown (2003); Bulliet (1975); Draper (2003); Law (1980); Roche (2004); and Van Sittert & Swart (2008).

66   See Worster & Crosby (1988, p. 290).

67   William Gervase Clarence-Smith, 'Southeast Asia and Southern Africa in the maritime horse trade of the Indian Ocean, c.1800–1914', in G. Bankoff & S. Swart, *Breeds of Empire: The 'Invention' of the Horse in the Philippines and Southern Africa, 1500–1950* (Uppsala: Nordic Institute of Asian Studies, 2007).

68   For a broader discussion, see Saul Dubow, ed., *Science and Society in Southern Africa* (Manchester: Manchester University Press, 2000); and J. Todd, *Colonial*

Technology: Science and the Transfer of Innovation to Australia (Cambridge: Cambridge University Press, 1995).

69   Similarly, South African muskets were adapted to local riding. They required a heavy trigger pull to prevent accidental discharge if either the musket or the rider (or both) dismounted precipitously and unexpectedly; see Storey (2008, p. 86).

70   See, for example, Bankoff & Swart (2007).

71   José Alvarez del Villar, *Men and Horses of Mexico: History and Practice of 'Charrería'*, trans. Margaret Fischer de Nicolin (Mexico City: Ediciones Lara, 1979).

72   Virginia deJohn Anderson's *Creatures of Empire: How Domestic Animals Transformed Early America* (Oxford: Oxford University Press, 2004) offers a good example. In examining the interactions of Indians, colonists and livestock in colonial North America, Anderson shows that liberated from the restraint of English animal husbandry, previously domesticated animals practically ran wild in America, and many cattle and pigs became feral, 'colonising' Indian territory on their own.

73   Donald Worster, 'Appendix: Doing environmental history', in Donald Worster & Alfred W. Crosby, eds, *The Ends of the Earth: Perspectives on Modern Environmental History* (Cambridge: Cambridge University Press, 1988), p. 289.

Chapter 2

1   H.C.V. Leibbrandt, ed., *Précis of the Archives of the Cape of Good Hope: Letters Despatched from the Cape, 1652–1662*, vol. I (Cape Town: W.A. Richards & Sons, 1900a), p. 31. A number of versions of Vereenigde Oost-Indische Compagnie (VOC) journals have been published, e.g. H.B. Thom, ed., *Journal of Jan van Riebeeck*, vol. I (Cape Town: A.A. Balkema, 1952). Of course, this is not solely Van Riebeeck's memoir, because information was sometimes dictated or authored by unknowns; see Leibbrandt (1900a).

2   Indeed, there is evidence of equids in west African archaeological sites dating back 2,000 years. African horses in the north include, for example, types that came to be known as the Western Sudan pony, the Dongola and the 'Abyssinian-Galla'.

3   Indeed, *Trypanosoma brucei brucei*, to which horses are particularly susceptible, was widespread; cattle, like humans, are unaffected. So the north-west penetration of horse owners was severely circumscribed; Ian Maudlin and John Hargrove, personal comments, April 2006.

4   In fact, one reason why early Arab traders did not extend their sphere of influence more widely was the transportation challenge through the fly belts.

Sixteenth-century Portuguese expeditions into the interior of East Africa failed because large numbers of their horses succumbed to trypanosomiasis.

5   Crosby (1986).

6   Parts of this chapter appeared in Sandra Swart, 'Riding High – Horses, Power and Settler Society, c.1654–1840', *Kronos*, 29 (2003); Sandra Swart '"Horses! Give me More Horses!" – White Settler Society and the Role of Horses in the Making of Early Modern South Africa', in Karen Raber and Treva J. Tucker, eds, *The Culture of the Horse: Status, Discipline, and Identity in the Early Modern World* (New York: Palgrave Macmillan, 2005); and Sandra Swart, 'Riding High – Horses, Power and Settler Society in Southern Africa, c.1654–1840', in Greg Bankoff and Sandra Swart, *Breeds of Empire: The 'Invention' of the Horse in the Philippines and Southern Africa, 1500–1950* (Copenhagen: NIAS Press, 2007).

7   See Storey (2008).

8   When European settlement began, most Khoikhoi inhabited the south-western Cape. Others, like the Namaqua, were in modern Namibia and the north-eastern Cape; the Korana were based along the Orange River.

9   Johan Anthoniszoon van Riebeeck (1619–77) joined the VOC and served as an assistant surgeon in the East Indies before undertaking the command of the initial Dutch settlement at the Cape. He died in Batavia in 1677.

10   He arrived in April with 80 VOC employees; by May the labour shortage compelled Van Riebeeck to ask for slaves to be sent to the Cape, a practice that began in 1658; R. Ross, *Cape of Torments: Slavery and Resistance in South Africa* (London: Routledge & Kegan Paul, 1983a).

11   For a discussion of the nomenclature, see Shula Marks, 'Khoisan resistance to the Dutch in the seventeenth and eighteenth centuries', *Journal of African History*, 13, 1972, pp. 55–80. Khoisan is an elision of the terms Khoikhoi and San. The name survives as an imprecise but practical reference to both the hunting and herding populations of the Cape (when differentiation is difficult, based on lack of specific sources). Indigenous herders of the south-western Cape were labelled 'Hottentots', now called Khoi, Khoikhoi or Khoekhoe. Bushman is preferred to San by many, because the latter may have been a derogatory Khoikhoi term. Thus, broadly, at the point of colonial contact, the Khoikhoi were pastoralists and the Bushmen were hunter-gatherers.

12   See Richard Elphick, *Kraal and Castle: Khoikhoi and the Founding of White South Africa* (New Haven: Yale University Press, 1977), pp. 90–110.

13   Oxen are technically mature castrated males, but actually the term just referred to working cattle regardless of age or gender. Oxen travelled at less than half the speed of horses and could not gallop for long periods. They could do harder, but much slower, work. Although oxen digested food more thoroughly by 'chewing the cud', the slow-moving four-stomach process of regurgitation meant they had less stamina than horses. In distinction to ungulates, which are ruminants, equids are cecal digesters and so their food is more rapidly digested, allowing for

immediate energy in case the horse needs to flee a predator and lending them their great speed.

14 Travelling by ox was a deeply disagreeable mode of transport to the uninitiated, as David Livingstone observed two centuries later; see David Livingstone, *Missionary Travels and Researches in South Africa* (London: John Murray, 1857); and William Burchell, *Travels in the Interior of Southern Africa*, vol. 2 (London: Batchworth, 1824), p. 188.

15 Monica Wilson & Leonard Thompson, *Oxford History of South Africa*, vol. I (Oxford: Clarendon Press, 1969), p. 166.

16 This tradition persisted. Later travellers commented on the 'Hottentot's' ability to ride the ox, at a 'walk, trot, or gallop' according to the 'will of its master'; Burchell (1824, p. 66).

17 Camels from Australia were a much later introduction.

18 H.C.V. Leibbrandt, ed., *Précis of the Archives of the Cape of Good Hope, January 1659–May 1662: Riebeeck's Journal,* part III (Cape Town: W.A. Richards & Sons, 1897b), entry for 11 December 1661, p. 317. From early in the eighteenth century mules were purposefully bred near grain-producing centres like Malmesbury.

19 See Thomas Dunlap, *Nature and the English Diaspora: Environment and History in the United States, Canada, Australia and New Zealand* (Cambridge: Cambridge University Press, 1999).

20 Leibbrandt (1900a, p. 670).

21 Thom (1952, entry for 16 November 1654, p. 272).

22 A.J.H. van der Walt, *Die Ausdehnung der Kolonie am Kap der Guten Hoffnung (1700–1779): Eine Historisch-ekonomische Untersuchung uber das Werden und Wesen des Pionierlebens im 18. Jahrhunderd* (Berlin: Ebering, 1928), p. 2.

23 Leibbrandt (1900a, entry for 4 May 1653, p. 152).

24 Leibbrandt (1900a, p. 152).

25 H.B. Thom, ed., *Journal of Jan van Riebeeck*, vol. II (Cape Town: A.A. Balkema, 1954), p. 116; S.F. du Plessis, 'Die verhaal van die dagverhaal van Jan van Riebeeck', D.Litt. thesis, University of Pretoria, 1934; *Dagverhaal van Jan van Riebeeck, Commandeur aan de Kaap de Goede Hoop* (Gravenhage: Nijhoff, 1892/1893), p. 434.

26 H.B. Thom, ed., *Journal of Jan van Riebeeck,* vol. III (Cape Town: A.A. Balkema, 1958), p. 446.

27 Later, a pair of these were recaptured (1655 and 1656) and brought to the Cape by the *Tulp*; the rest managed to evade capture.

28 The stallion was eaten by a lion a few days after arrival; Leibbrandt (1900a, p. 90). Sumbawa entered into treaty relations with the VOC in 1674, but supplied horses earlier and established itself as chief horse purveyor.

29 Leibbrandt (1900a, entry for 8 December 1854, pp. 406–7).

30 Thom (1952, pp. 272, 307).

31 Leibbrandt (1900a, p. 141).

32 Leibbrandt (1900a, p. 142).

33 H.C.V. Leibbrandt, ed., *Précis of the Archives of the Cape of Good Hope: Journal, 1662–1670* (Cape Town: W.A. Richards & Sons, 1901), entry for 11 January 1664, p. 90.

34 Nigel Penn, *The Forgotten Frontier* (Athens & Cape Town: Ohio University Press & Double Storey, 2005), p. 124. Horse – indeed, livestock – disease has attracted more interest from historians than other animal aspects: for a robust sample, see Brown (2008a; 2008b); Gilfoyle (2005); Beinart (2007, pp. 17–41); and Vandenbergh (2009).

35 They were advised, for example, to carry a bottle of the opium-based laudanum and administer it at once should their horse become sick (30 drops in a tumbler of water); *General Directory and Guide Book to the Cape of Good Hope and Its Dependencies* (Cape Town: Saul Solomon, 1869), p. 142.

36 Rat remains have been found in archaeological digs dating back to 700 CE; B.L. Penzhorn & R.C. Krecek, 'Veterinary parasitology in South Africa', *Veterinary Parasitology*, 71, 1997, pp. 69–76.

37 Vandenbergh (2009).

38 The main tsetse-transmitted trypanosomes of *Equidae* are *T. brucei*, *T. congolense* and *T. vivax*.

39 For a good discussion of the effects of these two diseases in particular, see Brown (2008a).

40 Incubation is just less than a week; morbidity is very high, but varies in relation to the number of insect vectors during the outbreak and the vulnerability of the host. The '*dunkop*' or pulmonary form is characterised by fever, coughing and nasal discharge, and means almost certain death. The '*dikkop*' form is characterised by longer incubation, the swelling of head and neck, fever, and death in half the cases. A mixed form exists. Donkeys suffered a mild form.

41 As Beinart and McGregor acknowledge: 'It is a weakness of past writings that indigenous and scientific, African and settler ideas are often considered separately'; W. Beinart & J. McGregor, eds, *Social History and African Environments* (Oxford, Athens & CapeTown: James Currey, Ohio University Press & David Philip, 2003), p. 3.

42 Dicke (1932); Wilson & Thompson (1969, p. 132).

43 A. Sparrman, *A Voyage to the Cape of Good Hope, towards the Antarctic Polar Circle, and around the World, but Chiefly into the Country of the Hottentots and Caffres, from the Year 1772 to 1776* (Cape Town: Van Riebeeck Society, 1975–77), pp. 216–17, 238.

44 Those who could not send their horses the long distance sent them to the Langeberg; Burchell (1824, p. 172).

45 Although this may have helped against the spreading of the disease, kraaling carried costs of its own, as horses suffered from malnourishment from the dry

summer pasturage and it was particularly hard on pregnant mares or those with young foals.

46   See the Cape Archives Repository, Cape Town (hereafter KAB), CO, 4015, 657, *Report from Field Cornet A. van Zyl*, 29 November 1842.

47   *Veterinary Journal*, 7, August 1878, p. 101.

48   Livestock were relocated in crises to avoid other infectious diseases like lungsickness in the mid-nineteenth century; Christian B. Andreas, 'The spread and impact of the lungsickness epizootic of 1853–57 in the Cape Colony and the Xhosa chiefdoms', *South African Historical Journal*, 53, 2005, pp. 50–72.

49   Van Riebeeck appointed Christiaan Jansz van Hoesum as master of the stable.

50   KAB, *Origineel Plakkaat Boek*, 1735; 1753, p. 82.

51   Company servants were initially prohibited from starting local industries and freedom of trade was forbidden because free enterprise was restricted to the VOC. Van Riebeeck argued that free burghers should be allowed to trade, farm and help with defence. In 1676 official VOC policy changed: it was agreed that a Dutch colony should be nurtured at the Cape to stimulate agricultural production.

52   The last quagga died in 1883 in an Amsterdam zoo.

53   Leibbrandt, H.C.V., ed., *Précis of the Archives of the Cape of Good Hope, January 1656–December 1658: Riebeeck's Journal*, part II (Cape Town: W.A. Richards & Sons, 1897a), pp. 33–34.

54   Gerrit van Spaan, *De Gelukzoeker* (Rotterdam: De Vries, 1752), p. 28; Thom (1958, entry for 14 December 1660, p. 300).

55   Thom (1958, entry for 14 December 1660, p. 300).

56   H.C.V. Leibbrandt, ed., *Précis of the Archives: Letters Despatched from the Cape, 1652–1662*, vol. III (Cape Town: W.A. Richards & Sons, 1900c), p. 129.

57   P. Kolbe, *Naaukeurige en Uitvoerige Beschryving van Kaap de Goede Hoop* (Amsterdam: B. Lakeman, 1727), p. 73.

58   This does not appear to have been the case without exception. Baines, for example, recorded that 'even the wild quaggas were dying of the horse-sickness' in March 1850; Thomas Baines, *Journal of Residence in Africa*, vol. II (Cape Town: Van Riebeeck Society, 1961), p. 217.

59   Barrow says some settlers did not eat quagga, as it so resembled the horse.

60   Sparrman (1975–77, pp. 216–17).

61   A span of zebra was even briefly utilised to run stagecoaches to Pietersburg at the end of the nineteenth century, while Captain Horace Hayes broke in a young Burchell's zebra in Pretoria in 1892. The Mazawattee Company also ran two four-in-hand teams of zebra for advertising purposes. See Clive Richardson, *The Horse Breakers* (London: Allen, 1998), pp. 121–22. As discussed in the next chapter, a professor of natural history at Edinburgh from 1882 to 1927, Cossar Ewart, crossed a zebra stallion with pony mares to disprove telegony. A secondary aim of these experiments was to produce a draught animal for South

Africa that was less subject to local diseases; see University of Edinburgh, Special Collections, L.14.29: W.J. Broderip, *Zoological Recreations* (London: H. Colburn, 1847).

62   Crossings persist to this day. In 2007 a zebra wandered across from De Hoop Nature Reserve and impregnated a surprised mare on the farm Die Kop near Swellendam; see *Landbouweekblad*, 'Sebra + perd = serd?', 1 June 2007.

63   H. Lichtenstein, *Travels in Southern Africa in the Years 1803, 1804, 1805, and 1806*, vol. II, trans. from the original German (London: Colburn, 1815), p. 162.

64   A 'hand' measures 4 inches or 10.16 cm.

65   Schreuder (1915).

66   Leibbrandt (1900c, p. 91).

67   H.C.V. Leibbrandt, ed., *Précis of the Archives of the Cape of Good Hope: Letters Despatched from the Cape, 1652–1662*, vol. II (Cape Town: W.A. Richards & Sons, 1900b), p. 1118.

68   Leibbrandt (1900c, p. 129).

69   Leibbrandt (1900c, entry for 17 February 1660, p. 133). Similarly, in West Africa, for example, horses were often used as symbolic demonstrations of power in contexts where they were of little military value; see Law (1980, p. 193).

70   Leibbrandt (1990c, pp. 89, 91).

71   Equally, Van Riebeeck was gratified by the 'fright and awe' stimulated by the 'first shot from his firelock'; Thom (1952, p. 270).

72   This use of horses endured. By the early nineteenth century, when the Bushmen suffered massive suppression, a traveller recorded: 'A troop of horsemen is the most alarming sight which can present itself to a kraal [homestead] of Bushmen in an open plain, as they then give themselves up for lost, knowing that under such circumstances, there is no escaping from these animals'; Burchell (1824, p. 187).

73   Storey (2008, p. 29).

74   At first the VOC had no large garrison and therefore relied on a few soldiers supplemented by local farmers and indigenous people – who volunteered or were compelled to join a commando. For a discussion of Cape defences at the time, see O.F. Mentzel, *Life at the Cape in the Mid-eighteenth Century*, trans. M. Greenlees ([1784], Cape Town: Darter Brothers, 1920), pp. 146–56.

75   The horse-based commando system extended into politics, culture and social mythology and is further discussed in Chapter 6. This has parallels with other African societies. In the case of West Africa, the dominance of cavalry had more than solely military implications; it had an important influence on the character of political structures and social institutions; see Law (1980, p. 184).

76   Only after 1806 were they expected to provide their own guns, and between 1722 and 1733 free blacks were also required to perform commando duty; Storey (2008, pp. 34–35).

77   Thom (1954, entry for 9 September 1658, p. 337).

78 Horse maiming was sometimes undoubtedly a form of social rebellion in Europe, for example. It was also a form of psychological terror, of symbolic murder that resulted from personal feuds between members of the same social class; see Roger Yates, Chris Powell & Piers Beirne, 'Horse maiming in the English countryside: Moral panic, human deviance, and the social construction of victimhood', *Society and Animals*, 9(1), 2001, pp. 1–23; and G. Elder, J. Wolch & J. Emel, 'Race, place, and the bounds of humanity', *Society and Animals*, 6(2), 1998, pp. 183–202.

79 Elder, Wolch & Emel (1998, p. 184).

80 B. Tuchman, *The Proud Tower* (New York: Macmillan, 1966). This is buttressed by psycho-social analysis by, for example, Freud, who described the horse as a symbol of power. Psychologists suggest that literally 'looking down on others' from the back of a horse may increase feelings of pride and self-esteem; D. Toth, 'The psychology of women and horses', in GaWaNí PonyBoy, ed., *Of Women and Horses* (Irvine: BowTie, 2000), p. 36.

81 As a rule, a horse at pasture requires an acre to sustain its nutritional needs, but this varies according to the type of horse, its energy output, the nature of the grass and seasonal climatic variation.

82 As observed in a 1603 preface to the *Anatomia and Medicina Equorum*: 'in order to sustain political societies, and protect the people who make up these societies, you cannot do without the horse'; quoted in Pia Cuneo, 'Beauty and the beast: Art and science in early modern European equine imagery', *Journal of Early Modern History*, 4(3–4), 2000, p. 269. Seventeenth-century European iconographic representations of the horse emphasised serenely regal control by (patrician) riders.

83 Lisa Jardine & Jerry Brotton, *Global Interests: Renaissance Art between East and West* (Ithaca: Cornell University Press, 2000), p. 145.

84 Although technically dressage stops at *piaffe* and *haute école* continues with the airs above ground, symbolising the ever-increasing degrees of collection.

85 L. Thompson, *A History of South Africa* (New Haven: Yale University Press, 1990), p. 35.

86 In any event, the various differentiated breeds were simply not available.

87 L. Guelke & R. Shell, 'An early colonial landed gentry: Land and wealth in the Cape Colony 1682–1731', *Journal of Historical Geography*, 9(3), 1983, pp. 265–86; see also Ross (1983a); Nigel Worden, *Slavery in Dutch South Africa* (Cambridge: Cambridge University Press, 1985); and Robert Shell, *Children of Bondage: A Social History of Slavery at the Cape of Good Hope, 1652–1838* (Johannesburg: Wits University Press, 1994).

88 The governor of the Cape Colony, Rijk Tulbagh, prepared a set of rules to govern the control of slaves in 1753.

89 They also dictated one's seat in church, one's place in funerals, and even whether or not one could use an open large umbrella; see C. Graham Botha, *General*

History and Social Life of the Cape of Good Hope (Cape Town: Struik, 1962), pp. 190, 196; and R. Ross, *Status and Respectability in the Cape Colony, 1750–1870* (Cambridge: Cambridge University Press, 1999), pp. 9–30.

90   Cited in Wayne Dooling, 'The making of a colonial elite: Property, family and landed stability in the Cape Colony, c.1750–1834', *Journal of Southern African Studies*, 31(1), 2005, p. 150.

91   They were a stable, self-reproducing elite from the eighteenth-century Cape, ruling the countryside until replaced (after an economic decline instigated by slave emancipation) by English-speaking merchants in the second third of the nineteenth century; Dooling (2005).

92   The literal meaning of *knechts* is 'retainer', but their duties changed over time, from manual labourers in the 1600s to overseers by the early eighteenth century; Shell (1994, p. 11); see also Shell (1994, p. 20). Slaves did ride horses, but they did not have the right to do so.

93   Nigel Worden, 'Armed with swords and ostrich feathers: Militarism and cultural revolution in the Cape slave uprising of 1808', in Richard Bessel, Nicholas Guyatt & Jane Rendall, eds, *War, Empire and Slavery, 1770–1830* (London: Palgrave, 2009).

94   The Spanish government had issued decrees forbidding Indians to own or ride horses. See also J.E. Sherow, 'Workings of the geodialectic: High plains Indians and their horses in the region of the Arkansas River Valley, 1800–1870', *Environmental History Review*, 16, 1992, pp. 61–84.

95   Sparrman (1975–77, p. 253).

96   Child (1967, p. 13).

97   Each (male white) *vrijburger* received 28 acres; they were expected to sell their produce to the VOC and adhere to the trade monopoly.

98   Horses were extremely expensive, worth five large oxen in peak condition. Sixteen horses were sold for (on average) £4 each: nine mares, two colts and five stallions.

99   Child (1967, p. 22).

100 G.M. Theal, *History and Ethnography of Africa South of the Zambesi*, vol. II (London: George Allen & Unwin, 1922), p. 323.

101 K.M. Jeffreys & S.D. Naude, eds, *Kaapse Argiefstukke: Kaapse Plakkaatboek, 1652–1795*, vol. I (Cape Town: Government Printer, 1944–49), entry for 22 January 1692, p. 262; entry for 19 October 1697, p. 301.

102 These animals are believed to have been of the early English Roadster breed. There is evidence that the name Roadster was synonymous with Hackney; M.H. Hayes, *Points of the Horse* (New York: Arco, 1969).

103 The spelling of the names of the various breeds of horses varied with usage, e.g. sometimes the Cape Horse is referred to and at others the Cape horse. This issue of spelling/terminology applies to the names of many of the breeds mentioned in this book.

104 Leibbrandt (1900c, pp. 89, 91).

105 The first 100 years saw no major new breed importations, resulting in a foundation stock of hardy ponies.

106 John Barrow, *An Account of Travels in the Interior of South Africa, in the Years 1797 and 1798*, vol. 1 (New York: Johnson Reprint, 1968), p. 36.

107 The horses of Spanish origin were taken from two French ships boarded during the Napoleonic wars, but others had already been imported into the Cape as early as 1797.

108 Eric Walker, *A History of Southern Africa* (London: Longman, 1965), p. 89.

109 W. Bird, *State of the Cape of Good Hope in 1822* (Cape Town: Struik, 1966), p. 99.

110 Alexander Crawford Lindsay, *Lives of the Lindsays; or, a Memoir of the Houses of Crawford and Balcarres*, vol. III (London: John Murray, 1849), p. 450.

111 M.H. Hayes, *Among Horses in South Africa* (London: Everett, 1900).

112 This 'peculiar pace' was first mentioned in 1806, but was labelled 'the bungher' (which could be a corruption of 'burgher'). It was contended that an English jockey soon '[got] rid of it'; Anon. *Gleanings in Africa, Exhibiting a Faithful and Correct View of the Manners and Customs of the Inhabitants of the Cape of Good Hope, and Surrounding Country* ([1806], New York: Negro University Press, 1969), p. 23. H. Rider Haggard referred to a sort of 'tripple' or ambling canter much affected by South African horses; see the first chapter of H. Rider Haggard, *Jess* ([1887], London: Smith & Elder, 1909); see also Chapter 4, 'Doctor Rodd' in H. Rider Haggard, *Finished* ([1917], London: Macdonald, 1962). This was later cherished as the traditional Boer riding style; see George Green, 'How to train a horse to triple', *Farmer's Weekly*, 24 December 1947.

113 An exception is Gordon Pirie, who has explored transport's historical role; see, for example, his 'Railways and labour migration to the Rand mines: Constraints and significance', *Journal of Southern African Studies*, 19, 1994, pp. 713–30; and 'Slaughter by steam: Railway subjugation of ox wagon transport in the eastern Cape and Transkei, 1886–1910', *International Journal of African Historical Studies*, 26, 1993, pp. 319–42.

114 Later, roads were entrusted to the supervision of the *heemraden*, and the services of locals (i.e. their slaves and horses) could be requisitioned to maintain the roads in rough and ready order.

115 This trend was further consolidated by the Kimberley diamond rush from 1867 onwards and the discovery of gold on the Witwatersrand in 1886.

116 James Ewart, *James Ewart's Journal, Covering His Stay at the Cape of Good Hope (1811–1814) & His Part in the Expedition to Florida and New Orleans (1814–1815)* (Cape Town: Struik, 1970), p. 92.

117 The technique was used elsewhere and at other times. T.E. Lawrence, for example, mentions the knee haltering of camels in the Middle East and it is still used today in parts of southern Africa.

118   Alfred W. Drayson, *Sporting Scenes amongst the Kaffirs of South Africa* (London: Routledge, 1858), p. 68.

119   Distances and relative speeds are discussed in Petrus Borcherds, *An Autobiographical Memoir of Petrus Borchardus Borcherds, esq.* (Cape Town: Robertson, 1861), pp. 43–45.

120   D. Neville, B. Sampson & C.G. Sampson, 'The frontier wagon track system in the Seacow River Valley, north-eastern Cape', *South African Archaeological Bulletin*, 49, 1994, pp. 65–72.

121   Tim Flannery, *The Future Eaters* (Sydney: Grove, 1994), p. 303.

122   Crosby (1986); Alfred W. Crosby, *The Columbian Exchange: Biological and Cultural Consequences of 1492* (Westport: Praeger, 2003).

123   Alfred W. Crosby, *Germs, Seeds and Animals: Studies in Ecological History* (New York: M.E. Sharpe, 1994), p. 29.

124   The tamed mounts transported by the Spanish to the Americas assumed a feral state in the New World and developed into the 'mustang'.

125   See, for example, Elizabeth Lawrence, 'Rodeo horses: The wild and the tame', in R. Willis, *Signifying Animals: Human Meaning in the Natural World* (London: Routledge, 1990), p. 223; and, more extensively, Elizabeth Lawrence, *Rodeo: An Anthropologist Looks at the Wild and the Tame* (Knoxville: University of Tennessee Press, 1981). See also Richard Slata, *Cowboys of the Americas* (New Haven: Yale University Press, 1990).

126   Moreover, pasturage was poor around the first settlement because much of the *fynbos* was unpalatable. What appeared to be grass was often from the *Restionaceae* family.

127   Particularly in the first decade of horse importation, equine existence was precarious; e.g. see Leibbrandt (1900a, p. 90).

Chapter 3

1   For instance, in the early twentieth century horses were used to produce a serum to prevent the bacterial infection diphtheria. Bacteria were injected into the horse, who then suffered an immune response that produced antibodies to the toxin. Blood was then collected from the horses to create the serum for humans.

2   'South Africa' per se did not exist in the nineteenth century, but it was a term loosely used to mean variously the geographic region (which later became consolidated as the country South Africa); the Cape; or even southern Africa. This chapter deploys it in the first sense, focusing mainly on the Cape Colony, but incorporating trends from areas across the Vaal and the Orange Rivers in the second half of the nineteenth century.

3   The horses of Spanish origin were taken from two French ships boarded during the Napoleonic wars.

4   The Cape pony, or Caper, was a name adopted in India for horses exported from
      the Cape. English-speaking settlers called it the 'Colonial', the 'South African' or
      the 'Boer horse', while Dutch speakers used the term 'Hantam' (an area in which
      horse breeding occurred). They were sometimes known as the Melck or Kotze
      horse (surnames of famous breeders), or even the Bossiekoppe (bushyheads or
      'thick headed', i.e. unrefined).

5   Wyndham (1924, p. 97); Worden (1985, p. 87); Ross (1983a, p. 18). In J. Suasso
      de Lima, *Cape Calendar and Directory, for the Leap Year, 1836* (Cape Town:
      J. Suasso de Lima, 1935), of the 'free blacks', six were coachmen, five were
      saddlers and one was advertised as a groom.

6   Cited in Leonard Guelke, 'Frontier settlement in early Dutch South Africa',
      Annals of the Association of American Geographers, 66(1), 1976, p. 30.

7   W. Derham, *A Visit to Cape Colony and Natal* (Bristol: Mardon, 1879), p. 76.
      The term 'Malay' has fluid meanings; on this, see A. Davids, *The Mosques of
      BoKaap* (Athlone: South African Institute of Arabic and Islamic Research,
      1980); V. Bickford-Smith, *Ethnic Pride and Racial Prejudice in Victorian Cape
      Town* (Johannesburg: Wits University Press, 1995), p. 69; and Chet Fransch,
      'Stellenbosch and the Muslim communities, 1866–1966', MA diss., University
      of Stellenbosch, 2009, pp. 17–22, 67–69.

8   Charles van Onselen, *New Babylon New Nineveh: Everyday Life on the
      Witwatersrand 1886–1914* (Johannesburg: Jonathan Ball, 2001), p. 176.

9   James Little, *South Africa: A Sketch Book of Men, Manners and Facts* (London:
      Sonnenschein, 1887), p. 404.

10   J.S. Mayson, *The Malays of Capetown* (Manchester: J. Galt, 1861), p. 36.

11   Sparrman (1975–77, vol. I, p. 253).

12   Drayson (1858, p. 15).

13   Storey (2008, pp. 72, 110, quoting James Chapman).

14   The paintings are not simply straightforward depictions of events, but also
      interpretive. Two key areas with paintings of colonial material culture are
      the south-western Cape and the KwaZulu-Natal Drakensberg. Many depict
      cattle raids by Bushmen, with horsemen striking back with muskets or rifles.
      In some, even the horses' reins and traces are portrayed; see Royden Yates,
      Anthony Manhire & John Parkington, 'Colonial era paintings in the rock
      art of the south-western Cape: Some preliminary observations', *Historical
      Archaeology in the Western Cape*, 1993, pp. 59–70; and P. Vinnicombe, 'General
      notes on Bushmen riders and the Bushmen's use of the assegai', *South African
      Archaeological Bulletin*, 15(58), 1960, p. 49. See also A.H. Manhire et al., 'Cattle,
      sheep and horses: A review of domestic animals in rock art of southern Africa', in
      Prehistoric Pastoralism in Southern Africa, Goodwin Series, vol. 5 (South African
      Archaeological Society, June 1986), pp. 22–30.

15   Pat Vinnicombe & John Wright, *Bushman Raiders of the Drakensberg 1840–1870*
      (Pietermartizburg: University of Natal Press, 1971).

16 Oral Testimony of Sello Mokoallo, quoted by P. Vinnicombe, 'Basotho oral knowledge: The last Bushman inhabitants of the Mashai District, Lesotho', in P. Mitchell & Benjamin Smith, eds, *The Eland's People: New Perspectives in the Rock Art of the Maloti-Drakensberg Bushmen: Essays in Memory of Patricia Vinnicombe* (Johannesburg: Wits University Press, 2009), p. 168.

17 Lewis, quoted in Tim Ingold, David Riches & James Woodburn, eds, *Hunters and Gatherers: Property, Power and Ideology*, vol. II (Oxford: Berg, 1997), p. 193.

18 Sam Challis, 'Taking the reins: The introduction of the horse in the nineteenth-century Maloti-Drakensberg and the protective medicine of baboons', in P. Mitchell & Benjamin Smith, eds, *The Eland's People: New Perspectives in the Rock Art of the Maloti-Drakensberg Bushmen: Essays in Memory of Patricia Vinnicombe* (Johannesburg: Wits University Press, 2009), pp. 104–7; C. Campbell, 'Art in crisis: Contact period rock art in the south-eastern mountains of southern Africa', MSc diss., University of the Witwatersrand, 1987; Patricia Vinnicombe, *People of the Eland: Rock Paintings of the Drakensberg Bushmen as a Reflection of Their Life and Thought* (Pietermaritzburg: University of Natal Press, 1976), p. 77.

19 Challis (2009, pp. 104–7).

20 These part-human, part-animal creatures showed humans and animals assuming one another's shapes during rituals in which shamans found a path into the spirit world; Ingold, Riches & Woodburn (1997, p. 196).

21 J.C. Hollmann, ed., *Customs and Beliefs of the /Xam Bushmen* (Johannesburg: Wits University Press, 2004). Moreover, baboons carried their young in a manner eerily reminiscent of horses and their human riders.

22 KAB, GH 8/8, 43, 21 August 1839.

23 George Thompson, *Travels and Adventures in Southern Africa* (London: Henry Colburn, 1827).

24 Lichtenstein (1815); see also Anon., *Sketches of India or, Observations Descriptive of the Scenery, etc. in Bengal ... Together with Notes on the Cape of Good-Hope, and St. Helena* ([1847], London: Black, Parbury & Allen, 1916), p. 74.

25 Peter Edwards, *The Horse Trade of Tudor and Stuart England* (Cambridge: Cambridge University Press, 1988).

26 Of course, challenges were presented in the seventeenth century by William Harvey, and there were dissenting voices like William Osmer, who dismissed the significance of blood in his 1756 treatise on horses.

27 For more on the history of breeding, see Derry (2006, pp. 4–25).

28 Raber and Tucker contend that the exotic 'orientalised' Other, to use Said's categorisation, was nationalised: the Arabian, Turk and Barb modified into the English Thoroughbred. Moreover, the continental *haute école* was replaced by specifically British styles. As Raber notes, '[w]hile the new horse culture might still be socially restrictive, as a metaphor and interpretive device it became an inclusive definition of Englishness'; see Raber & Tucker (2005, p. 36).

29   Nicholas Russell, 'Well-groomed or well-bred?', *History Today*, 39(1), 1989, p. 11.
      See also Russell (1986); and D. Landry, 'The bloody shouldered Arabian and
      early modern English culture', *Criticism*, 2004, pp. 41–69.

30   Donna Landry, *Noble Brutes: How Eastern Horses Transformed English Culture*
      (Baltimore: Johns Hopkins University Press, 2008), p. 77.

31   See Richard Nash, 'Honest English breed: The Thoroughbred as cultural
      metaphor', in Karen Raber & Treva J. Tucker, eds, *The Culture of the Horse:
      Status, Discipline, and Identity in the Early Modern World* (New York: Palgrave
      Macmillan, 2005).

32   For a discussion of how ideas about hereditary reflected notions of gender, class
      and race in the specific societies in which they operated, see Harriet Ritvo, *The
      Animal Estate: The English and Other Creatures in the Victorian Age* (Cambridge,
      MA: Harvard University Press, 1987).

33   Landry (2008, p. 3). Landry has made the elegant analysis that breeding from
      Eastern stock and absorbing Eastern notions of horsemanship helped in
      producing an imperial discourse.

34   Russell (2004, p. 219).

35   Kirsten McKenzie, *Scandal in the Colonies* (Melbourne: Melbourne University
      Press, 2004), p. 3.

36   Saul Dubow, *A Commonwealth of Knowledge* (Oxford: Oxford University Press,
      2006), pp. 22–23.

37   Dubow (2006, p. 2); and see W. Dooling, 'The decline of the Cape gentry', *Journal
      of African History*, 40, 1999, pp. 215–42.

38   With the end of VOC rule and the development of the Patriot movement
      from the late eighteenth century, the strata coming to be considered 'gentry'
      challenged the company that had controlled the Cape for over a century.

39   Robert Ross, 'The rise of the Cape gentry', *Journal of Southern African Studies*,
      9(2), 1983b, pp. 193–217.

40   Edna Bradlow, 'The culture of a colonial elite: The Cape of Good Hope in the
      1850s', *Victorian Studies*, 29(3), 1986, p. 391.

41   See, for example, Cowper Rose, *Four Years in Southern Africa* (London:
      Colburne & Bentley, 1829).

42   John Wedderburn Dunbar Moodie, *Ten Years in South Africa*, vol. 2 (London:
      R. Bentley, 1835), p. 27. By the end of the nineteenth century, however, new men
      and new money started to be drawn in; see John Pinfold, 'Horse racing and the
      upper classes in the nineteenth century', *Sport in History*, 28(3), September 2008,
      pp. 414–30.

43   'Letter from Mr William Duckitt to William Huskisson, Simons Town, Cape of
      Good Hope', 6 January 1801, in G.M. Theal, *Records of the Cape Colony: Copied
      for the Cape Government, from the Manuscript Documents in the Public Record
      Office, London, December 1799 to May 1801*, vol. 3 (London: Clowes, 1898),

pp. 389–90. Duckitt actually thought draught horses would be more useful – but acknowledged that people would only want them if they were 'pedigreed'.

44   Bird (1966). He also mentions the availability of mules, chiefly from Buenos Aires, at 200 Rd (rix dollars), and Spanish jacks selling at 500–1 000 Rd, p. 99.

45   This was to facilitate the embryonic export trade to India and Australia and helped form the foundation stock of the Waler, which usurped the Indian market for cavalry horses.

46   Ewart (1970, p. 23).

47   *Report of the Commissioners of Enquiry to Earl Bathurst, Cape Town, Cape of Good Hope, 2 October 1824*, in G.M. Theal, *Records of the Cape Colony: Copied for the Cape Government, from the Manuscript Documents in the Public Record Office, London, June to October 1824*, vol. 18 (London: Clowes, 1903b), p. 460.

48   Wyndham (1924, p. 16). Wyndham emigrated to South Africa in 1901 and worked under Milner. He tried to live as an English country gentleman, breeding horses in Standerton. A Unionist MP, he advocated stronger bonds with Britain.

49   This blood stock formed the foundation of the Melck stud, which from c.1808 to 1881 was very influential in southern Africa.

50   Barnard, Lady Anne, *The Cape Journals of Lady Anne Barnard, 1797–1798* (Cape Town: Van Riebeeck Society, 1994), p. 169.

51   W.H.C. Lichtenstein, *Foundation of the Cape, about the Bechuanas: Being a History of the Discovery and Colonisation of South Africa*, trans. O.H. Spohr ([1807, 1811], Cape Town: Balkema, 1973).

52   After the post-race celebration, one reveller fell into a pond and nearly drowned; London *Morning Chronicle*, 18 September 1797.

53   Anon. (1969, p. 23); *Cape Town Gazette*, 27 February 1802.

54   Anon. (1969, p. 258).

55   M.D. Teenstra, *De Vruchten Mijmer Werkzaamheden* (Cape Town: Van Riebeeck Society, 1943), p. 339.

56   William Burchell, *Travels in the Interior of Southern Africa*, vol. 1 (London: Longman, Hurst, Rees, Orme & Brown, 1822), p. 28.

57   Duff Gordon, Lady, *Letters from the Cape* (London: Macmillan, 1876), pp. 152–53. She also observed that the Malays predominated in the horse-hiring industry, p. 46.

58   Anon. (1969, p. 23); Burchell (1924, p. 163). Unlike many from the metropole, Burchell sided with the local Dutch population: 'there cannot be a greater proof of bad taste and thoughtless cruelty, than in viewing so beautiful an animal as the horse, so far to pervert all reason … as to consider that a mutilated stump is more handsome than the fine flowing brush which Nature … has wisely bestowed.'

59   Lady Anne Barnard, *The Cape Diaries of Lady Anne Barnard, 1799–1800*, vol. 1, ed. M. Lenta & B. le Cordeur (Cape Town: Van Riebeeck Society, 1999), pp. 311, 333–34, 359; Lady Anne Barnard, *The Letters of Lady Anne Barnard to Henry*

Dundas, from the Cape and Elsewhere, 1793–1803, ed. A.M. Lewin Robinson (Cape Town: Balkema, 1973), entry for September 1798. Interestingly, she also mentions oxen or bullock racing among the Khoikhoi, pp. 116, 123.

60   Barnard (1973, p. 169).

61   Barnard (1999, p. 237).

62   Quoted in Anthony Kendal Millar, *A Plantagenet in South Africa: Lord Charles Somerset* (Cape Town & London: Oxford University Press, 1965), p. 27.

63   *Cape Gazette*, August 1814.

64   For the Stellenbosch Turf Club, see KAB, CO, 3910, 105, 'Petition pertaining to the horse racing club of Stellenbosch', 1817; KAB, CO, 3927, 'Stewards of the turf club at Stellenbosch', 1824.

65   Wyndham (1924, p. 25).

66   The British returned the Cape Colony to Holland in 1803. Holland was at the time renamed the Batavian Republic.

67   Barnard (1999, p. 356). Indeed, the Melck and Coetzee names remained a signal of good blood. F.W. Reitz (1844–1934) a lawyer and statesman, even wrote an amusing piece of doggerel verse about the escape of a would-be bridegroom: '*Sij pêrd was geteeld bij Melck en Coetzee,/ Die bruid had 'n ander haar "jawoord" gegee."/Hij drukte haar hand; hij fluisterde iets;/ Hij dans na die deur; maar niemand merk iets;/Meteens sprong hij uit – sij pêrd stond gereed–/Die meisie is meê, en o! wat 'n leed!*'

68   In Paarl (1815); Uitenhage and Stellenbosch (1816); Graaff-Reinet (1821); Grahamstown (1823); Somerset East and Swellendam (1825); Cradock (1830s); Natal (1840s, with a Jockey Club in 1864); and Port Eizabeth Turf Club (1857).

69   Wyndham (1924, p. 34).

70   Wyndham (1924, p. 39).

71   A.E. Blount, *Notes on the Cape of Good Hope Made during an Excursion in that Colony in the Year 1820* (London: John Murray, 1821).

72   Alfred W. Cole, 'Extracts from idylls of a prince', in Nerine Desmond, ed., *Candlelight Poets of the Cape* (Cape Town: Howard Timmins, 1967), pp. 27–29.

73   Rose (1829, pp. 9–10).

74   Burchell (1822, p. 25).

75   Bird (1966, p. 163).

76   Wyndham (1924, p. 22).

77   Little (1887, p. 79). In Natal horses survived on small amounts of high pasture, but in low-lying areas they were vulnerable to horse sickness in summer. By the end of the nineteenth century there were only 54,485 horses in Natal, as opposed to 388,000 in the Cape. Interestingly, in Natal nearly half the horses belonged to the black population.

78   *South African Almanack and Reference Book, 1911–1912* (Cape Town: Argus, 1911), p. 196.

79 M. Horace Hayes, *Among Men and Horses* (London: T. Fisher Unwin, 1894), p. 220. A little later, across the Vaal and the Orange and over the Maluti Mountains, things were very different. Riding was certainly a marker of masculine identity in some other societies, as in the two Boer republics and Basutoland, functioning as a marker of militarised male identity, as will be explored in the following chapters.

80 Quoted by Sir Humphrey F. de Trafford in Millar (1965, p. 13).

81 H.A. Bryden, *Nature and Sport in South Africa* (London: Chapman & Hall, 1897), pp. 112–13.

82 Bryden (1897, p. 120).

83 Personal communication, Adrian Ryan.

84 *Report of the Commissioners of Inquiry to the Right Hon. William Huskisson upon the Police at the Cape of Good Hope, 10 May 1828*, in G.M. Theal, *Records of the Cape Colony: Copied for the Cape Government, from the Manuscript Documents in the Public Record Office, London, December 1827 to April 1831*, vol. 35 (London: Clowes, 1905e), p. 271.

85 *Cape Gazette*, in G.M. Theal, *Records of the Cape Colony: Copied for the Cape Government, from the Manuscript Documents in the Public Record Office, London, May 1823 to January 1824*, vol. 16 (London: Clowes, 1903a), p. 170.

86 Alan Lester, 'Reformulating identities: British settlers in early nineteenth-century South Africa', *Transactions of the Institute of British Geographers*, 23(4), 1998, p. 517.

87 Little (1887, pp. 29–30).

88 'Letter from Sir Rufane Shaw Donkin to Robert Wilmot Horton, Pall Mall', 23 June 1823, in Theal (1903a, p. 85).

89 G.M. Theal, *Records of the Cape Colony: Copied for the Cape Government, from the Manuscript Documents in the Public Record Office, London, 1 January to 6 February 1826*, vol. 25 (London: Clowes, 1905a), pp. 77–78.

90 And others, like Captain Christopher, who imported bloodstock to the Cape from England (selling them to, among others, the Van Reenens) and then exported Cape horses to India.

91 Martin Melck arrived at the Cape in 1746, bought himself Stellenbosch farms and increased his wealth by marrying two rich widows in succession; see Ross (1983b, p. 196).

92 'Letter from Mr D. van Reenen to Captain Hare, aide de camp to the governor', 28 September 1825, in G.M. Theal, *Records of the Cape Colony: Copied for the Cape Government, from the Manuscript Documents in the Public Record Office, London, August to November 1825*, vol. 23 (London: Clowes, 1904b), p. 182.

93 'Letter van Reenen to Captain Hare', 28 September 1825, in Theal (1904b, p. 182).

94 'Letter from J.J. Kotze to Landdrost J.W. Stoll', 1 October 1825, in Theal (1904b, p. 221).

95 'Letter from Mr William Duckitt to Lord Charles Somerset', 1 October 1825, in Theal (1904b, p. 221); G.M. Theal, *Records of the Cape Colony: Copied for the Cape Government, from the Manuscript Documents in the Public Record Office, London, June 1821 to August 1822*, vol. 14 (London: Clowes, 1902), p. 23; see also 'Letter to Huskisson', in Theal (1898, p. 390; and Barrow (1968, p. 67).

96 It was also safer for the elite breeders to invest in horseflesh than it was for small breeders, because the wealthy could stable their stock during horse sickness epidemics.

97 'Letter from Mr P. van der Byl to Captain Hare', 6 October 1825, in Theal (1904b, pp. 241–42).

98 Quoted in 'R.S. Donkin to inspector land's office, Cape of Good Hope', 6 May 1823, in Theal (1903a, p. 171).

99 Sir Rufane Shaw Donkin, *A Letter on the Government of the Cape of Good Hope, and on Certain Events which Have Occurred there of Late Years under the Administration of Lord Charles Somerset, Addressed Most Respectfully to Earl Bathurst* (London: Carpenter & Son, 1827), p. 115.

100 Another (coincidentally equine) cause of the bad blood between Somerset and the acting governor (who replaced him while he was in England and who levelled charges against him) was that Sir Rufane Donkin had shaken a horsewhip over Somerset's son, an army officer, in a threatening way; see Donkin (1827, pp. 98–99).

101 'Letter from James Stephen to R.W. Hay', 14 February 1827, in G.M. Theal, *Records of the Cape Colony: Copied for the Cape Government, from the Manuscript Documents in the Public Record Office, London, October 1824 to February 1825*, vol. 19 (London: Clowes, 1904a), p. 359; and 'Proclamation by His Excellency General the Right Hon. Lord Charles Henry Somerset', 23 May 1823, in G.M. Theal, *Records of the Cape Colony: Copied for the Cape Government, from the Manuscript Documents in the Public Record Office, 1 January to 24 February 1827*, vol. 30 (London: Clowes, 1905c), p. 359.

102 'Letter from the commissioners of enquiry to Earl Bathurst, George Town, Cape of Good Hope', 6 December 1823, in G.M. Theal, *Records of the Cape Colony: Copied for the Cape Government, from the Manuscript Documents in the Public Record Office, February to June 1826*, vol. 26 (London: Clowes, 1905b), p. 455; 'Letter from Earl Bathurst to Lord Charles Somerset, Colonial Office, London', 20 July 1823, in Theal (1905b, p. 139).

103 Theal (1905b, p. 458).

104 This venture was not without risk. In the same year, a Captain William Hollet spent £575 on eight young horses to import to the Cape and spent twice that amount on transport. Only one horse survived the journey.

105 For the sake of fiscal context, it is worth noting that Somerset received a salary of £10,000 per annum.

106 *Report of the Commissioners of Enquiry to Earl Bathurst, Cape Town, Cape of Good Hope, 2 October 1824*, in Theal (1903b, pp. 458, 468–71). The Widow Louw married Jacobus Redelinghuys in November 1818 (her first husband had died the year before). She became the owner of considerable property in the Hantam district, the value of which depended less upon the grazing available than the refuge it afforded horses 'during the fatal periods of the "distemper"' (horse sickness).

107 'Letter to R. Wilmot Horton, Cape of Good Hope', 1 November 1825, in Theal (1904b, p. 363); *Report of the Commissioners of Enquiry to Earl Bathurst, Cape Town, Cape of Good Hope*, 2 October 1824, in Theal (1903b, p. 462).

108 *Report of the Commissioners of Enquiry to Earl Bathurst, Cape Town, Cape of Good Hope*, 2 October 1824, in Theal (1903b, p. 465).

109 Walker (1965, pp. 167–68); also hinted at darkly in D'Escury's testimony; see Theal (1903b, p. 455).

110 KAB, GH 1/46, 1825; KAB, GH 1/58, 1826.

111 Some Hantam mares 'improved' by crosses with imported English horses were also purchased and a Thoroughbred stallion was offered for gratis servicing during the covering season.

112 'Proclamation by His Excellency General the Right Hon. Lord Charles Henry Somerset', 23 May 1823, in Theal (1905a, p. 177).

113 For a discussion on fencing, which gained real momentum later in the century, especially after 1883, see Lance van Sittert, 'Holding the line: The rural enclosure movement in the Cape Colony', *Journal of African History*, 43, 2002, pp. 95–118.

114 This procedure should not be confused with penectomy, which is the amputation of the penis, nor with vasectomy, which blocks the *vasa deferentia*.

115 Little (1887, p. 161).

116 *Cape of Good Hope Almanac and Annual Register 1860* (Cape Town: Van de Sandt & De Villiers, 1860). The era of more comprehensive road construction really began in the mid-nineteenth century with Ordinance no. 8 of 1843, with the formation of the central Road Board, to build roads and bridges and to make connections between the coastal regions and the interior.

117 For a cartload, computed for a half a mile, and so in proportion for longer distances; *Cape of Good Hope Almanac and Annual Register 1850* (Cape Town: Van de Sandt & De Villiers: 1850).

118 Oxen were preferred for draught except in the environs of Cape Town itself. Mules were not numerous. Donkeys had been imported from the Cape Verde Islands, and from early in the eighteenth century there were mules near grain-producing centres like the Malmesbury district; *Report of the Commissioners of Inquiry to the Right Hon. William Huskisson upon the Police at the Cape of Good Hope*, 10 May 1828, in Theal (1905e, p. 271).

119 Drayson (1858, p. 65).

120   Drayson (1858, pp. 70, 67). In fact, they relied on maize or 'Indian corn', oat hay and the veld itself.

121   Hayes (1894, p. 234).

122   A.G. Hales, *Campaign Pictures of the War in South Africa (1899–1900): Letters from the Front* (London: Cassell, 1901).

123   George Lacy, *Pictures of Travel, Sport, and Adventure* (London: C. Arthur Pearson, 1899), p. 408.

124   Hales (1901).

125   Their hardiness was illustrated in widely reported anecdotes such as a journey of a member of the Legislative Assembly who travelled from Colesberg to Cape Town in six days. It was said that 'no English-bred horse, fed according to English methods, could have accomplished such a ride as this'; see Lacy (1899, pp. 393, 395).

126   National Archives (United Kingdom), Young De Salis High Court Admiralty (HCA), 32-1697, part 1, letter 4-z-2; Father De Salis HCA 32-1697, part 1, letter 4-z-7.

127   'Patricius Africanus', 'Experiences in South Africa', *Irish Monthly*, 9(100), 1881, p. 534.

128   Lichtenstein (1815, pp. 79, 133).

129   Charles Thunberg, *Travels in Europe, Africa and Asia, Performed in the Years 1770 and 1779*, vol. 2 (London: 1793). Law (1980, p. 45) notes a similar phenomenon in West Africa, where mares had to feed themselves by grazing and were unpopular for riding.

130   Anon. (1916, p. 75).

131   Drayson (1858, p. 65).

132   Hales (1901).

133   *Argus Annual and South African Directory, 1890* (Cape Town: Argus, 1890), pp. 340–41. The rise of the veterinary profession in South Africa was at first an offshoot of the development of the profession abroad. A distinctive figure in his habitual frockcoat and top hat, Hutcheon qualified MRCVS at the Royal Veterinary College, Edinburgh in 1871 and was appointed as the second chief veterinary surgeon of the Cape of Good Hope in 1880, in succession to W.C. Branford.

134   *South African Almanack and Reference Book, 1911–1912* (1911, p. 196).

135   Wyndham (1924, p. 2). This was not unique to southern Africa. In Australia, for example, a horse could have a so-called 'station pedigree', which is to say that the sire was a Thoroughbred horse and the dam was given as a station mare that might or might not be Thoroughbred.

136   Ironically, left to their own devices, horses seem to have a natural incest taboo.

137   A mare could be returned to a stallion that serviced her previously to get a double measure of his traits.

138   Charles Darwin, for example, even compiled a list of cases where 'bad blood'
      polluted a whole gene line, causing it to produce tainted descendants forever.
      He made reference to Lord Morton's report to the Royal Society on a case of
      telegony in which an Arabian mare bore a hybrid to a quagga (*E. quagga*),
      and after that produced two colts by an Arabian horse. To his eyes, these colts
      resembled quaggas; Charles Darwin, *The Variations of Animals and Plants under
      Domestication* (New York: D. Appleton, 1896), pp. 8, 435.

139   See also Hermon Bumpus, 'Facts and theories of telegony', *American Naturalist*,
      33(396), 1899, pp. 917–22.

140   Leon Poliakov, *The Aryan Myth* (New York: Basic Books, 1974).

141   W. Grey Rattray, 'Horse breeding', *The SA Exhibition, Port Elizabeth, 1885* (Cape
      Town, 1886), p. 380.

142   Similar nineteenth-century prejudices against mules are recorded elsewhere; see
      Greene (2008, p. 31).

143   Ann Stoler, 'Carnal knowledge and imperial power: Gender, race, and morality
      in colonial Asia', in Micaela di Leonardo, ed., *Gender at the Crossroads of
      Knowledge* (Berkeley: University of California Press, 1991), p. 54.

144   C. Louis Leipoldt, *Bushveld Doctor* ([1937], Johannesburg: Lowry, 1980), p. 234.

145   The parallel between humans and horses 'contaminated' in this way was made
      explicitly by a professor at the University of Munich; see Ernst Rued, *Sex
      and Character* (London: William Heinemann, 1906), pp. 6, 158. Many of his
      colleagues internationally (such as Herbert Spencer, Francis Galton, Calaude
      Bermand and Eugene Kahn, later a professor of psychiatry at Yale) promoted
      this contention. These notions were later influential in the formulation of the
      German sterilisation laws intended to preclude the carriers of 'inferior' genes
      from infecting the Aryan gene pool.

146   See also R.W. Burkhardt, 'Closing the door on Lord Morton's mare: The rise and
      fall of telegony', *Studies in History of Biology*, 3, 1979, pp. 1–21.

147   *Argus Annual and South African Directory, 1890* (1890, p. 334).

148   *Argus Annual and South African Directory, 1890* (1890, p. 335). His physiological
      explanation was 'that the blood of the mother becomes inoculated with the
      character and peculiarities of the male, through the medium of the foetus,
      during its development in the uterus. The foetus … partakes of all the characters
      … of the male, and … when the male is of a different breed from the female, in
      proportion as the foetus partakes of the nature and physical peculiarities of the
      male, so will the blood of the female become contaminated, and herself a cross
      for a long time, if not for life, incapable of producing pure offspring'.

149   *Argus Annual and South African Directory, 1890* (1890, p. 336).

150   *Argus Annual and South African Directory, 1889* (Johannesburg, Cape Town &
      Pretoria: Argus Printing & Publishing, 1889), p. 328: 'In fact, a Thoroughbred
      horse implies that the animal is possessed of superior qualities of every

description, and his power of transmitting those superior qualities to his offspring surpasses that of any other breed of horses', p. 329.

151 *Argus Annual and South African Directory, 1889* (1889, p. 329).

152 *Argus Annual and South African Directory, 1890* (1890, p. 338).

153 Blood could be contaminated – by external vectors or by internal bad breeding – but it was occasionally used as a weapon to restore health; Natal Archives (hereafter NAB), CSO, 1559, 1897/8162, 'Resolution – transfusion of blood from the horse as a preventive of rinderpest', 12 October 1897.

154 Vandenbergh (2009).

155 Within present day KwaZulu-Natal and Mpumalanga.

156 There was flexibility in the term's usage: salted horses were those that had either survived being bitten by the tsetse fly or had survived horse sickness. Legend has it that such horses were easily identified by the white flecks in their coats (hence the name).

157 The label *goed gesout* meant the horse had demonstrated its immunity by travelling in disease-ridden areas after his/her first infection and surviving.

158 Hinnies are the progeny of donkey mothers and horse sires; mules are the offspring of male donkeys and female horses.

159 William Harvey Brown, *On the South African Frontier: The Adventures and Observations of an American in Mashonaland and Matabeleland* ([1899], Bulawayo: Rhodesiana Reprint Library, 1970), p. 314.

160 Of course, smaller-scale outbreaks may have occurred earlier; for a good discussion, see Vandenbergh (2009). If horses had managed to survive, they became comparatively inured to the disease. Equally, if their owners had been through an epidemic, they were more aware of the disease's dangers and were concomitantly more likely to stable, kraal or move their horses to higher ground. However, after a certain amount of time, horse owners became blasé, the regulations were softened, while concurrently the horses' physical resistance towards the disease declined as well, as fewer were 'salted' through past experience.

161 The numbers soon climbed. Remarkably, the census of 1865 recorded 226,610 horses in the Colony; see also T. Bayley, *Notes on the Horsesickness at the Cape of Good Hope, in 1854–55* (Cape Town: Saul Solomon, 1856), p. 41.

162 *The Argus Annual and South African Gazetteer 1889* (1889, p. 221).

163 Schreuder (1915, p. 47).

164 Bayley (1856, pp. 8–9).

165 G.M. Theal, *History of South Africa, from 1795–1872*, vol. 3 (London: George Allen & Unwin, 1916), p. 153.

166 Bayley (1856, pp. 41–42); see also KAB, GH 23/26, 118, 'Papers despatched to secretary of state, London. general despatches, Mr T.B. Bayley's notes on horse sickness, 1854–1855'.

167 Born in England in 1810 and having served in India, Bayley bought a Cape farm in 1844, renaming it The Oaks (after the English horse-racing event). Here he established a premier stud farm and even tried to construct a colonial stud book. This proved impossible at the time because horses were too widely dispersed and records of parentage were not routinely kept for mere utility horses. Bayley's own equine mortalities reached 43, nearly half of his stud. He sold his stud the very next year; see Wyndham (1924, p. 3); and E.H. Burrows, *Overberg Odyssey, People, Roads and Early Days* (Swellendam: self-published, 1994), p. 135.

168 Hayes (1900, pp. 49–50).

169 C. Rutherford, 'Horse sickness of South Africa', repr. from *Cape Times*, August 1885, p. 7.

170 Bayley (1856, pp. 8, 15).

171 This was the reverse of the process feared by early English breeders, who thought the damp and chill cooled the blood.

172 Lester (1998, p. 519); Greg Bankoff, 'A question of breeding: Zootechny and colonial attitudes toward the tropical environment in the late nineteenth-century Philippines', *Journal of Asian Studies*, 60(2), 2001, pp. 413–37.

173 Hayes (1900, p. 58).

174 Indeed, Bob Edgar wittily suggested this chapter be called: 'The ride and foal of the Cape horse'.

175 Theal (1902, p. 23). He wished to improve not the English Thoroughbred, but the draught horse. He claimed that the horses were so poor that farmers were reduced to using oxen. This meant that oxen were only sold for beef when past labour, and the meat was consequently tough and unpalatable; see 'Letter to Huskisson', in Theal (1898, p. 390); and Barrow (1801, p. 67).

176 G. Tylden, *Horses and Saddlery: An Account of the Animals Used by the British and Commonwealth Armies from the Seventeenth Century to the Present Day* (London: Allen, 1980), pp. 52–53, 58.

177 Clarence-Smith (2007, p. 24).

178 KAB, GH 1/260, 93, 'Papers received from secretary of state, London. General despatches, Major Apperley and Surgeon Rogers deputed to assist the local authorities in the Cape Colony in purchasing horses for India, 1857'. The horses cost at least £156,853 and almost as much again was spent on fodder and freight. In comparison, only 293 horses were exported in 1852 (value £9,657) and 213 in 1853 (value £8,414). To lend further perspective, wool exports were worth £95,145 and £110,498 in 1852 and 1853, respectively; see *Cape of Good Hope Almanac and Annual Register 1855* (Cape Town: Van de Sandt & De Villiers, 1855). KAB, CCP, CCP1/2/1/5, G3, 'Annexures to the votes and proceedings of the House of Assembly. Purchase of horses at the Cape of Good Hope for cavalry and artillery, for service in the Colony or in India, 1845–1857'; KAB, CCP1/2/1/5, G13, 'Papers relating to the supply of remount horses for the army in India, 1845–1858'; KAB, GH 23/16, 135, 'Papers despatched to secretary

of state, London: purchase of horses for the East India Company, 1846'; KAB, GH 23/19, 219, 'Papers despatched to secretary of state, London: purchase of horses for the Indian army, 1849'; KAB, CCP1/2/1/5, G13, 'Annexures to the votes and proceedings of the House of Assembly: additional papers relating to the supply of remount horses for the army in India, 1845–1858'.

179   Schreuder (1915, p. 39).

180   *Agricultural News and Farmer's Journal*, 7 February 1850. Tattersalls was the first bloodstock sales company, opening in 1766.

181   Rattray (1886, p. 370).

182   The state attempted breed improvement through the importation of Hackneys in 1888 and 1891. The Hackney, a fairly short-legged, powerful little animal, which stood above 14 to about 15.2 hands high, was a British horse breed.

183   Drayson (1858, p. 66).

184   Wyndham (1924, pp. 88–89).

185   *South African Almanack and Reference Book, 1911–1912* (1911, p. 197); see also KAB, AGR 133, 554, *Diseases of the Horses*, handbook by D. Hutcheon, 1893.

186   The name was derived from 'New South Wales'.

187   Because of the war, prices increased to £21 4s and £21 17s, respectively, in 1900; see *South African Year-Book, 1902–1903* (London, 1902), p. 469.

188   Hayes (1900, pp. 232–33).

189   Occasionally, other industries would adopt the vocabulary used by horse experts; e.g. 'purity of blood is the great essential towards producing Wool of [quality] … obtain Rams of *pure Saxon Breed*, or at least of *recent Saxon origin*'; *South African Directory and Almanac of 1834* (Cape Town, 1834), p. 128.

190   Hayes (1900, p. 72). Similarly, the director of Cape Agricultural Department noted in 1905 that 'the old Hantam horse seems almost doomed'.

191   *Argus Annual and South African Directory, 1890* (1890, pp. 341, 343).

Chapter 4

1   Thanks especially to Bob Edgar, Sam Challis, Richard Grove, Jesmael Mataga and Motlatsi Thabane; also to the archivists at Lesotho National Library and Archives (Maseru); the Morija Museum and Archives; the University of Lesotho (Roma) National Archives; and the National Archives, London. Some elements of this paper have appeared in Sandra Swart, '"Race" Horses – Horses and Social Dynamics in Post-Apartheid Southern Africa' in Distiller and Steyn (2004) and in Bankoff and Swart (2007).

2   *Volksblad*, 'Kis per helikopter na berg se kruin', 27 January 1996; Tefo Mothibeli, 'Basotho prepare for king's interment', *Saturday Star*, 20 January 1996; 'Dignitaries and masses pay final tribute to Moshoeshoe', *Saturday Star*, 27 January 1996.

3   For the symbolism of the riderless horse, and the hat and blanket on the saddle of the horse, see Scott Rosenberg, 'Promises of Moshoeshoe in culture, nationalism and identity in Lesotho, 1902–1966', Ph.D. thesis, Indiana University, 1998, p. 211.

4   Basutoland became the Kingdom of Lesotho on independence from the United Kingdom in 1966. 'Sesotho' refers to language and customs; 'Mosotho' to a person; 'Basotho' refers to people; 'Lesotho' refers to the country. I have used the term 'Basotho pony', but it is often referred to as 'Basuto pony'.

5   ANC daily news briefing, 13 July 1995, <http://www.anc. org.za/anc/newsbrief /1995/news0713>. The Lesotho monarch, owner of several racehorses, presented Mandela with the gift from the royal stable.

6   R. van de Geer & M. Wallis, *Government and Development in Rural Lesotho* (Morija: Morija Printing Works, 1982), p. 63; Tamolo Lekota, 'The state of the Basotho pony in Lesotho', <http://www.fao.org/DOCREP/006/Y3970E/y3970e08. htm>, accessed August 2005.

7   P. Savory, *Basuto Fireside Tales* (Cape Town: Howard Timmins, 1962). Horses are naturally absent from the older legends; see, for example, E. Jacottet, *The Treasury of Ba-Suto Lore* (London: Paul, Trench & Trubner, 1908); and M. Postma, *Tales from the Basotho* (Austin: University of Texas Press, 1974).

8   A form of woollen blanket associated with the upper class because of its high cost.

9   Senate Select Committee (hereafter SC), 5, 1927–28: *The Senate Report from the Select Committee on Horse-Breeding*, 28 May 1928, testimony of Frank Arthur Verney, chief veterinary officer, Basutoland.

10   Horse meat may be dried to make *lihoapa* (biltong).

11   To misquote Saki (H.H. Munro).

12   See Storey (2008).

13   Norman Etherington, *The Great Treks: The Transformation of Southern Africa* (London: Pearson Education, 2001), pp. 136, 340, 195.

14   Etherington (2001, p. 312). They may have originally acquired many of their guns, horses and riding techniques from their newly acquired clients, Khoi followers or Xhosa employed by farmers in the west of the region. The itinerant gunrunner Coenraad de Buys, for example, probably supplied the chief of the Rharhabe Xhosa with firearms and horses. Some Xhosa groups also acquired equestrian tactics and training from British clients, including a former sergeant of the Royal African Corps who became a minor chief; see Storey (2008, p. 56).

15   'Men' is used intentionally here. There is no historical or contemporary role of the horse among Basotho women; it was and remains largely a male preserve. In K. Limakatso Kendall, *Basali! Stories by and about Women in Lesotho* (Pietermaritzburg: University of Natal Press, 1995) other animals are mentioned, but not horses.

16　As Vail and others have stressed, people were less loyal to an 'ethnicity' than to a chief, with 'ethnicity' a teleological imposition; L. Vail, ed., *The Creation of Tribalism in Southern Africa* (London: James Currey, 1989).

17　See also L. Thompson, *Survival in Two Worlds: Moshoeshoe of Lesotho 1786–1870* (Oxford: Clarendon, 1975), p. 11.

18　'Basutoland' is used for clarity when referring to Moshoeshoe's kingdom prior to independence from Britain in 1966, even though the country was only officially called that in 1868.

19　Lawrence Green, *Karoo* (Cape Town: Howard Timmins, 1955), p. 200. On the 'Bastaards', see G.M. Theal, *Basutoland Records, 1833–1852*, vol. 1 ([1883], Cape Town: Struik, 1964a), pp. 1, 3, 8, 16, 22, 27, 294.

20　For discussion, see William Beinart, 'Settler accumulation in East Griqualand from the demise of the Griqua to the Natives Land Act', in W. Beinart, Peter Delius & Stanley Trapido, eds, *Putting a Plough to the Ground: Accumulation and Dispossession in Rural South Africa, 1850–1930* (Johannesburg: Ravan Press, 1986); Timothy Keegan, *Colonial South Africa and the Origins of the Racial Order* (Cape Town: David Philip, 1996); Susan Newton-King, *Masters and Servants on the Cape Eastern Frontier, 1760–1803* (Cambridge: Cambridge University Press, 1999); and Robert Ross, *Adam Kok's Griquas: A Study in the Development of Stratification in South Africa* (Cambridge: Cambridge University Press, 1976).

21　E. Casalis, *My Life in Basutoland*, trans. J. Brierley ([1889], Cape Town: Struik, 1971), p. 136.

22　Etherington (2001, p. 169).

23　Philip D. Curtin, 'Location in history: Argentina and South Africa in the nineteenth century', *Journal of World History*, 10(1), 1999, p. 69.

24　Joseph Orpen, *History of the Basutos of South Africa* (Cape Town: Cape Argus, 1857), pp. 72–73.

25　D.F. Ellenberger, *History of the Basuto, Ancient and Modern,* trans. J.C. MacGregor (New York: Negro University Press, 1969), p. 213.

26　William Lye & Colin Murray, *Transformations on the Highveld: The Tswana and Southern Sotho* (Cape Town: David Philip, 1980), p. 39.

27　'Letter from Chief Moshoeshoe to the British resident', 30 July 1849, in Theal (1964a, p. 256); 'Extracts from the work of the Rev. J.J. Freeman, *A Tour in South Africa*', 1851, in Theal (1964a, pp. 382–83).

28　Thompson (1975, p. 35).

29　Ellenberger (1969, p. 195); Peter Sanders, *Moshoeshoe: Chief of the Sotho* (London: Heinemann, 1975), p. 46.

30　Ellenberger (1969, p. 195); Elizabeth Eldredge, *A South African Kingdom: The Pursuit of Security in Nineteenth-century Lesotho* (Cambridge: Cambridge University Press, 1993), p. 71. Other reports say he received his first horse from a raid on a Boer farm; see Etherington (2001, p. 194).

31   G. Tylden, *A History of Thaba Bosiu: 'Mountain at Night'* (Morija: Morija Archives, 1950a), p. 8.

32   T. Arbousset, *Missionary Excursion into the Blue Mountains: Being an Account of King Moshoeshoe's Expedition from Thaba-Bosiu to the Sources of the Malibamatšo River in the Year 1840*, ed. & trans. D. Ambrose & A. Brutsch (Morija: Morija Archives, 1991), p. 90; Thompson (1975, p. 78).

33   Eldredge (1993, p. 26); Ellenberger (1969, p. 195); Sanders (1975, p. 46); see also R.W. Thornton, *The Origin and History of the Basotho Pony* (Morija: Morija Printing Works, 1936a); R.W. Thornton, *Hloleho le Historiea Pere ea Sesotho* (Morija: Morija Printing Works, 1936b); J.J. Grobbelaar, 'Die Vrystaatse Republiek en die Basoetoevraagstuk', *Archives Year Book* (Cape Town: Government Printers, 1939), p. 133; C.H. Malan, *South African Missions* (London: Nisbet, 1876), p. 14; D.B. Hook, *With Sword and Statute: On the Cape of Good Hope Frontier* (London: Greaves & Pass, 1905), p. 300; K.J. de Kok, *Empires of the Veld, Being Fragments of the Unwritten History of the Two Late Boer Republics* (Durban: Juta, 1904), p. 160; Godfrey Lagden, *The Basutos; The Mountaineers and Their Country*, vol. 1 (London: Hutchinson, 1909), p. 48; and Ellenberger (1969, p. 215).

34   Thomas Arbousset & F. Daumas, *Narrative of an Exploratory Tour to the North-East of the Colony of the Cape of Good Hope*, trans. John Croumbie Brown (Cape Town: A.S. Robertson, Saul Solomon, 1846).

35   Eugene Casalis, *The Basutos, or Twenty-Three Years in South Africa* ([1861], Cape Town: Struik, 1965), pp. 173–76.

36   Arbousset (1991, p. 124).

37   James Backhouse, *A Narrative of a Visit to the Mauritius and South Africa* (London: Hamilton Adams, 1844), p. 352.

38   Quoted in Eldredge (1993, p. 154).

39   Thompson (1975, p. 119).

40   G.M. Theal, *Basutoland Records, 1853–1861*, vol. 2 ([1883], Cape Town: Struik, 1964b), p. 212.

41   Orpen (1857, p. 7).

42   'Letter from the superintendent of the Wittebergen Native Reserve to the civil commissioner of Aliwal North', 21 March 1868, in G.M. Theal, *Basutoland Records, 1868*, vol. 4 (Maseru: Institute of Southern African Studies, National University of Lesotho, 2002a), p. 10; 'Letter from Chief Malapo to Sir Walter Currie', 2 April 1868, in Theal (2002a, p. 61); 'Letter from the president of the Orange Free State to the high commissioner', 28 April 1868, in Theal (2002a, p. 88); 'Letter from the superintendent of the Wittebergen Native Reserve to the civil commissioner of Aliwal North', 3 & 17 October 1868, in Theal (2002a, pp. 176, 181). For horses captured in war and political uprisings, see British Parliamentary Papers, C.2755, 1881, pp. 269–75.

43   Theal (1964a, p. 615).

44　*Minutes of Evidence, Special Commission on Laws and Customs of the Basutos and on the Operations of the Regulations Established for Their Government,* 4 December 1872, in G.M. Theal, *Basutoland Records, 1870–1872,* vol. 6 (Maseru: Institute of Southern African Studies, National University of Lesotho, 2002b), p. 241.

45　Arbousset (1991, p. 116).

46　See G. Tylden, *The Rise of the Basuto* (Cape Town: Juta, 1950b), p. 229; and Moloja, 'The story of the "Fetcani horde"', *Cape Quarterly Review,* 1 January 1882, p. 273.

47　Tylden (1950b, p. 229). Similarly, in America by the late seventeenth century the Caddo Indians' name for horses was '*cavali*', from the Spanish '*caballo*', because of their control of the equine regional trade; while the Choctaw had by the early eighteenth century developed the word '*isuba*' (from '*isi holba*' or 'resembling a deer'); see James Taylor Carson, 'Horses and the economy and culture of the Choctaw Indians, 1690–1840', *Ethnohistory,* 42(3), 1995, p. 497.

48　Tylden (1950b, p. 9).

49　Sanders (1975, p. 46); Ellenberger (1969, p. 195).

50　The British authorities recognised Moshoeshoe's land claims in 1842, as they desired a counterweight to the Boers.

51　Theal (1964a, p. 45).

52　'Philip to Hare', 12 July 1842, in Theal (1964a, pp. 44–46). For an interesting discussion, see Keegan (1996, pp. 248–49).

53　Keegan (1996, p. 251) notes that Moshoeshoe's views were often shaped by missionary advisers, particularly the enthusiastic evangelical imperialist Eugène Casalis.

54　Keegan (1996, pp. 256–57).

55　For a west African analysis, see Law (1980, p. 1).

56　'Extracts from the work of the Rev. J.J. Freeman, *A Tour in South Africa*', 1851, in Theal (1964a, p. 395).

57　Arbousset (1991, p. 113; see also pp. 58–69, 72, 91, 112, 161–65; and pp. 38, 95, 113, 114, 115–22, 147–48).

58　F. Maeder, *Journal de Mission Evangelque,* Morija Archives, entry for 15 January 1858, p. 33.

59　As late as the start of the twentieth century the assistant commissioner had to go so far as to discredit the myth formally; S. Barrett, *The Field,* July 1901.

60　Gill notes that in the nineteenth century marijuana figured among the main staples grown in Lesotho; Stephen J. Gill, *A Short History of Lesotho* (Morija: Morija Museum & Archives, 1993), pp. 7, 45.

61　Ellenberger (1969, p. 195); Thornton (1936a); Grobbelaar (1939, p. 133); Malan (1876, p. 14); Hook (1905, p. 300); De Kok (1904, p. 160).

62　Tylden (1950b, p. 9).

63　Casalis (1965, p. 170).

64   Theal (1964a, p. 381).

65   Theal (1964a, p. 629).

66   'Extracts from the work of the Rev. J.J. Freeman, *A Tour in South Africa*', 1851, in
      Theal (1964a, p. 381).

67   This was made more difficult after the Batlokoa incorporated horses and guns
      into their own arsenal; Anthony Atmore & Peter Sanders, 'Sotho arms and
      ammunition in the nineteenth century', *Journal of African History*, 12(4), 1971,
      p. 537.

68   Thompson (1975, pp. 240, 278).

69   Thornton (1936a, p. 8).

70   It formalised the loss to Basutoland of the area north of the Caledon and a
      significant portion between the Caledon and Orange Rivers, lost originally in the
      second Basotho war with the Boers.

71   Theal (1964b, p. iv).

72   Eldredge (1993, p. 72).

73   Geographic isolation played a role too – the Senqu-(Orange) and Senqunyane
      Valleys, for example, are isolated by mountain ranges. They therefore relied
      solely on horse transport for longer.

74   Estimated by the missionary Casalis, 'Despatch from Sir H.G. Smith to Earl
      Grey', 3 February 1848, in Theal (1964a).

75   Judith Kimble, *Migrant Labour and Colonial Rule in Basutoland, 1890–1930*,
      monograph no. 1 (Johannesburg: ISER, 1999), p. 16.

76   Arbousset (1991, p. 37); extract from 'A sketch of the principal events relative to
      the government of the Basutos since 1833' (supplied by Moshoshoe in 1852), in
      Theal (1964a, p. 2).

77   Arbousset (1991, pp. 37, 51).

78   Kimble (1999, p. 9).

79   Kimble (1999, pp. 13, 17).

80   Tylden (1950b, p. 118).

81   Timothy Keegan, 'Trade, accumulation and impoverishment: Mercantile capital
      and the economic transformation of Lesotho and the conquered territory,
      1870–1920', *Journal of Southern African Studies*, 12(2), 1986b, pp. 197–98.

82   *Mafisa*: a system of livestock lending that gives the manager rights to the
      animals' draught power while the owner retains the rights to their offspring.

83   Thompson (1975, pp. 194–95).

84   David B. Coplan & Tim Quinlan, 'A chief by the people: Nation versus state in
      Lesotho', *Journal of the International African Institute*, 67(1), 1997, p. 57.

85   Masopha was Moshoeshoe's third son.

86   J.M. Mohapeloa, *Government by Proxy: Ten Years of Cape Colony Rule in Lesotho,
      1871–1881* (Morija: Morija Printing Press, 1971), p. 15.

87   *Minutes of Meeting held at Maseru by the High Commissioner's Agent*, 16 August
      1871, in Theal (2002b, p. 95).

88   Thompson (1975, p. 196) notes that although their horses were sound, their weapons were not, as they were a mixture of Napoleonic war vintage and cheap Birmingham trade muskets. For a useful discussion of guns among the Basotho, particularly after the 1852 Sand River Convention, which prohibited the gun trade, see Atmore & Sanders (1971, pp. 535–44).

89   L. William Lye, ed., *Andrew Smith's Journal of His Expedition into the Interior of South Africa, 1834–36* (Cape Town: A.A. Balkema, 1975), p. 64.

90   M. Martin, *Basutoland: Its Legends and Customs* (New York: Negro University Press, 1969), p. 40.

91   Oral testimony taken by Constant Ficq, in 'Die betekenis van perde in die bewoning van die Lesotho-Hoogland', MA diss., RAU, 1988, pp. 85–86.

92   Thornton (1936a, p. 10); Tylden (1950b, p. 36).

93   Quoted in Thompson (1975, p. 194).

94   Thompson (1975, p. 195); Tylden (1950b, p. 59).

95   On the difference between cattle and horse as symbols, see, for example, in 1872, the 'Basotho [made] use of the word "reka" when they say buy a horse &c., but the cattle given in marriage are called the "bohadi"'; *Minutes of Evidence, Special Commission on the Laws and Customs of the Basutos and on the Operations of the Regulations Established for their Government*, 4 December 1872, in Theal (2002b, p. 233).

96   For the changing nature of *bohali*, see Colin Murray, 'The symbolism and politics of *bohali*: Household recruitment and marriage by installment in Lesotho', in E.J. Krige & J.L. Comaroff, eds, *Essays on African Marriage in Southern Africa* (Cape Town: Juta, 1981), p. 119.

97   The *molisana* is the 'herder' horse that the woman's father uses to fetch his cattle.

98   Even as late as 2003 interviewed women laughed and said they would ride 'only if they never hoped to get another boyfriend', although they conceded that they could ride in an emergency; personal communication in interviews, Malealea, December 2003.

99   Martin (1969, p. 40).

100   Ficq (1988, p. 113). For a historical focus on women in Lesotho, see Marc Epprecht, *'This Matter of Women Is Getting Very Bad': Gender, Development and Politics in Colonial Lesotho* (Pietermaritzburg: University of Natal Press, 2000).

101   Eldredge (1993, p. 72). Epprecht and others have commented that donkeys, on account of their destructive grazing habits, were the focus of a punitive campaign by the government in the 1920s and 1930s in Basutoland. The chiefs (at least ostensibly) supported the Basotho women (as the adults who used donkeys most) against the state on this issue, thus preserving donkeys; Marc Epprecht, personal comment and Epprecht (2000, pp. 48, 124).

102   Eldredge (1993, p. 151).

103   From almost the start of Moshoeshoe's rule, Basotho journeyed to work on farms and in the Cape's urban centres.

104 J.G. Fraser & James Briggs, *Sotho War Diaries, 1864–1865* (Cape Town: Human & Rousseau, 1985), p. 103; census returns for 1891, in Eldredge (1993, p. 71).

105 Eldredge (1993, p. 147). See Blue Books, G 41–74; G 27–73. The 'Basuto Horse' were irregular local troops in the 1870s and 1880s. Raised by the British from 1877, they served as 'horse-boys and breakers'; see Newnham Davis, *The Transvaal under the Queen* (London: Sands, 1900), pp. 94–96.

106 Hales (1901).

107 Pule Phoofolo, 'Face to face with famine: The BaSotho and the rinderpest, 1897–1899', *Journal of Southern African Studies*, 29(2), 2003, p. 510. For the experiences of Africans in the war, see Peter Warwick, *Black People and the South African War, 1899–1902* (Cambridge: Cambridge University Press, 1983).

108 This was a temporary reprieve and there was a long-term cost to pay: the large-scale unregulated trade spread equine and bovine disease.

109 Fraser emigrated to southern Africa in 1872 and began by buying horses in Basutoland for resale on the diamond fields. By 1880 the Fraser brothers were among the most successful traders in Basutoland and, with the uncertainty of the Gun War, bought out other traders, thereby consolidating their hold.

110 James Walton, *Father of Kindness and Father of Horses, Ramosa le Ralipere: A History of Frasers Limited* (Wepener: Frasers, 1958), p. 33; W. Nasson, 'Moving Lord Kitchener: Black military transport and supply work in the South African War, 1899–1902, with particular reference to the Cape Colony', *Journal of Southern African Studies*, 11(1), 1984, p. 33.

111 *South African Year Book, 1902–1903* (1902, p. 422).

112 Eldredge (1993, pp. 159–60).

113 B.C. Judd, 'With the CMR', *Nongquai*, June 1938.

114 Another interpretation might be that the Basotho trader is asking the remount officer for an exaggerated price by claiming that his stock is all 'salted'.

115 B. Paterson, 'A visit to Basutoland', *Sydney Morning Herald*, 15 December 1900.

116 Sessions (1903, pp. 19–20).

117 For example, Theal observes that the Basotho kept 'specially trained oxen' taught to act as 'leaders of the other cattle when out at pasture, and to race riderless from a distance [if summoned by a whistle or chant], sometimes several miles, to the home kraal'; G.M Theal, *History of SA before 1795*, vol. 1 (Cape Town: Struik, 1964c), pp. 67, 100, 154; vol. 2, pp. 210, 227. Possibly it was a custom acquired from the Khoi, who from the early eighteenth century were said to have trained oxen to herd, and even perhaps fight in battle; see Peter Kolbe, *The Present State of the Cape of Good Hope* (New York: Johnson Reprint, 1968), pp. xvi, 178, 286. One must be aware of the difference between a 'cattle complex' and other social phenomena, although it is inappropriate to explore the issue here; see, for example, with application to a different cultural group, Paul K. Bjerk, 'They poured themselves into the milk: Zulu political philosophy under Shaka', *Journal of African History*, 47(1), 2006, pp. 1–19.

118 B. Paterson, 'A visit to Basutoland', *Sydney Morning Herald,* 15 December 1900.

119 Right up until the present, this pervades the discourse on tourist-centred pony trekking.

120 B. Paterson, 'A visit to Basutoland', *Sydney Morning Herald,* 15 December 1900.

121 See H.B. Barclay, *The Role of the Horse in Man's Culture* (London: Allen, 1980), pp. xi, 17.

122 For example, in early 1899 a representative from the Bakwena (from Bechuanaland Protectorate) arrived to discuss bartering Basotho horses for Bakwena cattle. A Zulu deputation visited Basutoland the following month to trade Zulu cattle for Basotho horses; see Phoofolo (2003, p. 526).

123 Also referred to as the Basotho Pony and Basuto Pony/pony.

124 J.M. Christy, *Transvaal Agricultural Journal,* 1908; Schreuder (1915, p. 101).

125 Lesotho National Archives (hereafter LNA), S 5/7, 'Smyth to Clarke', 15 August 1889.

126 LNA, Cd. 3285, 6; LNA, Cd. 3729–20, 4; LNA, S5/34, 'Selborne to Sloley', 20 January 1908. Between 1907 and 1932 mainly Thoroughbred blood was introduced; see National Archives, Public Record Office, London, DO119/1096.

127 Colonial Office Basutoland, *Report for 1902–1903, Colonial Report Annual,* no. 408 (London: Colonial Office, 1903).

128 E.S. Rolland, 'Notes on the political and social position of the Basuto tribe', Aliwal North, 30 March 1868, in Theal (2002a, p. 48).

129 J.M. Mohapeloa, *Tentative British Imperialism, 1884–1910* (Morija: Morija Museum & Archives, 2002), pp. 123–24.

130 Crosby (2004, pp. 23, 48).

131 Tylden (1950b, p. 208).

132 Kimble and Grove have respectively revealed the importance of struggles over environmental issues in rural anti-colonial movements. In late nineteenth-century West Africa and in other British-controlled territories after the Second World War, peasants and their chiefs resisted the colonial state's control over environmental resources, which fostered closer co-operation with proto-nationalists; see D. Kimble, *A Political History of Ghana: The Rise of Gold Coast Nationalism* (Oxford: Oxford University Press, 1963); and Richard Grove, *Ecology, Climate and Empire: Colonialism and Global Environmental History, 1400–1940* (Cambridge: White Horse Press, 1997).

133 Francis Haines, 'The northward spread of horses among the Plains Indians', *American Anthropologist,* 40, 1938, pp. 429–37. After the Pueblo Rebellion of 1680 horses escaped Spanish corrals at Sante Fe and multiplied throughout the West, facilitated by local Indian trade that dispersed them across the Great Plains.

134 Carson (1995, p. 504).

135 In the same way, for example, Choctaw men of military age in a time of social crisis (with the collapse of deer hunting and traditional warfare) banded together

to form a body of mounted men in a national police force from 1823. They were thus able to retain a martial function and preserve 'traditional' equine practices; see Carson (1995, p. 503).

136   By the latter half of the 1880s horses had spread to the leisure domain, with pony racing becoming a popular pastime. The traveller Alice Blanche Balfour observed: 'The Basutos are great horse racers, racing barebacked, as they assert that girths interfere with the animals' breathing'; Alice Blanche Balfour, *Twelve Hundred Miles in a Waggon* (London: Edward Arnold, 1895), p. 56. This love of horse racing was remarked upon in the 1920s; Senate SC, 5, 1927–28: *The Senate Report from the Select Committee on Horse-Breeding*, 28 May 1928, testimony of Frank Arthur Verney, chief veterinary officer, Basutoland.

137   Thompson (1975, p. 194).

138   David Ambrose, *Summary of Events in Lesotho*, 3(1), 1996, National University of Lesotho, <http://www.trc.org.ls/events/events19.961.htm>.

139   Ambrose (1996).

Chapter 5

1   Parts of this chapter appeared in Sandra Swart, 'Horses in the South African War, 1899–1902', *Animals & Society*, 18, 4, 2010. Andrew 'Banjo' Barton Paterson (1864–1941) (his pseudonym, 'The Banjo', was the name of one of his father's racehorses) was a war correspondent for the Australian press. Upon disembarking in South Africa, on the strength of his reputation as a horseman, he gained entree into elite circles. His experiences of war were ambivalent: he was even hissed off platforms as 'pro-Boer', In this verse, he expressed his disquiet over the treatment of British-owned horses in the South African War.

2   For a good discussion of the ramifications, see Chamberlin (1996, p. 17). The oesophagus connects to the stomach at an oblique angle and at the junction is a muscular sphincter. Because of the angle and the strong sphincter, when the stomach bloats, the oesophagus is forced shut and the stomach contents and gas cannot be forced into the oesophagus. Untreated, the stomach will rupture and the horse will die.

3   There is a vast literature on the South African War; for a discussion of historiographical themes, see G. Cuthbertson, A. Grundlingh & M. Suttie, eds, *Writing a Wider War: Rethinking Gender, Race and Identity in the South African War, 1899–1902* (Athens & Cape Town: Ohio University Press & David Philip, 2002). For a comprehensive analysis, see W. Nasson, *The South African War, 1899–1902* (London: Arnold, 1999a).

4   The war had cost the British taxpayer more than £200,000,000, of which £15,329,306 was spent on horses, mules and donkeys; Royal Commission on

the War in South Africa, *Report, Minutes of Evidence and Appendices* (London, 1903), Cd. 1789–1792, p. 258.

5   The total was made up of 364,693 imperial and 82,742 colonial troops.

6   A. Grundlingh, 'The national women's monument: The making and mutation of meaning in Afrikaner memory of the South African War', in G. Cuthbertson, A. Grundlingh & M. Suttie, eds, *Writing a Wider War: Rethinking Gender, Race and Identity in the South African War, 1899–1902* (Athens & Cape Town: Ohio University Press & David Philip, 2002), p. 18.

7   Africans were used as mounted riflemen, especially in the guerrilla phase of the war; see W. Nasson, *Abraham Esau's War: A Black South African War in the Cape, 1899–1902* (Cambridge: Cambridge University Press, 1991); W. Nasson, *Uyadela Wen'osulapho: Black Participation in the Anglo-Boer War* (Randburg: Ravan Press, 1999b); Nasson (1999a, p. 279); I.R. Smith, *The Origins of the South African War 1899–1902* (New York & London: Longman, 1996), p. 9; and Warwick (1983).

8   Casualties may have been higher, as these statistics refer only to those animals paid for by the public purse, omitting those seized by troops locally; Royal Commission on the War in South Africa (1903, p. 97).

9   Frederick Smith, *A Veterinary History of the War in South Africa, 1899–1902* (London: H.W. Brown, 1919), p. 226. After qualifying, Smith (1857–1929) joined the British army in 1876 and served in India. From 1886 he was attached to the Army Veterinary School at Aldershot, transferring five years later to the Remount Department. He came to South Africa as a regular Army Veterinary Department officer in November 1899 and remained until 1905, serving as principal veterinary officer after the war. After his return to England he was appointed director general of the Army Veterinary Service in 1907, retiring in 1910, after which he dedicated himself to writing. *A Veterinary History of the War* was first published in the journal *Veterinary Record* over the period 1912–14, then as a book in 1919.

10   See Marquess of Anglesey, *A History of the British Cavalry*, vols. I–V (London: Leo Cooper, 1973–94).

11   There were still some successful cavalry charges in the South African War, and after the war Colonel Haig still maintained that it was a mistake to withdraw the *arme blanche* because although its 'actual use' was small, its 'moral effect was considerable'. This was countered by Sir Ian Hamilton, who noted that compared to a modern rifle, a sword or a lance 'can only be regarded as a mediaeval toy'; Royal Commission on the War in South Africa (1903, pp. 49–50).

12   Van der Merwe (2000).

13   'Banjo' Paterson, in his poem 'Johnny Boer'.

14   'Banjo' Paterson, 'French's cavalry and their work', *Sydney Morning Herald*, 12 February 1901.

15   As the war progressed, they often abandoned the *arme blanche* and used a rifle in place of a carbine.

16   War was declared on 11 October 1899.

17   *Agterryers* (or 'after riders'; i.e. 'those who ride behind') were Boer fighters' black retainers.

18   'Remounts' are supplies of fresh horses for those worn out or killed.

19   Paterson (1998, p. 19).

20   The government paid the owners an annual amount of 10s.

21   Oxen and mules were used for ordinary transport and provision. Oxen could haul heavier loads than mules and could simply graze on the veld, but they were slow. Mules, in contrast, were faster, but they were not as strong and their forage had to be carried for them. On the Boer side, some considered a strong riding mule for marches and a nimble little pony for action a good combination. The mule's stride was long and its gait shambling and, as Reitz observed, one soon longed for the easy seat of a horse; Deneys Reitz, *Commando: A Boer Journal of the Boer War* (Johannesburg: Jonathan Ball, 1990), pp. 226, 271.

22   Sessions (1903, pp. 19–20).

23   Smith (1919, p. 132); Sessions (1903, p. 18).

24   See Smith (1919, p. 132).

25   Sessions (1903, p. 19). Horses and guns were later commandeered. Guns could be hidden, while horses could not. However, the value of the horse could be disguised. The hair on the knees could be rubbed away to make the horse appear to be a confirmed stumbler, thus avoiding confiscation.

26   Title of a poem by 'Banjo' Paterson about the misery of transporting horses by sea.

27   M. Horace Hayes, *Horses on Board Ship: A Guide to Their Management* (London: Hurst & Blackett, 1902).

28   Smith (1919, p. 253).

29   L.S. Amery, ed., The Times *History of the War in South Africa*, vol. VI (London: Sampson Low Marston, 1909), pp. 650, 655–58; Natal Archives Repository (hereafter NAB), Cd. 963, *Report on the Working of the Army Remount Department*, pp. 10–14, 31–32.

30   Sessions (1903, p. 246); NAB, vol. 6, 'District veterinary surgeon – acting principal veterinary surgeon', 9 October 1900; NAB, Cd. 994, p. 18; NAB, PM, 22, 1901/1013, 'Horses shipped from Australia reported to be suffering from glanders', 1901; NAB, PM, 22, 1901/1185, 'Chief secretary, Queensland: Relative to horses shipped from Australia reported to be suffering from glanders', 1901; NAB, PVS, 4, 59/1900, 'Hutchinson: Regarding glanders amongst horses which arrived from Australia', 1900.

31   *Report by F. Duck as to the Condition of the Army Veterinary Department previous to the War in South Africa*, 11 May 1899, Royal Commission on the War in South Africa (1903, p. 100).

Endnotes

32 For an interesting discussion, see Johan Wassermann, 'A tale of two port cities: The relationship between Durban and New Orleans during the Anglo-Boer War', *Historia*, 49(1), 2004, pp. 27–47.

33 General Sir Charles Mansfield Clarke, in Royal Commission on the War in South Africa (1903, p. 97).

34 National Army Museum, United Kingdom, Laurence L. Maxwell Papers, 7402/30-8, 25 February 1900, MS. 'Stellenbosch, reporting on life at Stellenbosch, the remount station'.

35 NAB, MJPW, 79, LW4480/1900.

36 Smith (1919, p. 128).

37 Sessions (1903, p. 22).

38 Paterson (1998).

39 For an aggrieved account by a 'Stellenbosched' officer, see National Army Museum, UK, Laurence L. Maxwell Papers, 7402/30-8, 25 February 1900, MS. 'Stellenbosch'.

40 Both preceding quotes from Sessions (1903, pp. 39, 21).

41 Ben Viljoen, *My Reminiscences of the Anglo-Boer War* (London: Hood, Douglas & Howard, 1902), pp. 512–13.

42 Sessions (1903, pp. 8–9).

43 NAB, CSO, 1652, 1900/5324, 'Arrival of SS "Norfolk" from Buenos Ayres with horses under offer to military authorities', 1900.

44 Smith (1919, pp. 230–31); Free State Archives (hereafter VAB), Cd. 882, *Report on Horse Purchase in Austro-Hungary*, 1902.

45 Some estimates have it that 40,000 Australian horses were also imported into South Africa for the war; R.L. Wallace, *The Australians at the Boer War* (Canberra: Australian War Memorial & Australian Government Publishing Service, 1976), p. 39; National Archives, Pretoria, Public Records of the former Transvaal Province and its predecessors (hereafter TAB), MGP, 62, 577/01, 'Re – Prices for Australian horses', 1901.

46 Sessions (1903, p. 30).

47 See T.D. Pilcher, *Some Lessons of the Boer War 1899–1902* (London: Isbister, 1903), pp. 78–79.

48 Sessions (1903, pp. 99–101).

49 W.J. Gordon, *The Horse World of London* ([1893], London: Allen, 1971), p. 183.

50 J.P. Snyman, personal communication.

51 Smith (1919, p. 289).

52 Smith (1919, p. 277); National Archives, UK, PRO 30/57/22, 'Kitchener papers', parts 1–2, 22 November 1901, p. 207.

53 Viljoen (1902, p. 355).

54 Gardner Williams, *The Diamond Mines of South Africa*, vol. I (New York: B.F. Buck, 1905), p. 102.

55 Alfred J. Bethell, *Notes on South African Hunting and Notes on a Ride to the Victoria Falls of the Zambesi* ([1887], Bulawayo: Books of Rhodesia, 1976), p. 12.

56 Lord Randolph Churchill, *Men, Mines and Animals in South Africa* ([1893], Bulawayo: Rhodesiana Reprint Library, 1969), pp. 121–22. Sometimes one could negotiate for a guarantee on salted horses and receive a return of purchase money if it did succumb to horse sickness; Churchill (1969, p. 309).

57 Churchill (1969, p. 128).

58 Viljoen (1902, p. 226).

59 C.J. Becker, *Guide to the Transvaal* (Dublin: J. Dollard, 1878), p. 81.

60 Viljoen (1902, pp. 376–77).

61 F. Pretorius, *Life on Commando during the Anglo-Boer War* (Cape Town: Human & Rousseau, 1999), p. 40.

62 Viljoen (1902, pp. 213–14).

63 Reitz (1990, p. 81).

64 Viljoen (1902, p. 230).

65 H.W. Nevinson, *Ladysmith: The Diary of a Siege* (London: Methuen, 1900).

66 Reitz (1990, p. 27).

67 C.R. de Wet, *Three Years' War* (New York: Charles Scribner's Sons, 1902), p. 32.

68 For the preceding quotes, see Reitz (1990, pp. 64, 103 & 193, respectively).

69 H.F. Prevost Battersby, *In the Web of a War* (London: Methuen, 1900), p. 272.

70 *Report on the Army Veterinary Department in South Africa*, 'Ian Matthews, to Colonel Duff', 15 July 1900, Royal Commission on the War in South Africa (1903, p. 100). There was also a shortage of farriers.

71 Battersby (1900, pp. 272–73).

72 Sessions (1903, p. 233).

73 Viljoen (1902, pp. 31–32).

74 Cited in Anglesey (1973–94, vol. IV, p. 356).

75 Gale & Polden Ltd, *A Handbook of the Boer War* (London & Aldershot: Butler & Tanner, 1910), p. 192; see also Smith (1919, p. 39).

76 Horses carried saddlery, rifle, bucket, sword with scabbard, groundsheet, nosebags, rope, grooming kit, spare shoes and a variety of smaller items.

77 T. Pakenham, *The Boer War* (New York: Random House, 1979), p. 343.

78 Gale & Polden (1910, p. 166).

79 Reitz (1990, p. 217). For more on exhaustion, see National Archives, UK, PRO 30/57/22, 'Kitchener papers', parts 3–4, 22 November 1901; 20 April 1902.

80 Royal Commission on the War in South Africa (1903, p. 99).

81 J.Y.F. Blake, *A West Pointer with the Boers* (Boston: Angel Guardian Press, 1903), p. 241.

82 P.J. le Riche, ed., *Memoirs of General Ben Bouwer* (Pretoria: HSRC, 1980), p. 59.

83 C.J. Swanepoel, 'Hoe ry die Boere', *Tydskrif vir Volkskunde en Volkstaal*, 41(1), 1985, pp. 28–30. Boers tended to ride with only the left hand on the reins and they often favoured the control offered by a curb or Pelham bit as a consequence.

84 M. Horace Hayes, *Among Men and Horses* (London: T. Fisher Unwin, 1894), p. 29.

85 Reitz (1990, p. 1).

86 Just as in the case of West Africa, the dominance of cavalry had more than solely military implications; it had an important influence on the character of political structures and social institutions; see Law (1980, p. 184).

87 Hales (1901).

88 Lacy (1899, pp. 405–6).

89 G.M. Dorré, *Victorian Fiction and the Cult of the Horse* (Aldershot: Ashgate, 2006), p. 13.

90 Viljoen (1902, p. 518).

91 Cited in Anglesey (1973–94, vol. IV, p. 351).

92 Reitz (1990, p. 165); A.A. McLean, *Letters of the Late Major A.A. McLean, DSO, from the Date of His Leaving Australia for the Boer War, 6th November 1899, until the Conclusion of that Campaign, 1902* (Sydney: William Brooks, 1931), letter of 3 March 1900, p. 28; VAB, CO, 9, 685/01, 'Burial of dead horses by military', 1901.

93 Hales (1901).

94 For example, the evocative phrases such as the initial description of Black Beauty's home on a 'plantation of trees', the names given to the horse invoking his complexion and the slave narrative format, presenting a variety of masters' behaviours. Indeed, George Angell, founder of the Massachusetts Society for the Prevention of Cruelty to Animals (SPCA), gave free copies to cab drivers with the subtitle *The Uncle Tom's Cabin of the Horse*.

95 Like abolishing the use of bearing reins: the term 'bearing rein' is derived from 'mien; behaviour; carriage'. (Although critics contended ironically that the term might equally mean 'suffering without complaint'.) High-headed carriage was a mark of nobility: this was a very sought-after look, but it restricted proper breathing and made it harder to pull a load; see Peter Stoneley, 'Sentimental emasculations: *Uncle Tom's Cabin* and *Black Beauty*', *Nineteenth-century Literature*, 54(1), 1999, pp. 53–72.

96 See Sparrman (1975–77, pp. 126–27). In the first report to Holland, his name was not even mentioned, although attention was devoted to the 18 boxes of money salvaged. When Woltemade's body washed ashore in June 1773 he was buried without ceremony in an unmarked grave. Later, however, a VOC ship was named after him; his widow received compensation; in 1956 a statue was erected in his honour; and a commemorative stamp was issued in 1973.

97 Those like Dick Turpin's Black Bess appear to be later inventions teleologically imposed on the early eighteenth century.

98 There is some doubt about this, discussed in the final chapter. King's ride was to alert the British to the need for reinforcements against the Boers in Natal in 1842. Until recently, the name of his fellow rider, Ndongeni Ka Xoki, was

seldom mentioned and the name of the latter's horse is unknown. An equestrian monument to Dick King on the Victoria Embankment in Durban was erected in 1915.

99   Much of this was sheer myth making. Recent research has shown that Napoleon's famous horse, Marengo, may be a creation of the public imagination and that representations of the fiery little Arab stallion were drawn from several different horses. Equally revealing of the social significance of horsemanship as a signifier of power was that Napoleon was a mediocre rider, and his frequent involuntary descents were hidden from the public; see Jill Hamilton, *Marengo: The Myth of Napoleon's Horse* (London: Fourth Estate, 2000).

100 Cruelty to animals was banned in the Cape (1856); Natal (1874); the Orange Free State (1876); and the South African Republic (1888). The mother SPCA was founded in Cape Town in 1872.

101 Reitz (1990, p. 137). De Wet prayed to God to spare his Fleur, struck down by a foreign 'English disease' and then, when prayer failed, buried him on his farm.

102 After the war, some British officers returning home tried to place their war horses on state stud farms to ensure a happy retirement for their old comrades; TAB, LTG, 53, 68/5, 31 March 1903.

103 G. Fleming, 'The physical condition of horses for military purposes', Aldershot Military Society, London, 31 January 1889, p. 9.

104 'Banjo' Paterson, *The Bulletin*, 18 October 1902.

105 Pakenham (1979, p. 487).

106 Reitz (1990, pp. 16, 144).

107 Reitz (1990, p. 227).

108 The verses are a free translation to convey the atmosphere of the original poem. 'Voorslag', the name of the horse, literally means 'whiplash', but figuratively also 'live wire'. Interestingly, in terms of animal agency, one who is very efficient at performing certain tasks and can be relied on, especially when taking charge and using initiative is required, is often referred to as a '*voorslag*' in Afrikaans.

109 Viljoen (1902, p. 227).

110 Standertonner (pseudonym), 'Hendrik Prinsloo', *Huisgenoot*, 4 December 1936.

111 Viljoen (1902, p. 46).

112 Reitz (1990, p. 155).

113 Reitz (1990, p. 159).

114 Hales (1901).

115 Battersby (1900, pp. 217–18).

116 H.C. Hopkins, *Maar Een Soos Hy: Die Lewe van Kommandant C.A. van Niekerk* (Cape Town: Tafelberg, 1963), p. 53.

117 Viljoen (1902, p. 359).

118 Pretorius (1999, p. 284); Reitz (1990, p. 16).

119 TAB, MGP, 12, 1282/00, 'Asking that an order may be issued that horses who are in low condition may be taken to the site of burial and shot there', 26 July

1900; TAB, MGP, 13, 1522/00, 'Re: killing of horses', 2 August 1900; Reitz (1990, p. 207); E. Lee, *To the Bitter End* (London: Guild, 1985).

120 Reitz (1990, pp. 153, 161, 272, 258).

121 TAB, Preller Collection, 10, 'L. Botha to B.J. Viljoen', 21 November 1901, p. 45.

122 See Viljoen (1902, p. 207).

123 H. ver Loren van Themaat, *Twee Jaren in den Boerenoorlog* (Haarlem: H.D. Tjeenk Willink, 1903), p. 87.

124 Viljoen (1902, p. 220).

125 Reitz (1990, pp. 153, 170, 183–84, 200).

126 Reitz (1990, p. 221).

127 Battersby (1900, pp. 197–98).

128 Viljoen (1902, p. 503).

129 Sol T. Plaatje, *Mafeking Diary: A Black Man's View of a White Man's War* (Cambridge & London: Meridor Books, with James Currey, 1990), p. 108.

130 James Greenwood, *Odd People in Odd Places* (London: Frederick Warne, 1883), p. 214.

131 NAB, C4388, 'Anglo-Boer War: Slaughtering horses for consumption at Ladysmith', 1899–1902; NAB, 'Slaughtering horses for food, Siege of Ladysmith', 1899–1902.

132 Some horsemeat was consumed by those Africans allowed to buy it, mixed with oat bran and mealies; Pakenham (1979, pp. 407–8).

133 Nevinson (1900).

134 Herbert Watkins-Pitchford had been appointed principal veterinary surgeon by the Natal government four years previously; H. Watkins-Pitchford, *Besieged at Ladysmith: A Letter to His Wife, Written in Ladysmith during the Siege* (Pietermaritzburg: Shuter & Shooter, 1964), p. 107.

135 Battersby (1900, p. 21).

136 E. Oliver Ashe, *Besieged by the Boers: A Diary of the Siege of Kimberley* (London: Hutchinson, 1900), p. 111.

137 Ashe (1900, pp. 93–94).

138 Paterson (1998, pp. 30–31).

139 Ashe (1900, pp. 83–89, 98–99).

140 This was because of the ideology of empire, increasing wealth and faster communications; see Meurig Jones, 'A survey of memorials to the Second Anglo-Boer War in the United Kingdom and Eire', *Journal of the Africana Society*, 15, 1999.

141 Most early regimental memorials named only the officers and not the non-commissioned officers and men.

142 Reitz (1990, p. 307).

143 Contributions came variously from the London Metropolitan Drinking Trough Association; schools; businessmen; various military units; and individuals in England, Australia and North America.

144 J.J. van Tonder, *Sewentien Perd- en Ruitermonumente in Suid-Afrika* (Krugersdorp: self-published, 1971), pp. 75–85.
145 *New Orleans Times Democrat*, 'South African memorial to horses', 3 January 1909.
146 See, for example, *Die Bittereinder*, Danie de Jager, War Museum, Bloemfontein.
147 *Volksblad*, 9 October 1986, p. 5.
148 Rudyard Kipling, 'The lesson' (1903).
149 NAB, *Government House*, vol. 838, 'W. Hely-Hutchinson–A.G. Vansittart', 10 December 1900; NAB, Cd. 1792, Royal Commission on the War in South Africa (1903, pp. 97–98).
150 Royal Commission on the War in South Africa (1903, p. 47).
151 Royal Commission on the War in South Africa (1903, pp. 45–47).
152 A point Helen Bradford made about the fallacy of just 'adding women' to history; see H. Bradford, 'Women, gender and colonialism: Rethinking the history of the British Cape Colony and its frontier zones, c.1806–70', *Journal of African History*, 37(3), 1996, pp. 351–70.
153 'Banjo' Paterson, 'The last parade'.
154 Smith (1919, p. 297).

Chapter 6

1. The quote in the title is from correspondence in the South African National Archives Repository (hereafter SAB), Agriculture Education and Research division (hereafter LON), A173/13, 'P.J. Schreuder to W. Callender-Easby', 23 April 1946.
2. Hermann Giliomee, *The Afrikaners: Biography of a People* (Cape Town: Tafelberg, 2003), p. 322.
3. TAB, Lieutenant Governor (hereafter LTG), 53, 68/7, 'Director of agriculture to Milner', 30 October 1902.
4. TAB, High Commissioner (hereafter HC), 1.45, Col. Birbeck, 'Appreciation of the horse breeding problem in South Africa', October 1901.
5. In the former Orange Free State 90 per cent of homesteads and farm houses were damaged and a large proportion in the Transvaal were destroyed; see Giliomee (2003, p. 322).
6. TAB, Governor of the Transvaal Colony (hereafter GOV), 482, PS 129/01, 'Sir N.G. Lyttelton, commanding the forces in SA, to Milner', 31 March 1903; TAB, GOV, 40, GEN 272/03, 7 March 1903.
7. TAB, GOV, 492, PS 129/01, no. 66, Government Office, Bloemfontein, 23 May 1903, 'Colonial Secretary's Office to resident magistrates'.
8. TAB, Transvaal Agriculture Department (hereafter TAD), 438, G2107, 'Director of agriculture to commissioner of lands', 11 November 1904; SAB, secretary of

agriculture (hereafter LDB), 1037, R775, *Recommendations of Special Committee, Report on Resolutions of Natal Agricultural Union*, April 1911.

9.   John K. Hill, 'Horse breeding in South Africa', *South African News,* 2 September 1902, p. 3; indeed, Lord Methuen believed that 'Dams were generally of more importance than the Sires'; see TAB, GOV, 1223, PS 82/8/09, 'Meeting, Roberts Heights', 18 January 1909.

10.   TAB, LTG, 53, 68/11, 'Milner', 13 May 1903.

11.   Shula Marks & Stanley Trapido, 'Lord Milner and the South African state', *History Workshop,* 8, 1979, pp. 50–80.

12.   TAB, HC, 1.45, Col. Birbeck, 'Appreciation of the horse breeding problem in South Africa', October 1901.

13.   TAB, GOV, 482, PS 129/01, 'Milner to military secretary', 16 April 1903; TAB, TAD, 74, A372.

14.   TAB, GOV, 39, GEN 188/03, 'Colonial Office to War Office', 4 February 1903.

15.   TAB, GOV, 39, GEN 188/03, 'Colonial Office to War Office', 4 February 1903.

16.   TAB, LTG, 53, no. 68/7, 'Director of agriculture, Transvaal, to Milner', 30 October 1902.

17.   TAB, GOV, 490, 129/01, 'Milner to Chamberlain', 17 July 1903; TAB, GOV, 492, PS 129/01, no. 743, 'Milner', 22 December 1902.

18.   TAB, GOV, 40, GEN 272/03, 12 February 1903. After a meeting in Bloemfontein, a Stud Book was mooted and the Stud Book Association was established in 1905. In 1920 parliament promulgated an act to incorporate the South African Stud Book and affiliated societies to record and publish pedigrees of livestock (Registration of Pedigree Livestock Act No. 22 of 1920); SAB, LON, A173/27, vol. 1, 'Horses, national horse shows, conferences etc.' The Thoroughbred breed was excluded from the definition of 'livestock'.

19.   B.F.S. Baden-Powell, *War in Practice* (London: Isbister, 1903), p. 73; R.S.S. Baden-Powell, *Sport in War* (London: Heinemann, 1900), p. 49.

20.   TAB, GOV, 492, PS 129/01; TAB, GOV, 492, PS 129/01, 188, 'War Office to Colonial Office', 4 February 1903; TAB, LTG, 53, no. 67/56, 2, 2, 'Milner to Chamberlain', 27 June 1903.

21.   TAB, GOV, 492, PS 129/01, no. 743.

22.   TAB, HC, 1.45, Col. Birbeck, 'Appreciation of the horse breeding problem in South Africa', October 1901.

23.   TAB, GOV, 492, PS 129/01, no. 66.

24.   TAB, GOV, 492, PS 129/01, no. 66.

25.   TAB, GOV, 492, PS 129/01, no. 5590.

26.   TAB, GOV, 492, PS 129/01.

27.   TAB, GOV, 491, PS 129/01, no. 2078/02; TAB, GOV, 492, PS 129/01, no. 590; TAB, GOV, 492, PS 129/01, no. 540; TAB, LTG, 53, no. 67/55, 1903.

28.   TAB, GOV, 492, PS 129/01, no. 743.

29. KAB, Government House (hereafter GH), 1/502, 152, 'Papers received from secretary of state, improvements of breeds of horses in Ireland', 1909.
30. TAB, GOV, 491, PS 129/01, no. 484, 19 April 1902; TAB, GOV, 40, GEN 272/03, 12 February 1903; TAB, LTG, 53, no. 68/0, 30 March 1903; TAB, GOV, 40, GEN 272/03, 28 February 1903; TAB, GOV, 491, PS 129/01, no. 476, 18 June 1902; TAB, LTG, 53, no. 68/2; TAB, LTG, 53, no. 68/5.
31. TAB, GOV, 491, PS 129/01, no. 484, 4 June 1902.
32. VAB, under-secretary for Department of Agriculture (hereafter DA), 50 [2080.11.1910], Transvaal Agricultural Union, 'Distribution of military mares', secretary of Transvaal Agricultural Union, 1 August 1909
33. TAB, GOV, 1223, PS 82/8/09, 'Meeting, Roberts Heights', 18 January 1909.
34. TAB, TAD, 185, A 3314, 'Notice of removal of provincial quarantine under Government Notice no. 834 of 1903'; TAB, TAD, 185, A 3310, 'Notice of provisional quarantine under Government Notice no. 1257 of 1904'.
35. The control of livestock movement, in particular sick animals, had a long history. For example, in the Cape, mid-nineteenth-century glandered animals had to be kept shut up. Owners had to quarantine infected stock and inform the local magistrate/field-cornet and neighbours. If a horse escaped or was used for treading out grain, the human responsible faced a fine or even a gaol sentence (Lung-ziekte Act No. 1, 1853). The state could prohibit importation from particular countries. See KAB, GH, 1/162, 2841, 'Approval of Ordinance no. 5 of 1844 to prevent the spread of a horse disease called glanders', 1844.
36. Sol T. Plaatje, *Native Life in South Africa* ([1916], Johannesburg: Ravan Press, 2006), p. 85.
37. KAB, GH, 23/129, 282, General despatches: Laws re: horse-breeding, 'Merriman to Hely-Hutchinson', 24 November 1909.
38. *The Friend*, 'Horses for the army', 30 July 1909.
39. TAB, GOV, 1223, PS 82/8/09, 'Meeting, Roberts Heights', 18 January 1909; Methuen reiterated his position periodically; see SAB, LDB, 1037, R775, 'Methuen to governor general', 5 October 1911.
40. TAB, GOV, 1223, PS 82/8/09, 'Meeting, Roberts Heights', 18 January 1909. This was never a serious concern. Draught horses were never owned by a large sector of the public, but were deployed in pre-motor days for transport, military and police work, with agricultural work delegated to oxen. The promotion of heavy draught breeds in commercial agriculture was really a post-South African War initiative and was rapidly overtaken by mechanisation.
41. VAB, DA, 50 [2080.11.1910], 'Regulations'.
42. SAB, LDB, 1037, R775, 'Annual Conference of the Agricultural Union', Pietermaritzburg, 1911. In the Transvaal in 1911 the numbers were: stud stallions 3,840; brood mares 21,638; others 63,682; see SAB, LBD, 1037, R775.
43. *South African Year Book 1914* (London: Routledge, 1914), p. 183. Mules numbers were decreasing rapidly.

44. *South African Almanack and Reference Book, 1911–1912* (1911, p. 196). According to the 1904 census there were 2,409,804 humans in the Cape (of whom 318,544 were white males), but there were only 255,060 horses (or one per ten humans). Similarly, in the Transvaal there were 1,355,442 humans in 1904, as opposed to just 52,166 horses. Horses always remained more plentiful than donkeys and mules.

45. Hayes (1894, p. 232).

46. Senate SC, 5, 1927–28: *The Senate Report from the Select Committee on Horse-Breeding*, 28 May 1928, testimony of Frank Arthur Verney, chief veterinary officer, Basutoland, p. 22.

47. Senate SC, 5, 1927–28: *The Senate Report from the Select Committee on Horse-Breeding*, 28 May 1928, testimony of Frank Arthur Verney, chief veterinary officer, Basutoland, p. 22.

48. Little (1887, pp. 29–30).

49. The standard fee, plus insurance premium, to inoculate against horse sickness followed the value of the horse. For a horse valued at £10 it was £1 10s; for a horse worth £11 the fee was £1 12s (costing the state about 10s per dose for the serum). It was introduced into the Transvaal, first at a rate of two horses per owner, in 1911; the total number inoculated in 1912–1913 was 415, deaths were 65; see *South African Year Book 1914* (1914).

50. Senate SC, 5, 1927–28: *The Senate Report from the Select Committee on Horse-Breeding*, 28 May 1928, testimony of Frank Arthur Verney, chief veterinary officer, Basutoland, p. 22.

51. *South African Year Book 1914* (1914, p. 182); for example, the value of feathers exported in 1912 was £2,609,638.

52. Eldredge (1993, pp. 159–60).

53. In 1913 the state offered to subsidise farmers who owned premium stallions, as part of its move towards selling off its own tax-funded studs; SAB, LBD, 1037, R775, 'Ass. principal veterinary surgeon to secretary for agriculture', 30 January 1914; SAB, LDB, 1037, R775, vol. 1, 'Secretary of agriculture, proposed award of premiums to stallions', 13 September 1913.

54. SAB, governor-general, 1851, 54/337, 'Governor-general minute 842', 27 August 1913; Alex Robertson, 'Horse breeding in South Africa', *Rand Daily Mail*, 15 August 1914.

55. SAB, LBD, 1037, R775, Secretary for agriculture: *Promotion of Horse Breeding Report*, 1913. In 1914 there were about 719,000 horses in South Africa and little prospect of a burgeoning export trade. In comparison, for example, Australia had 2,279,000 horses and in the previous five years Australia managed to export £1,192,755 worth, compared to South Africa's £70,000 worth; *Rand Daily Mail*, 'Breeding remounts', 15 August 1914.

56. KAB, 3/CT, vol. 4/2/1/1/37, ref. 188/12; KAB, 3/KWT, vol. 4/1/280, ref. 2R/1/55.

57. KAB, 3/CT, 4/2/1/1/155, 1035/12, 'Motor car and Scotch cart accident', 1913.

58. Nasson (1984, p. 43).
59. *South African Almanack and Reference Book*, 1911–1912 (1911, p. 88); KAB, Justice Department (hereafter JUS), 72, 21155/09, 'Cape Town motor car regulations', 1909; KAB, 3/KWT, 4/1/30, AE7, 'Motor car regulations', 1912–14.
60. In contrast, a mid-nineteenth-century cab would travel at not less than 6 m/h; *General Directory and Guide Book to the Cape of Good Hope and Its Dependencies* (1869, p. 281).
61. *South African Almanack and Reference Book*, 1911–1912 (1911, p. 827). In 1906 the total cost of car importation was £99,500; by 1910 it had risen to £290,400.
62. From 370,000 in 1940 to 1.3 million in 1960.
63. It was not an easy shift from privately owned horse-drawn transport to electric public utility of trams on the Witwatersrand, for example. For the bumpy road to mechanised transport as a cog in the industrial state, see Van Onselen (2001, p. 202).
64. *Landbou Weekblad* was established in 1919. See, for example, Landbou Weekblad, 'Die outomobiel', 6 July 1921, p. 137.
65. Dooling (1999, p. 232).
66. For a brilliant discussion of donkeys in liminal areas, see Nancy Jacobs, 'The Great Bophuthatswana Donkey Massacre: Discourse on the ass and the politics of class and grass', *American Historical Review*, 106(2), 2001, pp. 485–507; see also T.E. Simalenga & A.B.D. Joubert, *Developing Agriculture with Animal Traction* (Alice: University of Fort Hare, 1997).
67. Paul Starkey, 'Animal power in South Africa: Some social and technological issues', workshop, NRI, Chatham, September 1994.
68. SAB, Board of Trade and Industry (hereafter RHN), 1469, 'Importation of mules'.
69. This occurred in other contexts. In America, for example, between 1850 and 1880 the number of urban horses grew because railway freight called for local delivery and fast-growing cities needed passenger services; McShane & Tarr (2007); see also Gordon (1971, p. 24).
70. Compiled from Department of Agriculture (1960–61).
71. SAB, LON, 291, A13/8, 'Breeding list', Division of Animal and Crop Production, Potchefstroom, 3 May 1946.
72. Paul Starkey (ed.), *Animal Power in South Africa: Empowering Rural Communities* (Gauteng: Development Bank of Southern Africa, 1995).
73. KAB, 3/GR 4/1/1/25, no. 8/7D (m).
74. KAB, 3/GR 4/1/1/25, no. 8/7D (m).
75. Shoeing horses was a monthly or six-weekly expense. In 1920 the average cost was 1/6d per shoe; KAB, 3/CT 4/2/1/1/387, no. 52/20. Even mules were shod; KAB, 3/CT 4/2/1/1/387, no. 52/20. A harness cost £10/15/- per set (English leather double-wagon harness); a double Scotch cart harness was priced at £17/15/- per set.

76. SAB, LON, 291, A13/8, 'Director of Agricultural Education and Research, the Percheron and Jack Stock Studs', 31 March 1946.

77. SAB, LON, 291, A13/8, 'Director of Agricultural Education and Research, the Percheron and Jack Stock Studs', 31 March 1946.

78. KAB, 3/KWT 4/1/209, S21/48, 'Keeping of horses in town', 1946; Provincial Administration no. 376, 24 September 1931.

79. KAB, 3/CT 4/1/4/61, no. B317/4.

80. SAB, LDB, 1037, R775, vol. 1, 19 October 1928.

81. John Brewer, *Black and Blue: Policing in South Africa* (Oxford: Oxford University Press, 1994), p. 19.

82. SAB, South African Police (hereafter SAP), 214, 13/64/31, 'Commissioner of the South African Police to director of agriculture', 12 August 1946. By 1937 the force leased a breeding farm, Grootdam, from the De Beers Mining Company stocked with 1,100 horses.

83. Commissioner of the South African Police, Annual Report (Pretoria: Government Printers, 1945), p. 8.+

84. SAB, SAP, 214, 13/64/31, 'Commissioner of the South African Police to director of agriculture', 12 August 1946.

85. Horses remained of use in stock-theft units (in areas inaccessible to cars) and in visible policing efforts, offering a higher vantage point and higher visibility.

86. See S. Swart, 'Desperate men: Rebellion and the politics of poverty in the 1914 rebellion', *South African Historical Journal*, 42, May 2000, pp. 161–75; S. Swart, '"You were men in war time": The manipulation of gender identity in war and peace', *Scientia Militaria*, 28(2), December 1998a, pp. 187–99; and S. Swart, 'A Boer and his gun and his wife are three things always together', *Journal of Southern African Studies*, 24(4), December 1998b, pp. 737–51.

87. J.K. O'Connor, *The Africander Rebellion* (London: Allen & Unwin, 1915), p. 12.

88. This was a widespread trend – albeit manifesting local idiosyncracy – evident, for example, in Britain; see David Cannadine, 'After the horse: Nobility and mobility in modern Britain', in N. Harte & R. Quinault, eds, Land and *Society in Britain, 1700–1914* (Manchester: Manchester University Press, 1996).

89. Today called Makwassie, near Wolmaransstad in North West Province.

90. Eric Rosenthal, *General De Wet* (Cape Town: Simondium, 1968), p. 250.

91. Senate SC, 5, 1927–28: *The Senate Report from the Select Committee on Horse-Breeding*, 28 May 1928, testimony of Frank Arthur Verney, chief veterinary officer, Basutoland, p. 22.

92. C.R. Swart was the last governor-general of the Union and the first state president from 1961 to 1967.

93. Translated from the original Afrikaans; cited in Van Tonder (1971).

94. Giliomee (2003, p. 375).

95. Standertonner (pseudonym), 'Hendrik Prinsloo: Held en ridder', *Huisgenoot*, 4 December 1936, p. 83.

96. Simon van Garderen, '"Ou Skaapvel": Die beroemde ryperd van Komdt. Prinsloo', *Huisgenoot*, 5 February 1937, p. 23.

97. Translated from the original Afrikaans, in Perdeboer (pseudonym), 'Die Voortrekker se perd', *Huisgenoot*, 11 December 1936, p. 75.

98. This dyad had a long history and outsiders also observed this trait. A Portuguese traveller observed in 1870: 'Die Boer op sy perd is 'n sentour ...'; quoted in O.J. Ferreira, ed., *Da Costa Leal in die Zuid-Afrikaanse Republiek* (Pretoria: Protea, 2008), p. 199.

99. C.A. Groenewald, 'Enkele herinnerings aan 'n groot digter: Eugène Marais', *Suiderstem*, 7 September 1937.

100. Hans Jurie Vermaas, *Sy Perd Staan Gereed* (Cape Town: Nasionale Pers, 1954). There were few similar novels among English speakers. One, *A Rooinek's Ride*, was written in 1951 for not only riders, but for 'the motorist, cyclist and the pedestrian', those 'in danger of forgetting that South Africa does not consist solely of a ... National road bounded on both sides by wire fences and ... telegraph poles'; J.B. Shephard, *A Rooinek's Ride* (Cape Town: Longman, Green, 1951).

101. H.J. Vermaas, *Die Perdedief* (Cape Town: Nasionale Boekhandel, 1960), p. 102.

102. Mikro (Christoffel Hermanus Kühn, 1903–1968) was the author of 111 books in many different genres. Born in the Williston district, he studied agriculture at Stellenbosch University. After several years as a teacher, he was editor of *Boerdery in Suid-Afrika*, 1956–60 and led the *Landdiensbeweging* (Farmers' Movement) of the Ministry of Agriculture until his retirement in 1964. His work frequently appeared in *Huisgenoot* and was widely recognised. He received the Hertzog Prize for Prose (1936); the W.A. Hofmeyr Prize (1956) for *Die Porselein Kat*; the Scheepers Prize for youth literature (1957) for *Die Jongste Ruiter*; and the National Publishers' Award (1961).

103. Mikro, *Die Jongste Ruiter* (Cape Town: Nasionale Boekhandel, 1954); *Die Kleingeld-Kommando* (Pretoria: Van Schaik, 1956); *Die Jongste Veldkornet* (Johannesburg: Simondium, 1963); *Die Ruiter in die Nag* (Cape Town, Bloemfontein & Port Elizabeth: Nasionale Pers, 1936).

104. Mikro's *Die Ruiter in die Nag* was so popular it was filmed in 1968.

105. Mikro, *Kaptein Gereke* (Cape Town, Bloemfontein & Port Elizabeth: Nasionale Pers, 1937).

106. Translated from the original Afrikaans, in Mikro (1937, pp. 201–2).

107. Translated from the original Afrikaans in Mikro, *Boerseun* (Bloemfontein, Cape Town & Port Elizabeth: Nasionale Pers, 1947), p. 22.

108. Translated from the original Afrikaans in Mikro (1947, p. 22).

109. See, for instance, Standertonner, 'Hendrik Prinsloo', *Huisgenoot*, 4 December 1936, p. 83.

110. Translated from the original Afrikaans in Perdeboer (pseudonym), 'Die voortrekker se perd', *Huisgenoot*, 11 December 1936, p. 107.

Endnotes

111. Mikro (1954, pp. 5, 10).
112. Translated from the original Afrikaans in Johann Bühr, 'Manne te perd', *Huisgenoot,* 16 October 1936, p. 22.
113. Translated from the original Afrikaans in 'Ou pantoffel' (pseudonym), 'Menings van ons lesers: Ook maar onder die pantoffel', *Landbouweekblad,* 23 December 1942, p. 29.
114. While still a teenager, the iconic Gonda Butters (later Betrix) competed under special licence to participate as an adult in both South Africa and Britain in 1958.
115. Horses, oxen and mules had strong masculine connotations in some communities; Starkey (1994, p. 6). For a comparison in North America, see Greene (2008, p. 39).
116. See Chapter 5 and Jacobs (2001).
117. G.J. Joubert, 'Velbroek die swarte', *Huisgenoot,* 8 October 1937, p. 20.
118. Certainly, this sub-text was not limited to such Afrikaner notions of horsemanship nor to the florescence of writing in the 1930s. An English-speaking member 'protested that it seemed a pity that the police horses at the Cape Town Cavalcade had been ridden by natives', because the whites were in the forces; SAB, LON, 290, A173/5, vol. 2, *Minutes of General Meeting of Horse and Mule Breeders Association,* 2 May 1944.
119. Translated from the original Afrikaans, in 'Heropbouing van ons perdestapel', *Boerdery in Suid-Afrika,* July 1934, p. 259.
120. KAB, JUS, 3/527/17 (part 3), *Police Inspector's Report,* Transvaal Native National Congress, Ebenezer Hall, Johannesburg, 12 June 1918, Solomon Plaatje's speech.
121. Jochem van Bruggen is credited with writing one of the first popular Afrikaans novels, *Ampie die Natuurkind* (Amsterdam: Swets & Zeitlinger, 1924). He won the prestigious Hertzog Prize for literature four times; J.P. Smuts, ''n Belangrike bydraer tot ons prosa: Van Bruggen, Ampie se skepper, gedenk', *Die Burger,* 'Boeke', 29 September 1989, p. 18.
122. Translated from the original Afrikaans in J. van Bruggen, *Die Sprinkaanbeampte van Sluis* (Cape Town: Van Schaik, 1998), p. 42.
123. Translated from the Afrikaans, Van Bruggen (1998, p. 44).
124. From this scene onwards, for the rest of the novel (a further 60 pages), the horse or descriptions of Lambertus on the horse are mentioned specifically at least 12 more times, underscoring the centrality of the animal in character development; Van Bruggen (1998, pp. 49, 51, 55, 58, 60, 62, 66, 74, 86, 96, 98, 99).
125. SAB, LON, 293, A173/31; SAB, LON, 293, A173/28.
126. SAB, LON, 290, A173/4.
127. W.J. van der Merwe, 'Horses: In defence of the American saddler', letters to the editor, *Farmer's Weekly,* 12 November 1947, p. 63.
128. *Farmer's Weekly,* 'Union's first horse textbook', 25 January 1949, p. 89.
129. *Farmer's Weekly,* 'Union's first horse textbook', 19 January 1949, p. 89.

130. SAB, LON, 293, A173/24, 'Central Agricultural Society to Dr Schreuder';
'Landboukollege en Proefplaas, Potchefstroom to Dr Schreuder', 11 January
1949; 'Northern Cape Agricultural Society to Dr Schreuder', 15 December 1948;
'Dr Schreuder to Worcester Landbougenootskap', 26 November 1947.

131. K.D. Mackenzie, 'Die Suid-Afrikaanse perd (Boerperd)', *Boerdery in Suid-Afrika*,
September 1933.

132. P.J. v.d. H. Schreuder & K.D. Mackenzie, 'Die heropbouing van ons perdestapel',
Boerdery in Suid-Afrika, April 1934.

133. P.J. v.d. H. Schreuder, 'Die boer en sy ryperd', *Boerdery in Suid-Afrika*, February
1934.

134. P.J. v.d. H. Schreuder & K.D. Mackenzie, 'Die heropbouing van ons perdestapel',
Boerdery in Suid-Afrika, April 1934.

135. Senate SC, 5, 1927–28: *The Senate Report from the Select Committee on Horse-
Breeding*, 28 May 1928.

136. Some optimistic Orange Free State breeders echoed arguments made by Lord
Charles Somerset a century earlier by suggesting that Thoroughbred horses, if
bred domestically, could be exported to India if there were a military crisis; SAB,
LDB, 18/9/, R2260, House of Assembly, Petition no. 478/27-1928. A protectionist
duty of £5 was imposed on every imported mule, mostly from Argentina (the
Horse and Mule Breeders Association lobbied futilely to double it); see SAB,
RHN, 1469, 'Importation of mules'.

137. This was considerable. To raise and train a Thoroughbred from foal to first
earning cost about £200.

138. SAB, LDB, 18/9/, R2260, *Report of the Select Committee on Horse Breeding*, 1932.

139. It also reflected a desire to derive more revenue from a lucrative industry:
£250,000 was exacted annually by provincial councils for racing.

140. SAB, LDB, 18/9/, R2260, 'Senator Munnik's plaint: Rapscallion horse importers',
19 March 1932, 'G.G. Munnik: Open letter to the minister of finance'.

141. SAB, LDB, 18/9/, R2260, 'Secretary of Jockey Club to minister of agriculture',
5 April 1932. In addition, the bill suggested that geldings not bred in South
Africa could not race. Existing geldings were grandfathered into the bill (the
term 'grandfather' was a trifle ironic, given the circumstances).

142. Senate, SC, 5, 1915–27, 'Union of SA, Horse Racing Bill', 11 November 1927.

143. Senate SC, 5, 1927–28, *The Senate Report from the Select Committee on Horse-
Breeding*, 28 May 1928.

144. Senate SC, 5, 1927–28, *The Senate Report from the Select Committee on Horse-
Breeding*, 28 May 1928, testimony of Frank Arthur Verney, chief veterinary
officer, Basutoland, p. 26.

145. Plaatje (2006, p. 96).

146. SAB, LON, 291, A13/8, 'Director of Agricultural Education and Research, the
Percheron and Jack Stock Studs', 31 March 1946. The areas into which Africans

had been moved did suffer land degradation due to overcrowding, precipitating anxieties about overgrazing by equids, especially donkeys.

147. SAB, LON, 291, A173/4, 'Eastern Border Farmers Association to minister for lands', 4 October 1937.

148. The department had contributed to some extent towards draught horse improvement, keeping Percherons at the agricultural schools.

149. 'Alpha', *Horse and Saddle in South Africa (a Vision)* (Cape Town: Maskew Miller, 1943).

150. SAB, LON, A173/13, 'P.J. Schreuder to W. Callender-Easby', 17 March 1944.

151. SAB, LON, A173/13, 'P.J. Schreuder to chairman, Registered Saddle Horse Society of SA', 15 April 1948.

152. Senate SC, 5,1927–28, *The Senate Report from the Select Committee on Horse-Breeding*, 28 May 1928, testimony of Sir Julius Jeppe, chairman of Jockey Club of South Africa, p. 71.

153. SAB, LON, 291, A173/8, vol. 3, 'Director of Agricultural Education and Research, the Percheron and Jack Stock Studs', 1 July 1947.

154. SAB, LON, A173/27, vol. 1, 'Horses, national horse shows, conferences etc.'

155. SAB, LON, A173/13, *Chairman's Report of the Horse and Mule Breeders Association of South Africa and Registered Saddle Horse Breeders Association of South Africa and Rhodesias*, 2 May 1944.

156. SAB, LON, 291, A173/4, 'To encourage farmers to own good stallions and encourage them further to retain their best young mares for breeding purposes'.

157. K.D. Mackenzie, 'Die Suid-Afrikaanse perd (Boerperd)', *Boerdery in Suid-Afrika*, September 1933.

158. SAB, LON, 291, A173/4, 'A.M. Bosman to secretary for agriculture', 12 October 1939.

159. P.J. v.d. H. Schreuder & K.D. Mackenzie, 'Die heropbouing van ons perdestapel', *Boerdery in Suid-Afrika*, April 1934.

160. SAB, LON, 291, A173/8, vol. 3, 'Director of Agricultural Education and Research, the Percheron and Jack Stock Studs', 1 July 1947.

161. SAB, LON, 300, A184/6.

162. Original emphasis; SAB, LON, 221, A120/57, 'Short course in horse husbandry', Glen College, principal's letter, 5 November 1946.

163. SAB, LON, 221, A120/57, 'Horse and Mule Breeders Association to chief, animal and crop industry', 19 September 1946; LON, 221, A120/57, 'Inclusion of horse shoeing in two-year diploma', 9 November 1950; LON, 221, A120/57, 'Short course in horse husbandry', 17 November 1948.

164. Only the minute industry of draught horse breeding remained largely in state hands; SAB, LON, 291, A13/8, 'Director of Agricultural Education and Research, the Percheron and Jack Stock Studs', 31 March 1946.

165. SAB, LON, 300, A184/6, 'Proposals for the improvement of horse breeding in the Western Province'.

166. SAB, LON, 221, A120/57, 'Short course in horse husbandry', 1946.
167. Karen Brown, 'Tropical medicine and animal diseases: Onderstepoort and the development of veterinary science in South Africa 1908–1950', *Journal of Southern African Studies*, 31(3), 2005, pp. 513–29.
168. R.A. Alexander, 'Immunisasie van perde en muile teen perdesiekte', *Boerdery in Suid-Afrika*, July 1934; R.A. Alexander, 'Perdesiekte', *Boerdery in Suid-Afrika*, September 1934. Later, well-funded research into equine disease was driven not by the state, but by the needs of the racing industry, focusing on diseases of Thoroughbreds; SAB, LON, 293, A173/33, 'G.S. Maré to secretary for agriculture', 27 March 1951.
169. SAB, LON, 291, A13/8, 'Director of Agricultural Education and Research, the Percheron and Jack Stock Studs', 31 March 1946.
170. SAB, LON, 293, A173/27, vol. 1, 'Horses, national horse shows, conferences etc.', speech by Schreuder, 'A national horse show', 3 March 1948.
171. Concurrently with a draught horse project, from 1934, Percherons, Grootfontein School, Potchefstroom, Cedara, Glen; LON, 293, A173/8, vol. 1(5), March 1934 to 6 November 1939.
172. Hennie Basson, 'Die cowboys van weleer', *SA Horseman*, May 2007, pp. 78–79.
173. SAB, LON, 293, A173/27, vol. 1, 'Horses, national horse shows, conferences etc.', letters, 1948.
174. SAB, LON, 293, A173/26, 'Horses: Horse breeding, films and books, journals and photos', 'Texas A and M, to Schreuder', 27 July 1949; 'L.W. van Vleet to Schreuder', 21 July 1949.
175. SAB, LON, 293, A173/27, 'P.J. Schreuder to S.P. Fouché', 8 August 1949; SAB, LON, 293, A173/27, vol. 1, 'Horses, national horse shows, conferences etc.', 'Schreuder to Fouché', 8 August 1949.
176. SAB, LON, 293, A173/26, 'Horses: Horse breeding, films and books, journals and photos', 'Schreuder to I. Truman Ward', 14 June 1949.
177. SABN, LON, 293, A173/26, 'Horses: Horse breeding, films and books, journals and photos', 1947.
178. Translated from the original Afrikaans; SAB, LON, 293, A173/26, 'Horses: Horse breeding, films and books, journals and photos', 'Schreuder to Senator W.P. Steenkamp', 8 October 1946.
179. SAB, LON, 293, A173/26, 'Horses: Horse breeding, films and books, journals and photos', Schreuder, 'Scenario: The horse on the farm', 1946.
180. SAB, LON, 293, A173/26, 'Horses: Horse breeding, films and books, journals and photos', 'Schreuder to librarian, Houses of Parliament', 4 January 1947.
181. *Huisgenoot*, 'Taaiste manne wat SA opgelewer het', 9 June 1950, pp. 26, 60–63.
182. SAB, LON, 293, A173/27, vol. 1, 'Horses, national horse shows, conferences etc.', Conferensie over Paardenfokkery, 6–8 September 1948.
183. SAB, LON, 293, A173/27, vol. 1, 'Horses, national horse shows, conferences etc.', Conferensie over Paardenfokkery, 6–8 September 1948.

184. SAB, LON, 293, A173/27, vol. 1, 'Horses, national horse shows, conferences etc.', speech by Schreuder, 'A national horse show', 3 March 1948.
185. SAB, LON, 291, A173/4, 'Meeting, horse improvement', 11 October 1939.
186. SAB, LON, A173/13, *Minutes of the Horse and Mule Breeders Society of SA*, 1 June 1949.
187. SAB, LON, A173/13, *Minutes of the Horse and Mule Breeders Society of SA*, 1 June 1949.
188. The full mechanisation of the South African Artillery officially began in 1935 and horse-drawn artillery made its last public appearance in 1936 at a Union Day parade.
189. The Horse and Mule Breeders Association did facilitate the export of 35,772 equines during the war, but post-war markets were restricted; *Die Middellander*, 'The part played by Middelburg Cape in the development of the riding horse industry in South Africa', 9 September 1983; SAB, LON, A173/13, 'W. Callender-Easby to P.J. Schreuder', 29 April 1946.
190. SAB, Department of Trade and Industry (hereafter HEN), 1372, 161/29/732, 'Greek government purchase of horses and mules', 24 January 1949; SAB, HEN, 1372, 161/29/732, 'Code telegram, secretary for external affairs, Pretoria, to SA Legation, Athens', 3 December 1948.
191. SAB, HEN, 1372, 161/29/732, 'Secretary for external affairs on Greek government purchase of horses and mules', 10 December 1948.
192. *Farmer's Weekly*, 'Union's first horse textbook', 25 January 1949, p. 89.
193. SAB, LON, 290, A173/5, vol. 2, *Minutes of General Meeting of Horse and Mule Breeders Association*, 2 May 1944; SAB, LON, 290, A173/7, 25 February 1948.
194. SAB, LON, 293, A173/27, vol. 1, 'Horses, national horse shows, conferences etc.', speech by Schreuder, 'A national horse show', 3 March 1948.
195. *Weet Wat Wat Is* (pseudonym), 'Trekker vs perd', *Landbou Weekblad*, 22 August 1945.
196. SAB, LON, A173/13, 'P.J. Schreuder to W. Callender-Easby', 23 April 1946.

Chapter 7

1   This chapter was published in a previous incarnation as Sandra Swart, "High Horses – Horses, Class and Socio-economic Change in South Africa", *Journal of Southern African Studies*, 34, 2, 2008.
2   This line from Emerson's poetic commentary on the rise of (American) consumerism seemed apposite; see Ralph Waldo Emerson, 'Ode, inscribed to W.H. Channing', in *Poems* (Boston: James Munroe, 1847).
3   The term *horsepower* gained currency in the late eighteenth and early nineteenth centuries in the context of a growing obsolescence of horses in an industrialising

Britain, with James Watt determining that a horse could do 33,000 foot-pounds of work a minute in drawing up coal from a coal pit.

4   The Horse and Mule Breeders Association did facilitate the export of 35,772 equines during the war, but post-war markets were restricted; see *Die Middellander*, 'The part played by Middelburg, Cape in the development of the riding horse industry in South Africa', 9 September 1983; SAB, LON, A173/13, 'W. Callender-Easby to P.J. Schreuder', 29 April 1946.

5   Vehicle numbers increased from 370,000 in 1940 to 1.3 million in 1960; W. Beinart, *Twentieth Century South Africa* (Oxford: Oxford University Press, 2001), p. 182.

6   SAB, LON, A 173/13, *Minutes of the Horse and Mule Breeders Association of SA*, 1 June 1949.

7   SAB, LON, A 173/13, *Minutes of the Horse and Mule Breeders Association of SA*, 1 June 1949.

8   SAB, LON, A173/13, 'P.J. Schreuder, to W. Callender-Easby', 23 April 1946.

9   The American Saddlebred in South Africa is now called the 'SA Saddlehorse'. The horses are also variously known as Saddle horses, Saddlers and Saddlebreds. Nomenclature adopted in this chapter tries to be chronologically rather than retroactively correct.

10   See P. Botha, 'The Saddle horse is alive and well in the Western Cape', *Farmer's Weekly*, 29 June 2001, p. 38. The phrase is repeated in Juliette Lewis, 'American Saddlebreds online', *Farmer's Weekly*, 30 August 2002, p. 45; and P. Swift & J. Szymanowski, *The Sporting Horse in Southern Africa* (South Africa: BoE Private Bank, 2001), p. 16.

11   This offers us a window into only one of the regnant rural paradigms. It is, of course, dangerous to homogenise rural life; analysts must be sensitive to the huge socio-economic variation that existed over time and area. In the South African context, for example, there were *houtkappers*, citrus growers, wine farmers, wool farmers and sugar cane farmers, to list but a few.

12   Oral interviews with Pieter Hugo, John Swart & Petro Botha; see also *Farmer's Weekly*, 'Stiff competition in American Saddler National Championships', 19 March 1958, p. 29.

13   One must be wary of the fallacy of *cum hoc ergo propter hoc*, as correlation is not necessarily causation. Nonetheless, there is ample evidence of the connection between upward mobility and the acquisition of Saddlers as status symbols.

14   The Afrikaans plural – Boerperde – is usually preferred.

15   L. Mumford, *Technics and Civilization* (New York: Harcourt & Brace, 1934), p. 105; T.J. Schlereth, 'Country stores, county fairs, and mail-order catalogues: Consumption in rural America', in Simon Bronner, ed., *Consuming Visions: Accumulation and Display of Goods in America, 1880–1920* (New York: W.W. Norton, 1989), p. 340. For American discussion, see D. Blanke, *Sowing the American Dream: How Consumer Culture Took Root in the Rural Midwest*

Endnotes

(Athens: Ohio University Press, 2000); R.P. Kline, *Consumers in the Country: Technology and Social Change in Rural America* (Athens: Ohio University Press, 2000); and T. Ownby, *American Dreams in Mississippi: Consumers, Poverty, and Culture 1830–1998* (Chapel Hill: University of North Carolina Press, 1999). In South African historiography, see, for example, Ross (1999), who proposes a new method that seeks to constitute 'a history of the markers of status', p. 3.

16 J. Lears, 'Beyond Veblen: Rethinking consumer culture in America', in Simon J. Bronner, ed., *Consuming Visions: Accumulation and Display of Goods in America, 1880–1920* (New York: W.W. Norton, 1989), pp. 73–97.

17 Moreover, as Adorno noted, it is not helpful to rarefy (and thereby implicitly criticise) 'display', when most cultural practices and goods contain elements of display (and therefore in so doing assail 'culture' itself); T. Adorno, 'Veblen's attack on culture' (1941), reprinted in T. Adorno, *Prisms*, trans S. & S. Weber (Cambridge, MA: MIT Press, 1981), pp. 73–94.

18 The sole area of the hoof could be encased in a system of pads to alleviate concussion; J. Murdoch, 'Shoeing for trueness of gaits', *Farmer's Weekly*, 26 January 2001.

19 A switch (hairpiece made by hand) could be braided into the existing hairs to lengthen the sweep of the tail. During the author's fieldwork in show stables at the Robertson Agricultural Show on 2 October 2004 false tails were lined up on pegs against the walls like models' hairpieces at a fashion show.

20 N. Clatworthy, 'Social-class and value factors in Saddle-horse showing', *Free Inquiry in Creative Sociology*, 9(2), 1981, pp. 135–38.

21 L. Kaplan, *American Saddle Horses in South Africa* (Cape Town: self-published, 1974), p. ix.

22 SAB, LON, A173/13, *Minutes of the Foundation Meeting of the Registered Saddle Horse Breeders Association of South Africa*, 23 November 1942. Note that 'saddle horses' in this context is a general term referring to horses used for riding, not draught, and should not be confused with the American Saddle horses, which, as we have seen, is a specific breed (thus indicating the general problems with nomenclature that have been noted in various footnotes throughout this book).

23 *Farmer's Weekly*, 'Fanie Fouché talks horses – but only if they are American five-gaiters', 12 June 1951. See Carol Birkby & L. de Wet, 'A brief history of SA Saddle horses', *Farmer's Weekly*, 8 August 2003, p. 12. Tradition has it that Fouché was making a phone call and while waiting to be connected purportedly glanced at a magazine photo of a Saddlebred; he immediately became intent on breeding them.

24 Fouché imported the first mares in 1947; thus for the first three decades all Saddlebreds were part-breds, being bred from South African mares; SAB, LON, A173/13, 'P.J. Schreuder to N.W. Dimock', 1 August 1947.

25 *Farmer's Weekly*, 'National futurity shows advocated for South Africa', 18 June 1952, p. 13.

26 By 1918 there were 231 tractors and by 1930 there were 3,684 in use nationwide; see S. Jones & A. Müller, *The South African Economy, 1910–90* (Basingstoke: Macmillan, 1992), p. 43. By the 1960s private car ownership boomed, absorbing 9 per cent of total private consumption expenditure; see H.T. Andrews et al., *South Africa in the Sixties: A Socio-economic Survey* (London: South Africa Foundation, 1962), p. 25. For a further brief note on mechanisation – an under-discussed phenomenon – see A. Jeeves & J. Crush, eds, *White Farms, Black Labour: The State and Agrarian Change in Southern Africa, 1910–1950* (Pietermaritzburg: University of Natal Press, 1997), p. 12.

27 C. Norden, 'The Boerperd', *Farmer's Weekly*, 26 February 1958, p. 29.

28 L. de Wet, 'A brief history of SA Saddle horses', *Farmer's Weekly*, 8 August 2003, p. 12; SAB, LON, A173/13, 'P.J. Schreuder to C.J. Cronon', 28 November 1947.

29 SAB, LON, A173/13, 'S.P. Fouché to P.J. Schreuder', 1 December 1947.

30 SAB, LON, A173/13, 'S.P. Fouché to P.J. Schreuder', 3 January 1948.

31 SAB, LDB, 1038 R775, vol. 4., V.107/31, 'Director of veterinary services to the secretary for agriculture and forestry', August 1945; SAB, LDB, 1038 R775, vol. 4, 'S.P. Fouché to director of veterinary services', 1 August 1945; SAB, LDB, 1038 R775, vol. 4, 'Secretary of agriculture to P.T. Retief', 6 November 1945; SAB, LDB, 1038 R775, vol. 4, 'US Dept Agriculture to director of veterinary services', 2 November 1945.

32 SAB, LDB, 1038 R775, vol. 4, 'Office of the minister of native affairs to minister of agriculture', 21 October 1946. However, the passage could be as low as £150 if managed correctly; SAB, LON, A173/13, 'P.J. Schreuder to P.J. Louw', 28 May 1946.

33 SAB, LDB, 1038 R775, vol. 4, 'Director of veterinary services to secretary for agriculture', 25 March 1947; SAB, LDB, 1038 R775, vol. 4, 'Minister of agriculture to Oppenheimer and son', n.d. (1946); 'Minister of agriculture to R. Barnett', n.d. (1946); 'V.H. Russ to secretary of agriculture', 29 October 1946.

34 J.S. Pansegrouw, 'Cult of the Saddle horse', *Farmer's Weekly*, 27 March 1940, p. 123.

35 SAB, LON, A173/13, P. J. Schreuder, 'Important importation of Saddlers ex USA', 31 July 1947.

36 SAB, LON, A173/13, 'P.J. Schreuder to C.E. Olivier', 31 August 1946.

37 SAB, LON, A173/13, P.J. Schreuder, 'Important importation of Saddlers ex USA', 31 July 1947.

38 E.C. Hugo, 'In defence of the Saddler', *Farmer's Weekly*, 10 December 1947, p. 63.

39 'Daily Rider' (pseudonym), 'Qualities of the American Saddler', *Farmer's Weekly*, 26 November 1947, p. 67.

40 'Alpha' (1943, p. 23).

41 B. Weyer-Henderson, 'In defence of the American Saddler', *Farmer's Weekly*, 12 November 1947; J. Versfeld, 'Importation of Saddlers', *Farmer's Weekly*, 26 November 1947, p. 67.

42   SAB, LON, A173/13, 'P.J. Schreuder to J.M. Ferreira', 24 November 1942.

43   C. Norden, 'The Boerperd', *Farmer's Weekly*, 26 February 1958, p. 29. Norden was a Middelburg (Cape Province) breeder. For a biography of this pioneering female equestrienne, see P. Hugo, 'To ride or not to ride … what a stupid question!', *South African Showhorse*, September 2004, pp. 133–39.

44   In a 1938 meeting of Orpen, Fouché, Louw, 'Koosie' Pansegrouw and Jack Oosthuizen in Colesberg, Orpen donated £8 towards starting the society, which became a reality in 1942.

45   SAB, LON, A173/13, 'P.J. Schreuder to Registered Saddle Horse Society of S.A.', 15 April 1948.

46   SAB, LON, A173/13, 'Proposed constitution of the Registered Saddle Horse Society of South Africa and Rhodesia'.

47   SAB, LON, A173/13, *Minutes of the Foundation Meeting of the Registered Saddle Horse Breeders Association of South Africa*, 23 November 1942.

48   SAB, LON, A173/13, *Newsletter No. 1, Horse and Mule Breeders Association of South Africa; and the Registered Saddle Horse Breeders Association of South Africa and Rhodesias; and Clydesdale Breeders Society of South Africa*, June 1945.

49   SAB, LON, A173/13, *Chairman's Report of the Horse and Mule Breeders Association of South Africa and Registered Saddle Horse Breeders Association of South Africa and Rhodesias*, 2 May 1944.

50   SAB, LON, A173/13, *Chairman's Report of the Registered Saddle Horse Breeders Association of South Africa and Rhodesias*, 1 May 1945.

51   SAB, LON, A173/13, *Minutes of the Registered Saddle Horse Breeders Association of South Africa*, 21 February 1945.

52   The minutes were taken in English and Afrikaans alternately; SAB, LON, A173/13, *Minutes of the Meeting of the American Saddle Horse Breeders Society of SA*, 7 February 1950, 10am. The committee included S.P. Fouché (chairman), J.S. Pansegrouw, J.H. van der Merwe, H. van Z. Kock, W.P van Notten, J.Z. Moolman, A.I. Moolman, E.L. Marais, J.P Botha, P J. Louw and B. Weyer-Henderson.

53   SAB, LON, A173/13, *Minutes of the Meeting of the American Saddle Horse Breeders Society of SA*, 7 February 1950, 2:30pm.

54   SAB, LON, A173/13, Minutes of the Meeting of the American Saddle Horse Breeders Society of SA, 7 February 1950.

55   The proposal was to have their own inspectors and this was vetoed by the state on the grounds that only the South African Stud Book could issue certificates of registration of pedigree (on pain of a fine of £500); SAB, LON, A173/13, 'H.W. Turpin (director of Agricultural Education and Research, Department of Agriculture) to American Saddle Horse Breeders Society of South Africa and Rhodesia', 25 March 1950. In Middelburg (15 October 1949) Pansegrouw had put forward a motion that breeders only register with this society and be discouraged from registering with the South African Stud Book; see SAB,

LON, A173/13, 'H.W. Turpin (director of Agricultural Education and Research, Department of Agriculture) to American Saddle Horse Breeders Society of South Africa and Rhodesia', 25 March 1950.

56   *Farmer's Weekly*, 'National futurity shows advocated for South Africa', 18 June 1952, pp. 12–13.

57   *Farmer's Weekly*, 'National futurity shows advocated for South Africa', 18 June 1952, p. 13.

58   C. Norden, 'The 1954 American Saddle Horse Championships of South Africa', South African Saddle Horse and Other Breeds, 51(2), April 1954; L. de Wet 'A brief history of SA Saddle horses', *Farmer's Weekly*, 8 August 2003, p. 13.

59   *Farmer's Weekly*, 'Union's first horse textbook', 19 January 1949, p. 89.

60   SAB, LON, A173/13, 'P.J. Schreuder to W.W. Dimock, University of Kentucky', 12 December 1946.

61   SAB, LON, A173/13, 'Schreuder to C.E. Olivier', 20 March 1946.

62   SAB, LON, A173/13, 'P.J. Schreuder to W. Callender-Easby', 23 April 1946.

63   P.J. Schreuder, 'Reply', *Farmer's Weekly*, 26 November 1947, p. 67.

64   P.J. Schreuder, 'The American Saddle horse', *Farmer's Weekly*, 10 September 1947, pp. 71–72. When the South African Stud Book Association was founded at the beginning of the twentieth century, English speakers were in the considerable majority and it took urging from agricultural extension workers and breed society staff to get significant numbers of Afrikaans-speaking breeders to adopt the paperwork of pedigree; F. van der Merwe, personal comment.

65   W.F. Versfeld, 'The fifth gait', *Farmer's Weekly*, 19 November 1947, p. 66.

66   G. Thomas, 'South African riding horses', *Farmer's Weekly*, 3 July 1946, p. 1433.

67   G. Thomas, 'South African riding horses', *Farmer's Weekly*, 3 July 1946, p. 1433.

68   J. Versfeld, 'Good South African breeds', *Farmer's Weekly*, 24 March 1948, p. 67.

69   J. van Zyl, 'Four paces only', *Farmer's Weekly*, 17 December 1947, p. 57.

70   W.F. Versfeld, 'The fifth gait', *Farmer's Weekly*, 19 November 1947, p. 66.

71   W.F. Versfeld, 'Artificial action', *Farmer's Weekly*, 10 December 1947, p. 63.

72   B. van der Meulen, 'Saddle horse types in South Africa', *Farmer's Weekly*, 12 December 1946, p. 81. He eccentrically maintained that imported French Percherons crossed with local horses would offer the 'true South African stamp'.

73   W.F. Versfeld, 'Types for South Africa', *Farmer's Weekly*, 8 October 1947.

74   M. du Plessis, 'Hantam and Saddler', *Farmer's Weekly*, 26 November 1947, p. 67.

75   B. Weyer-Henderson, 'In defence of the American Saddler', *Farmer's Weekly*, 12 November 1947.

76   *Farmer's Weekly*, 'National futurity shows advocated for South Africa', 18 June 1952, p. 15.

77   *Farmer's Weekly*, '"Ryperd", Saddlers and experts', 3 December 1947.

78   P.A. Myburgh, 'Achievements of five-gaiters', *Farmer's Weekly*, 27 August 1952, p. 19.

79   C. Norden, 'Pre-show training for riding classes', *Farmer's Weekly*, 4 April 1956, p. 23.

80   W.J. van der Merwe, 'In defence of the American Saddler', *Farmer's Weekly*, 12 November 1947.

81   M. Lievesley, 'The showy and versatile American Saddler', *Farmer's Weekly*, 2 March 1960, p. 23.

82   *Farmer's Weekly*, 'Our American Saddlers make a hit with Kentucky expert', 25 April 1956, p. 21.

83   M. Lievesley, 'The showy and versatile American Saddler', *Farmer's Weekly*, 2 March 1960, p. 22.

84   M. Lievesley, 'The showy and versatile American Saddler', *Farmer's Weekly*, 2 March 1960, p. 23.

85   E.C. Hugo, 'In defence of the Saddler', *Farmer's Weekly*, 10 December 1947, p. 63.

86   *Farmer's Weekly*, 'Our American Saddlers make a hit with Kentucky expert', 25 April 1956, p. 21.

87   For an example, see *Farmer's Weekly*, 'Stiff competition in American Saddler National Championships', 19 March 1958, p. 29.

88   H.N. Bekker, 'Standard of South African mounts', *Farmer's Weekly*, 25 January 1950.

89   *Farmer's Weekly*, 'Our American Saddlers make a hit with Kentucky expert', 25 April 1956, p. 21.

90   See *Farmer's Weekly*, 12 February 1958, p. 53. In 1952 Fouché's horses were going for £300 upwards. See L. de Wet, 'The trials, tripples and tributes of Isak Strauss', *South African Show Horse*, September 2004, p. 55.

91   R.W. Cloete, 'Virtues of the American Saddler', *Farmer's Weekly*, 8 April 1959, p. 45.

92   See, for example, *Farmer's Weekly*, 28 September 1955, p. 21.

93   *Farmer's Weekly*, 'How to take better horse photographs', 22 January 1958, p. 19. The breeders' letters also make reference to desire for 'kiekies' [snapshots] and portraits of horses; see SAB, LON, A173/13, 'Taillefer Retief to P.J. Schreuder', 26 February 1946.

94   His investigation appears to be as much satire as analysis, but he provided much of the original vocabulary of subsequent analyses and has the distinction of commenting directly on Saddle horses themselves; see T.B. Veblen, *The Theory of the Leisure Class: An Economic Study of Institutions* (New York: Macmillan, 1902). For a discussion of Veblen's contribution and limitations, see R. Mason, *Conspicuous Consumption: A Study of Exceptional Consumer Behaviour* (Hampshire: Gower, 1981).

95   There are various show classes for the Saddle horse with their own canons of beauty. For example, the 'three-gaited horse' performs walk, trot and collected canter, and the horse should show 'beauty, brilliance, elegance, refinement, expression and high action'. The 'five-gaited classes' have long flowing manes and

tails and show both ways of the show ring at walk, trot, canter, slow gait and the rack.

96   Veblen (1902, chap. 6).

97   Swift & Szymanowski (2001, p. 16).

98   SAB, LON, A173/13, 'P.J.S. (Department of Agriculture and Forestry) to Philip Myburgh', 10 September 1948; SAB, LON, A173/13, 'G.P. Steyn to P.J. Schreuder', 1 April 1948.

99   S. Jones, 'An agricultural revolution, 1950–1970: A rejoinder', *South African Journal of Economic History*, 15(1/2), September 2000, pp. 180–86. For a lead-up to this economic change, see N. Nattrass, 'Economic growth and transformation in the 1940s', in S. Dubow & A. Jeeves, eds, *South Africa's 1940s: Worlds of Possibilities* (Cape Town: Double Storey, 2005), pp. 20–43.

100 Beinart (2001, p. 181); see Department of Agriculture (1960–61, tables 35, 52 & 70).

101 As Dubow has successfully shown, the 1940s presented a plethora of possibilities: a place of rival imaginings, fluidity and socio-economic change; see S. Dubow, 'Introduction: South Africa's 1940s', in S. Dubow & A. Jeeves, eds, *South Africa's 1940s: Worlds of Possibilities* (Cape Town: Double Storey, 2005), p. 17.

102 D. O'Meara, *Forty Lost Years: The Apartheid State and the Politics of the National Party, 1948–1994* (Johannesburg: Ravan Press, 1996), p. 21.

103 Quoted in 'Jan Burger', *The Gulf Between* (Cape Town: Howard Timmins, 1960), p. 70.

104 'Jan Burger' (1960, p. 76).

105 'Jan Burger' (1960, p. 82); see also James T. Campbell, 'The Americanization of South Africa', in A. Offenburger, S. Rosenberg & C. Saunders, eds, *A South African and American Comparative Reader: The Best of Safundi and Other Selected Articles* (Nashville: Safundi, 2002), pp. 29–32.

106 D.W.J. Wijnholds, *Geld, Goud en Goedere: 'n Uiteensetting van Hedendaagse Ekonomiese Vraagstukke wat Suid-Afrika in die Besonder Raak* (Pretoria: Akademiese Pers, 1953), p. 99.

107 'Jan Burger' (1960, p. 82).

108 See K. du Pisani, 'Puritanism transformed: Afrikaner masculinities in the apartheid and post-apartheid period', in R. Morrell, ed., *Changing Men in Southern Africa* (Pietermaritzburg: University of Natal Press, 2001), pp. 157–75.

109 By 1910, 29 per cent of Afrikaners were urbanised; by 1936, 50 percent; and by 1960, 75 per cent; Giliomee (2003, p. 405).

110 D. O'Meara, *Volkskapitalisme: Class, Capital and Ideology in the Development of Afrikaner Nationalism 1834–48* (Johannesburg: Ravan Press, 1983), pp. 165–66.

111 During the 1920s and 1930s writers such as C.M. van der Heever celebrated the 'Boer' as the autochthonous figure in *plaasromans* (farm novels); J.M. Coetzee, *White Writing* (New Haven: Yale University Press, 1988), p. 83.

112 See Giliomee (2003, p. 374); and C.F.J. Muller, *Sonop in die Suide: Geboorte en Groei van die Nasionale Pers 1915–1948* (Cape Town: Nasionale Boekhandel, 1990).

113 See, for example, N. Hamman, 'Interesting townsmen in the Saddle-horse', *Farmer's Weekly*, 1 May 1940, p. 535; and *Farmer's Weekly*, 'National futurity shows advocated for South Africa', 18 June 1952, pp. 12–13.

114 SAB, LDB, 1038R775, vol. 4, 'Office of the minister of native affairs to private secretary of the minister of agriculture', 21 October 1946; John Swart, oral testimony, Stellenbosch, 5 January 2006; Frans van der Merwe, personal comment, 10 June 2007.

115 See Louise de Wet, 'A legendary breeder', *Farmer's Weekly*, 28 November 2003, p. 8; and Charl van Rooyen, 'Dekades oue teelbeleid werk', *Landbouweekblad*, 27 September 2002, pp. 36–37.

116 Beinart (2001, p. 185).

117 Two famous exceptions were Cecily Norden and Louise de Wet, both women who played a role in establishing the breed and showing regulations.

118 The magazine *Skouring* (show ring), devoted exclusively to Saddlebreds, appeared from 1963 until the 1970s.

119 R. Wrightman Fox & T.J. Jackson Lears, eds, *The Culture of Consumption: Critical Essays in American History, 1880–1980* (New York: Pantheon, 1983), p. xii.

120 Giliomee (2003, p. 544). Giliomee (2003, p. 42) relates an illustrative tale published in *Die Burger* in 1952. The Devil wants to eradicate his enemy's nation in Africa and tries to obliterate it by putting it under foreign rule, destroying its republics, sending it into rebellion and two global wars. The Devil concludes by saying: 'Only one thing remains: I shall make them prosperous and see if they can survive that.'

121 Giliomee (2003, p. 402). As late as 1939 there was no 'Afrikaans' commercial bank, no major finance house and no large industrial undertaking.

122 See T. Steenekamp, 'Discrimination and the economic position of the Afrikaner', *South African Journal of Economic History*, 5(1), 1990, pp. 49–66.

123 *Die Blanke Werker*, for example, was the mouthpiece of the Blanke Werkers Beskermingsbond (the Association for the Protection of White Workers), established in 1944. It disseminated nostalgic myths about earlier days when there were no class divisions and blamed capitalists for intra-Afrikaner dissent.

124 See O'Meara (1983, p. 54).

125 See O'Meara (1983, p. 54).

126 See, for example, D.F. Malan, University of Stellenbosch Library, D.F. Malan Collection, Malan, correspondence 1/1/1014, 'Malan to Eric Louw', 1933, quoted in Giliomee (2003, p. 405).

127 See, for example, O'Meara (1983, p. 54). In the horse-breeding world this was very evident in the discourse surrounding the Boerperd, which is discussed later in this chapter.

128 For a comparative case study in South Korea, see L. Nelson, *Measured Excess: Status, Gender, and Consumer Nationalism in South Korea* (New York: Columbia University Press, 2000).

129 F. Firat & N. Dholakia, *Consuming People: From Political Economy to Theatres of Consumption* (London: Routledge, 1998), p. 43.

130 See R. Lynes, *The Tastemakers: The Shaping of American Popular Taste* (New York: Dover, 1980); and Michele Lamont, *Money, Morals, and Manners: The Culture of the French and American Upper-middle Class* (Chicago: University of Chicago Press, 1992).

131 H. Marcuse, *One Dimensional Man* (Boston: Beacon Press, 1964), p. 9.

132 Cited in Beinart (2001, p. 183).

133 'Jan Burger' (1960, p. 78); see also *Huisgenoot*, 7 May 1965, pp. 42–43.

134 For an example, see *Farmer's Weekly*, 5 November 1958, p. 88.

135 *Farmer's Weekly*, 26 February 1958, p. 129.

136 See J.L. Sadie, 'Die ekonomiese faktor in die Afrikanergemeenskap', in H.W. van der Merwe, ed., *Identiteit en Verandering* (Cape Town: Tafelberg, 1974), p. 92. See also J.L. Sadie, *The Fall and Rise of Afrikaner Capitalism* (Stellenbosch: US Annale, 2002); and E.P du Plessis, *'n Volk Staan Op* (Cape Town: Human & Rousseau, 1964). In the 1930s workers made up the bulk of Afrikaners, but as Giliomee (2003, p. 42) has shown, they did not dominate organised labour leadership, at least in part because of reservations about capitalism itself, individualism and greed.

137 For discussion of this caricature, see T.D. Moodie, *The Rise of Afrikanerdom: Power, Apartheid, and the Afrikaner Civil Religion* (Berkeley: University of California Press, 1975), pp. 15, 90, 136, 168. On the residual legacy of this stereotype, see M. Shain, *The Roots of Anti-Semitism in South Africa* (Johannesburg: Wits University Press, 1994), pp. 55, 94.

138 On the lack of active materialism, see, for example, Carnegie Commission, *The Poor White Problem in South Africa*, vol. 1 (Stellenbosch, 1932), p. 116. For a more extended discussion, see S. Schirmer, 'White farmers and development in South Africa', *South African Historical Journal*, 52, 2005, pp. 82–101.

139 Firat & Dholakia (1988, p. 49). Of course, trade may have been looked down on, but there is plenty of evidence of Afrikaners in trade.

140 See C. van Onselen, 'Paternalism and violence on the maize farms of the south-western Transvaal, 1900–1950', in A. Jeeves & J. Crush, eds, *White Farms, Black Labour: The State and Agrarian Change in Southern Africa*, 1910–1950 (Pietermaritzburg: University of Natal Press, 1997), p. 210.

141 See *Rapport*, 17 February 1974; and Sadie (1974, p. 96).

142 Du Pisani (2001, p. 160).

143 See Du Pisani (2001, p. 161).

144 'Jan Burger' (1960, p. 38).

145 'Jan Burger' (1960, p. 23).

146 See also *Huisgenoot*, 12 July 1968; and *Huisgenoot*, 'Stand en klas by die
Afrikaners' (Standing and class among Afrikaners), 10 November 1961 &
17 November 1961; *Huisgenoot*, 9 October 1959, p. 24; and *Huisgenoot*,
8 January 1965, p. 50. It is a recurring concern, particularly over loss of central
cultural control and Americanisation, with the two usually linked. See, for
example, Henning Viljoen, 'Raka en Mammon in ons kraal', *De Kat*, 3 May 1988,
p. 116; *Beeld*, 'Onheilighede', editorial, 11 December 1989; and C.F.C. Coetzee,
'Beoordeling van die Vryheidstryd van die Afrikanervolk', *Patriot*, 7 May 1998
on the loss of religious underpinnings. See also Bruce Taylor, 'Geld is alles vir
die Afrikaner', *Beeld*, 22 November 1989, in which Erika Reynolds presented a
sociological analysis showing Afrikaners as the 'most materialist' of the language
groups; G. Bester, 'Afrikaners moet oordrewe materialisme los, sê Mulder', *Beeld*,
18 December 1995; and 'Gawie', 'Vryheid!', *Die Afrikaner*, 25 August 2005.
147 'Jan Burger' (1960, pp. 37–38).
148 Beinart (2001, p. 187).
149 The 1938 Eeufees, for example, mobilised popular energies (of which horses
were an integral part, symbolically part of the 'return of history'). On the
Eeufees, see A. Grundlingh, 'The politics of the past and of popular pursuits in
the construction of everyday Afrikaner nationalism, 1938–1948', in S. Dubow &
A. Jeeves, eds, *South Africa's 1940s: Worlds of Possibilities* (Cape Town: Double
Storey, 2005), p. 194.
150 S. van Schalkwyk, 'Gerrit van Schalkwyk', *South African Show Horse*,
championship edition, April 2005. For the racial dimension of horse breeding,
see Swart (2004, pp. 13–24).
151 Grundlingh (2005, p. 195).
152 Like the English Thoroughbred horse, the Saddler even had its own equivalent of
Burke's or Debrett's *Peerage* in Lee Kaplan's magisterial tome in which she sought
to trace the lineage of every Saddler in South Africa, listing show record and
ancestry; see Kaplan (1974).
153 Veblen (1902, pp. 68–101).
154 *Farmer's Weekly*, 'Our American Saddlers make a hit with Kentucky expert',
25 April 1956, p. 21.
155 'Alpha' (1943, pp. 56–57).
156 Firat & Dholakia (1988, p. 45).
157 Just as the *petit bourgeoisie* culture brokers had reacted against 'Englishness' in
the previous decades. O'Meara has shown that by the 1930s economic pressures
had alienated the *petit bourgeoisie*. Afrikaner urbanisation affected the clientele
of lawyers and traders, and the rural clergy felt the loss of members to urban
apostolic churches. The secular labour movement and capitalism required
mastery of English, so the affirmation of both language and culture symbolised
the struggle against imperialist power structures.
158 Grundlingh (2005).

159   C. Norden, 'The Boerperd', *Farmer's Weekly*, 26 February 1958, p. 29.

160   C. Norden, 'The Boerperd', *Farmer's Weekly*, 26 February 1958, p. 29.

161   W. Callender-Easby, T.R. Vimpany, A.S. van Wyk, J.Z. Moolman, P. v.d. Merwe & M.H. Wessels, 'Under the title: The National Horse Breeders Society of SA and Rhod., affiliated to the Registered Saddle Horse Breeders Society of S.A. and Rhod', SAB, LON A173/13, *Minutes of the Registered Saddle Horse Breeders Society of SA and Rhod.*, 22 September 1949.

162   SAB, LON, A173/13, 'Registered Saddle Horse Breeders Society of SA and Rhod', October 1949; SAB, LON, A173/13, *Minutes of the Registered Saddle Horse Breeders Society of SA and Rhod.*, Middelburg, 19 May 1948 and Bloemfontein, 1 June 1949.

163   <http://www.ansi.okstate.edu/breeds/horses/boer/>. See also Kaapse/Cape Boerperd Breeders Society, <http://www.capeboerperd.co.za/boerperd_breeders. htm> and SA Boerperd, <http://studbook.co.za/society/boerperd/boer.html>.

164   Renamed the 'South African Boerperd' in 1988 in keeping with a discourse of nation building.

165   <http://www.ansi.okstate.edu/breeds/horses/boer/index.htm>.

166   For a useful précis of the Cape Boerperd's lineage, see E. Marais, 'Kaapse Boerperd/Cape Boerperd', *South African Show Horse*, April 2005.

167   In 1996 the Department of Agriculture formally accepted the Historical Boerperd (with approximately 2,000 registered horses).

168   D. Jordaan, *Perdeteelt in Suid-Afrika* (Pretoria: self-published, 1997). All quotations from this work are translated by the present author.

169   Jordaan (1997, pp. 37, 11).

170   Jordaan (1997, p. 49).

171   Eugène Terre'Blanche, personal comment, letter to author, Rooigrond Prison, 4 December 2003.

172   Eugène Terre'Blanche, personal comment.

173   *Conservation of Early Domesticated Animals of Southern Africa*, conference proceedings, Willem Prinsloo Agricultural Museum, 3–4 March 1994; D.M. Joubert & W.M. Bosman, 'The Nooitgedacht pony', *South African Journal of Science*, 67(7), 1971, p. 366.

174   F. van der Merwe & J. Martin, unpublished paper, n.d. My thanks for a copy of this paper.

175   One may question this rationale, as the Basotho pony was itself developed from an Arab and Cape horse/Boerperd amalgamation. Perhaps a more likely reason was that the South African horse market of the time was reluctant to acquire 'native' stock.

176   There are about 150 internationally accepted 'breeds' of horses in the world, all belonging to the species *Equus caballus*.

177   This is not to say, of course, that there is no biological variation among different populations of horses.

178 G. Falk, 'The Saddle horse on the modern farm', *Farmer's Weekly*, 7 January 1953, p. 31.
179 Members of the society were debited for their subscription to *Farmer's Weekly*; J.D. Prinsloo, 'Saddle horses: AGM sets guidelines', *Farmer's Weekly*, 29 December 2000, p. 29. The community has grown with the globally accessible, American-based website <http://www.saddlebred.com>. See also Juliette Lewis, 'American Saddlebreds online', *Farmer's Weekly*, 30 August 2002.

Chapter 8

1 Although the Przewalski's horse has 66 chromosomes and the domestic horse 64, they are the only equids that can cross-breed and produce fertile offspring, which possess 65 chromosomes. Its classification is therefore hotly debated and is known variously as *Equus ferus przewalskii, Equus przewalskii* or *Equus caballus przewalski*.
2 Columbus's second voyage brought horses to the New World in 1493 and, over time, Hispaniola became a horse-raising hub; by 1511 horses had been brought to Puerto Rico, Jamaica and Cuba, and from these centres they were introduced to Central America and Mexico. Horses broke free from captivity or were sporadically turned loose on the range, forging self-sustaining feral populations.
3 This is echoed in the names '*cimarrón*' in Hispaniola, '*bagual*' in Argentina and '*mostrenco*' in Venezuela; see Tom McKnight, 'The feral horse in Anglo-America', *Geographical Review*, 49(4), 1959, pp. 506–25.
4 When feral they usually quickly acquired owners, often through state intervention; see, for example, VAB, director of land settlement (hereafter DLS), 13, A1265, 'Offer to purchase certain wild horses now running in Vrede district', 1902–1903; VAB, colonial secretary (hereafter CO), 99, 3817/02, 'Wild horses being handed over to Remount Department', 1902.
5 The only other well-known feral horses on the African continent are those of the Kondudo region in Ethiopia from which herd Emperor Haile Selassie was said to have obtained his first mount over a century ago. Their tiny herd – less than ten strong – roam 13 hectares on the flat grassland summit of a mountain.
6 William Scully, *Lodges in the Wilderness* (London: Herbert Jenkins, 1915), p. 226.
7 SAB, LDB, 1037, R775 vol. 1, 'Prime minster to minister of agriculture', 5 November 1924; Robert Broom, 'Note on *Equus capensis*', *Bulletin of the American Museum of Natural History*, 32(25), 1913, pp. 437–39. A more likely source was a ship with a cargo of horses wrecked about 25 km south of the Orange River mouth in the late nineteenth century.
8 *Sunday Times*, 'Mankind closing in on horses of Bot River', 9 August 1998. For a more scholarly discussion of their habits, see Van der Merwe (2007).

9   *Rapport*, 'Droogte bedreig die wilde woestyn perde van Namib', 14 February 1999; E.G. Cothran, E. van Dyk & F.J. van der Merwe, 'Genetic variation in the feral horses of the Namib Desert, Namibia', *Journal of the South African Veterinary Association*, 72(1), 2001, pp. 18–22; T. Greyling, 'The behavioural ecology of the feral horses in the Namib Naukluft Park', MSc diss., Potchefstroom University, 1994.

10 In 1986 a subsidiary of Anglo American handed over the northern part of the *Sperrgebiet* ('forbidden territory') to the Directorate of Nature Conservation.

11 A *droster* (from the Dutch *drossen*, to desert) was an escapee from the condition of unfree labour.

12 A point Helen Bradford made about the fallacy of just 'adding women' to history; see Bradford (1996).

13 Parts of this chapter have appeared in other forms as Sandra Swart, 'The World the Horses Made: A South African Case Study of Writing Animals into Social History', *International Review of Social History*, SS, 2, 2010.

14 For a broader discussion, see Sandra Swart, '"But where's the bloody horse?": Textuality and corporeality in the "animal turn"', *Journal of Literary Studies*, 23(3), 2007, pp. 271–92.

15 Eugene D. Genovese, *Roll, Jordan, Roll: The World the Slaves Made* (New York: Pantheon, 1974); Mechel Sobel, *The World They Made Together: Black and White Values in Eighteenth-century Virginia* (Princeton: Princeton University Press, 1987); Christopher Hill, *The World Turned Upside Down: Radical Ideas during the English Revolution* (Harmondsworth: Penguin, 1972). Hill (pp. 303–10) describes a time when ideas about animals were turned upside down with the rest of the world.

16 For discussion, see Ritvo (2004); and Fudge (2002).

17 Nash (1972, p. 363).

18 See Philip Armstrong, 'The postcolonial animal', *Society and Animals*, 10(4), 2002, pp. 413–19.

19 '[A]l is dit altyd baie moeilik om vooruit te sien wat 'n vosperd of 'n vrou sal doen'; Johann Buhr, 'Manne te perd', *Huisgenoot*, 16 October 1936, p. 22.

20 Royal Commission on the War in South Africa (1903, p. 97).

21 Bozzoli (1991); and Shula Marks, *Not Either an Experimental Doll* (Bloomington: Indiana University Press, 1987) are especially significant exemplars of this approach. Similarly, for the life story of a male from an oppressed group, see Van Onselen (1996).

22 Somerset might well not have made the whole journey and might have been substituted at the British camp at the Umgazi mouth.

23 Otto Mentzel, *Description of the Cape* (London, 1785), quoted in Nigel Worden, *The Chains that Bind Us: A History of Slavery at the Cape* (Cape Town: Juta, 1996), pp. 50–51.

24 This would defuse the methodological danger of seeing animals as synchronic and humans as diachronic.

25 Karl Marx, *The Eighteenth Brumaire of Louis Napoleon*, trans. D. de Leon ([1852], Chicago: Kerr, 1919).

26 Law (1980, p. vii). In a seminal work, Peter Edwards (2007) offers the best synopsis of the early English arena of the inter-species relationship that transformed the history of transportation, commerce, leisure, warfare, agriculture, art, and diplomacy. For a ground-breaking wider European perspective, see Raber & Tucker (2005). In North America, three publications offer recent, careful and nuanced studies; see McShane & Tarr (2007); Derry (2006); and Greene (2008).

27 Fisher (1973).

28 Webb (1993).

29 Legassick (1996).

30 Marx (1919, p. 15).

31 Timothy Mitchell, *Rule of Experts: Egypt, Techno-politics, Modernity* (Berkeley: University of California Press, 2002).

32 Indeed, modern dressage instructors and training manuals actually deploy the technical term 'resistance' to refer to a horse's non-compliance.

33 James Scott, *Weapons of the Weak: Everyday Forms of Peasant Resistance* (New Haven: Yale University Press, 1985).

34 Horses had a symbolic meaning that allowed people to exercise their 'weapons of the weak' upon them. Horse maiming, for example, allowed for a form of social rebellion. See Yates, Powell & Beirne (2001).

35 Eric Hobsbawm, 'Peasants and politics', *Journal of Peasant Studies*, 1(1), 1973, pp. 3–22.

36 Lady Anne Barnard, *The Letters of Lady Anne Barnard to Henry Dundas, from the Cape and Elsewhere, 1793–1803*, ed. A.M. Lewin Robinson (Cape Town: Balkema, 1973), p. 109.

37 Barnard (1973, pp. 68–69).

38 A horse's independence has even filtered into the human idiom in 'you can lead a horse to water but you can't make it drink'. Indeed, recently, a judge of the South African Supreme Court of Appeal ruled against a tourist claiming damages after a fall, blaming the horse's owners. The court ruled that the owners could not be held responsible for the horse's actions as 'horses will be horses'; see 'Judge finds a horse cannot be anything but a horse', *Sunday Times*, 3 September 2006.

39 Diamond (1999).

40 Storey (2008).

41 To use Goody's phrase; Jack Goody, *Technology, Tradition, and the State in Africa* (New York: Press Syndicate & Cambridge University Press, 1980), p. 39.

42 Here quoted from the 1917 edition, p. 418.

43   For a resonant recent analysis, see Peter Coates, 'The strange stillness of the past: Toward an environmental history of sound and noise', *Environmental History*, 10(4), 2005, pp. 636–65.

44   Battersby (1900, pp. 75, 217).

45   Scully (1915, p. 162).

46   Battersby (1900, pp. 75, 217).

47   This heeds, in a modest way, Febvre's call for a sensory history; see L. Febvre, 'Smells, tastes, and sounds', in his *The Problem of Unbelief in the Sixteenth Century* (Cambridge, MA: Harvard University Press, 1982). For up-to-date discussion, see Mark M. Smith, 'Producing sense, consuming sense, making sense: Perils and prospects for sensory history', *Journal of Social History*, 40(4), 2007, pp. 841–58; and Richard Cullen Rath, *How Early America Sounded* (Ithaca: Cornell University Press, 2003).

48   McShane & Tarr (2007).

49   Although only a small percentage of humans owned horses in many communities, in some – like Boer and Basotho communities in the nineteenth century – most men, at least, were mounted.

50   H. Carrington Bolton, 'The language used in talking to domestic animals', *American Anthropologist*, 10(4), 1897, pp. 97–113.

51   An incensed horse's ears flatten and an interested horse's ears prick forward.

52   Roy Porter, 'Foreword', in Alain Corbin, *The Foul and the Fragrant: Odour and the French Social Imagination* (London: Picador, 1994).

53   Again, there was a dark side to the aural and aromatic experience: during the South African War, for example, people became familiar with the 'foul whirr of flies where beasts have been slaughtered, the bitter odour from dead horse and mule'; Battersby (1900, p. 130).

54   The question of horse's and human's relative speed is enduring. The great Jesse Owens raced horses over a 100 yard distance and came first, but only because the horses reared at the sound of the starter's pistol, giving him an unfair advantage. There is no doubt that horses are much faster than humans and can sustain speed far longer.

55   Taking the horses seriously as living, breathing creatures reveals small, eccentric, but key facts, explored in Chapter 5, such as that horses find it impossible to vomit, which played a role in the reasons for British losses in the war in South Africa.

56   Since Darwin wrote *The Variation of Animals and Plants under Domestication* (1868), a large bibliography has been published on the relationship between humans and animals, known as domestication; see F.E. Zeuner, *A History of Domesticated Animals* (London: Hutchinson, 1963); Clutton-Brock (1989b); and S. Budiansky, *The Covenant of the Wild: Why Animals Chose Domestication* (New Haven: Yale University Press, 1999).

57   It was an idea hinted at by Austrian Nobel Prize winning ethnologist Konrad
      Lorenz, explicated by Raymond Coppinger and popularised by science writer
      Stephen Budiansky. They have suggested *agency* specifically for dogs in throwing
      in their lot with humans, and perhaps a comparable, although slightly different,
      argument could be made for horses; see Konrad Lorenz, *King Solomon's Ring:*
      New Light on Animal Ways (London: Methuen, 1982), pp. 115–16.

58   See, for example, T. Ingold, 'From trust to domination: An alternative history of
      human–animal relations', in A. Manning & J. Serpell, eds, *Animals and Human*
      Societies: Changing Perspectives (London: Routledge, 1994), which describes
      human–animal relationship as transformed from one of a mutually shared
      environment to unmitigated human domination.

59   Budiansky thus envisions it instead as a process of *co-evolution* between humans
      and animals.

60   However, even following Budiansky's argument, an alliance between two
      predators would have been more likely than a voluntary alliance between
      predator and prey. Furthermore, considering the problems encountered even by
      modern collectors trying to breed Przewalski's horses, it seems likely that horse
      keeping would have to have been relatively advanced before controlled breeding,
      and consequently domestication, was possible; see M.A. Levine, 'Botai and the
      origins of horse domestication', *Journal of Anthropological Archaeology*, 18, 1999,
      pp. 29–78.

61   Linda Nash, 'The agency of nature or the nature of agency', *Environmental*
      History, 10, 2005, pp. 67–69.

62   Tim Ingold, *The Perception of the Environment: Essays in Livelihood, Dwelling and*
      Skill (New York: Routledge, 2000).

63   Of course, simply couching it in scientific terms does not insulate the narrative
      from politics. Before 1950 whether or not something was introduced or
      native was not significant, but in 1970s that changed. Even an ostensibly
      neutral scientific account would be redolent with the politics of belonging and
      autochthony, discussed in the previous chapter. The political metaphors of non-
      native introduction abound even in scientific journal articles, e.g. 'ecological
      imperialism' versus 'biotic resistance', 'invasion', 'emigrant-immigrant species',
      'colonisation' and 'naturalisation'. For a South Africanist analysis, see Jean
      Comaroff & John Comaroff, 'Naturing the nation: Aliens, apocalypse and the
      postcolonial state', *Journal of Southern African Studies*, 27(3), September 2001,
      p. 627. See also T. Chris Smout, 'The alien species in 20th-century Britain:
      Constructing a new vermin', *Landscape Research*, 28(1), 2003, pp. 11–20;
      J. Jenschke, D. Strayer & S. Carpenter, 'Invasion success of vertebrates in Europe
      and North America', *Proceedings of the National Academy of Sciences of the*
      United States of America, 102(20), 2005, pp. 7198–202; and Steven Radosevich,
      M.M. Stubbs & Claudio Ghersa, 'Plant invasions: Process and patterns', *Weed*
      Science, 51(2), 2003, pp. 254–59.

64   In North America, for example, about one European vertebrate species was introduced per 10,000 human immigrants; see Jenschke, Strayer & Carpenter (2005).

65   Like the North American *Phagocata woodworthi*, a freshwater flatworm introduced into Loch Ness on the equipment used by monster hunters trying to find 'Nessie'.

66   Karl W. Butzer, 'Coastal eolian sands, paleosols, and pleistocene geoarchaeology of the southwestern Cape, South Africa', *Journal of Archaeological Science*, 31(12), 2004, pp. 1743–81; Richard G. Klein, 'A preliminary report on the "Middle Stone Age" open-air site of Duinefontein 2', *South African Archaeological Bulletin*, 31(121/122), 1976, pp. 12–20.

67   Radosevich, Stubbs & Ghersa (2003).

68   In one study, in the territories of male feral horses grass was allowed to regenerate to a greater height before being consumed than in nearby areas where there were open membership groups with broad home-range overlap; see D.I. Rubenstein, 'The ecology of equid social organization', in D.I. Rubenstein & R.W. Wrangham, eds, *Ecological Aspects of Social Evolution* (Princeton: Princeton University Press, 1986), pp. 282–302.

69   E. van Dyk & S. Neser, 'The spread of weeds into sensitive areas by seeds in horse faeces', *Journal of the South African Veterinary Association*, 7(3), 2000, pp. 173–74. Opportunistic immigrant plants that arrived with the imported horses and fodder and made a new home in South African soil include Brome grass (*Bromus*), *Cirsium arvense*; *Acanthospermum australe*; *Salsola kali*; *Inula graveolens*; and Russian *rolbossie*. *Speerdissel* (*Skotse dissel*), *kameeldoringbos* and *donkieklits* polluted sheep's wool. Under normal conditions, few non-native plant propagules would be deposited in the dung as horses fed on local forage.

70   That is, *Alternanthera pungens*; see Ernst van Jaarsveld, 'Kakiedubbeltjie, knapsekêrels en die Anglo-Boereooorlog', *Die Burger*, 2 June 2001.

71   M.J. Liddle & L.D. Chitty, 'The nutrient-budget of horse tracks on an English lowland heath', *Journal of Applied Ecology*, 18(3), 1981, pp. 841–48; T. Weaver & D. Dale, 'Trampling effects of hikers, motorcycles and horses in meadows and forests', *Journal of Applied Ecology*, 15, 1978, pp. 451–58; F.H. Frederick & J.M. Henderson, 'Impact force measurement using preloaded transducers', *American Journal of Veterinary Research*, 31, 1970, pp. 2279–83.

72   L. Bigot & N. Poinsot-Balaguer, 'Influence du pasturage d'une manade de chevaux de race Carmargue sur les communautés des invertébrés d'une sansouire', *Revue d'Ecologie et de Biologie du Sol*, 15, 1978, pp. 517–28.

73   Their food is more rapidly digested, allowing for immediate energy in case the need arises to flee a predator and allowing horses to survive on older, taller, denser foliage (with a high fibre:protein ratio) than would be sufficient for a cow, for example. This evolutionary adaptation, however, comes at a price. It means that there is reduced efficiency in absorption and thus horses need to graze continuously.

74   T.A. Hanley & K.A. Hanley, 'Food resource partitioning by sympatric ungulates on great basin rangeland', *Journal of Range Management*, 35, 1982, pp. 152–58; R.M. Hansen, 'Foods of free-roaming horses in southern New Mexico', *Journal of Range Management*, 29, 1976, p. 347; R. Hubbard & R. Hansen, 'Diets of wild horses, cattle and mule deer in the Piceance basin, Colorado', *Journal of Range Management*, 29, 1976, pp. 389–92.

75   Unlike other equids, such as donkeys, which *were* perceived to inflict environmental damage; see Jacobs (2001).

76   In the 1930s in Basutoland, bridle paths were linked to sheet erosion because pack animals (not solely horses) wandered from the track; Kate B. Showers, 'Soil erosion in the Kingdom of Lesotho: Origins and colonial response, 1830s–1950s', *Journal of Southern African Studies*, 15(2), 1989, pp. 276–77.

77   See Beinart (2003, p. 137); W. Beinart, 'Soil erosion, animals and pasture over the longer term: Environmental destruction in Southern Africa', in M. Leach & R. Mearns, eds, *The Lie of the Land: Challenging Received Wisdom on the African Environment* (Oxford: James Currey, 1996), pp. 54–72; J. Keay-Bright & J. Boardman, 'The influence of land management on soil erosion in the Sneeuberg Mountains, Central Karoo, South Africa', *Land Degradation & Development*, 18(4), 2006a, pp. 423–39; and J. Keay-Bright & J. Boardman, 'Changes in the distribution of degraded land over time in the Central Karoo, South Africa', *CATENA*, 67(1), 2006b, pp. 1–14.

78   For a selection of sources reflective of this enduring multiracial and multiregional development, see NAB, Attorney General's Office (hereafter AGO), 1/8/3, 8A/1856, 'Magistrate, Weenen forwards papers in the case of April, a coloured man, for horse theft', 1856; NAB, AGO, 1/8/5, 'A case of a Natal kafir being accused of horse theft by Basutos in Basutoland'; TAB, W222, 1880–1918, *Biografiese gegewens en korrespondensie oor Scotty Smith* (George Gordon Lennox); VAB, CO, 476, 5045/07, 'Horse alleged to have been stolen from Motlalefi, a native of Basutoland, and now in possession of one Bothma in the Orange River Colony', 1907; KAB, CSC, 1/2/1/8, 10, '*King vs Flink*, wounding and killing horses with intent to steal', 1831; KAB, GH, 23/97, 272, 'Movements of a band of Hottentots said to have stolen certain horses and mules and crossed

into British territory', 1906; and KAB, CO, 4096, 853, 'Postcon tractor mills, regarding horses stolen by kaffirs', 1857.

79   TAB, W222, 1880–1918, *Biografiese gegewens en korrespondensie oor Scotty Smith* (George Gordon Lennox).

80   'J.A. van Wyk (fieldcornet) to H. van de Graaff (landdrost of Tulbagh)', 3 May 1807, in G.M. Theal, *Records of the Cape Colony: Copied for the Cape Government, from the Manuscript Documents in the Public Record Office, London, February to June 1827*, vol. 31 (Government of Cape Colony, 1905d), p. 19.

81   *Minutes of Meeting held at Maseru by the High Commissioner's Agent*, 16 August 1871, in Theal (2002a, vol. vi, p. 95).

82   Herbert Gutman, in I. Berlin, ed., *Power and Culture: Essays on the American Working Class* (New York: Pantheon 1987), p. 50.

83   For lively discussion, see Jason Hribal, 'Animals, agency, and class: Writing the history of animals from below', *Human Ecology Forum*, 14(1), 2007, pp. 101–12.

84   Compiled from Department of Agriculture (1960–61).

85   There are comparative parallels to be made with other parts of the world. Indeed, India's 'Laws of Manu' associated horses with the highest caste and donkeys with the untouchables.

86   Marc Epprecht, personal comment; Epprecht (2000, pp. 48, 124).

87   Jacobs (2003, p. 201).

88   Quoted in Jacobs (2003, p. 203).

89   Today, Jacobs notes, in Kuruman a strong pro-donkey populism still lingers, redolent of moral significance to poor people, Christianity, the environment and democracy.

90   Their name only came into use in the twentieth century; Michael de Jongh, 'No fixed abode: The poorest of the poor and elusive identities in rural South Africa', *Journal of Southern African Studies*, 28(2), 2002, p. 448.

91   '*Ons is te arm om bruin mense te wees. Ons is die geel mense*'; see De Jongh (2002, p. 442). For identity politics and recent self-identification as San, see De Jongh (2002, p. 459). See also Michael de Jongh & Riana Steyn, 'Itinerancy as a way of life: The nomadic sheep-shearers of the South African Karoo', *Development Southern Africa*, 11(2), 1994, pp. 217–28; and C.J. van Vuuren, 'Horses, carts and taxis: Transportation and marginalisation in three South African communities', *South African Journal of Cultural History*, 13(1), 1999, pp. 90–103.

92   E.G. Malherbe, *Education and the Poor White: Report of the Carnegie Commission*, vol. III (Stellenbosch: Pro Ecclesia, 1932), p. 241.

93   Aldo Leopold, *A Sand County Almanac* (Oxford: Oxford University Press, 1966), p. 140.

94   J. Berger, *Wild Horses of the Great Basin: Social Competition and Population Size* (Chicago: University of Chicago Press, 1986).

95   Reitz (1990, p. 211).

Endnotes

96   Leonard Flemming, 'The romance of a new South African farm', *Journal of the Royal African Society*, 21(82), 1922, pp. 115–28.

97   G. Minkley & C. Rassool, 'Orality, memory, and social history in South Africa', in S. Nuttall & C. Coetzee, eds, *Negotiating the Past: The Making of Memory in South Africa* (Cape Town: Oxford University Press, 1998), p. 98.

98   Thompson (1966, p. 9).

99   For an example of a professional, see TAB, 34B/1922, *R. vs Charles Orton*; and Flemming (1922, pp. 115–28).

100 Charles Darwin, *The Expression of the Emotions in Man and Animals* ([1872], Oxford: Oxford University Press, 1998). Following Descartes and Skinner, one pole argues for animals as automatons, conditioned to respond automatically to stimuli. This changed as the rise of the hard sciences and the logical positivist climate in the twentieth century led to the marginalisation of animal emotions as unquantifiable and unverifiable.

101 Hribal (2007, pp. 101–12).

102 Scott (1985).

103 Lord Charles Somerset and his equine-induced career stumble was discussed in Chapter 3. William Branford was a Cape colonial veterinary surgeon who was struck from the Royal College of Veterinary Surgeons in 1880 after a mortifying court case over a lottery for a racehorse he owned; see Beinart (2003, p. 141).

104 For historiography of technology and technological determinism, see M.R. Smith & L. Marx, eds, *Does Technology Drive History?* (Cambridge, MA: MIT Press, 1994).

Bibliography

Archival sources

Cape Archives Repository (KAB)
Free State Archives Repository (VAB)
Lesotho National Archives (LNA)
Morija Museum and Archives
Natal Archives Repository (NAB)
National Archives Repository, Pretoria, Transvaal Archives (TAB)
National Archives, United Kingdom
National Army Museum, United Kingdom
South African National Archives Repository (SAB)

Printed sources

Adams, Jonathan & Thomas O. McShane, *The Myth of Wild Africa: Conservation without Illusions* (New York: W.W. Norton, 1992).

Adorno, T., 'Veblen's attack on culture', *Prisms*, trans. S. & S. Weber (Cambridge, MA: MIT Press, 1981).

'Alpha', *Horse and Saddle in South Africa (a Vision)* (Cape Town: Maskew Miller, 1943).

Ambrose, David, *Summary of Events in Lesotho*, 3(1), 1996, National University of Lesotho, <http://www.trc.org.ls/events/events19.961.htm>.

Amery, L.S., ed., The Times *History of the War in South Africa*, vol. VI (London: Sampson Low Marston, 1909).

Anderson, D. & R. Grove, eds, *Conservation in Africa* (Cambridge: Cambridge University Press, 1989).

Anderson, Virginia deJohn, *Creatures of Empire: How Domestic Animals Transformed Early America* (Oxford: Oxford University Press, 2004).

Andreas, Christian B., 'The spread and impact of the lungsickness epizootic of 1853–57 in the Cape Colony and the Xhosa chiefdoms', *South African Historical Journal*, 53, 2005, pp. 50–72.

Andrews, H.T. et al., *South Africa in the Sixties: A Socio-economic Survey* (London: South Africa Foundation, 1962).

Anglesey, Marquess of, *A History of the British Cavalry*, vols. I–V (London: Leo Cooper, 1973–94).

Anon., *Sketches of India or, Observations Descriptive of the Scenery, etc. in Bengal … Together with Notes on the Cape of Good-Hope, and St. Helena* ([1847], London: Black, Parbury & Allen, 1916).

——, *Gleanings in Africa, Exhibiting a Faithful and Correct View of the Manners and Customs of the Inhabitants of the Cape of Good Hope, and Surrounding Country* ([1806], New York: Negro University Press, 1969).

Anthony, D.W. & D.R. Brown 'The origins of horseback riding', *Antiquity*, 246, 1991, pp. 22–38.

Arbousset, T., *Missionary Excursion into the Blue Mountains: Being an Account of King Moshoeshoe's Expedition from Thaba-Bosiu to the Sources of the Malibamatšo River in the Year 1840*, ed. & trans. D. Ambrose & A. Brutsch (Morija: Morija Archives, 1991).

Arbousset, Thomas & F. Daumas, *Narrative of an Exploratory Tour to the North-East of the Colony of the Cape of Good Hope,* trans. John Croumbie Brown (Cape Town: A.S. Robertson, Saul Solomon, 1846).

Argus Annual and South African Directory, 1889 (Johannesburg, Cape Town & Pretoria: Argus Printing & Publishing, 1889).

Argus Annual and South African Directory, 1890 (Cape Town: Argus Printing & Publishing, 1890).

Aristotle, *Politics*, rev. Trevor J. Saunders; trans. T.A. Sinclair (London: Penguin, 1981).

Armstrong, Philip, 'The postcolonial animal', *Society and Animals*, 10(4), 2002, pp. 413–19.

Ashe, E. Oliver, *Besieged by the Boers: A Diary of the Siege of Kimberley* (London: Hutchinson, 1900).

Atmore, Anthony & Peter Sanders, 'Sotho arms and ammunition in the nineteenth century', *Journal of African History*, 12(4), 1971, pp. 517–30.

Backhouse, James, *A Narrative of a Visit to the Mauritius and South Africa* (London: Hamilton Adams, 1844).

Baden-Powell, B.F.S., *War in Practice* (London: Isbister, 1903).

Baden-Powell, R.S.S., *Sport in War* (London: Heinemann, 1900).

Baines, Thomas, *Journal of Residence in Africa*, vol. II (Cape Town: Van Riebeeck Society, 1961).

Baker, Steve, *Picturing the Beast: Animals, Identity, and Representation* (Chicago: University of Illinois Press, 2001).

Balfour, Alice Blanche, *Twelve Hundred Miles in a Waggon* (London: Edward Arnold, 1895).

Bankoff, Greg, 'A question of breeding: Zootechny and colonial attitudes toward the tropical environment in the late nineteenth-century Philippines', *Journal of Asian Studies*, 60(2), 2001, pp. 413–37.

Bankoff, Greg & Sandra Swart, *Breeds of Empire: The 'Invention' of the Horse in the Philippines and Southern Africa, 1500–1950* (Uppsala: Nordic Institute of Asian Studies, 2007).

Barclay, H.B., *The Role of the Horse in Man's Culture* (London: Allen, 1980).

Barnard, Lady Anne, *The Letters of Lady Anne Barnard to Henry Dundas, from the Cape and Elsewhere, 1793–1803*, ed. A.M. Lewin Robinson (Cape Town: Balkema, 1973).

—, *The Cape Journals of Lady Anne Barnard, 1797–1798* (Cape Town: Van Riebeeck Society, 1994).

—, *The Cape Diaries of Lady Anne Barnard, 1799–1800*, vol. 1, ed. M. Lenta & B. le Cordeur (Cape Town: Van Riebeeck Society, 1999).

Barrow, John, *An Account of Travels in the Interior of South Africa, in the Years 1797 and 1798*, vol. 1 (New York: Johnson Reprint, 1968).

Battersby, H.F. Prevost, *In the Web of a War* (London: Methuen, 1900).

Bayley, T., *Notes on the Horsesickness at the Cape of Good Hope, in 1854–55* (Cape Town: Saul Solomon, 1856).

Becker, C.J., *Guide to the Transvaal* (Dublin: J. Dollard, 1878).

Beinart, William, 'Settler accumulation in East Griqualand from the demise of the Griqua to the Natives Land Act', in W. Beinart, Peter Delius & Stanley Trapido, eds, *Putting a Plough to the Ground: Accumulation and Dispossession in Rural South Africa, 1850–1930* (Johannesburg: Ravan Press, 1986).

—, 'Soil erosion, animals and pasture over the longer term: Environmental destruction in Southern Africa', in M. Leach & R. Mearns, eds, *The Lie of the*

Land: Challenging Received Wisdom on the African Environment (Oxford: James Currey, 1996).

——, 'African history and environmental history', *African Affairs*, 99, 2000, pp. 269–302.

——, *Twentieth Century South Africa* (Oxford: Oxford University Press, 2001).

——, ed., *The Rise of Conservation in South Africa: Settlers, Livestock, and the Environment 1770–1950* (Oxford: Oxford University Press, 2003).

——, 'Transhumance, animal disease and environment in the Cape, South Africa', *South African Historical Journal*, 58(1), 2007, pp. 17–41.

Beinart, W., P. Delius & S. Trapido, eds, *Putting a Plough to the Ground: Accumulation and Dispossession in Rural South Africa, 1850–1930* (Johannesburg: Ravan Press, 1986).

Beinart, W. & J. McGregor, eds, *Social History and African Environments* (Oxford, Athens & Cape Town: James Currey, Ohio University Press & David Philip, 2003).

——, 'Introduction', in W. Beinart & J. McGregor, eds, *Social History and African Environments* (Oxford, Athens & Cape Town: James Currey, Ohio University Press & David Philip, 2003).

Beinart, William & E. Green Musselman, 'Scientific travellers, colonists, and Africans: Chains of knowledge and the Cape vernacular, 1770–1850', in William Beinart, ed., *The Rise of Conservation in South Africa: Settlers, Livestock, and the Environment 1770–1950* (Oxford: Oxford University Press, 2003).

Berger, J., 'Why look at animals?', in *About Looking* (London: Writers & Readers, 1980).

——, *Wild Horses of the Great Basin: Social Competition and Population Size* (Chicago: University of Chicago Press, 1986).

Berlin, I., ed., *Power and Culture: Essays on the American Working Class* (New York: Pantheon 1987).

Betrix, Gonda with J. Attwood-Wheeler, *Gonda Betrix: Jumping to Success* (Cape Town: Southern Book Publishers, 1991).

Bethell, Alfred J., *Notes on South African Hunting and Notes on a Ride to the Victoria Falls of the Zambesi* ([1887], Bulawayo: Books of Rhodesia, 1976).

Bickford-Smith, V., *Ethnic Pride and Racial Prejudice in Victorian Cape Town* (Johannesburg: Wits University Press, 1995).

Bigot, L. & N. Poinsot-Balaguer, 'Influence du pasturage d'une manade de chevaux de race Carmargue sur les communautés des invertébrés d'une sansouire', *Revue d'Ecologie et de Biologie du Sol*, 15, 1978, pp. 517–28.

Bird, W., *State of the Cape of Good Hope in 1822* (Cape Town: Struik, 1966).

Bjerk, Paul K., 'They poured themselves into the milk: Zulu political philosophy under Shaka', *Journal of African History*, 47(1), 2006, pp. 1–19.

Blake, J.Y.F., *A West Pointer with the Boers* (Boston: Angel Guardian Press, 1903).

Blanke, D., *Sowing the American Dream: How Consumer Culture Took Root in the Rural Midwest* (Athens: Ohio University Press, 2000).

Blount, A.E., *Notes on the Cape of Good Hope Made during an Excursion in that Colony in the Year 1820* (London: John Murray, 1821).

Boomgaard, Peter, *Frontiers of Fear: Tigers and People in the Malay World, 1600–1950* (New Haven: Yale University Press, 2001).

Borcherds, Petrus, *An Autobiographical Memoir of Petrus Borchardus Borcherds, esq.* (Cape Town: Robertson, 1861).

Boswell, James, *The Life of Samuel Johnson LL.D*, ed. George Birkbeck Hill (London: 1897, repr. Echo Library, 2006).

Botha, C. Graham, *General History and Social Life of the Cape of Good Hope* (Cape Town: Struik, 1962).

Bourdieu, Pierre, *Outline of a Theory of Practice* (translated R. Nice. Cambridge: Cambridge University Press, 1977).

Boyd, L. & K.A. Houpt, eds, *Przewalski's Horse: The History and Biology of an Endangered Species* (New York: State University of New York Press, 1994).

Bozzoli, B., *Women of Phokeng: Consciousness, Life Strategy and Migrancy in South Africa, 1900–1983* (Portsmouth: Heinemann, 1991).

Bradford, H., 'Women, gender and colonialism: Rethinking the history of the British Cape Colony and its frontier zones, c.1806–70', *Journal of African History*, 37(3), 1996, pp. 351–70.

Bradlow, Edna, 'The culture of a colonial elite: The Cape of Good Hope in the 1850s', *Victorian Studies*, 29(3), 1986, pp. 387–403.

Brewer, John, *Black and Blue: Policing in South Africa* (Oxford: Oxford University Press, 1994).

British Parliamentary Papers

Broderip, W.J., *Zoological Recreations* (London: H. Colburn, 1847).

Broom, Robert, 'Note on *Equus capensis*', *Bulletin of the American Museum of Natural History*, 32(25), 1913, pp. 437–39.

Brown, Karen, 'Political entomology: The insectile challenge to agricultural development in the Cape Colony 1895–1910', *Journal of Southern African Studies*, 29(2), 2003, pp. 529–49.

——, 'Tropical medicine and animal diseases: Onderstepoort and the development of veterinary science in South Africa 1908–1950', *Journal of Southern African Studies*, 31(3), 2005, pp. 513–29.

——, 'Frontiers of disease: Human desire and environmental realities in the rearing of horses in nineteenth- and twentieth-century South Africa', *African Historical Review*, 40(1), 2008a, pp. 30–57.

——, 'From Ubombo to Mkhuzi: Disease, colonial science, and the control of nagana (livestock trypanosomiasis) in Zululand, South Africa, c.1894–1953', *Journal of the History of Medicine and Allied Sciences*, 63(3), 2008b, pp. 285–322.

Brown, William Harvey, *On the South African Frontier: The Adventures and Observations of an American in Mashonaland and Matabeleland* ([1899], Bulawayo: Rhodesiana Reprint Library, 1970).

Bryden, H.A., *Nature and Sport in South Africa* (London: Chapman & Hall, 1897).

Budiansky, S., *The Covenant of the Wild: Why Animals Chose Domestication* (New Haven: Yale University Press, 1999).

Bulliet, Richard, *The Camel and the Wheel* (Cambridge: Harvard University Press, 1975).

Bumpus, Hermon, 'Facts and theories of telegony', *American Naturalist*, 33(396), 1899, pp. 917–22.

Bundy, Colin, *The Rise and Fall of the South African Peasantry* (London: Heinemann, 1979).

Burchell, William, *Travels in the Interior of Southern Africa*, vol. 1 (London: Longman, Hurst, Rees, Orme & Brown, 1822).

——, *Travels in the Interior of Southern Africa*, vol. 2 (London: Batchworth, 1824).

Burkhardt, R.W., 'Closing the door on Lord Morton's mare: The rise and fall of telegony', *Studies in History of Biology*, 3, 1979, pp. 1–21.

Burman, Jose, *To Horse and Away* (Cape Town: Human & Rousseau, 1993).

Burrows, E.H., *Overberg Odyssey, People, Roads and Early Days* (Swellendam: self-published, 1994).

Butzer, Karl W., 'Coastal eolian sands, paleosols, and pleistocene geoarchaeology of the southwestern Cape, South Africa', *Journal of Archaeological Science*, 31(12), 2004, pp. 1743–81.

Campbell, C., 'Art in crisis: Contact period rock art in the south-eastern mountains of southern Africa', MSc diss., University of the Witwatersrand, 1987.

Campbell, James T., 'The Americanization of South Africa', in A. Offenburger, S. Rosenberg & C. Saunders, eds, *A South African and American Comparative*

Reader: The Best of Safundi and Other Selected Articles (Nashville: Safundi, 2002), pp. 29–32.

Cannadine, David, 'After the horse: Nobility and mobility in modern Britain', in N. Harte & R. Quinault, eds, *Land and Society in Britain, 1700–1914* (Manchester: Manchester University Press, 1996).

Cape of Good Hope Almanac and Annual Register 1850 (Cape Town: Van de Sandt & De Villiers: 1850).

Cape of Good Hope Almanac and Annual Register 1855 (Cape Town: Van de Sandt & De Villiers, 1855).

Cape of Good Hope Almanac and Annual Register 1860 (Cape Town: Van de Sandt & De Villiers, 1860).

Carnegie Commission, *The Poor White Problem in South Africa*, vol. 1 (Stellenbosch, 1932).

Carrington Bolton, H., 'The language used in talking to domestic animals', *American Anthropologist*, 10(4), 1897, pp. 97–113.

Carruthers, E.J., 'The Pongola Game Reserve: An eco-political study', *Koedoe*, 28, 1985, pp. 1–16.

——, 'Game protection in the Transvaal, 1846 to 1926', *Archives Year Book for South African History* (Pretoria: Government Printer, 1995).

——, 'Nationhood and national parks: Comparative examples from the post-imperial experience', in T. Griffiths & L. Robin, eds, *Ecology and Empire: Environmental History of Settler Societies* (Edinburgh: Keele University Press, 1997).

Carruthers, J., *The Kruger National Park: A Social and Political History* (Pietermaritzburg: University of Natal Press, 1995).

Carson, James Taylor, 'Horses and the economy and culture of the Choctaw Indians, 1690–1840', *Ethnohistory*, 42(3), 1995, pp. 495–513.

Casalis, E., *My Life in Basutoland*, trans. J. Brierley ([1889], Cape Town: Struik, 1971).

Challis, Sam, 'Taking the reins: The introduction of the horse in the nineteenth-century Maloti-Drakensberg and the protective medicine of baboons', in P. Mitchell & Benjamin Smith, eds, *The Eland's People: New Perspectives in the Rock Art of the Maloti-Drakensberg Bushmen: Essays in Memory of Patricia Vinnicombe* (Johannesburg: Wits University Press, 2009).

Chamberlin, J. Edward, *Horse: How the Horse Has Shaped Civilizations* (New York: Blue Bridge, 2006).

Child, Daphne, *Saga of the South African Horse* (Cape Town: Howard Timmins, 1967).

Churchill, Lord Randolph, *Men, Mines and Animals in South Africa* ([1893], Bulawayo: Rhodesiana Reprint Library, 1969).

Clarence-Smith, William Gervase, 'Southeast Asia and Southern Africa in the maritime horse trade of the Indian Ocean, c.1800–1914', in G. Bankoff & S. Swart, *Breeds of Empire: The 'Invention' of the Horse in the Philippines and Southern Africa, 1500–1950* (Uppsala: Nordic Institute of Asian Studies, 2007).

Clatworthy, N., 'Social-class and value factors in Saddle-horse showing', *Free Inquiry in Creative Sociology*, 9(2), 1981, pp. 135–38.

Clutton-Brock, Juliet, *A Natural History of Domesticated Mammals* (Cambridge: Cambridge University Press, 1989a).

—, ed., *The Walking Larder: Patterns of Domestication, Pastoralism and Predation* (London: Unwin Hyman, 1989b).

Coates, Peter, 'The strange stillness of the past: Toward an environmental history of sound and noise', *Environmental History*, 10(4), 2005, pp. 636–65.

Coetzee, J.M., *White Writing* (New Haven: Yale University Press, 1988).

Cole, Alfred W., 'Extracts from idylls of a prince', in Nerine Desmond, ed., *Candlelight Poets of the Cape* (Cape Town: Howard Timmins, 1967).

Colonial Office Basutoland, *Report for 1902–1903*, *Colonial Report Annual*, no. 408 (London: Colonial Office, 1903).

Comaroff, Jean & John Comaroff, 'Naturing the nation: Aliens, apocalypse and the postcolonial state', *Journal of Southern African Studies*, 27(3), September 2001, pp. 627–51.

Commissioner of the South African Police, *Annual Report* (Pretoria: Government Printers, 1945).

Coplan, David B. & Tim Quinlan, 'A chief by the people: Nation versus state in Lesotho', *Journal of the International African Institute*, 67(1), 1997, pp. 27–60.

Cothran, E.G., E. van Dyk & F.J. van der Merwe, 'Genetic variation in the feral horses of the Namib Desert, Namibia', *Journal of the South African Veterinary Association*, 72(1), 2001, pp. 18–22.

Cronon, William, 'A place for stories: Nature, history, and narrative', *Journal of American History*, 78, 1992, pp. 1347–76.

—, ed., *Uncommon Ground: Rethinking the Human Place in Nature* (New York: W.W. Norton, 1996a).

——. 'The trouble with wilderness, or, getting back to the wrong nature', in William Cronon, ed., *Uncommon Ground* (New York: W.W. Norton, 1996b).

Crosby, Alfred, *Germs, Seeds and Animals: Studies in Ecological History* (New York: M.E. Sharpe, 1994).

——, *The Columbian Exchange: Biological and Cultural Consequences of 1492* (Westport: Praeger, 2003).

——, *Ecological Imperialism: The Biological Expansion of Europe, 900–1900* (Cambridge: Cambridge University Press, 2004).

Cubbin, A.E., 'An outline of game legislation in Natal, 1866–1912', *Journal of Natal and Zulu History*, 14, 1992, pp. 37–47.

Cuneo, Pia, 'Beauty and the beast: Art and science in early modern European equine imagery', *Journal of Early Modern History*, 4(3–4), 2000, pp. 269–321.

Curtin, Philip D., 'Location in history: Argentina and South Africa in the nineteenth century', *Journal of World History*, 10(1), 1999, pp. 41–92.

Cuthbertson, G., A. Grundlingh & M. Suttie, eds, *Writing a Wider War: Rethinking Gender, Race and Identity in the South African War, 1899–1902* (Athens & Cape Town: Ohio University Press & David Philip, 2002).

Dagverhaal van Jan van Riebeeck, Commandeur aan de Kaap de Goede Hoop (Gravenhage: Nijhoff, 1892/1893).

Darwin, C., *The Variations of Animals and Plants under Domestication* (New York: D. Appleton, 1896).

——, *The Expression of the Emotions in Man and Animals* ([1872], Oxford: Oxford University Press, 1998).

Davids, A., *The Mosques of BoKaap* (Athlone: South African Institute of Arabic and Islamic Research, 1980).

Davis, Newnham, *The Transvaal under the Queen* (London: Sands, 1900).

Debates of the House of Assembly, 1 (Pretoria: State Printer, 17 May 1916).

De Jongh, Michael, 'No fixed abode: The poorest of the poor and elusive identities in rural South Africa', *Journal of Southern African Studies*, 28(2), 2002, pp. 441–60.

De Jongh, Michael & Riana Steyn, 'Itinerancy as a way of life: The nomadic sheep-shearers of the South African Karoo', *Development Southern Africa*, 11(2), 1994, pp. 217–28.

De Kok, K.J., *Empires of the Veld, Being Fragments of the Unwritten History of the Two Late Boer Republics* (Durban: Juta, 1904).

De Lima, J. Suasso, *Cape Calendar and Directory, for the Leap Year, 1836* (Cape Town: J. Suasso de Lima, 1935).

Del Villar, José Alvarez, *Men and Horses of Mexico: History and Practice of 'Charrería'*, trans. Margaret Fischer de Nicolin (Mexico City: Ediciones Lara, 1979).

Department of Agriculture, *Handbook of Agricultural Statistics, 1904–1950* (Pretoria: Department of Agriculture, 1960–61).

Derham, W., *A Visit to Cape Colony and Natal* (Bristol: Mardon, 1879).

Derry, Margaret, *Horses in Society: A Story of Animal Breeding and Marketing Culture, 1800–1920* (Buffalo: University of Toronto Press, 2006).

De Wet, C.R., *Three Years' War* (New York: Charles Scribner's Sons, 1902).

Diamond, Jared, *Guns, Germs and Steel: The Fates of Human Societies* (London & New York: W.W. Norton, 1999).

Dicke, B.H., 'The tsetse-fly's influence on South African history', *South African Journal of Science*, 29, October 1932, pp. 792–96.

Donkin, Sir Rufane Shaw, *A Letter on the Government of the Cape of Good Hope, and on Certain Events which Have Occurred there of Late Years under the Administration of Lord Charles Somerset, Addressed Most Respectfully to Earl Bathurst* (London: Carpenter & Son, 1827).

Dooling, Wayne, 'The decline of the Cape gentry', *Journal of African History*, 40, 1999, pp. 215–42.

——, 'The making of a colonial elite: Property, family and landed stability in the Cape Colony, c.1750–1834', *Journal of Southern African Studies*, 31(1), 2005, pp. 147–62.

Dorré, G.M., *Victorian Fiction and the Cult of the Horse* (Aldershot: Ashgate, 2006).

Draper, Malcolm, 'Zen and the art of garden province maintenance: The soft intimacy of hard men in the wilderness of Kwa-Zulu-Natal, South Africa, 1952–1997', *Journal of Southern African Studies*, 24(4), 1998, pp. 801–28.

——, 'Going native? Trout and settling identity in a Rainbow Nation', *Historia*, 48, 2003, pp. 55–94.

Drayson, Alfred W., *Sporting Scenes amongst the Kaffirs of South Africa* (London: Routledge, 1858).

Dubow, Saul, ed., *Science and Society in Southern Africa* (Manchester: Manchester University Press, 2000).

——, 'Introduction: South Africa's 1940s', in S. Dubow & A. Jeeves, eds, *South Africa's 1940s: Worlds of Possibilities* (Cape Town: Double Storey, 2005).

——, *A Commonwealth of Knowledge* (Oxford: Oxford University Press, 2006).

Dubow, S. & A. Jeeves, eds, *South Africa's 1940s: Worlds of Possibilities* (Cape Town: Double Storey, 2005).

Dunlap, Thomas, *Nature and the English Diaspora: Environment and History in the United States, Canada, Australia and New Zealand* (Cambridge: Cambridge University Press, 1999).

Du Pisani, K., 'Puritanism transformed: Afrikaner masculinities in the apartheid and post-apartheid period', in R. Morrell, ed., *Changing Men in Southern Africa* (Pietermaritzburg: University of Natal Press, 2001).

Du Plessis, E.P., *'n Volk Staan Op* (Cape Town: Human & Rousseau, 1964).

Du Plessis, S.F. 'Die verhaal van die dagverhaal van Jan van Riebeeck', D.Litt. thesis, University of Pretoria, 1934.

Du Toit, Kobus, *Die Geskiedenis van die S.A. Boerperd*, draft manuscript, <http://www.boerperd.net/tuisblad.php>.

Edwards, Peter, *The Horse Trade of Tudor and Stuart England* (Cambridge: Cambridge University Press, 1988).

——, *Horse and Man in Early Modern England* (London: Hambledon Continuum, 2007).

Eldredge, Elizabeth, *A South African Kingdom: The Pursuit of Security in Nineteenth-century Lesotho* (Cambridge: Cambridge University Press, 1993).

Ellenberger, D.F., *History of the Basuto, Ancient and Modern,* trans. J.C. MacGregor (New York: Negro University Press, 1969).

Ellis, Stephen, 'Of elephants and men: Politics and nature conservation in South Africa', *Journal of Southern African Studies*, 20(1), 1994, pp. 53–69.

Elphick, Richard, *Kraal and Castle: Khoikhoi and the Founding of White South Africa* (New Haven: Yale University Press, 1977).

Emerson, Ralph Waldo, 'Ode, inscribed to W.H. Channing', in *Poems* (Boston: James Munroe, 1847).

Epprecht, Marc, *'This Matter of Women Is Getting Very Bad': Gender, Development and Politics in Colonial Lesotho* (Pietermaritzburg: University of Natal Press, 2000).

Etherington, Norman, *The Great Treks: The Transformation of Southern Africa* (London: Pearson Education, 2001).

Ewart, James, *James Ewart's Journal, Covering His Stay at the Cape of Good Hope (1811–1814) & His Part in the Expedition to Florida and New Orleans (1814–1815)* (Cape Town: Struik, 1970).

Febvre, L., 'Smells, tastes, and sounds', *The Problem of Unbelief in the Sixteenth Century* (Cambridge, MA: Harvard University Press, 1982).

Ferreira, O.J., ed., *Da Costa Leal in die Zuid-Afrikaanse Republiek* (Pretoria: Protea, 2008).

Bibiography

Ficq, Constant, 'Die betekenis van perde in die bewoning van die Lesotho-Hoogland',
MA diss., RAU, 1988.

Firat, F. & N. Dholakia, *Consuming People: From Political Economy to Theatres of
Consumption* (London: Routledge, 1998).

Fisher, Humphrey J., '"He swalloweth the ground with fierceness and rage": The
horse in the central Sudan, II: Its use', *Journal of African History*, 14(3), 1973,
pp. 355–79.

Flannery, Tim, *The Future Eaters* (Sydney: Grove, 1994).

Fleming, G., 'The physical condition of horses for military purposes', Aldershot
Military Society, London, 31 January 1889.

Flemming, Leonard, 'The romance of a new South African farm', *Journal of the Royal
African Society*, 21(82), 1922, pp. 115–28.

Fransch, Chet, 'Stellenbosch and the Muslim communities, 1866–1966', MA diss.,
University of Stellenbosch, 2009.

Fraser, J.G. & James Briggs, *Sotho War Diaries, 1864–1865* (Cape Town: Human &
Rousseau, 1985).

Frederick, F.H. & J.M. Henderson, 'Impact force measurement using preloaded
transducers', *American Journal of Veterinary Research*, 31, 1970, pp. 2279–83.

Freeman, Derek, *The Fateful Hoaxing of Margaret Mead: A Historical Analysis of Her
Samoan Research* (Boulder: Westview Press, 1999).

Fudge, Erica, 'A left-handed blow: Writing the history of animals', in Nigel Rothfels,
ed., *Representing Animals* (Bloomington: University of Indiana Press, 2003).

Gale & Polden Ltd, *A Handbook of the Boer War* (London & Aldershot: Butler &
Tanner, 1910).

Geertz, Clifford, *The Interpretation of Cultures* (New York: Basic Books, 1973).

General Directory and Guide Book to the Cape of Good Hope and Its Dependencies
(Cape Town: Saul Solomon, 1869).

Genovese, D., *Roll, Jordan, Roll: The World the Slaves Made* (New York: Pantheon,
1974).

Gilfoyle, D., 'Veterinary immunology as colonial science: Method and quantification
in the investigation of horsesickness in South Africa, c.1905–1945', *Journal of the
History of Medicine and Allied Sciences*, 61, 2005, pp. 26–65.

Giliomee, Hermann, *The Afrikaners: Biography of a People* (Cape Town: Tafelberg,
2003).

Gill, Stephen J., *A Short History of Lesotho* (Morija: Morija Museum & Archives, 1993).

311

Goody, Jack, *Technology, Tradition, and the State in Africa* (New York: Press Syndicate & Cambridge University Press, 1980).

Gordon, Lady Duff, *Letters from the Cape* (London: Macmillan, 1876).

Gordon, W.J., *The Horse World of London* ([1893], London: Allen, 1971).

Green, Lawrence, *Karoo* (Cape Town: Howard Timmins, 1955).

Greene, Ann, *Horses at Work: Harnessing Power in Industrial America* (Cambridge, MA: Harvard University Press, 2008).

Greenwood, James, *Odd People in Odd Places* (London: Frederick Warne, 1883).

Greyling, T., 'The behavioural ecology of the feral horses in the Namib Naukluft Park', MSc diss., Potchefstroom University, 1994.

Grobbelaar, Charmaine, *The Arabian Horse and Its Influence in South Africa* (Pretoria: Protea Book House, 2007).

Grobbelaar, J.J., 'Die Vrystaatse Republiek en die Basoetoevraagstuk', *Archives Year Book* (Cape Town: Government Printers, 1939).

Grove, Richard, *Ecology, Climate and Empire: Colonialism and Global Environmental History, 1400–1940* (Cambridge: White Horse Press, 1997).

Grundlingh, A., 'The National women's monument: The making and mutation of meaning in Afrikaner memory of the South African War', in G. Cuthbertson, A. Grundlingh & M. Suttie, eds, *Writing a Wider War: Rethinking Gender, Race and Identity in the South African War, 1899–1902* (Athens & Cape Town: Ohio University Press & David Philip, 2002).

——, 'The politics of the past and of popular pursuits in the construction of everyday Afrikaner nationalism, 1938–1948', in S. Dubow & A. Jeeves, eds, *South Africa's 1940s: Worlds of Possibilities* (Cape Town: Double Storey, 2005)

Guelke, Leonard, 'Frontier settlement in early Dutch South Africa', *Annals of the Association of American Geographers*, 66(1), 1976, pp. 25–42.

Guelke, L. & R. Shell, 'An early colonial landed gentry: Land and wealth in the Cape Colony 1682–1731', *Journal of Historical Geography*, 9(3), 1983, pp. 265–86.

Haggard, H. Rider, *Jess* ([1887], London: Smith & Elder, 1909).

——, *Finished* ([1917], London: Macdonald, 1962).

Haines, Francis, 'The northward spread of horses among the Plains Indians', *American Anthropologist*, 40, 1938, pp. 429–37.

Hales, A.G., *Campaign Pictures of the War in South Africa (1899–1900): Letters from the Front* (London: Cassell, 1901).

Hamilton, Jill, *Marengo: The Myth of Napoleon's Horse* (London: Fourth Estate, 2000).

Hanley, T.A. & K.A. Hanley, 'Food resource partitioning by sympatric ungulates on great basin rangeland', *Journal of Range Management*, 35, 1982, pp. 152–58.

Hansen, R.M., 'Foods of free-roaming horses in southern New Mexico', *Journal of Range Management*, 29, 1976, p. 347.

Hayes, M.H., *Among Men and Horses* (London: T. Fisher Unwin, 1894).

—, *Among Horses in South Africa* (London: Everett, 1900).

—, *Horses on Board Ship: A Guide to Their Management* (London: Hurst & Blackett, 1902).

—, *Points of the Horse* (New York: Arco, 1969).

Herodotus, *The Histories* (London: Penguin, 2003).

Hill, Christopher, *The World Turned Upside Down: Radical Ideas during the English Revolution* (Harmondsworth: Penguin, 1972).

Hobsbawm, Eric, 'Peasants and politics', *Journal of Peasant Studies*, 1(1), 1973, pp. 3–22.

—, *The Age of Extremes, 1914–1991* (London: Michael Joseph, 1994).

Hollmann, J.C., ed., *Customs and Beliefs of the /Xam Bushmen* (Johannesburg: Wits University Press, 2004).

Hook, D.B., *With Sword and Statute: On the Cape of Good Hope Frontier* (London: Greaves & Pass, 1905).

Hopkins, H.C., *Maar Een Soos Hy: Die Lewe van Kommandant C.A. van Niekerk* (Cape Town: Tafelberg, 1963).

Hribal, Jason, 'Animals, agency, and class: Writing the history of animals from below', *Human Ecology Forum*, 14(1), 2007, pp. 101–12.

Hubbard, R. & R. Hansen, 'Diets of wild horses, cattle and mule deer in the Piceance basin, Colorado', *Journal of Range Management*, 29, 1976, pp. 389–92.

Ingold, Tim, 'The animal in the study of humanity', in Tim Ingold, ed., *What Is an Animal?* (London: Routledge, 1988).

—, 'From trust to domination: An alternative history of human–animal relations', in A. Manning & J. Serpell, eds, *Animals and Human Societies: Changing Perspectives* (London: Routledge, 1994).

—, *The Perception of the Environment: Essays in Livelihood, Dwelling and Skill* (New York: Routledge, 2000).

Ingold, Tim, David Riches & James Woodburn, eds, *Hunters and Gatherers: Property, Power and Ideology*, vol. II (Oxford: Berg, 1997).

Jacobs, Nancy, 'The Great Bophuthatswana Donkey Massacre: Discourse on the ass and the politics of class and grass', *American Historical Review*, 106(2), 2001, pp. 485–507.

—, *Environment, Power, and Injustice: A South African History* (Cambridge: Cambridge University Press, 2003).

Jacottet, E., *The Treasury of Ba-Suto Lore* (London: Paul, Trench & Trubner, 1908).

'Jan Burger', *The Gulf Between* (Cape Town: Howard Timmins, 1960).

Jankovich, Miklós, *They Rode into Europe: The Fruitful Exchange in the Arts of Horsemanship between East and West*, trans. Anthony Dent (London: Long Riders' Guild Press, 1971).

Jansen, Thomas et al., 'Mitochondrial DNA and the origins of the domestic horse', *Proceedings of the National Academy of Sciences of the United States of America*, 99(16), 2002, pp. 10905–10.

Jardine, Lisa & Jerry Brotton, *Global Interests: Renaissance Art between East and West* (Ithaca: Cornell University Press, 2000).

Jenschke, J., D. Strayer & S. Carpenter, 'Invasion success of vertebrates in Europe and North America', *Proceedings of the National Academy of Sciences of the United States of America*, 102(20), 2005, pp. 7198–202.

Jones, Meurig, 'A survey of memorials to the Second Anglo-Boer War in the United Kingdom and Eire', *Journal of the Africana Society*, 15, 1999.

Jones, S., 'An agricultural revolution, 1950–1970: A rejoinder', *South African Journal of Economic History*, 15(1/2), September 2000, pp. 180–86.

Jones, S. & A. Müller, *The South African Economy, 1910–90* (Basingstoke: Macmillan, 1992).

Jordaan, D., *Perdeteelt in Suid-Afrika* (Pretoria: self-published, 1997).

Jeeves, A. & J. Crush, eds, *White Farms, Black Labour: The State and Agrarian Change in Southern Africa, 1910–1950* (Pietermaritzburg: University of Natal Press, 1997).

Jeffreys, K.M. & S.D. Naude, eds, *Kaapse Argiefstukke: Kaapse Plakkaatboek, 1652–1795*, vol. I (Cape Town: Government Printer, 1944–49).

Joubert, D.M. & W.M. Bosman, "The Nooitgedacht pony', *South African Journal of Science*, 67(7), 1971, pp. 366–73.

Kaplan, L., *American Saddle Horses in South Africa* (Cape Town: self-published, 1974).

Keay-Bright, J. & J. Boardman, 'The influence of land management on soil erosion in the Sneeuberg Mountains, Central Karoo, South Africa', *Land Degradation & Development*, 18(4), 2006a, pp. 423–39.

——, 'Changes in the distribution of degraded land over time in the Central Karoo, South Africa', *CATENA*, 67(1), 2006b, pp. 1–14.

Keegan, Timothy, *Rural Transformations in Industrializing South Africa: The Southern Highveld to 1914* (Basingstoke: Macmillan, 1986a).

——, 'Trade, accumulation and impoverishment: Mercantile capital and the economic transformation of Lesotho and the conquered territory, 1870–1920', *Journal of Southern African Studies*, 12(2), 1986b, pp. 196–216.

——, *Colonial South Africa and the Origins of the Racial Order* (Cape Town: David Philip, 1996).

Kendall, K. Limakatso, *Basali! Stories by and about Women in Lesotho* (Pietermaritzburg: University of Natal Press, 1995).

Kimble, D., *A Political History of Ghana: The Rise of Gold Coast Nationalism* (Oxford: Oxford University Press, 1963).

Kimble, Judith, *Migrant Labour and Colonial Rule in Basutoland, 1890–1930*, monograph no. 1 (Johannesburg: ISER, 1999).

Klein, Richard G., 'A preliminary report on the "Middle Stone Age" open-air site of Duinefontein 2', *South African Archaeological Bulletin*, 31(121/122), 1976, pp. 12–20.

Kline, R.P., *Consumers in the Country: Technology and Social Change in Rural America* (Athens: Ohio University Press, 2000).

Kolbe, P., *Naaukeurige en Uitvoerige Beschryving van Kaap de Goede Hoop* (Amsterdam: B. Lakeman, 1727).

——, *The Present State of the Cape of Good Hope* (New York: Johnson Reprint, 1968).

Lacy, George, *Pictures of Travel, Sport, and Adventure* (London: C. Arthur Pearson, 1899).

Lagden, Godfrey, *The Basutos; The Mountaineers and Their Country*, vol. 1 (London: Hutchinson, 1909).

Lamont, Michele, *Money, Morals, and Manners: The Culture of the French and American Upper-middle Class* (Chicago: University of Chicago Press, 1992).

Landry, D., 'The bloody shouldered Arabian and early modern English culture', *Criticism*, 2004, pp. 41–69.

——, *Noble Brutes: How Eastern Horses Transformed English Culture* (Baltimore: Johns Hopkins University Press, 2008).

Law, R., *The Horse in West Africa* (Oxford: Oxford University Press, 1980).

Lawrence, Elizabeth, *Rodeo: An Anthropologist Looks at the Wild and the Tame* (Knoxville: University of Tennessee Press, 1981).

——, 'Rodeo horses: The wild and the tame', in R. Willis, *Signifying Animals: Human Meaning in the Natural World* (London: Routledge, 1990).

Lears, J., 'Beyond Veblen: Rethinking consumer culture in America', in Simon J. Bronner, ed., *Consuming Visions: Accumulation and Display of Goods in America, 1880–1920* (New York: W.W. Norton, 1989).

Lee, E., *To the Bitter End* (London: Guild, 1985).

Legassick, Martin, 'Firearms, horses and Samorian army organization, 1870–1898', *Journal of African History*, 7(1), 1966, pp. 95–115.

Leibbrandt, H.C.V., ed., *Précis of the Archives of the Cape of Good Hope, January 1659–May 1662: Riebeeck's Journal*, part II (Cape Town: W.A. Richards & Sons, 1897a).

——, *Précis of the Archives of the Cape of Good Hope, January 1659–May 1662: Riebeeck's Journal*, part III (Cape Town: W.A. Richards & Sons, 1897b).

——, *Précis of the Archives of the Cape of Good Hope: Letters Despatched from the Cape, 1652–1662*, vol. I (Cape Town: W.A. Richards & Sons, 1900a).

——, *Précis of the Archives of the Cape of Good Hope, Letters Despatched from the Cape, 1652–1662*, vol. II (Cape Town: W.A. Richards & Sons, 1900b).

——, *Précis of the Archives of the Cape of Good Hope: Letters Despatched from the Cape, 1652–1662*, vol. III (Cape Town: W.A. Richards & Sons, 1900c).

——, *Précis of the Archives of the Cape of Good Hope: Journal, 1662–1670* (Cape Town: W.A. Richards & Sons, 1901).

Leipoldt, C. Louis, *Bushveld Doctor* ([1937], Johannesburg: Lowry, 1980).

Leopold, Aldo, *A Sand County Almanac* (Oxford: Oxford University Press, 1966).

Le Riche, P.J., ed., *Memoirs of General Ben Bouwer* (Pretoria: HSRC, 1980).

Lester, Alan, 'Reformulating identities: British settlers in early nineteenth-century South Africa', *Transactions of the Institute of British Geographers*, 23(4), 1998, pp. 151–31.

Levine, M.A., 'Botai and the origins of horse domestication', *Journal of Anthropological Archaeology*, 18, 1999, pp. 29–78.

Levine, M.A. et al., 'Palaeopathology and horse domestication', in G. Bailey & Charles R. Winder, eds, *Human Ecodynamics and Environmental Archaeology* (Oxford: Oxbow, 2000).

Levi-Strauss, Claude, *Totemism* (Boston: Beacon, 1963).

Lichtenstein, H., *Travels in Southern Africa in the Years 1803, 1804, 1805, and 1806*, vol. II, trans. from the original German (London: Colburn, 1815).

316

Lichtenstein, W.H.C., *Foundation of the Cape, about the Bechuanas: Being a History of the Discovery and Colonisation of South Africa*, trans. O.H. Spohr ([1807, 1811], Cape Town: Balkema, 1973).

Liddle, M.J. & L.D. Chitty, 'The nutrient-budget of horse tracks on an English lowland heath', *Journal of Applied Ecology*, 18(3), 1981, pp. 841–48.

Lindsay, Alexander Crawford, *Lives of the Lindsays; or, a Memoir of the Houses of Crawford and Balcarres*, vol. III (London: John Murray, 1849).

Little, James, *South Africa: A Sketch Book of Men, Manners and Facts* (London: Sonnenschein, 1887).

Livingstone, David, *Missionary Travels and Researches in South Africa* (London: John Murray, 1857).

Lorenz, Konrad, *King Solomon's Ring: New Light on Animal Ways* (London: Methuen, 1982).

Lye, L. William, ed., *Andrew Smith's Journal of His Expedition into the Interior of South Africa, 1834–36* (Cape Town: A.A. Balkema, 1975).

Lye, William & Colin Murray, *Transformations on the Highveld: The Tswana and Southern Sotho* (Cape Town: David Philip, 1980).

Lynes, R., *The Tastemakers: The Shaping of American Popular Taste* (New York: Dover, 1980).

MacKenzie, John, *The Empire of Nature: Hunting, Conservation and British Imperialism* (Manchester: Manchester University Press, 1988).

Maeder, F., *Journal de Mission Evangelque*, Morija Archives, 15 January 1858.

Malan, C.H., *South African Missions* (London: Nisbet, 1876).

Malherbe, E.G., *Education and the Poor White: Report of the Carnegie Commission*, vol. III (Stellenbosch: Pro Ecclesia, 1932).

Manhire, A.H. et al., 'Cattle, sheep and horses: A review of domestic animals in rock art of southern Africa', in *Prehistoric Pastoralism in Southern Africa*, Goodwin Series, vol. 5 (South African Archaeological Society, June 1986), pp. 22–30.

Marcuse, H., *One Dimensional Man* (Boston: Beacon Press, 1964).

Marks, Shula, 'Khoisan resistance to the Dutch in the seventeenth and eighteenth centuries', *Journal of African History*, 13, 1972, pp. 55–80.

——, *Not Either an Experimental Doll* (Bloomington: Indiana University Press, 1987).

Marks, Shula & Stanley Trapido, 'Lord Milner and the South African state', *History Workshop*, 8, 1979, pp. 50–80.

Martin, M., *Basutoland: Its Legends and Customs* (New York: Negro University Press, 1969).

Marx, Karl, *The Eighteenth Brumaire of Louis Napoleon*, trans. D. de Leon ([1852], Chicago: Kerr, 1919).

Mason, R., *Conspicuous Consumption: A Study of Exceptional Consumer Behaviour* (Hampshire: Gower, 1981).

Mayson, J.S., *The Malays of Capetown* (Manchester: J. Galt, 1861).

McKenzie, Kirsten, *Scandal in the Colonies* (Melbourne: Melbourne University Press, 2004).

McKnight, Tom, 'The feral horse in Anglo-America', *Geographical Review*, 49(4), 1959, pp. 506–25.

McLean, A.A., *Letters of the Late Major A.A. McLean, DSO, from the Date of His Leaving Australia for the Boer War, 6th November 1899, until the Conclusion of that Campaign, 1902* (Sydney: William Brooks, 1931).

McShane, Clay & Joel A. Tarr, *The Horse in the City: Living Machines in the Nineteenth Century* (Baltimore: Johns Hopkins University Press, 2007).

Melville, Elinor, *A Plague of Sheep: Environmental Consequences of the Conquest of Mexico* (Cambridge: Cambridge University Press, 1994).

Mentzel, O.F., *Life at the Cape in the Mid-eighteenth Century*, trans. M. Greenlees ([1784], Cape Town: Darter Brothers, 1920).

Mikro, *Die Ruiter in die Nag* (Cape Town, Bloemfontein & Port Elizabeth: Nasionale Pers, 1936).

—, *Kaptein Gereke* (Cape Town, Bloemfontein & Port Elizabeth: Nasionale Pers, 1937).

—, *Boerseun* (Bloemfontein, Cape Town & Port Elizabeth: Nasionale Pers, 1947).

—, *Die Jongste Ruiter* (Cape Town: Nasionale Boekhandel, 1954).

—, *Die Kleingeld-Kommando* (Pretoria: Van Schaik, 1956).

—, *Die Jongste Veldkornet* (Johannesburg: Simondium, 1963).

Millar, Anthony Kendal, *A Plantagenet in South Africa: Lord Charles Somerset* (Cape Town & London: Oxford University Press, 1965).

Minkley, G. & C. Rassool, 'Orality, memory, and social history in South Africa', in S. Nuttall & C. Coetzee, eds, *Negotiating the Past: The Making of Memory in South Africa* (Cape Town: Oxford University Press, 1998).

Mitchell, Timothy, *Rule of Experts: Egypt, Techno-politics, Modernity* (Berkeley: University of California Press, 2002).

Mohapeloa, J.M., *Government by Proxy: Ten Years of Cape Colony Rule in Lesotho, 1871–1881* (Morija: Morija Printing Press, 1971).

—, *Tentative British Imperialism, 1884–1910* (Morija: Morija Museum & Archives, 2002).

Moloja, 'The story of the "Fetcani horde"', *Cape Quarterly Review*, 1 January 1882, p. 273.

Moodie, John Wedderburn Dunbar, *Ten Years in South Africa*, vol. 2 (London: R. Bentley, 1835).

Moodie, T.D., *The Rise of Afrikanerdom: Power, Apartheid, and the Afrikaner Civil Religion* (Berkeley: University of California Press, 1975).

Muller, C.F.J., *Sonop in die Suide: Geboorte en Groei van die Nasionale Pers 1915–1948* (Cape Town: Nasionale Boekhandel, 1990).

Mullin, Molly, 'Mirrors and windows: Sociocultural studies of human–animal relationships', *Annual Review of Anthropology*, 28, 1999, pp. 201–24.

—, 'Animals and anthropology', *Society and Animals*, 10(4), 2002, pp. 387–93.

Mumford, L., *Technics and Civilization* (New York: Harcourt & Brace, 1934).

Murray, Colin, 'The symbolism and politics of *bohali*: Household recruitment and marriage by installment in Lesotho', in E.J. Krige & J.L. Comaroff, eds, *Essays on African Marriage in Southern Africa* (Cape Town: Juta, 1981).

Musselman, E. Green, 'Plant knowledge at the Cape: A study in African and European collaboration', *International Journal of African Historical Studies*, 36, 2003, pp. 367–92.

Nash, Linda, 'The agency of nature or the nature of agency', *Environmental History*, 10, 2005, pp. 67–69.

Nash, Richard, 'Honest English breed: The Thoroughbred as cultural metaphor', in Karen Raber & Treva J. Tucker, eds, *The Culture of the Horse: Status, Discipline, and Identity in the Early Modern World* (New York: Palgrave Macmillan, 2005).

Nash, Roderick, 'American environmental history: A new teaching frontier', *Pacific History Review*, 41, 1972, pp. 362–72.

Nasson, W., 'Moving Lord Kitchener: Black military transport and supply work in the South African War, 1899–1902, with particular reference to the Cape Colony', *Journal of Southern African Studies*, 11(1), 1984, pp. 25–51.

—, *Abraham Esau's War: A Black South African War in the Cape, 1899–1902* (Cambridge: Cambridge University Press, 1991).

—, *The South African War, 1899–1902* (London: Arnold, 1999a).

—, *Uyadela Wen'osulapho: Black Participation in the Anglo-Boer War* (Randburg: Ravan Press, 1999b).

Nattrass, N., 'Economic growth and transformation in the 1940s', in S. Dubow &
    A. Jeeves, eds, *South Africa's 1940s: Worlds of Possibilities* (Cape Town: Double
    Storey, 2005).

Nel, J.J., 'Perdeteelt in Suid-Afrika, 1652–1752', MA diss., University of Stellenbosch,
    1930.

Nelson, L., *Measured Excess: Status, Gender, and Consumer Nationalism in South Korea*
    (New York: Columbia University Press, 2000).

Neville, D., B. Sampson & C.G. Sampson, 'The frontier wagon track system in the
    Seacow River Valley, north-eastern Cape', *South African Archaeological Bulletin*,
    49, 1994, pp. 65–72.

Nevinson, H.W., *Ladysmith: The Diary of a Siege* (London: Methuen, 1900).

Newton-King, Susan, *Masters and Servants on the Cape Eastern Frontier, 1760–1803*
    (Cambridge: Cambridge University Press, 1999).

Norden, C., 'The 1954 American Saddle Horse Championships of South Africa', *South
    African Saddle Horse and Other Breeds*, 51(2), April 1954.

Novick, Peter, *Noble Dream: The 'Objectivity Question' and the American Historical
    Profession* (Cambridge: Cambridge University Press, 1988).

O'Connor, J.K., *The Africander Rebellion* (London: Allen & Unwin, 1915).

*Official Yearbook of the Union of South Africa and of Basutholand, Bechuanland
    Protectorate and Swaziland, 1931–1932*, vol. 14 (Pretoria: Government Printer,
    1933).

O'Meara, D., *Volkskapitalisme: Class, Capital and Ideology in the Development of
    Afrikaner Nationalism 1834–48* (Johannesburg: Ravan Press, 1983).

——, *Forty Lost Years: The Apartheid State and the Politics of the National Party,
    1948–1994* (Johannesburg: Ravan Press, 1996).

Orpen, Joseph, *History of the Basutos of South Africa* (Cape Town: Cape Argus, 1857).

Ownby, T., *American Dreams in Mississippi: Consumers, Poverty, and Culture 1830–
    1998* (Chapel Hill: University of North Carolina Press, 1999).

Pakenham, T., *The Boer War* (New York: Random House, 1979).

Pama, C., *Regency Cape Town: Daily Life in the Early Eighteen-thirties with hitherto
    Unpublished Johannesburg Album of Sketches by Sir Charles D'Oyly* (Cape Town:
    Tafelberg, 1975).

Paterson, Andrew Barton 'Banjo', *Happy Dispatches* ([1934], Sydney: University of
    Sydney, 1998).

'Patricius Africanus', 'Experiences in South Africa', *Irish Monthly*, 9(100), 1881,
    pp. 532–35.

Penn, Nigel, *The Forgotten Frontier* (Athens & Cape Town: Ohio University Press & Double Storey, 2005).

Penzhorn, B.L. & R.C. Krecek, 'Veterinary parasitology in South Africa', *Veterinary Parasitology*, 71, 1997, pp. 69–76.

Philo, Chris & Chris Wilbert, eds, *Animal Spaces, Beastly Places: New Geographies of Human–Animal Relations* (London: Routledge, 2000).

Phineas, Charles, 'Household pets and urban alienation', *Journal of Social History*, 7, 1973/74, pp. 338–43.

Phoofolo, Pule, 'Face to face with famine: The BaSotho and the rinderpest, 1897–1899', *Journal of Southern African Studies*, 29(2), 2003, pp. 503–27.

Piggott, S., *Wagon, Chariot and Carriage* (London: Thames & Hudson, 1992).

Pilcher, T.D., *Some Lessons of the Boer War 1899–1902* (London: Isbister, 1903).

Pinfold, John, 'Horse racing and the upper classes in the nineteenth century', *Sport in History*, 28(3), September 2008, pp. 414–30.

Pirie, Gordon, 'Railways and labour migration to the Rand mines: Constraints and significance', *Journal of Southern African Studies*, 19, 1994, pp. 713–30.

——, 'Slaughter by steam: Railway subjugation of ox wagon transport in the eastern Cape and Transkei, 1886–1910', *International Journal of African Historical Studies*, 26, 1993, pp. 319–42.

Plaatje, Sol T., *Mafeking Diary: A Black Man's View of a White Man's War* (Cambridge & London: Meridor Books, with James Currey, 1990).

——, *Native Life in South Africa* ([1916], Johannesburg: Ravan Press, 2006).

Poliakov, Leon, *The Aryan Myth* (New York: Basic Books, 1974).

Porter, Roy, 'Foreword', in Alain Corbin, *The Foul and the Fragrant: Odour and the French Social Imagination* (London: Picador, 1994).

Postma, M., *Tales from the Basotho* (Austin: University of Texas Press, 1974).

Pretorius, F., *Life on Commando during the Anglo-Boer War* (Cape Town: Human & Rousseau, 1999).

Raber, Karen & Treva J. Tucker, eds, *The Culture of the Horse: Status, Discipline, and Identity in the Early Modern World* (New York: Palgrave Macmillan, 2005).

Radosevich, Steven, M.M. Stubbs & Claudio Ghersa, 'Plant invasions: Process and patterns', *Weed Science*, 51(2), 2003, pp. 254–59.

Rath, Richard Cullen, *How Early America Sounded* (Ithaca: Cornell University Press, 2003).

Rattray, W. Grey, 'Horse breeding', *The SA Exhibition, Port Elizabeth, 1885* (Cape Town, 1886).

Reitz, Deneys, *Commando: A Boer Journal of the Boer War* ([1929], Johannesburg: Jonathan Ball, 1990).

Renfrew, C., *Archaeology and Language: The Puzzle of Indo-European Origins* (London: Jonathan Cape, 1987).

Richardson, Clive, *The Horse Breakers* (London: Allen, 1998).

Ritvo, Harriet, *The Animal Estate: The English and Other Creatures in the Victorian Age* (Cambridge, MA: Harvard University Press, 1987).

——, 'History and Animal Studies', *Society & Animals*, 10(4), 2002, pp. 403–6.

——, 'Animal planet', *Environmental History*, 9(2), 2004, pp. 204–20.

Roche, C., 'Ornaments of the desert: Springbok treks in the Cape Colony, 1774–1908', MA diss., University of Cape Town, 2004.

Roche, Daniel, 'Montaigne cavalier: Un témoin de la culture équestre dans la France du XVIe siècle', in Bernard Barbiche & Yves-Marie Bercé, eds, *Études sur l'ancienne France offertes en hommage à Michel Antoine* (Paris: École des Chartes, 2003).

Rose, Cowper, *Four Years in Southern Africa* (London: Colburne & Bentley, 1829).

Rosenberg, Scott, 'Promises of Moshoeshoe in culture, nationalism and identity in Lesotho, 1902–1966', Ph.D. thesis, Indiana University, 1998.

Ross, R., *Adam Kok's Griquas: A Study in the Development of Stratification in South Africa* (Cambridge: Cambridge University Press, 1976).

——, *Cape of Torments: Slavery and Resistance in South Africa* (London: Routledge & Kegan Paul, 1983a).

——, 'The rise of the Cape gentry', *Journal of Southern African Studies*, 9(2), 1983b, pp. 193–217.

——, *Status and Respectability in the Cape Colony, 1750–1870* (Cambridge: Cambridge University Press, 1999).

Rosenthal, Eric. *General De Wet* (Cape Town: Simondium, 1968).

Rothfels, Nigel, ed., *Representing Animals* (Bloomington: University of Indiana Press, 2003).

Royal Commission on the War in South Africa, *Report, Minutes of Evidence and Appendices* (London, 1903).

Rubenstein, D.I., 'The ecology of equid social organization', in D.I. Rubenstein & R.W. Wrangham, eds, *Ecological Aspects of Social Evolution* (Princeton: Princeton University Press, 1986).

Rued, Ernst, *Sex and Character* (London: William Heinemann, 1906).

Russell, Nicholas, *Like Engend'ring Like: Heredity and Animal Breeding in Early Modern England* (London: Cambridge University Press, 1986).

——, 'Well-groomed or well-bred?', *History Today*, 39(1), 1989, pp. 10–12.

Sadie, J.L., 'Die ekonomiese faktor in die Afrikanergemeenskap', in H.W. van der Merwe, ed., *Identiteit en Verandering* (Cape Town: Tafelberg, 1974).

——, *The Fall and Rise of Afrikaner Capitalism* (Stellenbosch: US Annale, 2002).

Sanders, Peter, *Moshoeshoe: Chief of the Sotho* (London: Heinemann, 1975).

Savory, P., *Basuto Fireside Tales* (Cape Town: Howard Timmins, 1962).

Schama, Simon, *Landscape and Memory* (New York: Alfred A. Knopf, 1995).

Schirmer, S., 'White farmers and development in South Africa', *South African Historical Journal*, 52, 2005, pp. 82–101.

Schreuder, P.J., 'The Cape horse: Its origin, breeding and development in the Union of South Africa', Ph.D. thesis, Cornell University, 1915.

Scott, James, *Weapons of the Weak: Everyday Forms of Peasant Resistance* (New Haven: Yale University Press, 1985).

Scully, William, *Lodges in the Wilderness* (London: Herbert Jenkins, 1915).

Sessions, Harold, *Two Years with the Remount Commission* (London: Chapman & Hall, 1903).

Shain, M., *The Roots of Anti-Semitism in South Africa* (Johannesburg: Wits University Press, 1994).

Shaw, I., 'Egyptians, Hyksos and military technology: Causes, effects or catalysts?', in A.J. Shortland, ed., *The Social Context of Technological Change: Egypt and the Near East, 1650–1550 BC* (Oxford: Oxbow, 2001).

Shell, Robert, *Children of Bondage: A Social History of Slavery at the Cape of Good Hope, 1652–1838* (Johannesburg: Wits University Press, 1994).

Shephard, J.B., *A Rooinek's Ride* (Cape Town: Longman, Green, 1951).

Sherow, J.E., 'Workings of the geodialectic: High plains Indians and their horses in the region of the Arkansas River Valley, 1800–1870', *Environmental History Review*, 16, 1992, pp. 61–84.

Showers, Kate B., 'Soil erosion in the Kingdom of Lesotho: Origins and colonial response, 1830s–1950s', *Journal of Southern African Studies*, 15(2), 1989, pp. 263–86.

Simalenga, T.E. & A.B.D. Joubert, *Developing Agriculture with Animal Traction* (Alice: University of Fort Hare, 1997).

Slata, Richard, *Cowboys of the Americas* (New Haven: Yale University Press, 1990).

Smith, Frederick, *A Veterinary History of the War in South Africa, 1899–1902* (London: H.W. Brown, 1919).

Smith, I.R., *The Origins of the South African War 1899–1902* (New York & London: Longman, 1996).

Smith, Mark M., 'Producing sense, consuming sense, making sense: Perils and prospects for sensory history', *Journal of Social History*, 40(4), 2007, pp. 841–58.

Smith, M.R. & L. Marx, eds, *Does Technology Drive History?* (Cambridge, MA: MIT Press, 1994).

Smith, Neil, 'The production of nature', in George Robertson et al., eds, *Future Natural Nature/Science/Culture* (London & New York: Routledge, 1996).

Smout, T. Chris, 'The alien species in 20th-century Britain: Constructing a new vermin', *Landscape Research*, 28(1), 2003, pp. 11–20.

Sobel, Mechel, *The World They Made Together: Black and White Values in Eighteenth-century Virginia* (Princeton: Princeton University Press, 1987).

South African Almanack and Reference Book, 1911–1912 (Cape Town: Argus, 1911).

South African Directory and Almanac of 1834 (Cape Town, 1834).

South African Year-Book, 1902–1903 (London, 1902).

South African Year Book 1914 (London: Routledge, 1914).

Sparrman, A., *A Voyage to the Cape of Good Hope, towards the Antarctic Polar Circle, and around the World, but Chiefly into the Country of the Hottentots and Caffres, from the Year 1772 to 1776* (Cape Town: Van Riebeeck Society, 1975–77).

Starkey, Paul (ed.), *Animal Power in South Africa: Empowering Rural Communities* (Gauteng: Development Bank of Southern Africa, 1995).

Steenekamp, T., 'Discrimination and the economic position of the Afrikaner', *South African Journal of Economic History*, 5(1), 1990, pp. 49–66.

Steyn, Phia & André Wessels, 'The roots of contemporary governmental and non-governmental environmental activities in South Africa, 1654–1972', *New Contree*, 45, 1999, pp. 77–80.

Stoler, Ann, 'Carnal knowledge and imperial power: Gender, race, and morality in colonial Asia', in Micaela di Leonardo, ed., *Gender at the Crossroads of Knowledge* (Berkeley: University of California Press, 1991).

Stoneley, Peter, 'Sentimental emasculations: *Uncle Tom's Cabin* and *Black Beauty*', *Nineteenth-century Literature*, 54(1), 1999, pp. 53–72.

Storey, William, *Guns, Race, and Power in Colonial South Africa* (Cambridge: Cambridge University Press, 2008).

Swanepoel, C.J., 'Hoe ry die Boere', *Tydskrif vir Volkskunde en Volkstaal*, 41(1), 1985, pp. 28–30.

Swart, Sandra, '"You were men in war time": The manipulation of gender identity in war and peace', *Scientia Militaria*, 28(2), December 1998a, pp. 187–99.

——, 'A Boer and his gun and his wife are three things always together', *Journal of Southern African Studies*, 24(4), December 1998b, pp. 737–51.

——, 'Desperate men: Rebellion and the politics of poverty in the 1914 rebellion', *South African Historical Journal*, 42, May 2000, pp. 161–75.

——, '"Race" horses: Horses and social dynamics in post-apartheid southern Africa', in N. Distiller & M. Steyn, eds, *Under Construction: Race and Identity in South Africa Today* (London: Heinemann, 2004).

——, '"Horses! Give me more horses": White settler society and the role of horses in the making of early modern South Africa', in Karen Raber & Treva J. Tucker, eds, *The Culture of the Horse: Discipline, and Identity in the Early Modern World* (New York: Palgrave Macmillan, 2005).

——, '"But where's the bloody horse?": Textuality and corporeality in the "animal turn"', *Journal of Literary Studies*, 23(3), 2007, pp. 271–92.

——, '"High horses": Horses, class and socio-economic change in South Africa', *Journal of Southern African Studies*, 33(4), 2008, pp. 193–213.

——, 'Horses in the South African War, 1899–1902', *Animals & Society*, 18, 4, 2010.

——, 'The World the Horses Made: A South African Case Study of Writing Animals into Social History', *International Review of Social History*, SS, 2, 2010.

Swift, P. & J. Szymanowski, *The Sporting Horse in Southern Africa* (South Africa: BoE Private Bank, 2001).

Taylor, Alan, 'Unnatural inequalities: Social and environmental histories', *Environmental History*, 1(4), 1996, pp. 6–19.

Teenstra, M.D., *De Vruchten Mijmer Werkzaamheden* (Cape Town: Van Riebeeck Society, 1943).

Theal, George McCall, *History of South Africa, from 1795–1872*, vol. 3 (London: George Allen & Unwin, 1916).

——, *History and Ethnography of Africa South of the Zambesi*, vol. II (London: George Allen & Unwin, 1922).

——, *Basutoland Records, 1833–1852*, vol. 1 ([1883], Cape Town: Struik, 1964a).

——, *Basutoland Records, 1853–1861*, vol. 2 ([1883], Cape Town: Struik, 1964b).

——, *History of SA before 1795*, vols. 1 & 2 (Cape Town: Struik, 1964c).

——, *Basutoland Records, 1868*, vol. 4 (Maseru: Institute of Southern African Studies, National University of Lesotho, 2002a).

——, *Basutoland Records, 1870–72*, vol. 6 (Maseru: Institute of Southern African Studies, National University of Lesotho, 2002b).

——, *Records of the Cape Colony: Copied for the Cape Government, from the Manuscript Documents in the Public Record Office, London, December 1799 to May 1801*, vol. 3 (London: Clowes, 1898).

——, *Records of the Cape Colony: Copied for the Cape Government, from the Manuscript Documents in the Public Record Office, London, June 1821 to August 1822*, vol. 14 (London: Clowes, 1902).

——, *Records of the Cape Colony: Copied for the Cape Government, from the Manuscript Documents in the Public Record Office, London, May 1823 to January 1824*, vol. 16 (London: Clowes, 1903a).

——, *Records of the Cape Colony: Copied for the Cape Government, from the Manuscript Documents in the Public Record Office, London, June to October 1824*, vol. 18 (London: Clowes, 1903b).

——, *Records of the Cape Colony: Copied for the Cape Government, from the Manuscript Documents in the Public Record Office, London, October 1824 to February 1825*, vol. 19 (London: Clowes, 1904a).

——, *Records of the Cape Colony: Copied for the Cape Government, from the Manuscript Documents in the Public Record Office, London, August to November 1825*, vol. 23 (London: Clowes, 1904b).

——, *Records of the Cape Colony: Copied for the Cape Government, from the Manuscript Documents in the Public Record Office, London, 1 January to 6 February 1826*, vol. 25 (London: Clowes, 1905a).

——, *Records of the Cape Colony: Copied for the Cape Government, from the Manuscript Documents in the Public Record Office, London, February to June 1826*, vol. 26 (London: Clowes, 1905b).

——, *Records of the Cape Colony: Copied for the Cape Government, from the Manuscript Documents in the Public Record Office, London, 1 January to 24 February 1827*, vol. 30 (London: Clowes, 1905c).

——, *Records of the Cape Colony: Copied for the Cape Government, from the Manuscript Documents in the Public Record Office, London, February to June 1827*, vol. 31 (Government of Cape Colony, 1905d).

——, *Records of the Cape Colony: Copied for the Cape Government, from the Manuscript Documents in the Public Record Office, London, December 1827 to April 1831*, vol. 35 (London: Clowes, 1905e).

Thom, H.B., ed., *Journal of Jan van Riebeeck*, vol. I (Cape Town: A.A. Balkema, 1952).

——, *Journal of Jan van Riebeeck*, vol. II (Cape Town: A.A. Balkema, 1954).

——, *Journal of Jan van Riebeeck*, vol. III (Cape Town: A.A. Balkema, 1958).

Thompson, E.P., *The Making of the English Working Class* (New York: Vintage, 1966).

——, *Customs in Common: Studies in Traditional Popular Culture* (New York: New Press, 1993).

Thompson, George, *Travels and Adventures in Southern Africa* (London: Henry Colburn, 1827).

Thompson, L., *Survival in Two Worlds: Moshoeshoe of Lesotho 1786–1870* (Oxford: Clarendon, 1975).

——, *A History of South Africa* (New Haven: Yale University Press, 1990).

Thornton, R.W., *The Origin and History of the Basotho Pony* (Morija: Morija Printing Works, 1936a).

——, *Hloleho le Historiea Pere ea Sesotho* (Morija: Morija Printing Works, 1936b).

Thunberg, Charles, *Travels in Europe, Africa and Asia, Performed in the Years 1770 and 1779*, vol. 2 (London: 1793).

Todd, J., *Colonial Technology: Science and the Transfer of Innovation to Australia* (Cambridge: Cambridge University Press, 1995).

Toth, D., 'The psychology of women and horses', in GaWaNí PonyBoy, ed., *Of Women and Horses* (Irvine: BowTie, 2000).

Tuchman, B., *The Proud Tower* (New York: Macmillan, 1966).

Tylden, G., *A History of Thaba Bosiu: 'Mountain at Night'* (Morija: Morija Archives, 1950a).

——, *The Rise of the Basuto* (Cape Town: Juta, 1950b).

——, *Horses and Saddlery: An Account of the Animals Used by the British and Commonwealth Armies from the Seventeenth Century to the Present Day* (London: Allen, 1980).

Vail, L., ed., *The Creation of Tribalism in Southern Africa* (London: James Currey, 1989).

Van Bruggen, Jochem, *Ampie die Natuurkind* (Amsterdam: Swets & Zeitlinger, 1924).

——, *Die Sprinkaanbeampte van Sluis* (Cape Town: Van Schaik, 1998).

Van de Geer, R. & M. Wallis, *Government and Development in Rural Lesotho* (Morija: Morija Printing Works, 1982).

Vandenbergh, S.J.E., 'The story of a disease: A social history of African horsesickness, c.1850–1920', MA diss., University of Stellenbosch, 2009.

Van der Merwe, F.J., *Perde van die Anglo-Boereoorlog/Horses of the Anglo Boer War* (Kleinmond: self-published, 2000).

Van der Walt, A.J.H. *Die Ausdehnung der Kolonie am Kap der Guten Hoffnung (1700–1779): Eine Historisch-ekonomische Untersuchung uber das Werden und Wesen des Pionierlebens im 18. Jahrhunderd* (Berlin: Ebering, 1928).

Van Dyk, E. & S. Neser, 'The spread of weeds into sensitive areas by seeds in horse faeces', *Journal of the South African Veterinary Association*, 7(3), 2000, pp. 173–74.

Van Onselen, Charles, *The Seed Is Mine: The Life of Kas Maine, a South African Sharecropper 1894–1985* (New York: Hill & Wang, 1996).

—, 'Paternalism and violence on the maize farms of the south-western Transvaal, 1900–1950', in Jeeves and Crush, eds, *White Farms, Black Labour: The State and Agrarian Change in Southern Africa, 1910–1950* (Pietermaritzburg: University of Natal Press, 1997).

—, *New Babylon New Nineveh: Everyday Life on the Witwatersrand 1886–1914* (Johannesburg: Jonathan Ball, 2001).

Van Sittert, Lance, 'Holding the line: The rural enclosure movement in the Cape Colony', *Journal of African History*, 43, 2002, pp. 95–118.

—, 'Writing and teaching the history of the land and environment in Africa in the twenty-first century', report on conference session, *South African Historical Journal*, 50, 2004, pp. 223–24.

Van Sittert, L. & S. Swart, eds, *Canis Familiaris: A Dog History of Southern Africa* (Leiden: Brill, 2008).

Van Spaan, Gerrit, *De Gelukzoeker* (Rotterdam: De Vries, 1752).

Van Themaat, H. ver Loren, *Twee Jaren in den Boerenoorlog* (Haarlem: H.D. Tjeenk Willink, 1903).

Van Tonder, J.J., *Sewentien Perd- en Ruitermonumente in Suid-Afrika* (Krugersdorp: self-published, 1971).

Van Vuuren, C.J., 'Horses, carts and taxis: Transportation and marginalisation in three South African communities', *South African Journal of Cultural History*, 13(1), 1999, pp. 90–103.

Veblen, T.B., *The Theory of the Leisure Class: An Economic Study of Institutions* (New York: Macmillan, 1902).

Vermaas, Hans Jurie, *Sy Perd Staan Gereed* (Cape Town: Nasionale Pers, 1954).

—, *Die Perdedief* (Cape Town: Nasionale Boekhandel, 1960).

Vilà, Carles et al., 'Widespread origins of domestic horse lineages', *Science*, 291(5503), 2001, pp. 474–77.

Viljoen, Ben, *My Reminiscences of the Anglo-Boer War* (London: Hood, Douglas & Howard, 1902).

Vinnicombe, P., 'General notes on Bushmen riders and the Bushmen's use of the assegai', *South African Archaeological Bulletin*, 15(58), 1960, p. 49.

——, *People of the Eland: Rock Paintings of the Drakensberg Bushmen as a Reflection of Their Life and Thought* (Pietermaritzburg: University of Natal Press, 1976).

——, 'Basotho oral knowledge: The last Bushman inhabitants of the Mashai District, Lesotho', in P. Mitchell & Benjamin Smith, eds, *The Eland's People: New Perspectives in the Rock Art of the Maloti-Drakensberg Bushmen: Essays in Memory of Patricia Vinnicombe* (Johannesburg: Wits University Press, 2009).

Vinnicombe, Pat & John Wright, *Bushman Raiders of the Drakensberg 1840–1870* (Pietermartizburg: University of Natal Press, 1971).

Walker, Eric, *A History of Southern Africa* (London: Longman, 1965).

Wallace, R.L., *The Australians at the Boer War* (Canberra: Australian War Memorial & Australian Government Publishing Service, 1976).

Walton, James, *Father of Kindness and Father of Horses, Ramosa le Ralipere: A History of Frasers Limited* (Wepener: Frasers, 1958).

Warwick, Peter, *Black People and the South African War, 1899–1902* (Cambridge; Cambridge University Press, 1983).

Wassermann, Johan, 'A tale of two port cities: The relationship between Durban and New Orleans during the Anglo-Boer War', *Historia*, 49(1), 2004, pp. 27–47.

Watkins-Pitchford, H., *Besieged at Ladysmith: A Letter to His Wife, Written in Ladysmith during the Siege* (Pietermaritzburg: Shuter & Shooter, 1964).

Weaver, T. & D. Dale, 'Trampling effects of hikers, motorcycles and horses in meadows and forests', *Journal of Applied Ecology*, 15, 1978, pp. 451–58.

Webb, James, 'The horse and slave trade between the Western Sahara and Senegambia', *Journal of African History*, 34(2), 1993, pp. 221–46.

Wijnholds, D.W.J., *Geld, Goud en Goedere: 'n Uiteensetting van Hedendaagse Ekonomiese Vraagstukke wat Suid-Afrika in die Besonder Raak* (Pretoria: Akademiese Pers, 1953).

Williams, Gardner, *The Diamond Mines of South Africa*, vol. I (New York: B.F. Buck, 1905).

Wilson, Monica & Leonard Thompson, *Oxford History of South Africa*, vol. I (Oxford: Clarendon Press, 1969).

Wolch, J. & J. Emel, *Animal Geographies: Place, Politics, and Identity in the Nature–Culture Borderlands* (London & New York: Verso, 1998).

Woodward, Wendy, 'Social subjects: Representations of dogs in South African fiction in English', in L. van Sittert & Sandra Swart, eds, *Canis Familiaris: A Dog History of Southern Africa* (Leiden: Brill, 2008).

Worden, Nigel, *Slavery in Dutch South Africa* (Cambridge: Cambridge University Press, 1985).

——, *The Chains that Bind Us: A History of Slavery at the Cape* (Cape Town: Juta, 1996).

——, 'Armed with swords and ostrich feathers: Militarism and cultural revolution in the Cape slave uprising of 1808', in Richard Bessel, Nicholas Guyatt & Jane Rendall, eds, *War, Empire and Slavery, 1770–1830* (London: Palgrave, 2009).

Worster, Donald, *Nature's Economy: A History of Ecological Ideas* (Cambridge: Cambridge University Press, 1985).

——, 'Appendix: Doing environmental history', in D. Worster & Alfred W. Crosby, eds, *The Ends of the Earth: Perspectives on Modern Environmental History* (Cambridge: Cambridge University Press, 1988).

Worster, Donald & Alfred W. Crosby, eds, *The Ends of the Earth: Perspectives on Modern Environmental History* (Cambridge: Cambridge University Press, 1988).

Wrightman Fox, R. & T.J. Jackson Lears, eds, *The Culture of Consumption: Critical Essays in American History, 1880–1980* (New York: Pantheon, 1983).

Wyndham, H.A., *The Early History of the Thoroughbred Horse in South Africa* (London: Humphrey Milford & Oxford University Press, 1924).

Yates, Roger, Chris Powell & Piers Beirne. 'Horse maiming in the English countryside: Moral panic, human deviance, and the social construction of victimhood', *Society and Animals*, 9(1), 2001, pp. 1–23.

Yates, Royden, Anthony Manhire & John Parkington, 'Colonial era paintings in the rock art of the south-western Cape: Some preliminary observations', *Historical Archaeology in the Western Cape*, 1993, pp. 59–70.

Zeuner, F.E., *A History of Domesticated Animals* (London: Hutchinson, 1963).

Permissions

Sections of Chapter 1 appeared as Sandra Swart, "'But where's the bloody horse?": Textuality and corporeality in the "animal turn'", *Journal of Literary Studies*, 23(3), June 2007. My grateful thanks for permission to reprint portions of this article. A small section in Chapter 1 appeared in an earlier incarnation in Sandra Swart, Albert Grundlingh, Christopher Saunders and Howard Phillips, 'Environment, Heritage, Resistance and Health: Newer Historiagraphical Directions', in Robert Ross, Anne Mager and Bill Nasson (eds.), *The Cambridge History of South Africa, Vol. 2: From 1886 to the End of Apartheid* (Cambridge University Press, New York, 2011).

Some parts of Chapters 2 and 3 appeared in Sandra Swart, 'Riding high: Horses, power and settler society, c.1654–1840', *Kronos*, 29, 2003; Sandra Swart "'Horses! Give me more horses!": White settler society and the role of horses in the making of early modern South Africa', in Karen Raber & Treva J. Tucker, eds, *The Culture of the Horse: Status, Discipline, and Identity in the Early Modern World* (New York: Palgrave Macmillan, 2005); and Sandra Swart, 'Riding high: Horses, power and settler society in southern Africa, c.1654–1840', in Greg Bankoff & Sandra Swart, *Breeds of Empire: The 'Invention' of the Horse in the Philippines and Southern Africa, 1500–1950* (Copenhagen: Nordic Institute of Asian Studies Press, 2007). My grateful thanks for permission to reprint portions of these publications.

Some elements of Chapter 4 appeared in Sandra Swart, 'The "ox that deceives": The meanings of the "Basotho pony" in Southern Africa', in Greg Bankoff & Sandra Swart, *Breeds of Empire: The 'Invention' of the Horse in the Philippines and Southern Africa, 1500–1950* (Copenhagen: Nordic Institute of Asian Studies Press, 2007) and in Sandra Swart, "'Race" horses: Horses and social dynamics in post-apartheid southern Africa', in N. Distiller & M. Steyn, eds, *Under Construction: Race and Identity in South Africa Today* (London: Heinemann, 2004).

Chapter 5 was published in an altered form in Sandra Swart, 'Horses in the South African War, 1899–1902', *Animals & Society*, 17(3), 2010. Grateful thanks for permission to include it here.

Permissions

Chapter 6 was delivered in a different incarnation to the Agricultural History Society, MIT, Cambridge, Massachusetts, in June 2006.

Chapter 7 was published in a previous incarnation as Sandra Swart, '"High horses": Horses, class and socio-economic change in South Africa', *Journal of Southern African Studies*, 34(1), 2008. My grateful thanks for permission to republish it.

Some sections of chapter 8 were published in Sandra Swart, 'The world the horses made: A South African case study of writing animals into social history', *International Review of Social History*, 55(2), 2010. My grateful thanks for permission to republish them.

Index

Riding High

Index

Index

Index

Index

Lowveld 68, 86, 115, 167
Truter, Hendrick 120
tsetse fly 8, 23, 114–115
Tswana 30, 78
Tulbagh 166

United Nations Relief and Rehabilitation
   Administration 169
   UN Charter 181
United Party 182
United States of America 111–112*fig*,
   146, 167, 169, 172–178, 180–181,
   183–184, 187–188, 192
   American Saddle Horse Breeders'
   Association 174
   Kentucky 174, 188
   Missouri 174
   Saddle horse registry 174
   Tennessee 188
   Virginia 174
urbanisation 4, 146–147, 152, 157, 182,
   200, 206, 220

van Bruggen, Jochem 161
van den Heever, Toon 154
van Onselen, Charles 185
van Schalkwyk, Gerrit 186
van der Stel, Simon 31
van Reenen
   Dirk 49, 52
   Jacobus 49, 52, 58
   Sebastiaan 49, 52
Van Riebeeck, Jan 19–22, 24–27, 58, 121,
   168
Van Sittert, Lance 8–9
Veblen, T.B. 180, 186
Vereenigde Oost-Indische Compagnie
   (voc) 18–19, 21, 24, 26–32, 37, 39,
   78, 86, 107, 123
   and wage labour economy 20
Vermaas, Hans Jurie 154–155

Verney, Frank Arthur 164
Viljoen, General 114–115, 118, 127, 130
Visser, A.G. 126, 154, 168
von Wolf, Baron Hansheinrich 195
voortrekkers 8, 154, 157, 181, 189, 199

W
Wasserman, Johan 109
Webb, Jim 9
Wellington 146
Welsh Pony and Cob Society 141
West Africa 9, 18, 86
White, General 130
wild/feral horses 194, 209, 211–212, 216,
   220
   African wild ass 18, 194
   Asiatic wild ass 194
   Burchell's zebra 25
   domestic horse 18, 194
   equus capensis 195, 210
   Grevy's zebra 194
   Kiang 194
   mountain zebra 25, 194
   Kaapsehoop 196, 220
   mustang 111, 194–195
   Bot River 195, 220
   Namib Desert horse 195–196, 220
   plains zebra 194
   Przewalski's horse 194
   quagga 24–26, 220
   strandveld, Gansbaai 196, 220
   zebra 18, 23–26, 39, 66, 75, 139, 220
wildlife protection 9
Woltemade, Wolraad 123–124, 199
women's history 6, 198–199
   emancipation of women 159
   narratives/life stories 199
Worcester 138, 166
Worden, Nigel 29
Worster, Donald 13, 17
Wright, F.B. 162, 177

Wyndham, Hugh Archibald 49, 53

Xenophon 13
Xhosa 20, 43, 79, 207

Yonge, Sir George 51

Zandveld 23, 220
Zulu 92, 97–98
Zululand 23
Zydensteicker 83